Music in Our World

An Active-Listening Approach

Music in Our World

An Active-Listening Approach

Gary White

David Stuart

Elyn Aviva

Boston   Burr Ridge, IL   Dubuque, IA   Madison, WI   New York
San Francisco   St. Louis   Bangkok   Bogotá   Caracas   Lisbon
London   Madrid   Mexico City   Milan   New Delhi   Seoul
Singapore   Sydney   Taipei   Toronto

McGraw-Hill Higher Education ✖

A Division of The McGraw-Hill Companies

MUSIC IN OUR WORLD: AN ACTIVE-LISTENING APPROACH
Published by McGraw-Hill, an imprint of the The McGraw-Hill
Companies, Inc. 1221 Avenue of the Americas, New York, NY, 10020.

This book is printed on acid-free paper.

1 2 3 4 5 6 7 8 9 0 DOC/DOC 0 9 8 7 6 5 4 3 2 1 0

ISBN 0-07-027212-3

Editorial director: *Phillip A. Butcher*
Sponsoring editor: *Christopher Freitag*
Developmental editor: *JoElaine Retzler*
Marketing manager: *David S. Patterson*
Project manager: *Rebecca Nordbrock*
Production supervisor: *Michael McCormick*
Senior designer: *Jennifer McQueen Hollingsworth*
Supplement coordinator: *Jason Greve*
Interior designer: *Joel Davies/ZGraphics*
Cover images: *Lindsay Hebberd/Corbis*
            Neal Preston/Corbis
            Photodisc
Compositor: *A-R Editions, Inc.*
Typeface: *New Aster*
Printer: *R. R. Donnelley & Sons Company*

Library of Congress Cataloging-in-Publication Data

White, Gary
    Music in our world : an active-listening approach / Gary White, David Stuart,
    Elyn Aviva.
      p. cm.
    Includes index.
    ISBN 0-07-027212-3 (softcover : alk. paper)
    1. Music appreciation. I. Stuart, David (David H.) II. Aviva, Elyn. III. Title.

MT6.W4146 M93 2001
781.1'7--dc21
                                                      00-033923

www.mhhe.com

TABLE OF CONTENTS

Listening Activities xvii

About the Authors xix

Preface xxi

Audience xxi

Approach xxi

Content and Organization xxii

Supplements xxiv

Acknowledgments xxiv

PART I Introduction to Active Listening 2

PRELUDE Active Listening 4

Dolphin Dreams, Jonathan Goldman

Step One 6

Step Two 6

Jonathan Goldman and the Creation of *Dolphin Dreams* 8

Is *Dolphin Dreams* Music? 8

Summary 9

Applying What You Have Learned 9

Important Terms 9

Musician Mentioned 9

Further Listening Resources 10

CHAPTER 1 Music in Society 11

Simple Gifts, Elder Joseph Brackett
Appalachian Spring, Aaron Copland

Early Humans 12

Language 13

Music 14

Setting   14
Purpose   16
   Work Songs   17
   Motivational Music   18
   Background Music   18
   Art Music   19

Call and
Response   18

The Changing Functions of Music   19
Simple Gifts   21
The United Society of Believers in Christ's Second
Appearing (Shakers)   21
Summary   26
Applying What You Have Learned   27
Important Terms   28
Musicians Mentioned   28
Further Listening Resources   28

The Suite   25

Historical
Periods   27

CHAPTER 2   Our Response to Music   30

Exodus and *Redemption Song,* Bob Marley

Physical Responses   31
Emotional Responses   32
Cognitive Responses   33
Spiritual Responses   34
The Music of Bob Marley—Setting and Purpose   39
Brief History and Politics of Jamaica   39
Rastafari   40
Musical Roots of Reggae   41
Bob Marley   42
Listening to the Songs   44
Exodus   45
Redemption Song   47
Response to the Music   49
Summary   49
Applying What You Have Learned   49
Important Terms   51
Musicians and Ensembles Mentioned   51
Further Listening Resources   51

Four Categories
of Human
Attributes   36

History of
Reggae   42

PART II   Rhythm in Music   52

CHAPTER 3   Beat, Accent, and Tempo   54

Grand Entry Song, Powwow Music

Beat   55

Accent   55

Tempo   55

The Powwow—Setting and Purpose   55

    Powwow Music   57

    Powwow Dance   58

    The Form of a Powwow Song   60

    A Typical Powwow   61

Listening to a Grand Entry Song   66

Little Otter Singers (from the Mille Lacs Reservation in Minnesota)   67

Response to the Music   70

Summary   70

Applying What You Have Learned   70

Important Terms   71

Musicians and Ensembles Mentioned   71

Further Listening Resources   71

History of Powwow   57

CHAPTER 4   Meter   73

Klezmer Music—*Bay a Glezele Mashke* and *Oy, Abram!* Traditional

Meter   74

Division of the Beat   75

Klezmer Music   76

    The Rise of Eastern European Jewish Communities   76

    Origins of the Klezmer Tradition   77

    The *Klezmorim* and Their Music   78

    Klezmer in the United States   78

    Meter in Klezmer Music   80

Response to the Music   83

Summary   84

Applying What You Have Learned   84

Important Terms   85

Musicians Mentioned   85

Further Listening Resources   85

The Jewish Diaspora   76

History of Klezmer Music   79

CHAPTER 5   Polyrhythm   86

Shango, Babatunde Olatunji

Polyrhythm   87

Polyrhythm in African Music   87

Sub-Saharan Africa   88

The Importance of Music in Sub-Saharan
Africa   90

Percussion Instruments in West African Music   90

Babatunde Olatunji—West African Music in the
West   93

Response to the Music   95

Summary   96

Applying What You Have Learned   96

Important Terms   96

Musicians Mentioned   97

Further Listening Resources   97

History of
Sub-Saharan
African
Music   90

PART III   Melody in Music   98

CHAPTER 6   Vocal Melody   100

De sancta Maria, Hildegard of Bingen

Sound and Pitch   101

Scales   102

Melody   103

Phrase   104

Vocal Melody   104

Introduction to *De Sancta Maria*   104

Hildegard of Bingen   104

Music in the Middle Ages   108

Gregorian Chant   109

Hildegard's Music   113

Symphonia Harmonie Caelestium Revelationum   113

Listening to *De sancta Maria* (For the Virgin Mary)   115

Response to the Music   118

Summary   119

Applying What You Have Learned   119

Important Terms   120

Musicians and Ensembles Mentioned   121

Further Listening Resources   121

The Cosmic
Symphony   109

The Medieval
Period   111

CHAPTER 7   Instrumental Melody   122

Máru-Bihág, Ravi Shankar

Instrumental Melody   123

The Indian Subcontinent   123
The Music of India   124
   Northern and Southern Styles   127
   Raga and *Tala*   127
   Instruments of Indian Classical Music   130
   Ravi Shankar   132
   The Impact of Indian Classical Music in the West   132
   The Impact of Western Music in India   134
Listening to *Máru-Bihág*   134
Response to the Music   136
Summary   137
Applying What You Have Learned   137
Important Terms   138
Musicians Mentioned   138
Further Listening Resources   139

Sacred Dance   126

Improvisation 128

History of *Raga*   129

CHAPTER 8   Vocal Melody in Opera   140

La Bohème, Act II, Giacomo Puccini

Drama and Music   141
Western Opera   142
   Brief History of Western Opera   142
   The Operatic Singer   146
   Melody in Opera   147
   Giacomo Puccini   147
Listening to *La Bohème*   151
   Puccini's Music   151
   Plot Synopsis of *La Bohème*   151
Response to the Music   164
Summary   165
Applying What You Have Learned   165
Important Terms   166
Musicians Mentioned   166
Further Listening Resources   166

Major Opera Composers   143

The Romantic Period   144

Operatic Voices   146

Rent   152

PART IV   Harmony in Music   168

CHAPTER 9   Harmony   170

The Four Seasons—Spring, Antonio Vivaldi
Tonal Harmony   171

Chords   171
Harmonic Progression   172
Harmonic Tension and Release   173
Diatonic Scales   173
Diatonic and Chromatic Harmony   173
Antonio Vivaldi   174
The Music of Vivaldi in Recent Times   178
Vivaldi's *Four Seasons*   178
Musical Materials of *Spring*   180
Vivaldi's Orchestra   182
Listening to *Spring*   183
Response to the Music   185
Summary   185
Applying What You Have Learned   185
Important Terms   187
Musicians and Ensembles Mentioned   187
Further Listening Resources   188

The Ospedale
della Pietà   175

The Baroque
Period   177

The "Early Music"
Movement   179

CHAPTER 10   Harmonizing   189

This Land Is Your Land, Woody Guthrie
Bring Me Little Water Silvy, Leadbelly: Huddie Ledbetter

Harmonizing   190
Woody Guthrie   191
Leadbelly (Huddie Ledbetter)   195
Sweet Honey in the Rock   197
Response to the Music   199
Summary   199
Applying What You Have Learned   200
Important Terms   201
Musicians and Ensembles Mentioned   201
Further Listening Resources   201

American
Vernacular
Music   191

PART V   Dynamics, Timbre, and Texture in Music   204

CHAPTER 11   A Western Ensemble: The Symphony Orchestra   206

The Young Person's Guide to the Orchestra, Benjamin Britten

Ensembles   207
Small Ensembles   207
Large Ensembles   207

The Symphony Orchestra   207

   String Section   210

   Woodwind Section   211

   Brass Section   211

   Percussion Section   212

Benjamin Britten   212

The Young Person's Guide to the Orchestra   214

   Textures in *The Young Person's Guide to the Orchestra*   219

   Dynamics in *The Young Person's Guide to the Orchestra*   221

Response to the Music   223

Summary   224

Applying What You Have Learned   224

Important Terms   225

Musicians and Ensembles Mentioned   225

Further Listening Resources   226

Ensembles Around the World   208

The Modern Period   214

Henry Purcell   216

CHAPTER 12   A Non-Western Ensemble: The Balinese *Gamelan*   227

Gending Petegak, Sekehe Gender Bharata Muni, Sading

Place and Time: Bali   228

Gamelan   230

   The Instruments   230

   Performers and Instrument Makers   232

   Gamelan Performances   232

   Gamelan Music in the West   232

   Wayang Kulit: Shadow-Puppet Theater   233

   Gender Wayang: Instrumental Ensemble   234

   Musical Materials   235

   Gamelan Compositions   236

Listening to *Gending Petegak*   236

Response to the Music   237

Summary   238

Applying What You Have Learned   238

Important Terms   239

Musicians and Ensembles Mentioned   239

Further Listening Resources   239

History of Indonesia   229

CHAPTER 13   In the Recording Studio   240

Animal Crackers, Matt Ryan

The Impact of Recording Technology on Music   241
   Early History of Recording   241
   Records to Compact Disks   242
   The Emergence of Recording Engineering   243
   Multitrack Recording and "Effects"   244
   Multitrack Tape Recorders   244
   Echo and Reverberation   245
   Delay and Flanging   245
   Compressors, Expanders, and Limiters   245
Producing a Commercial Recording   248
   Preproduction   248
   Recording   248
   Mixdown   248
   Postproduction   249
Listening to a Digital Studio Recording: *Animal Crackers*   250
"Ensembles" in Commercial Recorded Music   252
Music in a Postmodern World   253
Response to the Music   254
Summary   254
Applying What You Have Learned   254
Important Terms   256
Musicians and Ensembles Mentioned   256
Further Listening Resources   257

Mr. Edison's
Phonograph   242

History of Popular
Music in the
U. S.   247

The Recording
Studio   249

PART VI   Form in Music   258

CHAPTER 14   Sectional Forms I   260

Huachos, Eduardo Villaroel and J. Mercado

Elements of Form: Repetition   261
Repeated Sections   263
Elements of Form: Contrast   263
Sectional Form   264
   Strophic Forms   264
   Verse and Chorus Form   265
A Sectional Work from the Andes   266
   South America   266
   People of the Andes Mountains   266
   The Music of the Andes   268
Listening to *Huachos*   272
Response to the Music   274

History of
the Inca   271

Hocket   272

Summary 274
Applying What You Have Learned 274
Important Terms 275
Musicians and Ensembles Mentioned 275
Further Listening Resources 276

CHAPTER 15 Sectional Forms II 277

Symphony No. 39, Franz Joseph Haydn

Elements of Form: Variation 278
Types of Sections 278
 Thematic Sections 279
 Introductions 279
 Connecting Sections—Transitions and Interludes 279
 Concluding Sections: Codas and Codettas 280
Sectional Forms 280
Sonata Form 282
 Exposition 282
 Development 282
 Recapitulation 283
The Complete Classical Sonata 283
The Symphony 285
Franz Joseph Haydn 288
Response to the Music 295
Summary 295
Applying What You Have Learned 295
Important Terms 296
Musicians and Ensembles Mentioned 296
Further Listening Resources 296

The Classical Period 284

Musical Performance in Vienna 286

CHAPTER 16 Continuous Forms I 297

Sultan Veled Peshrev, Dogan Ergin

Continuity 298
Pattern-Based Continuous Forms 298
Turkey 299
 Classical Music of Turkey 301
  Makam 302
  The Instruments 303
 Sufism 303
  The Whirling Dervishes 304
  Sema 305

Turkish History 300

Closing the *Tekkes:* Sufi Prayer Lodges 306

Listening to *Sultan Veled Peshrev*   306
Response to the Music   309
Summary   309
Applying What You Have Learned   309
Important Terms   310
Musicians and Ensembles Mentioned   310
Further Listening Resources   311

CHAPTER 17   Continuous Forms II   312

Absalon, fili mi, Josquin Desprez

Text-Based Continuous Forms   313   History of
Motet   313   the Motet   313
Josquin Desprez   314
Listening to *Absalon, fili mi*   314   The Renaissance
Response to the Music   319   Period   315
Summary   319
Applying What You Have Learned   319
Important Terms   320
Musicians and Ensembles Mentioned   320
Further Listening Resources   320

CHAPTER 18   Improvisation and Form   322

Suite Thursday, Duke Ellington and Billy Strayhorn

Development of Jazz   323   History of
    Form in Jazz   325   Jazz   325
Duke Ellington   326
    Duke Ellington's Early Years   326
    Ellington as a Bandleader   329
    Ellington the Composer   330
    Duke Ellington and the Suite   331
Listening to *Suite Thursday*   331
Response to the Music   337
Summary   338
Applying What You Have Learned   338
Important Terms   339
Musicians and Ensembles Mentioned   339
Further Listening Resources   339

Appendix A: Pronunciation Guide   341

Appendix B: Musician Biographies   346

Endnotes   373

Index   379

LISTENING ACTIVITIES

Dolphin Dreams, Jonathan Goldman: Studio-produced sonic landscape 6

Simple Gifts, Elder Joseph Brackett: Nineteenth-century Shaker hymn 25

Appalachian Spring (Simple Gifts), Aaron Copland: Twentieth-century North American ballet 26

Exodus, Bob Marley and the Wailers: Jamaican reggae music 46

Redemption Song, Bob Marley: Jamaican reggae music 48

Grand Entry Song, Little Otter Singers: Native American (Ojibwe) powwow music 68

Bay a Glezele Mashke, Klezmer Conservatory Band: Traditional klezmer music 80

Oy, Abram!, Klezmer Conservatory Band: Yiddish folksong 81

Shango (Chant to the God of Thunder), Babatunde Olatunji: Nigerian ritual music 94

De sancta Maria (For the Virgin Mary), Hildegard of Bingen: Medieval German religious music 116

Máru-Bihág, Ravi Shankar: North Indian classical music 135

La Bohème, End of Act II, Giacomo Puccini: Nineteenth-century Italian opera 154

The Four Seasons—Spring, Antonio Vivaldi: Eighteenth-century Italian orchestral music 183

This Land Is Your Land, Woody Guthrie: Twentieth-century North American folk music 194

Bring Me Little Water Silvy, Leadbelly (Huddie Ledbetter): Twentieth-century African American work song 198

The Young Person's Guide to the Orchestra, Benjamin Britten: Twentieth-century English orchestral music 217, 222

Gending Petegak, Sekehe Gender Bharata Muni, Sading: Balinese puppet theater music 236

Animal Crackers, Axigally: Digital studio recording 250

Listening again to **This Land Is Your Land,** Woody Guthrie: Twentieth-century North American folk music 262

Listening again to **Redemption Song,** Bob Marley: Jamaican reggae music 262

Listening again to **Grand Entry Song,** Little Otter Singers: Native American (Ojibwe) powwow music 263

Listening again to **Oy, Abram!,** Klezmer Conservatory Band: Yiddish folksong 264

Listening again to **Bring Me Little Water Silvy,** Leadbelly (Huddie Ledbetter): Twentieth-century African American work song 265

Huachos (Tramps), Eduardo Villaroel and J. Mercado: Music of the high Andes (Bolivia) 273

Symphony No. 39, Franz Joseph Haydn: Eighteenth-century Viennese orchestral music   289

Sultan Veled Peshrev, Dogan Ergin: Turkish religious processional music   308

Absalon, fili mi, Josquin Desprez: Sixteenth-century French motet   317

Suite Thursday, Duke Ellington and Billy Strayhorn: Twentieth-century North American big band jazz   333

Gary White holds a Ph.D. in Music Composition from Michigan State University. At his retirement in 1994 he was Distinguished Professor of Music at Iowa State University, where he developed and administered the music theory curriculum and established the electronic and computer music studio. For a number of years he was also in charge of music listening courses for the general student at Iowa State.

Dr. White is the composer of over fifty published musical compositions and the author of *Music First!* (a music fundamentals textbook) and *Instrumental Arranging* (a textbook for orchestration and arranging), both published by McGraw-Hill. He has been awarded the U.C. Berkeley Medal by the University of California at Berkeley, was named a National Arts Associate by Sigma Alpha Iota, and has held a MacDowell Colony Fellowship. His compositions have won many prizes and awards, including the Toon van Balkom Prize and the Shenandoah/Percussion Plus Prize.

David Stuart is Associate Professor of Music at Iowa State University and principal trombonist of the Des Moines Symphony Orchestra. He received his DMA in trombone pedagogy and performance from the University of Iowa and studied at the Akademie für Musik und darstellende Kunst in Vienna, Austria.

Dr. Stuart teaches the low brass studio at Iowa State University, the undergraduate nonmajor music listening course, and a course on the history of rock 'n' roll. Iowa State named him an Outstanding Teacher at the Introductory Level in 1999. He is currently pursuing research on the influence of Celtic folk music on recent popular music.

Dr. Stuart has written articles for the *International Trombone Association Journal, National Association of College Wind and Percussion Teachers,* and *The School Musician,* and several publications for the Yamaha Corporation. He is the editor of an Italian baroque chamber music series published by Nova Music, London. Dr. Stuart is a Yamaha performing artist.

Elyn Aviva is an anthropologist as well as a professional writer and editor. She earned a Ph.D. in cultural anthropology from Princeton University and a master of divinity degree from Iliff School of

Theology. She has been a tribal planner for the Kickapoo Tribe of Kansas, worked as the editor of an international high-technology newsletter, taught religious studies, and published a book on the Camino de Santiago, a 1,000-year-old pilgrimage road across northern Spain.

Dr. Aviva has a long-standing interest in comparative religion and has published articles in various national magazines on labyrinths, pilgrimage, sacred sites in Europe, and the reinvention of tradition. She is an avid listener to musics from all parts of the world and enjoys exploring their cultural context.

Audience

Music in Our World: An Active-Listening Approach is a textbook designed for any introductory music listening course. These courses are usually single-semester or single-quarter courses and often carry titles such as Music Appreciation, Introduction to Music, Music Listening, or Survey of Music Literature. Because of the cultural and historical background accompanying the music examples, *Music in Our World* would also be suitable as the musical part of a general humanities course. Since it provides a self-contained course of study, it could also be appropriate for individuals who want to expand their musical background.

Approach

This textbook assumes that the student has no specialized knowledge of or training in music. The core of the book is an active-listening approach that focuses on the elements of music (rhythm, melody, harmony, dynamics, timbre, and texture) and applies them to examples drawn from world music.

We live in a society filled with music, but most of this music is merely heard rather than listened to with active attention. In *Music in Our World* students will develop active-listening skills that they can apply to all the music to which they choose to listen. The active-listening approach in this book is a method for focusing the student's attention on specific musical elements of the works being listened to. Listening guides provide detailed timelines to lead students through this active-listening process.

An asterisk "*" preceding a name means that there is more information in Appendix B.

Emphasis on the elements of music has proved highly successful in developing musicianship skills in methods such as the *Orff Schulwerk*. In *Music in Our World*, the emphasis on elements is applied to the development of listening skills. This approach is an effective way to organize a course in active listening because each of the elements in turn becomes the focus for listening. Students initially learn to listen to these elements in a variety of musical styles, from a variety of cultures, and later use these skills to identify larger formal patterns in music.

Although we organize the book around the musical elements, we don't ignore the cultural and historical context of the music

By *Western* we mean the Western European cultural community, including the United States. We do not mean a specific geographical location. Native American societies, for example, live in "the West" but are not historically European cultures.

examples. For instance, when we use Native American powwow music as the example for learning about beat, we provide ample background on the role of the powwow and powwow music in Native American cultures. This background will enable students to appreciate powwow music within its own cultural context. The discussion of Hildegard of Bingen's *De sancta Maria*—selected as an example of vocal melody—includes information about the composer's cultural milieu; it also places her music in the chronological sequence of Western European art music. This chronological sequence is central to the understanding of the historical development of Western musical culture, although it is not relevant for the music of many other cultures.

We believe that the elements approach, together with cultural and historical background, provides an effective way to develop active-listening skills while imparting a broad-based knowledge and appreciation of the wide variety of the world's music.

We are living at a unique time in world history. Rapid transportation gives us contact with people from many different cultural backgrounds. Television, movies, and recordings bring the world's cultures into our living rooms every day. The impact of the Internet, which allows us to share information, including visual and aural materials, worldwide, is just beginning to be felt. Cultural contact has always led to cross-pollination, but this cross-pollination is much more rapid and pervasive today than ever before. This suggests that it is time for a new approach to the teaching of music appreciation. *Music in Our World* is in tune with this reality and provides a resource that instructors can use to structure courses that truly meet the needs of the current generation of students.

Content and Organization

The textbook is organized around the six elements of music. After an introduction to active listening (prelude) and an examination of the place of music within society (Chapter 1) and of our individual responses to music (Chapter 2), students are introduced to each element in turn. After becoming thoroughly familiar with these elements and learning to recognize them in diverse music examples, students learn to listen to the elements in combination and to identify larger musical patterns.

Cultural and historical background is provided in each chapter for the chosen music example; in addition, relevant information is provided about the performers and composer. The chapters provide pertinent cultural and historical background so that students will be better able to appreciate the music as it is experienced in its culture of origin. By putting disparate musics side by side, we learn about their similarities as well as their differences.

Each topic in the textbook is illustrated by carefully selected music examples. Detailed listening guides with accurate timings in minutes and seconds call attention to the features of the work that the student is to concentrate on during a given listening session. Later in the textbook, some of these music examples are listened to again with new listening guides that focus attention on additional musical elements.

Each chapter has a section called "Applying What You Have Learned." In these sections the students are asked a series of questions that encourage them to listen again to music examples that they have listened to in previous chapters. By applying what they have just learned, they are able to deepen their appreciation of the music. Other questions lead the students to apply what they have learned to music they listen to outside the classroom. Still others suggest short research projects. At the discretion of the instructor, some of these questions can be the basis of class discussion, whereas others can be assigned as homework.

Another special feature of *Music in Our World* is a series of enrichment boxes. These boxes present more detailed information about the topics under discussion: for example, the development of musical instruments, biographical details on musicians and other people mentioned in the main narrative, additional cultural-historic background, and summaries of stylistic periods in Western European art music.

Music in Our World includes many names and terms, some of which may not be familiar to students, so we have included a pronunciation guide (Appendix A) at the back of the book. Appendix B provides additional biographical information about many of the composers and performers mentioned in the book.

Marginal notes throughout the text provide immediately accessible definitions of terminology. Numerous photographs, graphics, and charts are also provided. This attractive multidimensional format is in keeping with the way we acquire information from contemporary print and electronic media. It also gives instructors considerable freedom to structure the materials to fit their own tastes and the level of the students in the course.

It is important that all the music students are asked to listen to is easily available. For this reason, two CDs come bound with the book. These CDs contain the selections in the detailed listening guides.

We have selected musical works on the basis of their suitability to illustrate the concepts and develop the active-listening skills that are the core of our approach. Our choices and our way of organizing them were also guided by our desire to show similarities and differences among musical works and to provide rich, varied listening experiences throughout the course. We have chosen music from recordings available in any well-stocked music shop in the United States. We have excluded current popular music (the top forty, the music on the charts) since this music changes rapidly and would soon be dated. For the music of non-Western European cultures, we have chosen examples that lie somewhere between ethnomusicological field recordings and highly syncretic popular recordings.

Thus we offer a carefully selected sample of the world's music, ranging from the twelfth century to the present. This sampling is representative of the music from which students will probably choose their listening experiences. Our goal has been to affirm the richness of the world's music. Although we concentrate on only twenty-three works, we suggest a wider range of possible listening activities in "Further Listening Resources" at the end of each chapter. Instructors are encouraged to include still other listening activities.

The reader will notice quoted passages in the text. Citations are provided in Endnotes, page 373.

Supplements

For students, the twenty-three works in the listening guides are included in the two CDs that accompany this book. As noted above, additional listening is suggested at the end of each chapter, providing the student with a list of CDs and videos that may be checked out of a library or purchased at a music shop.

For the instructor, in addition to the Website, the *Instructor's Manual* provides supplementary resources. These resources include discussion questions and exercises beyond those in "Applying What You Have Learned." Additional information and anecdotes about musical styles, instruments, composers, and performers are also provided, along with a bank of examination questions. Further audiovisual resources are also suggested.

The Online Learning Center for *Music in Our World* is an Internet-based resource for students and faculty that provides an extensive selection of material, including self-graded quizzes, free listening software, discussion questions, and online access to the *Instructor's Manual.* The OLC is located at http://www.mhhe.com/miow.

Acknowledgments

We wish to thank Chris Freitag and JoElaine Retzler, our editors at McGraw-Hill, for their support for this project. They had a vision of what this book could become, a vision that we hope we have finally fulfilled. Gary and Elyn wish to thank each other for their mutual support, encouragement, and patience. David wishes to thank Dixie Bjurstrom and Robert Fuqua for their assistance. We all wish to thank John Galm, Chaitanya Kabir, Hankus Netsky, Quentin Navia, Pete Gahbow, and Mike Pace for their invaluable assistance. We also want to thank the students at Iowa State University who have provided input and enthusiasm for this book while it was a work in progress.

The reviewers of the manuscript contributed many helpful suggestions. Our sincerest thanks are extended to Claire Detels, University of Arkansas; Dana F. Everson, Delta College; Judith Glyde, University of Colorado–Boulder; David Knowles, Mississippi Gulf Coast Community College; Jean L. Kreiling, Bridgewater State College; Robert Pringle, Trinidad State Junior College; Floyd Slotterback, Northern Michigan University; Janet Sturman, University of Arizona; Joan Van Liew, Carl Sandburg College; Robert J. Ward, Oklahoma State University; John M. Ware, Virginia Union University; and Larry Weed, Valencia Community College.

Music in
Our World

An Active-Listening Approach

Introduction

to Active Listening

You, the student, have probably chosen this course for one or more of the following reasons. You may have a love of music and want to understand it better. You may have a hunger for new musical experiences. You may have intellectual curiosity about how music works—how it creates the powerful emotions you experience when you are listening. You may simply be fulfilling a requirement in your curriculum. Whatever your reason or reasons, we hope to provide a framework that will help you and your instructor travel broadly and in some depth into the fascinating world of music.

AFP/Corbis

PRELUDE   Active Listening   **4**
Dolphin Dreams, Jonathan Goldman

CHAPTER 1   Music in Society   **11**
Simple Gifts, Elder Joseph Brackett
Appalachian Spring, Aaron Copland

CHAPTER 2   Our Response to Music   **30**
Exodus and *Redemption Song,* Bob Marley

Active Listening

💿 ***Dolphin Dreams,*** Jonathan Goldman

Stuart Westmorland/Corbis

The art of music is so deep and profound that to approach it very seriously only is not enough. One must approach music with a serious vigor and, at the same time, with a great, affectionate joy.

*NADIA BOULANGER (1887–1979)
COMPOSITION TEACHER AND CONDUCTOR

4

"Before the Common Era" (*B.C.E.*) is now often used as a substitute for B.C. (before Christ). Similarly, *C.E.* (Common Era) is now often used instead of A.D. (*anno Domini*) which stands for "in the year of our Lord"—the Christian era.

If you were simply to read this book without listening to any of the music selections, you could achieve a good intellectual knowledge of music, but that would not be satisfying. Words are not enough. You need to listen repeatedly to the music that we have selected as examples. As the Greek philosopher Heraclitus (c. 540–c. 480 B.C.E.) said, "Much learning does not teach understanding." Real understanding will occur when you alternate listening and reading—when you allow your subjective impressions to be informed by the information we provide. Repeated listening takes time. Much of your "study" time in this course will be devoted to listening. We will provide detailed listening guides to direct your attention to important features of the works, but it will also be very important for you to spend time listening without looking at the book.

Most of the time we are not particularly conscious of our sound environment. We listen to what we want (or need) and ignore the rest. For example, if you are in conversation with another person, you probably ignore background noises, music, or even other people talking. A distinction we, the authors, make in this book is the

Hearing music
Tony Freeman/Photo Edit

Listening to music
Jeff Greenberg/Photo Edit

Boldfaced words
are listed under
"Important Terms"
at the end of the
chapter.

difference between **hearing** and **listening.** Hearing is the passive act of receiving and registering the sounds that reach your ears. Listening requires your active attention.

The purpose of this book is to teach you to listen to music with deeper understanding and appreciation. Throughout the book we will direct your attention to various aspects of the music you will hear. Our intent is to make your music listening experience more active and involved.

LISTENING ACTIVITY

Dolphin Dreams (Jonathan Goldman) [CD 1, track 1]

We begin with a short experiment in **active listening.** This work, an excerpt from a CD called *Dolphin Dreams,* created by Jonathan Goldman, is a mixture of several layers of natural sound. Don't concern yourself at this point with whether or not *Dolphin Dreams* is a piece of music, though that is a very interesting question. Our intent in this exercise is to focus on the act of listening versus the act of hearing.

Step One

Before beginning this listening exercise, find a comfortable position and relax. You may find that closing your eyes will help you to focus on what you are about to hear. As you listen to the excerpt from *Dolphin Dreams,* try to identify the sounds you hear. Some sounds will be familiar to you; others may not. Be prepared to make a mental list of the sound sources you recognize on the first hearing. Now, begin listening to the excerpt (CD 1, track 1).

What sounds were you able to recognize? How many different sounds did you hear? Compare your mental list with the list given in step two.

Step Two

Here are the sounds found in *Dolphin Dreams:*

Ocean

Seagulls

Human heartbeat

Chorus singing a wordless lullaby

Underlying chant: the Sanskrit mantra "om"

Dolphin sounds

Now, listen again with the complete list in front of you and see how many sounds you can identify. (Note: some of the sounds are not present at the beginning of the excerpt.)

Were you able to identify all the sounds on the list on the first hearing? On the second hearing? If you identified additional sounds in your second hearing, your enjoyment in listening to *Dolphin Dreams* may have been enhanced. You may need several hearings to find all the sounds in this complex mixture. As you move deeper into the work and become aware of all the various sounds, you are moving toward **active listening** as opposed to merely hearing.

The "wordless lullaby" is a simple melody similar to those found in lullabies throughout the world. The Sanskrit mantra is a single pitch sung on the syllable "om." Hindu sages believe that chanting "om" can bring enlightenment and a sense of well-being. Chanting mantras such as "om" continues to be a central part of the religious experience of many people in India. This practice has spread widely

Meditating by the Ganges River, India
Robert Holmes/Corbis

throughout the world and is used in the United States in several forms of meditation.

Jonathan Goldman and the Creation of *Dolphin Dreams*

Jonathan Goldman began creating *Dolphin Dreams* in 1988, when his wife was pregnant. He wanted to create a sonic environment to be used during the birth of their child. He says, "This sonic environment would contain the sounds present in an experience swimming with dolphins, which I felt would enhance the birthing process." (Details of the production process are described on pages 252–253.) The Goldmans' son, Joshua, was born to the sonics in this recording and, Goldman reports, ". . . since then, thousands of babies throughout the planet have been born to *Dolphin Dreams*. It has been used successfully in hospitals, in birthing clinics, and at home births. It also seems to be great at calming and balancing newborn infants, children, and adults."

Goldman began his musical career as a rock 'n' roll musician but later shifted to studying psychoacoustics: how sound affects the brain. Goldman is a composer, producer, and creator of award-winning music, as well as a widely read author. He is a member of several professional societies that study the relationship between sound and healing, and he teaches workshops on the topic throughout the United States and Europe.

Is *Dolphin Dreams* Music?

Jonathan Goldman swimming with a dolphin
Spirit Music

A question that we asked you to set aside at the beginning of this listening exercise was whether or not *Dolphin Dreams* is a piece of music. Now that you are more familiar with the work, we ask you to think about this question. *Dolphin Dreams* is probably very different from music you have been familiar with, but is it simply music of a different sort, or is it something entirely different? If it is not music, what is it?

What is your definition of music? One standard definition is that music is an art whose medium is sound and time. Does *Dolphin Dreams* fit that definition? You may find a class discussion of these issues interesting and enlightening.

Summary

Hearing is the act of receiving and registering the sounds that reach your ears. Listening requires your active attention and involves an attempt to understand and appreciate the sounds. As you direct your attention to various sounds, you will notice more and more details. Your aural experience will become more rewarding and pleasurable. Active listening will help you to achieve a richer and more enjoyable musical life.

Applying What You Have Learned

In each chapter of this book you will find a section called "Applying What You Have Learned." These sections provide opportunities for you to listen again to previous musical selections or to do other exercises to use your newly acquired active-listening skills. Your instructor may use material from these sections in class or make outside assignments based on some of these exercises.

1. Create an "ear map" of *Dolphin Dreams,* indicating precisely (in minutes and seconds) when you first hear each of the sounds listed on pages 6 and 7. Use your CD player's time display for this or a watch that indicates seconds. Now list on your "ear map" the other sounds you are also able to hear at each of the points you listed above.

2. Goldman intentionally selected a variety of sounds to achieve a certain effect. Can you recall intentionally using sound in this way? If so, what kinds of sounds and for what purposes? (For example, you might have used sounds to help you sleep, to wake you up, to help you study, etc.)

Important Terms

hearing 6   listening 6   active listening 7

Names preceded
by * have short
biographies in
Appendix B, page 346

Musician Mentioned

*Jonathan Goldman

Further Listening Resources

Other recordings by Jonathan Goldman include: *Gateways: Men's Drumming and Chanting, Angel of Sound, Song of Saraswati, Trance Tara,* and *Chakra Chants,* which won the 1999 Visionary Awards for "Best Healing Meditation Music" and "Album of the Year."

Similar works include *Spectrum Suite* by Steven Halpern.

CHAPTER 1

Music in Society

- 💿 *Simple Gifts,* Elder Joseph Brackett
- 💿 *Appalachian Spring,* Aaron Copland

Culver Pictures

What science cannot declare, art can suggest; what art suggests silently, poetry speaks aloud; but what poetry fails to explain in words, music can express.

*HAZRAT INAYAT KHAN (1882–1927)
FOUNDER, SUFI ORDER OF THE WEST

Music from all societies and times has reflected the culture in which it developed. Humans have created music to express their strongest emotions and deepest spiritual feelings. In ceremonies and rituals, while working in the fields or at sea, and while relaxing, men and women have made music. They have danced, sung, and adapted natural objects to create music by striking, scraping, plucking, or blowing through them.

People have taught each other music, either formally through classes and apprenticeships or informally through group participation and repetition. They have passed music on from generation to generation, in writing or orally. Originally transmission took place in person, but now it often occurs by means of computers and recordings.

Music has the power to generate emotion. It may excite passions, calm fears, inspire actions, or even draw tears. Music is a central part of the human experience. In this chapter we will examine music in its social context; in the next chapter we will consider our individual responses to music.

There is a wide diversity of musical styles throughout the world. Social, geographical, and political conditions as well as group philosophies shape the music preferred by different societies. Not only does music reflect the values of a society—it can also be a force for change.

Since the beginning of human societies, people have created music to express themselves. The oldest known musical instrument, a fragment of a Neanderthal bone flute, is believed to be at least 43,000 years old. A Cro-Magnon carved bone flute, discovered in 1986, is about 30,000 years old. Some scientists have even speculated that music predated speech.

Early Humans

Neanderthal is the name given to early humans of the Paleolithic Period whose first skeletal remains were found in the Neander Valley (*Thal*, or *Tal*, is the German word for "valley") in the Rhein province. Although scientists once believed these early distant relatives of humans to be brutish creatures whose only sounds were grunts, the discovery of a bone flute fragment in Slovenia in 1996 is changing our ideas about Neanderthals and about the beginnings of music.

Cro-Magnon is the name given to anatomically modern humans who lived in Europe and the Middle East from about 40,000 to 30,000 years ago until the end of the Pleistocene epoch some 10,000 years ago. Much more is known about their culture than that of any other prehistoric humans. A number of locations in Europe have yielded beautifully made Cro-Magnon stone tools as well as artifacts of bone and wood. Burial sites reveal that these groups engaged in a variety of ritual activities and made music.

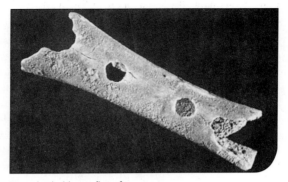

Neanderthal bone flute fragment
Ivan Turic, Slovenian Academy of Sciences, Ljubljana

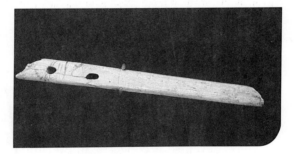

30,000-year-old Cro-Magnon carved bone flute
Hank Morgan

Language

Music is unlike language, which has fixed, shared meanings for every word; language conveys specific meaning through commonly accepted sounds and written symbols. Words, the symbols of language, have a direct correlation to ideas, places, and things. We say that language is denotative because words have definite meanings. Language is also connotative: our spoken and written communications often carry implied or associated meanings that go beyond the explicit "face value" of the words.

   Words refer to things we can point to (a chair, a dog) and to abstract ideas (such as truth or beauty) that we can talk about because they have (more or less) agreed-upon meanings. Sometimes we say that a particular language is "musical," but this refers to the way it sounds (perhaps it seems melodic to our ears, like someone singing), not to the way it "means."

Music

We also speak of the "language of music," but this is a kind of language different from spoken or written language. Music communicates in a more oblique fashion than words. Even though there may be general agreement about the purpose or general character of a piece of music, it is impossible to put into words precisely what the music "means."

The composer and conductor Leonard Bernstein observed that "there have been more words written about Ludwig van Beethoven's *Eroica* symphony than there are notes in it; in fact I should imagine that the proportion of words to notes, if anyone could get an accurate count, would be flabbergasting. And yet, has anyone ever successfully 'explained' the *Eroica*?"

Music, like the other arts, springs from our desire to create works that reflect our feelings, thoughts, ideas, and emotions.

Setting

Many questions can be asked about music in society, such as where it takes place, when it is performed, by whom, who is the audience, what is being performed, and why. The answers will vary not only from society to society but also within a society.

Music occurs in a variety of **settings.** We hear music at church, at athletic events, at concerts, in our homes, in elevators, in shopping malls, and in many other places. Some settings are formal—for example, a symphony concert. Others are informal, such as a bar or club. Some are group settings while others are individual settings.

Think about the difference between hearing a piece of rock music on your personal CD player and hearing the same music at a large rock concert. Listening to music with earphones puts you and the sounds in a very private space; you are not with other people, and you are not watching the performers. At a rock concert, on the other hand, you are part of a large, enthusiastic group of people, perhaps singing along, perhaps jumping up and down or dancing, perhaps holding up a lit cigarette lighter. You experience the music and your fellow participants, the performers onstage, and perhaps a state-of-the-art light and laser show. The setting in which we hear music is an important part of our experience of the music.

There is evidence that the Sumerians used music in **ceremonial settings** as early as 2400 B.C.E. Hymns were sung to accompany many rituals and festivals. Stone carvings show musical performances that included both singers and instruments. People played string instruments resembling the modern harp and hoop drums. Musicians were divided into two castes: those who performed

A *hymn* is a song of praise to God.

A page from Beethoven's *Eroica* Symphony

music in the service of gods and kings, and those who performed laments.

The following excerpt from a Sumerian poem extols the value of music.

Music's Ministry
To fill with joy the temple court,
And chase the city's gloom away,
The heart to still, the passions calm,
Of weeping eyes and tears to stay.

A *shaman* (the term comes from the Siberian Tungu tribe) is a person who goes into a trance in order to heal the sick or for other purposes. Today, the term is often used, more generally, for people who enter a trance or ecstatic state to remove a threat to an individual or a community.

The *mass* is the central Catholic religious service.

Music has been used to enhance religious ceremonies in all cultures, and music is often composed especially to accompany religious rites. In Siberian shamanic practices a drum is beaten to alter the shaman's state of consciousness so that he or she can "enter" the spirit world. The music for the requiem mass in the Roman Catholic liturgy and the chanting of Buddhist monks are other examples of music that occurs in a religious ceremonial setting.

Music is a significant part of the secular ceremonial life of any culture. Many official state functions are accompanied by music, which helps "set the stage" and makes the ceremonies more solemn. Consider, for example, the use of music as a part of the celebration of national events in the United States such as Independence Day (July 4) and Memorial Day. On these days there are likely to be parades with marching bands, outdoor concerts, and music to accompany ceremonies and gatherings.

Purpose

To ask why a piece of music was created raises a fundamental question: what is the intention of the music? What is its **purpose**?

Sumerian musicians with drum
Erich Lessing/ART Resource, N.Y.

Music is created for many purposes. These purposes include:

Religion (music for the Catholic mass; Buddhist ceremonial chanting)

Spirituality (New Age meditative music; music created to promote inner healing)

Group cohesion (a national anthem; a sports team's theme)

Utilitarian effects (helping a group coordinate physical labor; taking people's minds off of the difficulty of their work)

Communicating verbal and nonverbal messages

Entertainment (rock 'n' roll, hip-hop)

Motivation (protest songs; marches)

Artistic expression (music for its own sake—music that doesn't "do" but simply "is")

New Age is a general term for a diverse group of popular social movements in the latter half of the twentieth century, drawing on ancient spiritual concepts, especially from Eastern and Native American traditions.

Many of these purposes overlap. For example, if a piece of music is composed for a military setting, the "rat-tat-tat" of the drum helps the troops march together and also may serve to inspire them.

Much of the music of all cultures is **utilitarian:** that is, it serves a purpose beyond simply being listened to for its own sake. Military marches, work songs, sea chanteys, and aerobic exercise music all help us move in rhythm and make our tasks more efficient, easier, and more pleasurable. The strong rhythmic component of music gives it a compelling link to dance and other physical activities. Music is often used to help synchronize the movement of groups of people.

Work Songs

Work songs and **sea chanteys** have long been used throughout the world to help make mundane tasks more efficient and pleasant. This music was also a way for people to exert some control in environments where their control was otherwise limited. Singing the strong rhythms of these songs helped workers set and keep a pace and coordinate their movements. Usually the melodies were simple and repetitive, and the rhythms were driving and exciting. Often these songs were performed as **call and response.**

When seamen on early sailing ships fought the drag of line and anchor, they coordinated their efforts by singing together in rhythm with their work. Chanteying fell into disuse on English ships during the eighteenth century but reemerged on American ships in the early nineteenth century. These fast American ships had a great spread of canvas and a smaller crew. Singing chanteys allowed the work to be done by fewer hands, since sailors could more precisely coordinate the pulling of ropes. The chanteyman stood close to the mast, and the gang (the sailors) laid hold of the rope. The chanteyman sang his first line, and then all the sailors hauled and sang together on the response line.

Motivational Music

Music has been used to motivate and create unity of purpose in crowds throughout history and around the world. Armies often sang as they went into battle, and the sound of drums, bugles, or bagpipes raised the spirits of soldiers and struck fear into the hearts of their opponents. In the United States, protest songs and spirituals were an important part of the civil rights movement; these songs provided solidarity and support during difficult times. Singing and chanting at athletic events is another example of **motivational music,** as is a rousing rendition of a national anthem.

Background Music

Background music may be defined as music that people are supposed to hear but not listen to while they are engaged in some other activity. Music can provide a pleasant background. It can also be used to cover up less desirable sounds, such as machinery or unwanted conversation.

Call and Response

The kind of singing in which a group (chorus) answers a single voice (soloist) is called *call-and-response* or *responsorial* singing. Call-and-response singing is usually characterized by short melodies sung by a vocal soloist and answered immediately by another singer or a group. This technique is common in work songs around the world. It was also an important part of music of the early Christian church (e.g., in Gregorian chant, see page 109), where its purpose was ceremonial and the responses were preestablished. Call and response is also characteristic of instrumental jazz and related styles; in this case, it was derived from African call-and-response singing, in which the responses were often improvised.

Modern sailors hoisting a sail
Natalie Fobes/Corbis

Source: THE FAR SIDE © 1990
FarWorks, Inc. Reprinted with permission. All rights reserved.

Background music for films and
television makes scenes come alive
with an intensity that is not possible
with visual imagery alone. We are so
accustomed to music as part of multi-
media presentations that a spectacular
sight like Niagara Falls or Notre Dame
cathedral in Paris might seem a bit dis-
appointing without background music.

The background music we hear in
elevators, restaurants, and supermar-
kets is designed to stimulate buying,
provide a relaxing environment for
dining or shopping, and influence the
emotions of those who hear it. The
Muzak Corporation has provided this
kind of music for commercial appli-
cations for nearly fifty years and has
been so successful that Muzak has become a generic term, like
Kleenex for facial tissue or Xerox for photocopies.

Studies have found that the productivity of workers is improved
when certain types of background music are played in offices and
manufacturing plants. While many musicians refer to Muzak
derogatorily as "elevator music," no one denies the commercial success and power of background music in many contexts.

Art Music

Although we can appreciate music "for its own sake" even when it
is incidental to another activity, appreciation is more likely when
music is the focus of our attention. **Art music** is performed primarily for its intrinsic value. When you attend a symphony orchestra
concert (see page 207), a piano recital, or a performance of classical Indian music (see page 124), you are expected to remain very
quiet and listen attentively. The concert hall was created as a setting
for undisturbed listening, and appropriate audience behavior—
silence—is an important part of the setting. While art music exists
for its own sake and has no external utilitarian purpose, the moti-
vations of an individual listener may include achieving elite status,
participating in the social setting of the concert hall, and having a
deeply satisfying musical experience.

The Changing Functions of Music

Music has a wonderful flexibility and attractiveness that enable it
to shift from one social function to another. In the Middle Ages,

Arthur Rubinstein
Corbis-Bettman

popular street melodies were brought into the church and used as the basis for religious music. For example, *L'Homme armé* ("The Armed Man"), a popular fifteenth-century melody, was used by a number of composers as the basis for the music for masses.

Sea chanteys, originally sung by hardworking sailors, have been picked up and sung by popular Irish music groups, as well as by groups of friends singing together informally. Here the function changes to entertainment, or perhaps—depending on the musical arrangement—to art music. Bob Dylan's protest songs of the 1960s have remained popular, long after what he was protesting about has been forgotten. Johannes Brahms's "Lullaby" was composed as an art song, but it has been hummed for generations by mothers to put their babies to sleep.

The purpose of a piece of music often changes when the setting changes. Think about what happens when an excerpt from a classical symphony is used as background music for a television commercial. This music, which originally had an artistic purpose, has now taken on a utilitarian purpose—to sell something. It is interesting to consider why classical music is chosen for some commercials and not for others. For example, when a classical piece plays in the background of a commercial for a luxury automobile, what is the company trying to communicate about the vehicle? How would the message change if rock music were chosen?

Modern technology is, of course, partly responsible for this shifting of functions. We don't have to go to a monastery to hear Gregorian chant; instead, we can buy a CD and listen to the music at home while we study—we can even watch monks chanting on a video. We don't need to go to Jamaica to hear reggae; we can turn on the radio and listen to it while we do dishes. By changing the original setting, we often change the function of a piece of music.

Simple Gifts

As we have pointed out, music often changes function when the setting is changed. The American Shaker **hymn** tune *Simple Gifts* is a good example. In its original form it was performed as a part of Shaker religious services. As an important theme in the ballet *Appalachian Spring* by the American composer Aaron Copland, an orchestral setting of the tune *Simple Gifts* became music to accompany dance. When Copland scored some of the music for full symphony orchestra, the result was concert music.

> To *score* music is to write or arrange it for a specific performance medium, such as orchestra.

The United Society of Believers in Christ's Second Appearing (Shakers)

The **Shakers** are members of a religious movement founded in 1772 by a young married woman named Ann Lee, later known as "Mother Ann." They are a group that splintered from an English Quaker community and came to the United States to live together without being persecuted. They were not entirely successful in this, however, since attacks continued to be made upon them in the United States during the nineteenth century. Their radical views of the Second Coming, their ecstatic worship services (which earned them the name "Shaking Quakers"), and the gender equality they practiced in communal governance put them increasingly outside mainstream Christian ideology.

> *Second Coming* refers to the Christian belief about the coming of Christ as a judge of human behavior on the "last day"—the end of the world.

Music and dance were important in the Shakers' religious services. Their hymns expressed the "Inner Light," a concept that was central to their faith; and their dances expressed the ecstasy generated as this light came into their being. The text for the hymn *Simple Gifts* alludes to the central importance of the Shakers' dancing prayer:

Illumination of the text for *Simple Gifts* by Sister Karlyn Cauley
© 1983; licensee Little Creatures, Inc.

'Tis the gift to be simple, 'Tis the gift to be free,
'Tis the gift to come down where you ought to be,
And when we find ourselves in the place just right,
'Twill be in the valley of love and delight.

When true simplicity is gained
To bow and to bend we shan't be ashamed,
To turn, turn will be our delight,
'Till by turning, turning we come round right.

The Believers, as the Shakers called themselves, usually played no musical instruments in worship services, convinced that instruments would be too stimulating and would interfere with direct inspiration. For the same reason they refused to use trained professional choirs, which they felt also excluded common people "from full participation in religious worship." For the Shakers, the central purpose of singing was to help members unite in worship. They developed songs of their own, based on "the World's" music—which

Shakers of New Lebanon, New York, 1873
Culver Pictures

was Anglo-American folk melody. These familiar, well-loved songs enabled even the least musically gifted to sing songs of worship. They did not simply copy these folk melodies, however; they changed, converted, and elaborated on them, guided by "divine inspiration."

The Shakers established communal farms from Maine to Indiana. At their peak, 6,000 Shakers lived in nineteen communities. At the height of the Shakers' popularity in the mid-1800s, tourists (whom the Shakers called "the World's People") came from all over to visit their communities and watch their worship services.

Their belief in celibacy, extreme simplicity, leadership equality between the sexes, communal ownership of property, God as a male–female duality, the Second Coming of Christ as a woman, and direct personal experience of God's presence set them apart from other Christian groups. In order to survive economically and to publicize their beliefs, they developed simple, functional furniture designs that have remained popular today. Their beautifully produced crafts, music, dancing, and books became quite successful.

The Shakers were very hardworking and were devoted to conservation and excellence in craftsmanship. They experimented with cross-breeding livestock and developed a leading agricultural experimental station at Pleasant Hill, Kentucky, where they also built the first municipal water system in the state. Their ingenuity resulted in many inventions, including the circular saw and the common clothespin.

By the late nineteenth century, however, their lifestyle was less attractive. The Shakers' emphasis on celibacy made it impossible to maintain the communities except through conversion or adoption. In 1965 the remaining Shakers in New Hampshire decided to admit no new members, although the community at Sabbathday Lake in Maine continues to accept converts. The communities at Pleasant Hill and South Union, Kentucky, have been turned into "living history" farms and museums.

Although the Shakers are nearly extinct, interest in Shaker beliefs and practices has been growing in recent years, as people search for ways to simplify and purify their lives. Websites have sprung up, making the writings of the Shaker leaders and prophets available to a new generation.

A *suite* is a collection of pieces intended to be played together.

In the following musical excerpts, the Shaker hymn *Simple Gifts* is used in two distinct ways. As a hymn sung by actual Shakers, it has a religious function. However, when the American composer Aaron Copland used this hymn tune in the final section of his ballet *Appalachian Spring, Ballet for Martha* (1944), the music is used to accompany dance, so it has a utilitarian function. The ballet was originally titled *Ballet for Martha*, having been composed for the modern dancer Martha Graham and her company. Copland also used music from this ballet (including the hymn tune) in a **suite** called *Appalachian Spring*, for full orchestra. In this context, the *Simple Gifts* melody functions as art music. The suite was created shortly after the ballet was composed. It was first performed by the New York Philharmonic, conducted by Artur Rodzinski, on 4 October 1945; and it was awarded the Pulitzer Prize for Music that same year.

Copland was a conductor, speaker, pianist, author, and much-admired teacher. His compositions include ballets, operas, film scores, orchestral and chamber music, piano and choral music, and songs. He was born in 1900 in Brooklyn, and as a young man he studied music in New York and Paris. During his "Americana" period, he composed popular pieces that include the cowboy ballets *Rodeo* and *Billy the Kid*, as well as *Twelve Poems of Emily Dickinson* (a composition for voice and piano) and two sets of *Old American Songs*. He was notable for his use of folk motifs and folklike motifs in grand, sweeping works, such as *Appalachian Spring*.

The Suite

In Europe as early as 1557, the word *suite* was used to designate a group of dance pieces. Pairing a slow dance with a livelier one is a tradition that extends back at least to the Renaissance period (1450–1600). Dance pairs called *Tanz* ("dance") and *Nachtanz* ("after dance") were gliding dances and leaping dances, respectively. In the baroque period (1600–1750), the suite consisted of four or more movements. One common pattern of four movements is *allemande, courante, saraband,* and *gigue.*

Dramatic Suite

A *dramatic suite* is an arrangement of excerpts from a larger dramatic work such as a ballet, an opera, or the incidental music for a play. Such a suite is often excerpted by the composer from the larger dramatic work to facilitate concert performance. One example is the *Nutcracker Suite*, excerpts from the popular Christmas ballet *The Nutcracker*, by Pyotr Il'yich Tchaikovsky. The suite from *Appalachian Spring* is another example.

LISTENING ACTIVITY

Simple Gifts, Elder Joseph Brackett [CD 1, track 2]

In this recording you will hear the original hymn tune sung by Sisters Elizabeth Dunn, Elsie McCool, Mildred Barker, Minnie Green, Marie Burgess, and Frances Carr of the Sabbathday Lake United Society of Shakers. It is sung as it would be sung in their services—as an unaccompanied melody. This song is said to have come as an inspiration (a "gift") to Elder Joseph Brackett in 1848. The Shakers describe him singing *Simple Gifts* while turning, his coattails flying out behind him.

Time	Text
0:00	'Tis the gift to be simple, 'Tis the gift to be free, 'Tis the gift to come down where you ought to be, And when we find ourselves in the place just right, 'Twill be in the valley of love and delight.
0:16	[The first section of the song is repeated.]
0:33	When true simplicity is gained To bow and to bend we shan't be ashamed, To turn, turn will be our delight, 'Till by turning, turning we come round right.
0:49	[The second section of the song is repeated.]

LISTENING ACTIVITY

Appalachian Spring, Ballet for Martha: Simple Gifts, Aaron Copland [CD 1, track 3]

This ballet is the story of preparations for a wedding in a Pennsylvania farming community. The use of the Shaker melody is a bit ironic, since the Shakers were celibate. The ballet was scored for thirteen instruments—the maximum number of players that could fit comfortably in the hall at the Library of Congress where the premiere took place on 30 October 1944. *Appalachian Spring, Ballet for Martha,* received the New York Music Critics Circle Award as the outstanding theatrical work of the 1944–1945 season. This performance was recorded in 1973 at the Thirtieth Street Studio in New York City. Aaron Copland was the conductor.

Time	Musical Event
0:00	First part of the hymn tune played softly by a clarinet with background in the strings.
0:15	Second part of the hymn tune. Other instruments are added.
0:28	Short connecting section.
0:33	First part of the hymn tune again. Gradually, more and more instruments are added.
0:47	Second part of the hymn tune.
1:00	Background material in the harp; then lower strings play first part of the hymn tune.
1:16	Overlapping statements of the first part of the hymn tune.
1:42	Short connecting section.
1:50	First part of the hymn tune.
2:02	Second part of the hymn tune.
2:15	Both parts of the hymn tune played at the same time. Gradually dying away to the end.

Strings is a general name for all the string instruments in the orchestra: violins, violas, violoncellos (cellos), and basses. See page 210 for information about the instruments.

Lower strings are the cellos and basses.

Summary

Music is a vital part of all human cultures and has been for over 43,000 years. While we often speak of the "language of music,"

music differs from spoken language in that it is not concrete and it is not denotative. In this chapter we have discussed some settings in which music occurs, and we have also noted the purposes music serves in various settings. These purposes may overlap. In addition, the purpose of a given piece may shift when the setting is changed. The Shaker hymn *Simple Gifts,* which was originally meant to be sung in religious services, became music to accompany dance in Aaron Copland's *Appalachian Spring, Ballet for Martha,* and then became art music in the suite from *Appalachian Spring.*

Applying What You Have Learned

1. Listen again to *Dolphin Dreams.* The CD jacket mentions that it was originally created to accompany childbirth. Can you imagine other settings where *Dolphin Dreams* might be

Historical Periods

Since the nineteenth century, musicologists (historians of music) have been interested in when a particular style of Western European art music came into existence and when it was no longer of general interest. In contrast, many other cultures think of their musical styles as having always existed and themselves as participating in a basically unchanging musical culture. In other words, they emphasize tradition instead of musical innovation or change.

In the nineteenth century, musicologists felt that the history of Western music of necessity followed Western European cultural history. This led to the division of this music into stylistic periods that are still used today, although a given period often includes very different kinds of music. While scholars disagree on the exact dates of these periods, most agree on the following approximations:

500	1450	1600	1750	1825	1900
Medieval Period	Renaissance Period	Baroque Period	Classical Period	Romantic Period	**Modern Period**

Aaron Copland's suite from *Appalachian Spring* is an example of what is referred to as modern Western European art music because European musical forms (the ballet and the suite) influenced it, because it was written "for its own sake," and because it was composed in the modern period. Throughout this book, we

will provide some details about the historical context of the works we are studying. When we are dealing with Western European art music, you will see the chart above with the historical period of the given music highlighted. Similar enrichment boxes will provide appropriate contexts for non-Western music.

used appropriately? What purpose would it serve in a different setting?

2. Listen to Copland's orchestral suite *Appalachian Spring*
    (CBS MK 42430 or any other recording) and compare it
    with the excerpt from the original ballet on CD 1, track 3.
    How does the orchestral version differ from the original?
    Which do you prefer? Can you hear how the music has
    become art music in this new setting?

3. Listen to some of the pieces suggested in Further Listening
    Resources (below) or others that your instructor suggests.
    Discuss each piece from the viewpoint of setting and
    purpose.

Important Terms

setting 14

ceremonial setting 14

purpose 16

utilitarian 17

work song 17

sea chantey 17

call and response 17

motivational music 18

background music 18

art music 19

hymn 21

Shakers 21

suite 24

Musicians Mentioned

Names preceded by *
have short biographies
in Appendix B, page
346.

*Leonard Bernstein

*Ludwig van Beethoven

*Bob Dylan

*Johannes Brahms

*Aaron Copland

Sister Elizabeth Dunn

Sister Elsie McCool

Sister Mildred Barker

Sister Minnie Green

Sister Marie Burgess

Sister Frances Carr

*Elder Joseph Brackett

Further Listening Resources

Mozart, *Requiem Mass,* Bavarian Radio, Leonard Bernstein, DG
427 353-2.

International Folk Dance Music Collection Laserlight 15 145 (Samba
de Brazil); 15 162.

Pete Seeger, Woody Guthrie, Josh White: *Talking Union,* Folkways,
FH 5285.

Beethoven, Symphony No. 3 in E-flat (*Eroica*), Leonard Bernstein conducting, New York Philharmonic, Sony SMK 47514.

Various artists, *Songs of Protest*, Wea/Atlantic/Rhino.

Generations of Folk, Vol. 2: *Protest and Politics*, Vanguard.

Various artists, *Negro Work Songs and Calls*, Rounder Select.

Southern Journey, Vol. 1: *Voices from the American South—Blues, Ballads, Hymns, Reels, Shouts, Chanteys and Work Songs*, Uni/Rounder.

Johnny Collins, *Shanties and Songs of the Sea*, Arc (UK).

Various artists, *Sea Songs and Shanties—from the Last Days*, Saydisc (UK).

Our Response to Music

Exodus and *Redemption Song,* Bob Marley

Phil Schermeister/Corbis

One learns practically nothing about the actual functioning of music by sitting in mute surrender before it.

*R. MURRY SCHAFER (B. 1933)

COMPOSER AND WRITER

In Chapter 1 we concentrated on music in society—its functions and the settings in which it is performed or heard. In this chapter we look at our individual responses to music. Individual responses to music can be grouped into four general categories: physical, emotional, cognitive, and spiritual. We will examine each of these responses in turn and then explore our individual responses to the music of Bob Marley. Our personal responses are unique. They reflect our life experiences and our personal understanding of the music we hear.

Physical Responses

Determined in part by the norms of your society and the patterns you picked up from adults when you were a child, **physical responses** to music are wide-ranging and include both subtle and obvious effects.

Watusi dance, Rwanda
Super Stock

Many of our physical responses to music are quite obvious. We dance, march, tap our feet, and move or sway to certain kinds of music. It is easy to observe an infant's physical response to music, even though that response may be uncoordinated. Babies will become quite active, moving their arms and legs when lively music is played. This kind of physical response to music is innate. We respond in spite of ourselves and often without being aware. For example, we may not realize that we are tapping our feet in time with music.

Latin music dance concert, New York City
Hazel Hankin/Stock Boston

Other physical responses are less obvious. When soothing music is played, we relax and become quiet. (Studies have found that cattle produce more milk when soothing music is played to them, and surgery patients recovered faster if soothing music was played during the surgery.) We respond to music that is interesting to us with increased attention and a generally increased level of physical tension. In addition, we respond to some music with an increase or decrease of tension that may not be apparent to others but which we can clearly recognize once our attention is directed to it.

Studies have also found other physical responses to music, such as changes in heart rate, respiration, and brain-wave patterns. These subtler effects are determined, for the most part, by the degree to which the listener is familiar with the style of the music. You are not likely to respond to music in an unfamiliar style in the same way as to music you have much experience with.

Emotional Responses

Music is capable of arousing strong **emotional responses.** What are these emotions? We have seen lists that include anger, anxiety, awe, despair, enthusiasm, excitement, fear, love, joy, frustration, gratitude, grief, happiness, hope, hate, hopelessness, passion, pleasure, pride, sadness, and sorrow—to name a few. There are innumerable shades and combinations of these emotions.

It is not uncommon to see an audience moved to tears by the power of music. Patriotic and martial music has long been known to inspire emotional reactions in troops and citizens. Consider the emotional reaction of winners at the Olympic Games as they stand on the platform to receive their medals and then hear their national anthem played in their honor: they almost always weep. Or consider the surge of emotion felt by students at a sports event when they hear their school song. Music therapists draw on the emotional and physical power of music to improve the well-being of their clients. Music therapy is now practiced in hundreds of hospitals and rehabilitation centers. Protest singers around the world have also drawn upon the emotional power of music to rouse people to action against perceived injustice.

The emotions we feel while listening to music are determined in part by the nature of the music, of course, but even more by our individual associations and experiences with the particular style and the piece itself. For example, a piece of music you associate with a particular event such as a wedding, a funeral, or your first date will carry an emotional meaning for you that is quite different from the emotion it arouses in someone else.

Music that is totally unlike anything you have heard before is unlikely to elicit the same emotional reaction from you as it would from a person steeped in the traditions of that music. Music that is pleasing to the ears of younger listeners may be jarring or irritating to their parents—and vice versa. Thus, your emotional responses are unlikely to be in total agreement with those of other listeners, and it is not possible to assign a single emotion to a piece of music. Nevertheless, the power of music to evoke emotional responses is undeniable.

Indian classical dancer
Lindsay Hebberd/Corbis

Lauryn Hill performs at music video awards
Reuters Newmedia/Corbis

Native American children
Lindsay Hebberd/Corbis

Cognitive Responses

Cognitive responses are a result of our thinking about music. When we listen to a specific piece of music, we often think of what we know about the performers, the composers, the instruments, or the setting and purpose. This knowledge can be both formal and informal.

Your informal knowledge of familiar music was acquired by your direct experiences with the music. Informal knowledge might consist of recognition of the piece or recognition of the same performer in a new piece, or a set of expectations about how a piece in a given style will sound. Since this knowledge was gained informally, you may have difficulty verbalizing it.

You may have added formal understanding to that informal knowledge by reading about the music. You may be unable to verbalize what you understand informally about a piece of music, but formal knowledge is acquired verbally (by reading, hearing a lecture, etc.) and can be talked about. For instance, you may have learned something about the given piece of music, such as biographical details about the composer (e.g., Beethoven was deaf later in life), or the history of the song (a Beatles' piece performed by many different groups), or the reputation of the performers (for example, the mystique of The Grateful Dead's concerts). This is formal understanding, and you can think about and discuss these details with others.

For music that is totally unfamiliar, you will have neither formal nor informal knowledge. As a result, your cognitive response may be curiosity or lack of interest. In this case, formal knowledge will greatly enhance your cognitive response. You will be able to think about what you are listening to and become a more active listener.

One of the goals of this course is to increase your formal knowledge about both familiar and unfamiliar music by providing information about the pieces you will study and also by providing cultural and social background.

Spiritual Responses

The word *spiritual* often brings religion to mind. However, there is a distinct difference between religion and spirituality. Broadly speaking, *religion* refers to structures, creeds, sacred texts, church buildings—the whole organized establishment that maintains a particular faith community. *Spirituality,* on the other hand, refers to personal experience of a particular kind—personal experience connected with transcendent values, with deepest meaning, with whatever you find most important in your life.

If you are a member of a religious faith, many of your most important values are likely to reflect the tenets of your religious community. However, some of your deeply held values may go beyond those tenets to include, for example, concern for the environment or concern for social justice, even if your faith community does not have teachings pertaining to those concerns. If you are not a mem-

Church choir singing
Nathan Benn/Corbis

ber of any religious community, you may still have deeply held spiritual values that are the result of your social background and cultural experience. You may have had a kind of spiritual experience on a wilderness backpacking trip or in shared community with others.

Some music has the power to connect with your transcendent values. We say that such music is "uplifting." It transports us to other dimensions of experience in ways that go beyond a simple emotional response. The power of music to move us in that way has long been recognized by religious organizations, which use music precisely because of its power to "lift us up" spiritually.

Even more than physical, emotional, or cognitive responses, **spiritual responses** depend on intimate experience with the cultural context of the music. Your spiritual response to a given piece of music is likely to be unlike that of another person because of your unique background and experiences. This will be true even if the other person shares your culture and even has similar religious convictions.

For example, the Hispanic Christian hymn *De Colores* speaks deeply and directly to the experience of Hispanic Christians. For traditional Puerto Rican–American Catholics, for example, the piece speaks to their social, economic, and spiritual connection to the land—as well as to God's promise to be present to God's people, as demonstrated by the rainbow. *De Colores* is now included in many Protestant hymnals and is often sung by Anglo Christians.

De Colores (first verse)

De colores, de colores se visten los campos en la primavera.	All the colors, yes, the colors we see in the springtime with all of its flowers.
De colores, de colores son los pajaritos que vienen de a fuera.	All the colors, when the sunlight shines out through a rift in the cloud and it showers.
De colores, de colores es al arco iris que vemos lucir.	All the colors, as a rainbow appears when a storm cloud is touched by the sun.
Y por eso los grandes amores de muchos colores me gustan a mi.	All the colors abound for the whole world around and for everyone under the sun.

Source: English version by David Arkin, Hodgin Press. In *Singing the Living Tradition,* the Unitarian Universalist Hymnal (Boston: Beacon Press, 1993), p. 305.

(Literal translation: In colors, in colors the fields bloom in spring. In colors, in colors the little birds fly from afar. In colors, in colors the rainbow arcs so clearly. And for this reason, these great loves of many colors are pleasing to me.)

However, it will not move a non-Hispanic in quite the same way it would a member of the Hispanic community, simply because of cultural differences—differences in language, differences in response to the issues surrounding skin color in our society, and differences in musical background and taste.

In the rest of this chapter we will examine the music of the Jamaican reggae musician and composer Bob Marley, the first musical superstar to come out of the third world. Marley's music began the 1960s reggae movement that has since spread around the world. His music is an excellent demonstration of how listeners will respond to music in different ways based on their backgrounds, the setting in which the music is performed, and the music's perceived purpose.

Four Categories of Human Attributes

Many of the world's religious traditions divide human attributes into four general categories that are similar to our four categories of human response to music. These attributes are described as if they were discrete categories, but in actual experience, of course, the categories overlap.

In Cabala (Kabbala), the mystical branch of Judaism, one finds the following description: "This arrangement [the Tree of Life] operates throughout the four divisions of a man [sic]

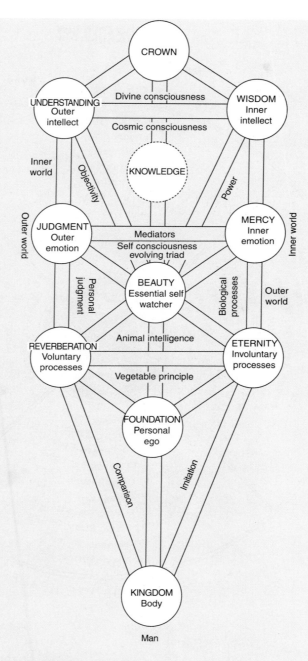

The Cabalistic representation of man

Source: Z'ev ben Shimon Halevi, Introduction to the Cabala Tree of Life *(York Beach, Maine: Samuel Weiser, 1972), Figure 2-5, p. 185. Used by permission.*

THE FOUR-FOLD WAY

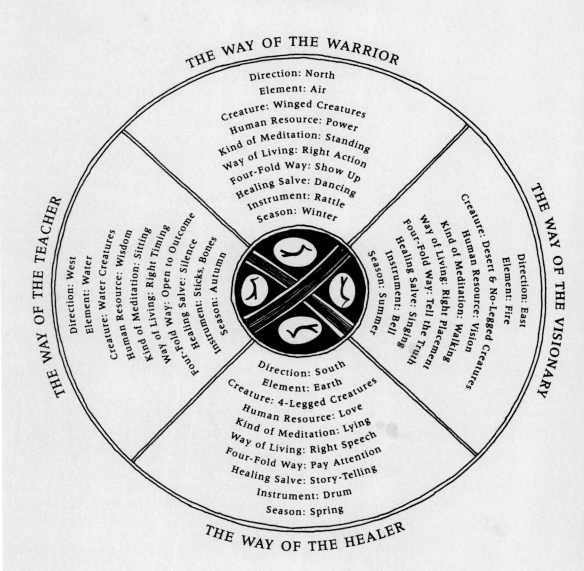

THE WAY OF THE WARRIOR

Direction: North
Element: Air
Creature: Winged Creatures
Human Resource: Power
Kind of Meditation: Standing
Way of Living: Right Action
Four-Fold Way: Show Up
Healing Salve: Dancing
Instrument: Rattle
Season: Winter

THE WAY OF THE TEACHER

Direction: West
Element: Water
Creature: Water Creatures
Human Resource: Wisdom
Kind of Meditation: Sitting
Way of Living: Right Timing
Four-Fold Way: Open to Outcome
Healing Salve: Silence
Instrument: Sticks, Bones
Season: Autumn

THE WAY OF THE VISIONARY

Direction: East
Element: Fire
Creature: Desert & No-Legged Creatures
Human Resource: Vision
Kind of Meditation: Walking
Way of Living: Right Placement
Four-Fold Way: Tell the Truth
Healing Salve: Singing
Instrument: Bell
Season: Summer

Direction: South
Element: Earth
Creature: 4-Legged Creatures
Human Resource: Love
Kind of Meditation: Lying
Way of Living: Right Speech
Four-Fold Way: Pay Attention
Healing Salve: Story-Telling
Instrument: Drum
Season: Spring

THE WAY OF THE HEALER

represented in the Assiatic, Yetziratic, Briatic and Atziluthic levels of the Tree: or in more human terms, the physical, emotional, intellectual and spiritual aspects of his nature."

Hazrat Inayat Khan, who is credited with bringing Sufism (see page 303) to the West in the early twentieth century, describes the four "magnetisms" as follows: "One of the aspects of personal magnetism is physical magnetism. . . . The second aspect of magnetism is the magnetism of mind. . . . The third aspect of magnetism is the magnetism of heart. . . . The fourth and highest aspect of magnetism is the magnetism of the soul."

The anthropologist Angeles Arrien makes a similar observation concerning the religions of indigenous peoples: "My research has demonstrated that virtually all shamanic traditions draw on the power of four archetypes in order to live in harmony and balance with our environment and with our own inner nature: the Warrior, the Healer, the Visionary, and the Teacher."

In the Hindu tradition we find the following description: "If we envisage the cosmos not merely as an unconscious mechanism but as a creative process, as the manifestation of a conscious power, we are led to search for an active or conscious substratum for each of the perceptible continua. . . . The substratum of space is existence (sat), the substratum of time is experience or enjoyment (ananda), and the substratum of thought is consciousness (cit). . . . The formless Immensity that appears to be the innermost nature of things can be grasped as the void, the silence, the absolute darkness, which lies beyond mind, beyond intellect, and can be realized as the substratum of man's [sic] own nature, as his own Self, his own Soul (atman)."

The Swiss psychologist Carl Jung (1875–1961) describes the four functions of consciousness as sensation, feeling, thinking, and intuition. Sensation corresponds to the physical responses, feeling corresponds to emotional responses, thinking corresponds to cognitive responses, and intuition corresponds to spiritual responses.

It appears that our physical, emotional, cognitive, and spiritual responses to music may indeed be part of our fundamental nature.

The Music of Bob Marley — Setting and Purpose

Bob Marley stands in the long line of protest singers who have sung about injustice, oppression, and discrimination. In order to understand his music and its message (as opposed to simply enjoying hearing it), you must know something about the culture from which the music came. The history, politics, and religion of the island republic of Jamaica all played a significant part in shaping Marley's music.

Brief History and Politics of Jamaica

Jamaica is an island slightly smaller than the state of Connecticut, located south of Cuba and west of Haiti in the island group called the West Indies. Its capital city is Kingston. Columbus claimed this island as Spanish territory in 1494, and it was ruled by Spain until the British seized it in 1655. Under Spanish rule the native Arawak

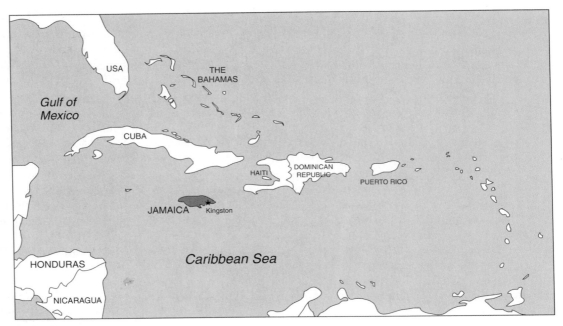

The West Indies

Indians died out. Slaves from Africa were brought in to work the sugar plantations in their place, and by 1690 these slaves numbered approximately 40,000. Their numbers continued to grow, reaching over 200,000 by 1790. Slavery was finally abolished in 1838, but racial tension continued between the black Jamaican majority, most of whom lived in extreme poverty, and the British rulers. Jamaica was made an independent member of the British Commonwealth in 1962.

The ancestry of well over three-quarters of the Jamaican population, including people of multiracial backgrounds, is West African. The official language is English, but most of the black population speaks a Creole dialect that blends English with French, Portuguese, and various ancestral West African languages. Although black Jamaicans make up a large majority of the population, the political leadership of the republic has continued to be white. Political unrest has been nearly constant, particularly around the time of elections. It has recently centered on the rivalry between a socialist party and a moderate party, both led by white politicians.

Rastafari

The chief religions of African Jamaicans blend elements of Protestant Christianity with elements of West African beliefs and rituals. A number of religious movements that move well beyond traditional

Haile Selassie
Culver Pictures

Christianity have sprung up from time to time. A major religious and cultural movement began among poorer Jamaican blacks in the 1930s, based on the belief that the emperor of Ethiopia, Haile Selassie ("Might of the Trinity"), was the messiah and that Ethiopia was the promised land for people of African descent. This movement was called **Rastafari** after Ras Tafari ("Prince to be Feared"), the original name of Haile Selassie.

It is not unusual for people in desperate circumstances such as poverty and oppression to turn to religion as a source of hope. The central tenets of Rastafari are the divinity of Haile Selassie, the eventual return of all believers to Africa (and to Ethiopia in particular), the superiority of black people, and a belief that Rastafarians never die. These beliefs are supported by numerous texts from the Christian and Hebrew Bibles and by certain historical events that are interpreted as fulfillments of biblical prophecy.

Rastafarians oppose the use of sharp objects on the body and hence never cut their hair. Instead they train it in long, twisted locks called dreadlocks, radiating out from their scalps. They make ritual use of marijuana, which they call *ganja*. Bob Marley is the best known of the Rastafarians and is responsible, through his music, for bringing this religious movement to the attention of the outside world.

Musical Roots of Reggae

Reggae is a popular music of Jamaican origin that developed in the 1960s among the poor black population of Kingston. The word *reggae* comes from *rege-rege*, a Jamaican-English term meaning ragged clothing. Many of the highly political songs sung by reggae musicians are strongly influenced by the tenets of the Rastafari movement, and many of the original reggae musicians wore the characteristic dreadlocks of the Rastafarians. Reggae developed out of West Indies popular music, Jamaican folk songs, and African American music. The lyrics expressed the feelings of an oppressed black majority in the political powder keg of Kingston.

Reggae, fueled by the immense popularity of Bob Marley and the Wailers, spread around the world in the 1970s. As it became an

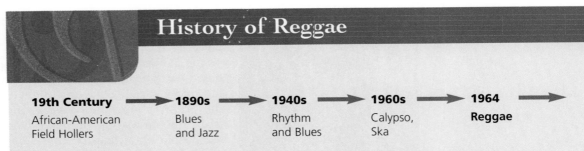

History of Reggae

19th Century ➡ **1890s** ➡ **1940s** ➡ **1960s** ➡ **1964** ➡

African-American   Blues   Rhythm   Calypso,   **Reggae**
Field Hollers   and Jazz   and Blues   Ska

Reggae resulted from the cross-fertilization of a number of ethnic musics. It was influenced by rhythm and blues, a popular African American music of the 1940s through the 1960s. Rhythm and blues was predominantly a vocal music with rhythm-section accompaniment that was used for dancing. It came from the long history of African American music in the United States, including blues and jazz. The immediate precursors of reggae were West Indies calypso music, a song style that was characterized by witty social commentary; *ska* music, a popular Jamaican dance music of the early 1960s (not to be confused with the cur-rent *ska* movement); and the folk music of Jamaica called *mento*. Reggae resulted when a springy rhythm from the West Indies was combined with the characteristic melodic and harmonic structure of African American rhythm and blues and with the close harmony of rhythm-and-blues singing groups. The lyrics of reggae expressed the feelings of oppression that were endemic among black Jamaicans. In later years, reggae spread worldwide and came into contact with other musical, political, and cultural influences. It is no longer only a vehicle for Rastafarian philosophy and social protest.

international style, it changed, taking on some characteristics of American and British rock as well as the distinctive elements of local cultures in Africa and the Far East. This created a further blending of musical influences. Reggae continues to influence the pop music scene to the present day. The Grammy-award-winning hip-hop artist Lauryn Hill used elements of reggae in her 1998 album, *The Miseducation of Lauryn Hill,* and reggae groups continue to proliferate worldwide.

Bob Marley

Bob Marley (Robert Nesta Marley)—singer, songwriter, and recording artist—was the child of a black Jamaican mother and a British father. He was born in 1945 in Nine Miles, a remote village in rural Jamaica. His mother was nineteen and his father fifty-one. Marley grew up in the home of his maternal grandfather. He came to Kingston at age nine to live in a violent ghetto called Trenchtown. There he later joined up with Bunny Wailer and Peter Tosh to form the Wailin' Wailers. Their first song, *Simmer Down,* was a reaction to gang violence in Trenchtown. It became a hit in Jamaica in 1964.

Wailin' Wailers: Bunny
Wailer, Bob Marley, and
Peter Tosh
Michael Ochs Archives

In the early 1970s the group connected with Chris Blackwell, the founder of Island Records. Blackwell was experienced in promoting rock musicians, and he launched their first two albums, *Catch a Fire* and *Burnin'*, in 1972. It was these recordings that established the international reputation of the group. Since Bunny Wailer and Peter Tosh were reluctant to go on tour to promote their recordings—something all rock groups are expected to do—Blackwell brought Bob Marley to the fore as the star of the group. They became known as "Bob Marley and the Wailers" from that time on. Bunny Wailer and Peter Tosh left the group in 1974. Marley continued to record and perform with a female backup group called the "I-Threes" (which included Marley's wife, Rita). By 1975 Bob Marley had achieved an international reputation rivalling that of British and American rock stars—the first third world artist to achieve such distinction. By this time all the members of the Wailers group had converted to Rastafari.

In 1976 Bob Marley entered into the turbulent politics of the island by scheduling a concert on behalf of Michael Manley of the ruling PNP political party. On the day before the concert, seven armed men broke into Marley's home and attempted to assassinate him. In spite of sustaining several gunshot wounds, Marley performed the concert. Then he moved to Miami, Florida, for his own protection. He returned in 1978 to attempt a reconciliation between the opposing political forces. The opposing leaders, Michael Manley and Edward Seaga, with Marley in between, linked arms on the concert stage as a gesture of peace. This historic concert, called "One Love," marked a high point in Bob Marley's career. Marley was also the featured performer in the concert celebrating the African nation of Zimbabwe's independence from British colonial rule on 18 April 1980.

Bob Marley
Monika Anderson/Stock Boston

At a 1981 concert in Central Park in New York City, shortly after he had been diagnosed with cancer of the liver, lungs, and brain, Bob Marley collapsed onstage. He died on 11 May 1981 in a Miami hospital at age thirty-six. When Marley was asked near the end of his life to sum up his special message, he replied, "Truth, peace, love, music, and liberty." One month before his death, Marley was awarded the Order of Merit by the Jamaican government.

Marley's funeral, which was attended by both the nation's prime minister and the leader of the opposition party, drew tens of thousands of devoted followers. It was the largest funeral in Jamaican history. His body rests in a mausoleum high on a hill in the tiny town of his birth, Nine Miles, Jamaica.

Bob Marley became famous throughout the world, but he never forgot his roots. It is said that at one time he was financially supporting as many as 4,000 people in Jamaica. Today he is thought of as a prophet by the Jamaican Rastafarians. They believe that he, like Haile Selassie, continues to live.

With this background in mind, let's prepare to listen to Bob Marley's *Exodus* and *Redemption Song*.

Listening to the Songs

The songs of Bob Marley are good examples of how music can evoke different responses from listeners with different backgrounds and experience. The song *Exodus*, for example, was wildly successful internationally as a piece of dance music in clubs and discos. Most dancers were only vaguely aware of the lyrics and completely unaware of their deeper meaning. Their response was a purely physical response—dancing. The words themselves might generate little response from some listeners, while for others, particularly those of black Jamaican heritage, these words were a rallying cry for black unity and the ultimate liberation of the black Jamaicans. This latter reaction falls clearly into the category of emotional responses.

Our detailed analysis of the lyrics of *Exodus* will show their relationship to the Rastafarian movement and will enable you to respond cognitively. You will be able to think about the lyrics in their social context. For Rastafarians, this song is experienced within a religious context, and their response falls within the spiritual category. Rastafarians are likely to dance, feel emotion, think about this music, and respond spiritually, so of all listeners, they would respond most completely.

In Chapter 1 we learned that music occurs in various settings and has different functions, and that a change in setting often changes the function. Sung by a group of Rastafarians, *Exodus* might have two functions—political protest and spirituality—much like some African-American spirituals sung during the civil rights movement. Marley's purpose in writing this song must have been, at least in part, to motivate the Jamaican people toward a move back to Africa. Played in a discotheque, however, the song loses the original function and becomes music for entertainment.

Exodus

Exodus, which you will soon be listening to, is the title song of Bob Marley's 1977 album. The album contains three songs (*Exodus, Waitin' in Vain,* and *Jamming*) that were huge successes as single recordings. The lyrics of *Exodus* are a statement of one of the fundamental principles of Rastafari.

The opening line, "Exodus, movement of Jah people," demonstrates two important Rastafarian concepts. "Exodus" is a reference to the second book of the Hebrew Bible (also known as the Old Testament), which describes Moses' call by God to rescue the Israelites from bondage in Egypt and move them to a promised land in Israel. "Jah" is a Rastafarian term for God (Yahweh), so this reference is to "God's people." The term comes from Psalm 68, verse 4: "Sing unto God, sing praises to his name: extol him that rideth upon the heavens by his name JAH, and rejoice before him." The line "Send us another Brother Moses gonna cross Red Sea" is a reference to the parting of the Red Sea in Exodus 14, verses 21–22. Rastafarians draw a parallel between the Hebrew Exodus and their own longed-for departure for Africa.

In the lines, "We know where we're going, we know where we're from. We're leaving Babylon, we're going to our fatherland," the reference is to leaving Jamaica and going to Africa. Rastafarians called Jamaica "Babylon," referring back to the Babylonian captivity of the Jewish people, as well as to a country associated with sinful extravagance and sensual pleasure.

LISTENING ACTIVITY

Reggae: *Exodus* (Bob Marley and the Wailers) [CD 1, track 4]

Note: The lyric as sung on this recording deviates considerably from the published version of the lyric.

Time	Text
0:00	(Introduction)
0:22	Exodus, movement of Jah people, oh yeah. (unintelligible) . . . and let me tell you this.
0:36	Men and people will fight ya down (Tell me why?) when ya see Jah light. (laugh) Let me tell you, if you're not wrong (Then why?) ev'rything is all right. So we gonna walk, all right, through the roads of creation. We're the generation (Tell me why.) trod through great tribulation. (2x)
1:05	Exodus, (all right) movement of Jah people. (O yeah, o yeah, all right) Exodus, movement of Jah people. (O yeah, yeah, yeah, yeah, yeah)
1:35	Open your eyes and look within. Are you satisfied with the life you're living? We know where we're going, we know where we're from. We're leaving Babylon, we're going to our fatherland.
2:03	Exodus, movement of Jah people. (O yeah) (Movement of Jah people.) Send us another Brother Moses (Movement of Jah people.) Gonna cross the Red Sea. (Movement of Jah people.)

Send us another Brother Moses
(Movement of Jah people.)
Gonna cross the Red Sea.
(Movement of Jah people.)
Exodus, (all right) movement of Jah people. (O yeah)
Exodus, Exodus, (all right, o yeah) etc.

3:30   Move! Move! Move! Move! Move! Move!

3:52   Open your eyes and look within.
Are you satisfied with the life you're living?
We know where we're going, we know where we're from.
We're leaving Babylon, we're going to the father's land.

4:20   Exodus, (all right) movement of Jah people.
Exodus, movement of Jah people.
Movement of Jah people. (4x)

4:59   Move! Move! Move! Move! Move! Move! Move!

5:25   Yeah, time to break down oppression.
(incoherent) . . .
Wipe away transgression.
Set the captives free.

5:39   Exodus, (all right, all right) movement of Jah people.
Exodus, movement of Jah people.
Movement of Jah people. (several times)
(Move! Move! Move!) (several times)
Movement of Jah people. (several times)

Source: *Exodus*—words and music by Bob Marley. Copyright © 1977 Fifty-Six Hope Road Music Ltd./Odnil Music Ltd./Blue Mountain Music Ltd. All rights controlled by Rykomusic, Inc. (ASCAP). International copyright secured. All rights reserved. Used by permission.

Redemption Song

Redemption Song is from the album *Uprising* (1980). It is an unusual solo performance by Bob Marley.

The opening lines, "Old pirates, yes, they rob I, Sold I to the merchant ships, minutes after they took I from the bottomless pit," describes the stealing of native West Africans by pirates and their sale to merchant ships. This is a historical fact (see History and Politics of Jamaica, page 39). Note also the grammatically unusual use of the repeated word "I." Rastafarians almost never use the words "me," "you," or "we." "Me" becomes "I," "you" becomes "I," and "we" is "I and I." This construction emphasizes the essential oneness of all the "Jah people."

The line in the chorus, " 'Cause all I ever had, redemption songs," is Marley's statement that he viewed his entire creative output in the context of the deliverance of black Jamaicans from the poverty and oppression of their lives in Jamaica. "Redemption" means "freedom from captivity." For example, Exodus 6, verse 6, says: "Wherefore say unto the children of Israel, I [am] the LORD, and I will bring you out from under the burdens of the Egyptians, and I will rid you out of their bondage, and I will *redeem* you with a stretched out arm, and with great judgments." This idea is underlined in Marley's second verse, which begins: "Emancipate yourselves from mental slavery. . . ."

"How long shall they kill our prophets, While we stand aside and look? Yes, some say it's just a part of it. We've got to fulfill the book," refers to a frequent discussion among Rastafarians about when the return to Africa will occur. Some place it in the near future, while others believe that it will come only when the prophecies of the Bible (the "book") are fulfilled.

LISTENING ACTIVITY

Redemption Song (Bob Marley) [CD 1, track 5]

Time	Text
0:00	(Guitar)
0:17	Old pirates, yes, they rob I, Sold I to the merchant ships minutes after they took I from the bottomless pit. But my hand was made strong by the hand of the Almighty. We forward in this generation triumphantly.
0:51	Won't you help to sing these songs of freedom? 'Cause all I ever had, redemption songs, redemption songs.
1:13	Emancipate yourselves from mental slavery, None but ourselves can free our minds. Have no fear for atomic energy, 'Cause none of them can stop the time. How long shall they kill our prophets While we stand aside and look? Oh, some say it's just a part of it. We've got to fulfill the book.

1:47   Won't you help to sing these songs of freedom?
            'Cause all I ever had, redemption songs,
                redemption songs, redemption songs.

2:13   (Guitar)

2:29   Emancipate yourselves from mental slavery,
            None but ourselves can free our minds.
            Have no fear for atomic energy,
            'Cause none of them can stop the time.
            How long shall they kill our prophets
            While we stand aside and look?
            Yes, some say it's just a part of it.
            We've got to fulfill the book.

3:02   Won't you help to sing these songs of freedom?
            'Cause all I ever had, redemption songs,
            All I ever had! redemption songs,
            These songs of freedom, songs of freedom.

Response to the Music

Now that you have heard these two examples of reggae, consider your emotional, physical, cognitive, and spiritual responses. If you were familiar with this music before, think about how your responses have changed with your increased knowledge about the music and its cultural context.

Summary

In this chapter you learned about four personal responses to music: physical responses, emotional responses, cognitive responses, and spiritual responses. These responses usually occur together; they are unique for each individual since we all have different experiences and backgrounds. It is likely that these four responses are a part of our fundamental nature. You also listened to two examples of Jamaican reggae by Bob Marley and learned about their historical and cultural background.

Applying What You Have Learned

1. Bob Marley's *Exodus* (CD 1, track 4) was a hit recording in discotheques. Compare how the lyric might be perceived when heard on a dance floor with how it might be perceived

as a Rastafarian anthem. Would the words be taken in different ways in the two settings?

2. Listen again to the hymn setting of *Simple Gifts* (CD 1, track 2). This hymn is performed as it is sung in church services by the Shakers, who bring a particular set of beliefs to their singing—beliefs that you may or may not share. Think about your physical, emotional, cognitive, and spiritual responses to the music. How might your responses be different from those of the Shakers, who danced to the hymn? How does what you now know about the Shakers and their music affect your response to the music?

3. Compare your physical, emotional, cognitive, and spiritual responses to *Simple Gifts* (CD 1, track 2) with your responses to Bob Marley's *Redemption Song* (CD 1, track 5). Why do you think your responses are different—or not different?

4. Now listen again to the excerpt from *Appalachian Spring* (CD 1, track 3). How do your physical, emotional, cognitive, and spiritual responses to the suite differ from your responses to the hymn (CD 1, track 2)? Why do you think your responses are different or not different?

5. Can you think of a piece of music that you listen to with only a single response (physical, emotional, cognitive, or spiritual)? What is that response? What about that piece causes your response to be so singularly focused?

6. Do you have your own favorite pieces of reggae music? How will your responses to those pieces be altered now that you know more about the background of reggae?

7. Make a list of settings (concerts, church music events, home, etc.) where you have actively listened to music as opposed to passively hearing it. Where have your responses been primarily physical? Emotional? Cognitive? Spiritual? What have been your primary responses to music in the past? Do you see them changing in the future? Why or why not?

8. Listen to several of your favorite musical pieces. Make a list of the emotions these pieces evoked in you. Were you surprised by the emotions on the list?

Important Terms

physical responses 31   spiritual responses 34
emotional responses 32   Rastafarianism 40
cognitive responses 33   reggae 41

Musicians and Ensembles Mentioned

Names preceded by *
have short biographies
in Appendix B, page
346.

*Bob Marley
*Lauryn Hill
*Bunny Wailer
*Peter Tosh
*Wailin' Wailers
Rita Marley

Further Listening Resources

Listen to some of the following recordings or to others that you or your instructor might suggest. Consider this music in terms of setting, purpose, and your own responses.

The Jolly Boys, *Pop 'n' Mento.* Rykodisk RCD-10185.
Bob Marley and the Wailers, *Songs of Freedom: The Complete Bob. Marley Collection.* Tuff Gong/Island Records 314-512280-2.
Jimmy Cliff, *The Harder They Come.* Mango Records 162-539202-2.
Toots and the Maytals, *Reggae Got Soul.* Mango Records 162-539374-2.
Bob Marley, Lauryn Hill, Erykah Badu, and Chuck D., *Chant Down Babylon.* Uni/Island Records.

Video:

Bob Marley and the Wailers, *The Bob Marley Story—Caribbean Nights.* A documentary on the life of Bob Marley. Island Visual Arts 440-082-373-2.

The following music was originally performed in a variety of different settings and for various purposes. Notice your individual physical, emotional, cognitive, and spiritual responses.

Mickey Hart, *Planet Drum.* Rykodisk RCD 10206.
Gyuto Monks, *Freedom Chants from the Roof of the World.* Rykodisk RCD 20113.
Ravi Shankar, *Unique Ravi Shankar.* Chhanda Dhara, SNCD70991.
Hildegard von Bingen, *Ordo Virtuum.* Sequentia.

Rhythm

in Music

Rhythm is a general term used to describe the motion of music in time. Our response to rhythm is physical: we tap our feet; we move our bodies; we dance or march. We feel the rhythm and we respond, usually with pleasure. We don't have to think about our response to rhythm at all—it is automatic.

We experience rhythm in many aspects of life. Our heartbeat produces a regular rhythm; our breathing (usually) has a regular rhythm; we can hear a rhythm in the pattering of rain; most machines produce a regular rhythm. On a larger scale, we experience the rhythmic alternation of day and night, the ebb and flow of tides, the waxing and waning of the moon, and the rhythm of the seasons. It is no wonder, therefore, that our response to rhythm is deeply imprinted in our bodies—in the muscles themselves.

In this section you will learn some basic elements of rhythm: beat, accent, meter, and tempo. You will also learn how rhythm helps to structure music.

Gregg Mancuso/Stock Boston

CHAPTER 3   Beat, Accent, and Tempo   **54**
Grand Entry Song, Powwow Music

CHAPTER 4   Meter **73**
Klezmer Music: *Bay a Glezele Mashke,* Traditional
Oy, Abram!, Traditional

CHAPTER 5   Polyrhythm   **86**
Shango, Babatunde Olatunji

Beat, Accent, and Tempo

🔘 *Grand Entry Song,* Powwow Music

Lindsay Hebberd/Corbis

W*e always say that our drum is the heartbeat of our Indian people.*

CLEVLAND HOLY ELK BOY
SIOUX ELDER

As we noted in the introduction to this part of the book, **rhythm** is a general term used to describe the motion of music in time. In this chapter we will introduce several aspects of rhythm, including beat, accent, and tempo.

Beat

One of our primary physical reactions to music is response to the **beat.** Beats are regular pulses that are the basis for measuring time in music. Perhaps because an infant listens to its mother's pulse while still in the womb, beat seems to be an essential element of music. When people march or dance, it is the beat that keeps them moving together in step. When you tap your foot or clap your hands along with a piece of music you are responding to its beat.

Beat may be overtly expressed in the music or only sensed by the musicians and listeners. For example, in a marching band the beat is marked by the bass drum, which plays on each beat, whereas in a choral ensemble the beat is not marked but only sensed. Whether the beat is heard or only sensed, it is a principal organizing factor in most music.

Accent

Beats that are emphasized are said to be **accented.** A common way to accent a particular beat is to have a louder musical event on it. For example, if you are clapping along with the beat of a piece of music, you can accent one beat by clapping louder.

Tempo

Beat may be relatively fast or slow. The speed of the beat is referred to as the **tempo** of the music. In the West we often refer to tempo in terms of the number of beats per minute. Musicians set a tempo by using their knowledge of musical style, by following directions in the score, and by considering their personal preferences. In ensembles with a leader, that person sets the tempo. In this chapter we will consider beat, tempo, and accent in the powwow music of Native Americans.

The Powwow — Setting and Purpose

A good example of ceremonial music is the music of the Native American **powwow,** an event that typically draws together members of numerous tribes for singing, dancing, and competitions. The powwow developed out of the summer reunions that many North

American Indian tribes held in earlier centuries. These reunions included social activities and religious ceremonies. The term *powwow* was derived from *pauau,* an Algonquin word for a gathering of medicine men and spiritual leaders in a curing ceremony. European explorers attended these events, mispronounced the name as "powwow," and thought it referred to "any large gathering of Indian people."

Beginning in the late 1800s, the United States government did all it could to repress Native American culture and traditions, and this included discouraging powwow gatherings. Despite these efforts, the dances did not die out. After World War II, attitudes began changing. Veterans, who were considered the "warriors" of the tribes, returned from battle and were honored at powwows. During the 1960s, Native Americans began to take new pride in their rich cultural heritage. "Today's proliferation of powwows is the strongest evidence of this cultural rejuvenation."

Although the powwow still has a strong religious element, its overriding importance today is as an expression of Native American identity. Native Americans are proud of their heritage and seek to keep the traditional ways alive in spite of the almost overwhelming influence of the dominant European-American culture. People of all ages participate in the powwow, and families travel together throughout the summer to different powwows to meet friends and relatives. Songs and dances are passed from one tribe to another—another indication of how the powwow provides an opportunity for friendly interchange among tribes.

While some religious and social dances and songs are specific to a given tribe, others are considered **intertribal** and are the common property of all Native Americans. It is thought that contemporary powwow dances originated with the Oklahoma Ponca and the Nebraska Omaha and Pawnee. The intertribal songs and dances are the basis for competitions, held both for musicians (drummers and singers) and for dancers. These competitions often carry prizes, but the element of competition appears to be low-key and friendly by Anglo standards (compared with college and professional football games, for example). Important effects of the competitions are ensuring that the performances achieve reasonable standards, that traditions are kept alive, and that interest keeps growing. A good dancer can win enough to help pay for the expenses of travel and for **regalia** (traditional clothing required for the dance competitions).

A powwow, however, is not just about competition and maintaining traditions. Some powwows, called "friendship powwows," don't even have competitions. As Grace Gillette, executive director of the highly successful Denver March Pow*Wow, says, the powwow is "a time to get together, dance, and have fun."

History of Powwow

Although chronology is not important to most Native American people (who have traditionally focused more on seasons and cycles than on linear history), we know that once there were no intertribal powwows but now there are, and they are growing in scope and popularity. The form of the modern powwow has developed over time, and it includes new dances such as the jingle dance and the grass dance. How these two dances became powwow dances tells us a great deal about the culture of the powwow.

The origin legend of the grass dance differs from tribe to tribe. One story is that a disabled young man, who could not fully use his legs, wanted to do the things other grown men of his tribe could do. He was told to "seek a vision." He went into the Great Plains on a vision quest and watched the tall prairie grass blowing in the wind. In his vision, he saw himself dancing like the grass. He went back to his tribe, and the elders interpreted his vision. They put prairie grass on him (now, dancers use yarn fringe), and he began to dance. The original style of the grass dance resembled a stumbling person, just about to fall but never falling. A different story is that victorious Nebraska Omaha and Pawnee warriors danced with scalps attached to their belts; later, braided sweet grass was substituted, and later still, yarn.

According to one legend about the jingle dress dance, a medicine man who couldn't cure his people of European diseases sought a vision. In a dream he saw his daughter and three friends dancing, wearing dresses with carved cone-shaped wooden ornaments. They sang healing songs as they danced, and they healed the sick. When he awoke, the medicine man carved wooden cones and attached them to a dress for his daughter. She danced, and the people were healed. Now the jingles are made from the lids of snuff (dipping tobacco) tins, available precut from Native American craft suppliers. At one time the jingle dance almost died out along with many other ceremonial dances. But in the 1980s it made the transition into a powwow dance, and since then it has become an increasingly popular dance style.

Powwow Music

Powwow music consists of singing and drumming, with the accompaniment of the many jingles, deer hooves, rattles, and bells that are part of the dancers' regalia. In powwow music several people usually play a single drum at the same time; they sit in a circle with the drum in the middle. This circle of singers and drummers is also called a **drum.** Each member of the drum holds a single beater, which is a long stick wrapped with rawhide on the end that hits the drum. All the members of the drum play and sing together, and the pattern they play on the drum is the underlying beat of the music. The beat of the drum is the primary organizing factor for both singers and dancers. All participants are guided by the beat.

The **lead singer,** who also starts singing the song, sets the tempo. The text of many songs consists entirely of **vocables,** such as "yo-he-yo" or "we-yo-he-ye." These vocables have no linguistic meaning; they are, however, considered an important part of the song and are not changed from performance to performance.

At certain points in the song one or more members of the drum will strike the drum very hard to produce accented beats, called **honor beats.** According to Mike Pace, treasurer of the Delaware Tribe of Oklahoma, the honor beats are ". . . an acknowledgment to the Creator and the warriors. It is a point in the song that honors . . . the sacrifices of our warriors so that we may continue to live well while we live here on earth." Pete Gahbow, lead singer of the Little Otter Singers, explains that in dance competitions the honor beats also serve as a signal for the dancers, to help them keep count of the number of repetitions.

The members of a drum are traditionally men ranging from adolescents through tribal elders. Drumming and singing have usually been the domain of men, while women participated only in the dancing. In recent years, however, this has been changing: one often sees women singing along with the drums, standing behind the seated singers and drummers. Another recent innovation is the appearance of all-female drum groups. Being a member of a drum has many personal rewards, including a sense of belonging (the group often feels like a family), a sense of group identity, an enhanced awareness of one's spirituality, and a specific link to one's traditional culture.

The music of the powwow is transmitted from musician to musician by oral tradition. Older singers teach the songs to younger singers as they are initiated into the drum. Members of one drum listen to and learn the songs of other drums. It is important that members of a drum be able to precisely sing and play the songs that are used in competition dancing since the dancers rely on accurate renditions. In recent times oral transmission has been augmented by commercial and amateur tape recordings that are passed from drum to drum. This also enables the drums to expand their repertoire to include currently popular songs.

Powwow Dance

There are distinctive dance styles for men and women, indicative of a culture where the roles of men and women are quite different. According to Linda Raczek, author of *Rainy's Powwow,* powwow dancers choose their own dances when they are young—often about eight years old. Sometimes a dance is handed down from one generation to the next, but often children are free to choose whatever

Kicking Woman Drum
Chris Roberts

A *bustle* is a large, flat, circular (or fan-shaped) framework covered with feathers or yarn and attached to the back of a dancer's regalia.

style appeals to them. Usually a child will keep that dance style for life. The choice is not made lightly, since it is an important coming-of-age ritual.

Dancers (whether tiny tots or adults) are costumed elaborately. As with the dances themselves, there are distinctive regalia for men and women. The attire depends on the chosen dance, but it is always handmade and quite intricate. Regalia for women will include fringed and beaded buckskin dresses, embroidered cloth dresses with matching shawls, and fabric dresses covered with the twisted metal cones called jingles. Men's regalia will include handsomely beaded buckskin pants and shirts, eye-catching feather or yarn bustles, and embroidered cloth tunics and pants. Elaborate head coverings, ranging from feathers to fur hats, are also part of the dancers' regalia. The members of the drums, on the other hand, are usually dressed in work clothes and wear farm hats or cowboy hats. Some members of a drum will also be dancers and will be wearing their regalia.

Men usually dance alone and are more athletic than women; women traditionally dance two, three, or four abreast, coordinating their steps. In recent times more active dances for women have appeared in the competitions and, while there are still separate styles for men and women, some of the dances for women have become much more theatrical and showy. Several dance styles—jingle dancing and fancy shawl dancing, for example—allow young women to express their individuality and dance alone. Children are welcome participants in the dancing and in the competitions. They are costumed as elaborately as the adults and usually dance with the women in group dancing.

All the dancers circle slowly clockwise around the center of the arena, which holds the drums. In larger powwows the drums may be stationed around the outside of an arena, allowing the entire floor space to be occupied by dancers. Several drums are usually invited to a powwow. A very large powwow, such as the Denver March Pow*Wow, may have as many as sixty or seventy drums. They alternate with each other, allowing the singers to rest their voices from the strenuous, demanding singing style.

The master of ceremonies (emcee) announces each song and gives the name of the drum that is performing. Since non–Native Americans often attend powwows, the emcee may also give brief explanations to help the audience appreciate the event. In addition, the emcee provides occasional humor to lighten the spirits of audience and participants alike. A popular emcee is greatly respected on the powwow circuit, and most emcees are professionals.

The Form of a Powwow Song

Powwow dancers
Tom Bean/Corbis

A typical intertribal powwow song begins with the lead singer establishing the tempo by beating softly on the drum. The members of the drum join in on this beat, and after it is well established, the lead singer sings an opening phrase, called the **lead.** The other members of the drum immediately pick up the song and continue singing it. This section of the song is called the **second.** In the **Southern style** of drumming, there is a break in the song about the midpoint, and several (usually three) honor beats occur. The song then continues with what is called the **second chorus.** (There is nothing actually called the "first chorus," but it is understood to be the lead and second.) In the **Northern style** of drumming, the honor beats usually occur during the second chorus, not before it.

When one rendition of the song is completed, the drumming may continue for a while without any singing. Then the lead singer begins the song again, and the entire pattern is repeated. There are usually three or four repetitions of the same song in a single performance.

Form of a Typical Song (Southern Style)

Lead	Second	Honor Beats	Second Chorus
Lead	Second	Honor Beats	Second Chorus
Lead	Second	Honor Beats	Second Chorus
Lead	Second	Honor Beats	Second Chorus

Form of a Typical Song (Northern Style)

Lead	Second	Second Chorus with Honor Beats
Lead	Second	Second Chorus with Honor Beats
Lead	Second	Second Chorus with Honor Beats
Lead	Second	Second Chorus with Honor Beats

The Northern style is tense and high-pitched, requiring considerable effort on the part of the singers. The Southern style is much more relaxed and lower in pitch. As Mike Pace has explained, "There are no really old Northern singers—they can't pitch that high."

The late Harry Buffalohead, a lead singer with the Ponca tribe, found the vocal effort worthwhile: "When I'm singing I don't see nothing, I don't hear nothing—just a great feeling of joy. When it's all over with, then I'm back in reality—aches and pains. But when I'm singing I have a great feeling. I wish I could feel like that all the time."

The tempo of the drums differs, depending on the dance. Grass dances and straight dances usually have the slowest tempo. Northern traditional, Northern shawl, and jingle dress dances are somewhat faster. Fancy dances and ruffle dances are fastest.

A Typical Powwow

Every powwow is a unique event organized by the tribe that is hosting it and lasting several days. There are no hard-and-fast rules for the order of events, but the following outline will give you a general flavor of a powwow.

Many powwows are held out of doors in wooded or other natural settings. When the powwow takes place in nature, the circular arena (the powwow grounds) will be an open space of cleared flat ground without any trees or other obstructions that would get in the way of the dancers. The focal point of the arena is the announcer's booth, a raised platform equipped with loudspeakers, on one edge of the arena. This is the nerve center of the powwow, and all activities are directed from this area. Around the central core are places for folding chairs or bleachers, and areas for booths that sell Native American handicrafts, materials for making regalia, and food. The powwow, after all, is an important expression of many aspects of Native American culture—not just music and dance.

In an adjacent area there will be campsites for groups—including established family sites, which may have some permanent structures such as sheltered cooking and eating areas. Some individuals and families bring recreational vehicles and mobile homes to the campsites so that they can live on the grounds during the powwow.

There are also public parking areas, usually at some distance from the actual powwow grounds, to accommodate the many visitors who attend these events. Native American tribes are welcoming to non-Indian guests and make them feel at home, so long as they observe the rules of behavior. Generally these rules amount to showing respect for the powwow and its participants and not consuming alcohol or drugs.

Before the actual beginning of the powwow, informal social dances called **gourd dances** may be performed. The gourd dances come from the Kiowa tradition. They are men's dances. The dancers stand in a line, shake rattles, and sing while performing a slow shuffling dance step. The dancers belong to gourd dancing societies that honor tribal members who are veterans of the United States armed forces—modern "tribal warriors." These dances are for the dancers' own enjoyment, but they are open to the public as well. Nonveterans can also participate.

Grand Entry. On each day of the powwow, the "formal" dancing begins with a **grand entry song.** Rules usually require that any dancer who is going to participate in the dance competitions must also participate in the grand entry. The dancers enter in a single line and dance in a clockwise spiral that moves gradually toward the center of the arena while the drums play and sing. In a large powwow there will be several hundred dancers (the Denver Pow*Wow has had as many as 1,500), and the grand entry continues until all have entered. Excitement builds as the arena gradually fills with dancers. Finally, the space is completely filled and the dance ends. The grand entry is one of the most spectacular powwow events.

Grand Entry, Rocky Boy Reservation, Montana
David Harvey/ National Geographic Image Collection

There is a traditional order for the dancers' entrance. The first to enter will be a group of men dressed in military uniforms and carrying the United States and other flags. These men will all be veterans of the armed forces. They are given the honor of leading the dancers because (as noted above) they are considered the warriors of the tribe. This mixing of Native American and non–Native American elements may seem strange to non-Indians, but it is a part of the powwow tradition. The honor guard will station itself near the announcer's booth and remain there during the grand entry.

Next to enter are the head men dancers, then the head women dancers, followed by Indian princesses and other honored guests of the powwow. To be designated as a head dancer, a princess, or an honored guest is the highest honor the powwow organizers can bestow. Following the honored group, the other dancers enter, usually grouped according to the style of the dances they will perform and, hence, the type of regalia they wear. In some powwows one will see family groups dancing together in the grand entry.

Clowns may also participate in the grand entry. The clowns will usually be dressed in some caricature of the traditional regalia, with balloons instead of feathers and other amusing variations on the attire of the other dancers. They inject humor into the setting and remind the participants that a powwow is partly a recreational event as well as a serious ritual. Many Native American tribes have a time-honored tradition of ceremonial clowns, and the powwow clowns may come out of that tradition.

Flag Song. The next event will be a song honoring the flag of the United States. This patriotic part of the powwow is treated with great solemnity. The **flag song** is similar in style to other powwow songs—it is not the United States' national anthem or any other non–Native American patriotic song.

The Blessing. Next, a tribal elder will take the microphone and offer a **blessing prayer** upon the powwow and all its participants. This prayer is usually delivered in the speaker's Native American tongue. Some elders provide translations and commentaries about parts of the prayer for those who do not understand the tribal language. Many in the audience will be English speakers or speak other tribal languages, so the translation is very helpful. It is not at all uncommon for this blessing prayer to include a mixture of Christian and native religious elements.

Memorial Prayer Song. Some powwows will continue with a **memorial prayer song** in honor of tribal members who have recently died or to mark the anniversaries of their deaths.

Round Dances and Intertribal Dances. The arena is now cleared, and the central program of dances begins. These will usually be **round dances, war dances,** and **intertribal dances** for large groups. The war dances are meant to honor warriors and veterans, to remember those who cannot dance for themselves, and to entertain. The announcer will describe each type of dance and introduce the drum that will be performing. The dancers may be in full regalia or in simpler clothes, usually jeans and work shirts. Au-

Ceremonial flag bearers, Tom Christian, Sioux
Chris Roberts

Cultural celebration, Onondaga Nation, Iroquois Conf., NY
Lawrence Migdale/Stock Boston

dience members, whether Native American or not, may be invited to
participate in some of these dances.

The Competition Dances. Certain kinds of competition have been
a part of most Native American cultures. For example, many com-
petitive athletic events and games are a part of each tribe's daily life.
The idea of a dance competition is a natural addition that has come
to the powwow in recent years. There are several categories of com-
petitive dances for women and men of all ages, and each dance has
its particular pattern of steps and its distinctive regalia.

Dance contestants are judged on footwork; stopping on time with
the beat; authenticity, originality, and craftsmanship of regalia; the
dancer's affinity to the dance style; and "attitude," seriousness, and
sincerity. Judges believe it is very important for the dancer to "feel"
the dance spiritually, rather than just following a choreographed routine. While the categories remain somewhat in flux and individual
powwows may vary, a typical set of competition dances may include
cloth, buckskin, jingle dress, and fancy shawl dance for women; and
straight, northern traditional, grass, fancy, and ruffle dances for men.

Children's Dances. Many powwows feature children's versions of
each of the dances mentioned above. Children as young as age three
or four may compete for prizes in these children's dances. The
children's dances are an important way that the younger generation

A young jingle dancer
Ben Marra

of Native Americans is trained to follow in the traditions of the tribe. The children's dances are charming to watch and are a favorite of many audience members.

Awarding of Prizes. In the dance competitions, prizes are awarded in each category. These are cash prizes (ranging from $150 to $2,500) and other gifts that are sometimes quite significant, often totalling $10,000, depending on the resources of the powwow sponsors. Skilled dancers can often earn a good income from prizes won in competitions on the summer powwow circuit. The prizes are awarded in a public ceremony at the end of each competition.

The Giveaway. Generosity is highly valued in most Native American tribes. Some Northwest Coast tribes had a ritual called *potlatch* in which a family would literally give away everything it owned. A similar generosity is seen in the **giveaway** that concludes each powwow. Dancers and other honored guests are often given expensive Pendleton wool blankets, shawls, beads, other jewelry, and even cash. There may be opportunities for members of the audience to make cash contributions to the powwow or to particular individuals who are in need of assistance. The authors recall a particularly moving giveaway to support the expensive medical treatments that a young girl needed desperately. The tiny, frail girl, in full traditional regalia, was awarded a large sum of cash in a ceremony that brought tears to the eyes of everyone present.

Listening to a Grand Entry Song

An *ethnomusicologist* is a scholar who studies music in a sociocultural context.

Thomas Vennum, Jr., senior **ethnomusicologist** of the Office of Folklife Programs for the Smithsonian Institution, wrote the following description of the opening of the "Honor the Earth Powwow":

> It is a warm night in July 1990. The Ojibway [also spelled Ojibwe] and their neighbors, the Menominee and Winnebago, are gathered for a powwow in a natural amphitheater set deep in the Wisconsin forest. Hundreds of people of all ages are scattered at various campfires and cookouts. Despite the commotion, the woods are alive with wildlife. Earlier someone had spotted an eagle overhead—a sign that the event is blessed. In the center of the amphitheater is a drum arbor, covered with boughs of pine, yet still open to the sky.
>
> The singers sit in a circle in the drum arbor, beating on a single large drum, singing, in high-pitched voices, songs that are as old as

anything in the community, as well as others newly composed for the occasion. To be accepted as a singer on the drum is a great honor. The dancers, elaborately costumed, move clockwise around the drum arbor, celebrating the birth of the four winds. To be able to dance in one's finest homemade regalia is an affirmation and renewal of the culture's deepest roots. Each piece of fur on a costume honors some animal, each feather some bird. The dancers wear bells on their ankles, and the women have metal cones [jingles] sewn in rows on their dresses. All is sound and movement as the powwow begins to pulse.

The sound of drums rings through the air. For hundreds or thousands of years, Indian people have gathered on nights like this to celebrate life, to honor the earth, and to thank the creator with song, dance, and drum. They gather in a circle because the circle is a symbol of life's eternal rhythm, as well as a door into sacred space. So much that is fundamental about life is circular. The earth, the sun, the moon, even the cycle of life from season to season is round, as one returns each year to where one began the year before, and, of course, the drum is round.

As dusk turns to night, James "Pipe" Moustache, the spiritual leader of the Lac Court Oreilles Ojibway, rises wearing a full eagle-feathered bonnet and begins, in his native tongue, to invoke the great spirit, Gitchi-Manidoo, to look favorably upon his people as they sing and dance to honor the earth for what it provides them. The situation is particularly sensitive to the Ojibway this year, for mineral discoveries by large corporations threaten to spoil the beauty of Indian Country and pollute the lakes and streams where they harvest wild rice.

Pipe finishes his lengthy invocation with a hefty "*Mi-Iw*" (Enough), the traditional Ojibway conclusion for oratory. The emcee announces, "Little Otter, take it away."

Little Otter Singers (from the Mille Lacs Reservation in Minnesota)

The original members of the Little Otter Singers—also called the Little Otter Drum, because drumming and singing are inseparable—started playing together at the Ojibwe tribal school in 1979, when Pete Gahbow (lead singer) was fourteen. Then they went to school in Duluth and needed a new name for the drum. As they crossed the Little Otter Creek, outside of Duluth, Pete and Larry Smallwood came up with "Little Otter Singers." According to Pete, "We thought it was a cool name at the time." Since then, they have made a "pretty good name" for themselves, placing in several important national competitions, as well as being included on three CDs, making three of their own, and having an excerpt from one of their songs in the Walt Disney film *Iron Will*.

Pete has been lead singer for the group for twenty years. He learned to sing with his father when he was quite little. His father and older members of the community had a drum, called the Mille Lacs Singers, and Pete grew up surrounded by the music. "Dad would take the old drum out nearly every evening," he reports. (Pete's father was tribal chairman for twenty years.) The drum is still a family affair: three of Pete's brothers and two of his sons sing. His sons, who are fourteen and sixteen years old, have also started their own drum group.

The Little Otter Singers has from six to ten members, depending on where it is drumming. They perform as host drum at local powwows and as invited drum across the country. Recently, they drummed on the steps of the United States Supreme Court to support the Wabanoon Run—a group of Native Americans (including one of Pete's brothers) who ran from Wisconsin to Washington, D.C., in the winter of 1998 to publicize the Court's review of their hunting and fishing treaty rights. According to Pete, these rights are vital for the continuation of traditional Native American ways of life. (The tribes won.) The Singers drum during the annual ceremonial cycle on the reservation (twelve weekends in spring and twelve weekends in fall). They also travel nearly every weekend during the mid-June to November powwow circuit.

Over the years, drumming and singing styles have changed, according to Pete. Honor beats, for example, were quite popular about ten years ago but are not so popular now, at least not among the Ojibwe. For a while, the Little Otter Singers added Ojibwe words to songs, but now they sing many with vocables instead. Pete says, "Music changes, but [the spirit] stays the same." They are also starting to perform more of the Mille-Lacs-style seasonal songs traditionally sung on the reservation. As Pete points out, the Little Otter Singers know how to sing the songs properly, and they want to preserve them.

LISTENING ACTIVITY

Grand Entry Song, Honor the Earth Powwow
(Little Otter Singers) [CD 1, track 6]

A *drumkeeper* is responsible for getting the drum to the powwow; a *drumwarmer* is responsible for keeping the drum in tune.

This recording was made in July 1990 at the annual Honor the Earth Powwow, deep in the Wisconsin forest. At that time, the Little Otter Singers included several family members—Pete Gahbow (lead), Art Gahbow (Pete's father, now deceased), Jared Gahbow, Bill Gahbow (drumkeeper and drum-warmer 1), and Erik Gahbow (drumwarmer 2)—along with Tom Benjamin (drumwarmer 3), Larry Smallwood, Darrell Moose, Ron White, and Joe Cominghay.

Grand Entry Song is a Canadian Ojibwe song they learned from the Lake of the Woods Singers, Ontario. It was "given" to Pete Gahbow's uncle, Ben Sam, who "gave" it to the Little Otter Singers. When they learned that the Honor the Earth Powwow recording was going to be sold commercially, Pete was quite concerned. *Grand Entry Song* wasn't their "personal" song, so he didn't feel it was right for the Little Otter Singers to be the ones singing it on a commercial tape. But, after much effort, Mickey Hart (who was producing the recording) and the ethnomusicologist Thomas Vennum worked it out with the Lake of the Woods Singers. Pete says, "Since the song was social, not sacred, we finally decided it would be OK for them to use the recording."

Pete begins by setting a moderate tempo on the drum and is soon joined by his father and other drum members. His high-pitched lead announces the song to the other singers, who repeat it. After the initial statement, the song is repeated four times. There is no pause between repetitions—the lead singer begins the next statement immediately upon the conclusion of the previous statement, as is typical of Northern style. The honor beats occur within the second part of the song (second chorus) rather than between the parts—this is also typical of Northern style.

Time	Event
0:00	Emcee announces the song, with background of drumbeats.
0:09	Lead—Lead singer starts song (first statement).
0:13	Second—Drum joins in singing.
0:36	Second chorus—Second melody with honor beats around 0:44+.
0:59	Lead—Lead singer again (second statement).
1:03	Second—Drum joins in.
1:25	Second chorus—Second melody, again with honor beats.
1:48	Lead—Lead singer (third statement).
1:57	Second—Drum.
2:13	Second chorus—Second melody with honor beats.
2:36	Lead—Lead singer (fourth statement).
2:40	Second—Drum.
3:02	Second chorus—Second melody with honor beats.

3:24   Lead—Lead singer (fifth statement).

3:27   Second—Drum.

3:50   Second chorus—Second melody with honor beats.

4:03   Recording fades.

Response to the Music

After you have heard *Grand Entry Song,* take some time to reflect on your personal responses. The music is intended to be danced to. Did it generate a strong physical response in you? What were your emotional responses while you listened? Intellectual responses? Spiritual responses? How do you think your responses might differ from those of the people participating in or watching the Honor the Earth Powwow?

Summary

In this chapter we introduced three important aspects of rhythm in music: beat, tempo, and accent. We have seen how beat and accent operate in the powwow music of Native Americans. We have also learned about the structure of powwow music. Finally, we have learned about the elements of a typical powwow and some aspects of Native American culture and values.

Applying What You Have Learned

1. Listen again to *Exodus* (CD 1, track 4), paying particular attention to the beat. Is the tempo of this music faster or slower than the tempo of *Grand Entry Song* (CD 1, track 6)? Are some beats more accented than others?

2. Write a short essay on your physical, emotional, cognitive, and spiritual responses to *Grand Entry Song.* How might they be different from those of the participants in the Honor the Earth Powwow? Do you think your responses would be different if you were at the powwow? Why?

3. Listen again to *Dolphin Dreams* (CD 1, track 1). Can you identify a beat in this piece? If so, what element creates that beat? Compare the tempo with that of *Exodus* and *Grand Entry Song.* Is it faster or slower? How important is rhythm in *Dolphin Dreams*?

4. Choose several musical pieces that you know well. In each case identify the beat and compare tempos with other pieces of music. Are some beats more accented than others?

5. How much of your enjoyment of music is centered on the beat? Are there types of music you dislike because of their tempo?

6. Compare the tempo of *Simple Gifts* (CD 1, track 2) with that of the same tune in *Appalachian Spring* (CD 1, track 3). Which tempo (if either) is faster?

7. Distinctive rhythmic styles and tempos characterize various forms of popular music (rock, Latin American, reggae, etc.). How much of your preference for one or another of these styles is due to your preference for the characteristic rhythms of the style? Can you describe how you identify these musical styles by their characteristic rhythms?

Important Terms

beat 55
accented beat 55
tempo 55
powwow 55
intertribal song 56
regalia 56
drum 57
lead singer 58
vocables 58
honor beats 58

lead 60
second 60
Southern style 60
second chorus 60
Northern style 61
gourd dance 62
grand entry 62
flag song 64
blessing prayer 64

memorial prayer
song 64
round dances 64
war dances 64
intertribal dances
64
giveaway 66
ethnomusicologist
66

Musicians and Ensembles Mentioned

Names preceded by * have short biographies in Appendix B, page 346.

*Mike Pace
*Pete Gahbow
*Harry Buffalohead
*Little Otter Singers
*Mickey Hart

Further Listening Resources

Little Otter Singers, *Little Otter* (Sunshine Records, Winnipeg, Canada); *Jammin' with Little Otter* (Panther Productions/Native Creative, Minnesota); *Way Up North with Little Otter* (Noc Bay Productions, Escanaba, MI); and a new one released in 2000, in which they sing traditional Mille-Lacs-style seasonal songs.

R. Carlos Nakai, *Desert Dance* (Celestial Harmonies 13033-2). This recording of flute music, composed by Nakai, is another kind of Native American music. The flute was used as a courting instrument in some Plains Indian tribes. Nakai, who is trained in Western music, combines traditional melodies with his own compositions in many of his other popular recordings.

Video

Into the Circle: An Introduction to Native American Powwows (Full Circle Communications, Tulsa, Oklahoma, [918] 589-8849) is an excellent introduction to the powwow and its music.

Meter

🎵 **Klezmer Music: *Bay a Glezele Mashke,*** Traditional

🎵 ***Oy, Abram!,*** Traditional

Peter Turnley/Corbis

*W*e never rehearsed. All the music was done in the studio. *The whole pay was fifteen dollars a musician to play three hours and make four sides [two 78-rpm records].*

*DAVE TARRAS
KLEZMER MUSICIAN

I n Chapter 3 you learned about beat, accent, and tempo in the powwow music of Native Americans. In this chapter we will continue our study of the rhythmic dimension of music by examining the role of meter. Meter is a central organizing factor in the rhythm of most Western music. In later chapters you will learn how rhythm is organized in non-Western music, for example, the Indian *tala* (see Chapter 7).

Meter

Meter is a regular pattern of accented and unaccented beats. In Western notational systems, one unit of the pattern is called a **measure** or a **bar.** Measures are indicated in Western musical notation by vertical lines called **bar lines.** Normally the first beat of each measure is accented.

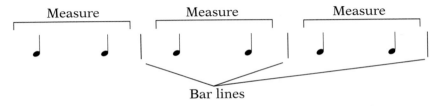

Measures of music

Most Western music has regular patterns of accents, and the number of beats in a pattern determines the meter. If there are two beats in the pattern, the meter is called **duple meter.**

>   —   >   —   >   —   >   —

1   2   1   2   1   2   1   2   Etc.

Duple meter

If there are three beats in the pattern, the meter is called **triple meter.**

>   —   —   >   —   —   >   —   —   >   —   —

1   2   3   1   2   3   1   2   3   1   2   3   Etc.

Triple meter

A four-beat meter is called **quadruple meter.**

> — — — > — — — > — — — > — — —

1　2　3　4　1　2　3　4　1　2　3　4　1　2　3　4　Etc.

Quadruple meter

Duple and quadruple meters are often difficult to distinguish from each other, since two measures of duple meter are equal to one measure of quadruple meter. Later, in Part IV, we will consider the effect of harmony on the perception of meter, and the distinction between duple and quadruple meter will become clearer. For now, however, we will concentrate on the role of accent in creating meter.

Division of the Beat

In the rhythmic life of music, many events are faster than the beat. When two or more events happen within a single beat, we say that the beat is divided. In Western music there are two basic divisions of the beat. When the beat is divided into two equal parts, we call it **simple division.** When the beat is divided in three equal parts, we call it **compound division.**

	>	—	—	—	
Beats:	1	2	3	4	Etc.
Simple division:	| |	| |	| |	|	
Compound division:	| | |	| | |	| | |	| |	

Simple and compound division of a beat

Arturo Toscanini, conducting
Archive Photos

The complete designation of meter includes both the number of beats in the measure and the way the beats are divided. For example, duple-simple meter has two beats per measure, and the beats are divided into two parts. Duple-compound meter has two beats per measure, and the beats are divided into three parts. Musicians use meter as a primary means of coordinating their performances. The motions that the conductor of a band or an orchestra makes with the baton indicate the meter to the musicians, and this helps them play together.

In this chapter you will learn how meter functions in a popular style of music known as klezmer music.

Klezmer Music

Yiddish is a Germanic language spoken by many Jews of Central and Eastern European ancestry.

Klezmer is a **Yiddish** word derived from the Hebrew *kle* (meaning "instruments") and *zemer* ("song"). **"Klezmer music"** is a recently coined term referring to what was originally Eastern European Jewish dance music, probably originating in the Middle Ages. The musicians who play this music are called **klezmorim.**

How did traditional Eastern European Jewish dance music become a contemporary global phenomenon? To understand this requires a short history.

The Rise of Eastern European Jewish Communities

As early as the tenth century C.E., Jewish communities were established on both sides of the Rhine River in Germany. This region was

The Jewish Diaspora

In 63 B.C.E. the Romans conquered the Jews, a people who had originated in Judaea near the modern state of Israel. In spite of two revolts, Judaea remained a part of the Roman Empire until its fall in 410 C.E. Jews gradually migrated, as merchants and traders, over most of the empire. The adoption of Christianity as the state religion of the Roman Empire in the fourth century C.E. brought increasing pressure on the Jewish populations. Various laws were passed limiting the freedom of Jews: property ownership was restricted; they were forced to wear distinguishing badges; and they were confined in particular quarters known as ghettos. Actual expulsions of Jews were carried out in England (1290), France (1394), Spain (1492), and Portugal (1497). In Spain thousands of Jews were forced to convert to Christianity or face death. Many of the Jews who were expelled were later allowed to return, however, because it was found that they were vital to economic and intellectual life.

Since the Catholic Church forbade Christians to engage in lending money with interest, this role fell to the Jews. They became well known as moneylenders and dealers in international trade. In this way some Jews accumulated considerable wealth. Not all Jews engaged in trade, however. Many were small shopkeepers and farmers. Jews have always honored learning, and some Jews became well known as doctors, intellectuals, artists, and musicians. Their communities flourished and attained high levels of intellectual and cultural life, although they remained outsiders because of their religion and their distinctive culture.

called *Ashkenaz* in Yiddish; hence the common designation of Eastern European Jews as **Ashkenazi** Jews (as opposed to **Sephardic** Jews, who originally settled in Spain and Portugal). From the Rhine the Ashkenazi spread to the east, where they continued to speak their distinctive German dialect.

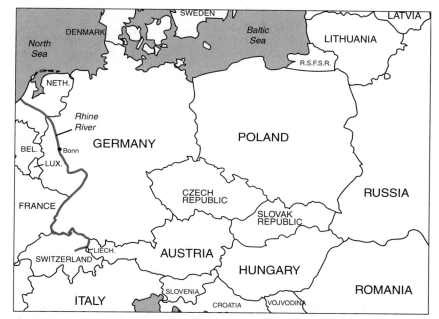

The Ashkenaz

Origins of the Klezmer Tradition

It is probable that the klezmer tradition began in Germany in the Middle Ages, eventually spreading eastward as itinerant Ashkenazi musicians moved from town to town, playing at celebrations and festivals. What we now call klezmer music traces its roots primarily to Moldova, the southern Ukraine, Bukovina (a region of Austrian Galicia), and parts of Romania.

There is some disagreement about the importance of various musical influences on the formation of klezmer. According to Henry Sapoznik, the most important music of the Ashkenazi Jews was the largely vocal music of the synagogues (Jewish community centers and houses of worship), especially the singing of the cantor. Sapoznik believes that klezmer music was profoundly influenced by the scales, inflections, and improvisational style of this cantorial

A *cantor* is a synagogue official trained to lead the congregation in prayer; he or she also sings or chants liturgical music.

music, which *klezmorim* adapted to the instrumental medium. Some other experts, however, minimize the influence of synagogue music on klezmer, placing more importance on regional non-Jewish dance traditions, including Greek, Moldovan, Ukranian, Romanian, and Gypsy music.

Everyone does agree, however, that the enthusiastic dancing, wordless melodic chanting, clapping, and foot stamping of the Hasidim influenced traditional klezmer music. This charismatic, populist Jewish religious movement originated in the second half of the 1700s and had a great influence on klezmer; Hasidim often employed *klezmorim* to "further enliven their gatherings."

Klezmer music was popular with the non-Jewish population, particularly the Polish nobility. Klezmer bands were invited to play for weddings and banquets, as well as on market days. The musical repertoire of the *klezmorim* was thus expanded to include Polish waltzes and mazurkas, and even light classical music.

A *mazurka* is a Polish folk dance.

The *Klezmorim* and Their Music

The musicians collectively known as *klezmorim* played whatever instruments were available, including the violin (fiddle), *strohfiedel* (folk xylophone), flute, bass, *tsimbl* (hammered dulcimer), a small accordion, clarinets, trumpets, tubas, and drums. Since its primary function was to provide music for celebrations, the vast majority of klezmer music is dances and marches. A second genre, known as *doina,* is a free rhapsodic music often used as an introduction to a dance. Traditional klezmer music is often characterized by a "wailing sound reminiscent of weeping," a "laugh-like instrumental sound," and a "sob-like 'catch'," which set it apart from non-Jewish music.

Klezmer in the United States

Millions of Ashkenazi Jews emigrated from Eastern Europe to the United States between 1880 and 1924, motivated by social and political upheavals in their homelands. Many of them were fleeing intense persecution in the form of *pogroms* (organized massacres of Jewish people) that occurred in the late nineteenth and early twentieth centuries, just as had occurred during the Middle Ages. The Ashkenazi naturally brought their culture with them, including their music. Many of them settled in the New York area, where strong Jewish communities soon sprang up. As in Europe, klezmer musicians were in great demand for traditional weddings and other celebrations. Because of the changing tastes of American Jews, however, American popular music, ragtime, and jazz soon influenced klezmer music. This influence went both ways: traditional Eastern European dance melodies

The Klezmer Conservatory Band

were also combined with popular American rhythms.

The rise of the recording industry in the 1920s brought klezmer music to the attention of the non-Jewish population. Although its popularity diminished during World War II, a minor revival began in the 1950s, and there were attempts to fuse klezmer with the rock and Latin music of that era. The major renewal of interest began in the 1970s. Many klezmer bands have since sprung up in the United States, and klezmer music has even become

History of Klezmer Music

16th Century ➡	19th Century ➡	20th Century ➡	1920s ➡	1970s ➡
Earliest references to klezmer-style music.	Hasidism in Eastern Europe encourages ecstatic music and dance.	Jewish musicians move to the United States.	Klezmer takes on elements of jazz and popular music.	Revitalization of klezmer.

We know more about the cultural context of early klezmer music than we know about the music itself. From the sixteenth through the early nineteenth century, Ashkenazi Judaism began to take several different forms, including the *Haskalah* enlightenment movement in Western Europe, which stressed cultural (not religious) assimilation; the northern European

Msnagdim, an intellectual movement that discouraged music and dance; and the Hasidic movement, which encouraged enthusiastic dancing and chanting wordless melodies. Ba'al Shem Tov started the Hasidic phenomenon in Eastern Europe in the latter half of the 1700s. This charismatic movement encouraged Jews to express their piety in ecstatic fervor through music and dance. The *klezmorim* often played at Hasidic gatherings—both influencing and being influenced by this enthusiastic spirit. It was among the Hasidim that Yiddish (and klezmer) continued to flourish.

Several million Jews immigrated to the United States between 1880 and 1924. Some were klezmer musicians, and many of these found work as musicians (though not playing klezmer) in American Yiddish theater and in vaudeville. In the 1920s a new style of klezmer music developed, one that "fused" traditional Eastern European dance melodies with popular American rhythms. This genre, the "oriental fox-trot" "inspired not only Jewish musicians but also such important African American artists as Duke Ellington and Fats Waller." Some of these "Afro-Judaic" songs became big hits.

After the late 1930s American Jewish audiences and musicians were less interested in their Eastern European roots, and traditional music faded in popularity or was transformed into a kind of slick swing music. In the 1960s few young musicians knew about klezmer. But then some of these younger Jewish musicians began looking for their musical roots, and they rediscovered klezmer. Since the 1970s *klezmorim* have revived the klezmer music of the early twentieth century by learning from older musicians and by listening to old recordings and attempting to re-create them as exactly as possible. Other groups chart new (or perhaps not so new, given klezmer's eclectic history) klezmer improvisational-jazz territory.

popular again in Europe, as well as in Australia, Mexico, and Japan. Modern *klezmorim* may play traditional music or a type of "fusion" music that mixes traditional klezmer with Latin and jazz.

Meter in Klezmer Music

Most klezmer music is in duple-simple or quadruple-simple meter. There are examples of triple-simple meter, but there appears to be very little compound meter in this music.

LISTENING ACTIVITY

Bay a Glezele Mashke (Traditional) [CD 1, track 7]

In the 1980s the Klezmer Conservatory Band (KCB) recorded the arrangement of *Bay a Glezele Mashke* you will hear. The KCB learned *Bay a Glezele Mashke* from a recording made in the 1920s by Harry Kandel's Philadelphia-based orchestra. The fifteen-piece KCB is directed by Hankus Netsky, a descendant of several Philadelphian klezmer orchestra musicians of the 1920s. Netsky, who formed the internationally renowned KCB in 1980, is a multi-instrumentalist and composer, as well as an instructor in jazz and contemporary improvisation at the

New England Conservatory of Music in Boston. The Klezmer Conservatory Band has been featured in several films.

Modern *klezmorim* have found the hundreds of early klezmer recordings a veritable treasure chest of material. *Bay a Glezele Mashke*—which translates as "Over a Glass of Whiskey"—is a typical example. The piece is a fast and frantic klezmer march in duple-simple meter. The emphasis on clarinet, saxophone, trumpet, trombone, and drums is quite appropriate for the march style.

Time	Event
0:00	The cymbal crash after the first three melody notes signals the beginning of the first measure of duple-simple meter. The tempo is quite fast. If you listen to the lower (bass) instruments, you will hear the beat clearly. Klezmer musicians know this pattern as the "oompah" beat, a typical pattern in klezmer music. Count "one," "two" with this repeating pattern and you will hear the duple-simple meter.
0:21	First section is repeated. Now listen to the instruments "between" the melody and the bass, and you will hear the division of the beats. Count "one-and-two-and" and notice that these instruments are often playing twice as fast as the lower instruments.
0:42	Second section. Duple-simple meter continues.
1:09	Third section. Listen to the woodblock and notice that it is playing a pattern derived from the division of the beat.
1:37	Second section is repeated.

LISTENING ACTIVITY

Oy, Abram! (Traditional) [CD 1, track 8]

Oy, Abram! is an example of a Yiddish folksong performed in traditional klezmer style. There are two distinct tempos in this piece: the song itself is slow, while the instrumental introduction and interludes between verses are much faster. The meter is quadruple-simple for both the faster and the slower material.

Notice how the transition is made between the faster and slower sections. In each case the singer holds the fourth beat of the final measure in the faster tempo, and the beat stops for a moment. The instrumental ensemble then establishes the new, slower tempo.

An *introduction* is music that comes before the main part of a piece. An *interlude* is music that occurs between major sections. A *verse* is the music for one stanza of a poem.

This variant of a traditional humorous love song is based on a 1920s recording by Isa Kremer. The arrangement is by the Klezmer Conservatory Band, directed by Hankus Netsky, with Judy Bressler performing the vocal. Translation of the Yiddish lyrics is by David E. Fishman.

Time	Musical Event	Text	Translation
0:00	Instrumental introduction		
0:11	Verse I	Oy, Abram! Ikh ken on dir nit zayn!	Oh, Abram! I can't live without you.
		Ikh on dir un du on mir	I without you and you without me,
		Kenen mir beyde nit zayn.	That could never be.
		Gedenkstu, gedenkstu, bay bem toyer	Do you remember when we stood at the gate
		Hostu mer gezogt a sod in oyer	How you whispered a secret in my ear?
		Oy vey, Rivkele	Oh, Rivkele!
		Gib zhe mir dayn piskele!	Give me your lips! (repeat)
0:48	Instrumental interlude		
0:59	Verse II	Oy, Abram! Ikh ken on dir nit zayn!	Oh, Abram! I can't live without you.
		Ikh on dir un du on mir	I without you and you without me,
		Vi a kliamke on a tir	Like a doorknob without a door.
		Gedenkstu, gedenkstu, bay der tir	Do you remember when we stood at the door?

		Hostu mikh tsugekvetsht tsu dir	You pressed me close to you and said:
		Oy vey, Rivkenyu	Oh, Rivkenyu
		Gib zhe mer dayn piskenyu!	Give me your lips! (repeat)
1:40	Instrumental interlude		
1:51	Verse III	Oy, Abram! Ikh ken on dir nit zayn!	Oh, Abram! I can't live without you.
		Ikh on dir un du on mir	I without you and you without me,
		Kenen mir beyde nit zayn.	That could never be.
		Gedenkstu, gedenkstu, dos royte kleydl	Do you remember my red dress?
		Oy, bin ikh geven a sheyne meydl!	Ah, I was such a pretty girl—and you said:
		Oy vey, Rivkele	Oh, Rivkele!
		Gib zhe mir dayn piskele!	Give me your lips! (repeat)
2:34	Instrumental coda		

A coda *is music that concludes a piece of music.*

Source: David Fishman, trans., "Oy, Abram!" in liner notes for the CD titled *Klez: The Klezmer Conservatory Band*, directed by Hankus Netsky, with Judy Bressler performing the vocal; Vanguard VCD-79449. Reprinted with permission of the Klezmer Conservatory Band.

Response to the Music

Reflect on your responses to this music. You probably had a strong physical response to *Bay a Glezele Mashke*. This music (unlike *Oy, Abram!*) has marching or dancing as its primary purpose. How do you respond physically, emotionally, and spiritually to these two very different klezmer pieces? Did the translation of *Oy, Abram!* help you to understand the emotional tone of the music? What effect does knowledge of the history of klezmer have on your responses?

Summary

In this chapter you have learned about meter in music. The three most common meters in Western music are duple, triple, and quadruple. We also identify meter by the division of the beat, which may be simple or compound. We have learned about klezmer, the modern term for a popular kind of music that originated among Eastern European Jews in the Middle Ages.

Applying What You Have Learned

1. Can you hear any variations in tempo in *Bay a Glezele Mashke* (CD 1, track 7)? If so, where do they occur?

2. Listen to *Simple Gifts* [CD 1, track 2]. The first line of the first verse is quoted here with the beats indicated above the words:

    4   **1** 2   3   4   **1** 2   3

    'Tis the gift to be simple, 'Tis the gift to be free,

    Copy the next three lines of the song (page 25) and mark the beats in the same way as above. What is the meter of this song? Find places where there is more than one syllable per beat. Is the division of the beat simple or compound? Give the complete designation for the meter.

3. Notice that the melody of *Simple Gifts* doesn't begin on the first beat of a measure. This is also true of the beginning of *Bay a Glezele Mashke* [CD 1, track 7]. It is very common for a piece of music to begin in this way. The beats before the first full measure are called the **anacrusis,** but musicians usually refer to them as "pickup beats" or "upbeats." Make a list of other pieces of music you know that begin with pickup beats.

4. Listen to the excerpt from *Appalachian Spring* [CD 1, track 3]. Is this music in the same meter as *Simple Gifts?*

5. Listen to *Redemption Song* [CD 1, track 5] and try to determine the meter. (It is most clear in the introduction, before Bob Marley begins singing.) Listen to the beginning of the song. Is there an anacrusis?

6. For the next few days, whenever you listen to music, try to determine the meter. It will be more obvious in some cases than in others. Make a list of the meters that you hear. What do you find to be the predominant meter in the music you listen to?

7. For the next few days, listen for the division of the beat in the music you listen to. From your observations, would you say that simple or compound division predominates in the music you listen to?

Important Terms

meter 74
measure or bar 74
bar line 74
duple meter 74
triple meter 74
quadruple meter 75

simple division 75
compound division 75
klezmer 76
klezmer music 76
Yiddish 76

klezmorim 76
Ashkenazi 77
Sephardic 77
doina 78
anacrusis 84

Musicians Mentioned

Names preceded by * have short biographies in Appendix B, page 346.

*Hankus Netsky
Isa Kremer
Judy Bressler

Further Listening Resources

If this brief introduction to klezmer music has whetted your appetite for more, you may want to listen to some of the following historical recordings. These are reissues of early 78 rpm records and have all the limitations of early recordings. They are, nevertheless, valuable and interesting listening experiences.

Klezmer Music 1910–1942 (Global Village). This CD includes several recordings by Abe Schwartz, a bandleader in New York Yiddish theater, who was one of the first musicians to produce klezmer recordings.

Klezmer Pioneers: European and American 1905–1952 (Rounder Records).

King of the Klezmer Clarinet (Rounder Records). Recordings of the klezmer clarinetist Naftule Brandwein.

Yiddish-American Klezmer Music 1925–1956 (Yazoo). Recordings made by the klezmer clarinetist Dave Tarras (who is quoted at the beginning of this chapter).

For modern adaptations and extensions of klezmer music, the following CDs are recommended:

The Klezmatics, *Rhythm and Jews* (Flying Fish Records).

The Klezmatics, *Jews with Horns* (Xenophile Records).

New Orleans Klezmer All-Stars (Gert Town).

Polyrhythm

🔴 *Shango,* Babatunde Olatunji

Christine Osborne/Corbis

Where I come from we say that rhythm is the soul of life
because the whole universe revolves around rhythm, and
when we get out of rhythm, that's when we get into trouble.
For this reason the drum, next to the human voice, is our
most important instrument.

*BABATUNDE OLATUNJI
AFRICAN DRUMMER AND EDUCATOR

Polyrhythm

As you learned in Chapter 4, rhythm in most Western music is organized around meter. The music of some other cultures, however, has a very different organization. For example, the classical music of India uses a system based on a rhythmic pattern called a *tala* (see Chapter 7). In this chapter we will look at the rhythmic structure of a piece of West African music. While the various rhythmic layers are tightly coordinated, there doesn't appear to be a single metrical structure that ties them together. In fact, each layer may have its own rhythmic structure. The Western term for this kind of rhythmic organization is **polyrhythm** (*poly* means "many"; thus, "many rhythms").

In polyrhythmic music the organizing factor is usually a common rhythmic unit that is too rapid to be perceived as a beat. This rhythmic unit acts as the division or subdivision of a beat, and different layers in the rhythm may have different numbers of divisions and thus different beat speeds. In the chart below, the rapid rhythmic unit is shown as a series of squares with drumbeats for two rhythmic layers shown as black dots.

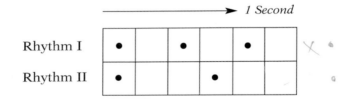

You can see that rhythm I divides the time (1 second) into three beats while rhythm II divides it into two beats. Although the rhythmic structure of African music is considerably more complex than this simple example, you can see the principle involved. If you want to produce a polyrhythm yourself, you can establish a rapid unit (for example, six units per second) and tap the upper part with one hand while tapping the lower part with the other hand.

Polyrhythm in African Music

The individual rhythms in African music tend to be fairly simple and repetitive, but when several of these rhythms occur at the same time, the result is very complex to Western ears. The primary reason for this apparent complexity is that the various patterns usually differ in length. In Western terms, there is no place to "draw the

bar line" in African music, and no single meter governs the music.
When people dance to this music, each layer of the rhythm corresponds to the movements of one or another of the dancers. Here is
a simple illustration of African rhythm.

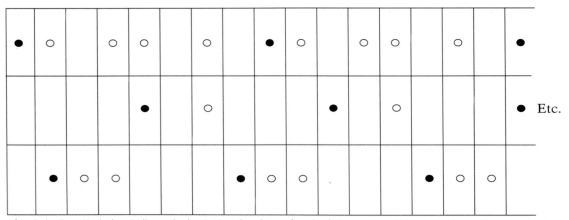

African rhythm. Black dots indicate the beginning drumbeat of each of the patterns. White dots show other drumbeats within the pattern.

While all the patterns observe the same basic time unit, the first
pattern repeats after eight units and the second and third patterns
repeat after six units. Also, the second and third patterns begin at
different times. There are almost always two—and there may be as
many as five or six—different rhythmic patterns being played at the
same time, by different drummers. As a result, African drumming
presents an interesting challenge to listeners who are unaccus-
tomed to identifying such complex patterns. From the African perspective, these complex rhythmic patterns resemble a rose—each
individual rhythm is like a petal, and together they form the flower.

We will now learn more about Sub-Saharan Africa and listen to
a piece of music performed by Babatunde Olatunji, a Yoruba from
Nigeria, a part of West Africa.

Sub-Saharan Africa

The continent of Africa can be divided into the northern and southern regions, which are separated by the Sahara Desert. The region
north of the Sahara (Egypt, Libya, Morocco, etc.) is largely Islamic,
with a distinctive ethnic population base. The music of the northern region is related more to Middle Eastern music than to music
south of the Sahara. Sub-Saharan Africa is divided into over thirty
countries with some 400 languages, but this division is a product of

European colonization in the nineteenth century rather than a natural grouping of peoples. Before the coming of European rule, highly developed African states already existed, based on ethnic and language groups. Sub-Saharan Africa can be subdivided into West Africa, Congo-Zaire, South Africa, and Zimbabwe.

Africa

The Importance of Music in Sub-Saharan Africa

Music is a constant in the everyday life of traditional Sub-Saharan Africans. Nearly everyone sings, dances, and plays musical instruments. Music is a part of ceremonies to celebrate birth, initiation, marriage, and death. Singing and dancing mark important events in the culture. The sound of drums is a companion to everyday life throughout the region.

Percussion Instruments in West African Music

Indigenous means native to, originating in a particular region.

Although a wide variety of musical instruments of all types is found in Africa, the **percussion** instruments—instruments sounded by being struck—are the most prevalent. There are numerous classification systems for indigenous instruments based on purpose, materials, religious association, ethnic affiliation, etc. For the sake of simplicity we will use the standard Western classification system. In this system, West African percussion instruments can be placed in two categories. Some instruments are **idiophones,** instruments that produce sound by vibration of the materials they are made of. These instruments are played by being struck with a beater,

History of Sub-Saharan African Music

Relatively little is known about the history of Sub-Saharan African music because many Sub-Saharan cultures had no indigenous written language until well into the nineteenth century. Instead, they had a highly developed, sophisticated set of oral traditions, the preservation of which was an important aspect of communal cultural life. Accounts of European slave traders from the sixteenth through the nineteenth centuries agree very well with recent observations by ethnomusicologists, providing strong circumstantial evidence of a relatively unchanging musical culture. In 1620 Richard Jobson described formal processions accompanied by music. Jobson reported that every village had professional musicians, who were similar to present-day master drummers. His descriptions of instruments and performance styles are also like those of present-day Africa. Olaudah Equiano, one of the first Africans to write a book in English—*The Interesting Narrative of the Life of Olaudah Equiano, or Gustavus Vassa the African. Written by Himself* (1789)—observed, "We are almost a nation of dancers, musicians, and poets." Thomas Bowdich, writing in 1817, described great public dances, accompanied by drums and other instruments, that are remarkably similar to those observed in the twentieth century. On this basis, we can say with some degree of certainty that the music of Africa remained relatively unchanged until the impact of Western culture began to be felt in the nineteenth and twentieth centuries.

scraped, shaken, or struck together. Other instruments are **membranophones,** instruments that produce sound through vibration of a stretched skin or membrane. These instruments are typically sounded by being struck with a stick or the hand.

West African Idiophones. The *agogo,* or *gong-gongs,* are hollow metal instruments that are struck with a stick. They resemble a simple bell without a clapper. Some are single instruments, but they often come in pairs that are joined together. In such a pair, the higher-sounding instrument is called the male *agogo,* and the lower-sounding instrument is called the female.

   Xylophones consist of a set of wooden bars of various sizes that are struck with a beater. In some xylophones, the bars are suspended over resonators, which amplify the sound of the bars.

   Rattles, which produce sound when shaken, are made of many different materials, including gourds, wood, and metal. Some African rattles have a network of beads draped around a gourd. These are called *shakere* in Yoruba.

Agogos
Royalty Free/Corbis

The term **membranophone** refers to the large group of instruments we commonly call **drums.** The player sounds a drum by striking the head with a beater or the hands. The head is made of a stretched animal skin. The body of the drum may be a hollow log; a gourd; a frame of wood, metal, or clay; or even a discarded metal container. Some drums have two drumheads; others have only one. Drums come in all sizes, producing a wide variety of sounds. Differences in sound are important to the effectiveness of a drum ensemble. The listener needs to be able to distinguish among the sounds of the various drums that are playing together to hear the various patterns in the polyrhythm.

Talking Drums. In many parts of Africa, drums are used to communicate over distances.

Xylophone
James Marshall/Corbis

Nigerian shaman holding a rattle
Paul Almasy/Corbis

This is possible because many Sub-Saharan languages are tonal languages (as is Chinese). Yoruba, for example, has six different **tones**—that is, relative pitches. In tonal languages, the meaning of a word depends on the tones applied to different syllables. A variety of instruments, including drums—and even the guitar—can be used as surrogates for speech because they can be made to imitate the tonal patterns of words. Drummers mimic the inflections of speech so completely that their drumming becomes a recognizable code, which can be deciphered by others. Context is, of course, extremely important, since "many words may share the same number of syllables and tonal contours." A "word" (a drummed tonal pattern) followed by a stereotypic drumming formula is easier to recognize. Great distances can be spanned by this method, because the sound of drums carries very well and other drummers pick up and relay the messages they receive.

Drums may also be used in ceremonial settings to "drum" the name of a dancer, to "drum" a historic text, or to honor a high official. These **talking drums** are associated with magic and myth. They are often hidden away out of sight and moved only during the night.

Shakere, rattles, and drums
Dan Peha/The Viesti Collection

Talking drum player
Brian Vikander/Corbis

Babatunde Olatunji— West African Music in the West

More than any other musician, Babatunde Olatunji has been responsible for the present interest in West African music in the United States. Olatunji was born and raised in Nigeria; he arrived in the United States in 1950 on a Rotary Educational Foundation scholarship. He earned an undergraduate degree from Morehouse College in Atlanta, Georgia. Facing racism and a pervasive ignorance about African culture, Olatunji set out to educate Americans about his native land. Music proved to be a powerful tool in this process. Olatunji's lectures and concerts were in constant demand and also became a source of income for him. His 1958 album, *Drums of Passion,* was the first commercially available recording of African music in the United States. *Shango* (Chant to the God of Thunder), which you will listen to in this chapter, is the final track in that album.

During the 1960s Olatunji met Martin Luther King, Jr., and Malcolm X, and he became an active force in the American civil rights movement. He also opened the Olatunji Center for African Culture in Harlem, in New York City. This center introduced many young Americans to African drumming and African culture. His group, "Drums of Passion," was invited to perform at the New York World's Fair of 1964 and appeared on national television programs such as *The Tonight Show,* the *Mike Douglas Show,* and the *Bell Telephone Hour.* He has composed music for Broadway plays and films, including *Raisin in the Sun* and *She's Gotta Have It.*

In 1985 Olatunji began a collaboration with Mickey Hart, drummer for The Grateful Dead. He opened many Grateful Dead concerts over the years, and in 1991 he joined Mickey Hart and other percussionists in recording the best-selling album *Planet Drum.* In 1998 he was nominated for a Grammy Award for his recording *Love Drum Talk.* Olatunji teaches at Esalen Institute in Big Sur, California; at the Omega Institute in Rhinebeck, New York; and in many universities throughout the world.

LISTENING ACTIVITY

Shango (Chant to the God of Thunder) [CD 1, track 9]

Olatunji gives the following description of the Shango ritual: "The Yoruba tribesmen who worship the god of thunder sing and dance vigorously during the Shango ritual. The Spirit enters their bodies as they dance to the powerful, complex rhythmic patterns. They are overpowered and sometimes collapse. The religious effect is so great that the dancers expose themselves to fire without danger. They do not feel the fire nor do their bodies show evidence of being burned. The chanting, accompanied by the rhythm of the drum, gongs, and rattles, seem to transform them."

West African drummers
*Xavier Rossi/Gamma
Liaison*

As you prepare to listen to *Shango,* keep the following images in mind.

With thunder and lightning, Shango, the God of Thunder and the deified King of Old Oyo, revisits the earth, as his devotees chant his invocationary praise. Listen, as Babatunde invokes him:

> *Shango, protect me! Gatekeeper of the passenger train. Today belongs to the passengers; tomorrow belongs to the gatekeeper.*
> *Shango, you lap blood*
> *Like the cat that laps palm oil*
> *Costumed like the acrobatic masquerade,* labala,
> *With the cloth of death,*

Shango, you are the death that drips, drips, drips
Like indigo dye dripping from an adire cloth.

Source: Excerpted from "Shango" song lyrics and from liner notes of *Olatunji! Drums of Passion,* written by Akin Akiwowo and Babatunde Olatunji. Liner notes reprinted by permission of Sony Music Entertainment.

Time	Musical Event
0:00	Free introduction on drums and *agogo*. No beat is established here.
0:13	First singer enters against the drum and *agogo* background.
0:30	Response by second singer. A call-and-response pattern is established.
0:47	First singer repeats opening, "Shango . . ."
0:59	Both voices.
1:06	Tempo is established by a regular drumbeat.
1:09	Second rhythmic pattern on clapping sticks is added.
1:12	Third pattern on *agogo*.
1:16	Fourth pattern on *shakere*.

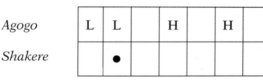

Agogo	L	L		H		H		L	L		H
Shakere		•						•			

L = low bell
H = high bell

Agogo and *shakere* patterns

Time	Musical Event
1:22	Fifth pattern on drum. There is a gradual transformation of the repeated rhythmic patterns throughout the remainder of the work.
1:56	Voice enters again.
2:38	Speaking, shouting, and trilling vocal sounds.
3:37	First singer repeats, "Shango . . ."
4:42	Women begin singing.
6:35	Slow fade begins, indicating that the ritual would continue.

Response to the Music

In its original setting *Shango* is part of a religious ritual. All participants in the ritual would be dancing, singing, or playing musical instruments. We have just listened as passive spectators to a recorded version of the music. This change of setting causes us to view the music as an object to be contemplated rather than as an experience to be shared with others. One result of Olatunji's bringing West African music to the United States is that this ceremonial music has become concert music. As such, it has changed its setting and purpose. We cannot fully grasp the effect this music would have on the Yoruba tribesmen who perform the ritual, but we can use our imaginations to try to place ourselves in the original setting. In this way we can better appreciate the music.

What are your physical, emotional, and spiritual responses to the music? How successful were you in imagining the original setting? Did learning about the culture from which the music comes enhance your enjoyment?

Summary

In this chapter we have learned about the complex polyrhythmic structure of West African drumming. We have learned to listen actively to the multilayered rhythms. We have also learned about a number of West African musical instruments, including specific membranophones and idiophones.

Applying What You Have Learned

1. Listen again to *Grand Entry Song* [CD 1, track 6]. Compare this music with *Shango*. Both works involve drumming and singing to accompany a dance. What other similarities do you observe? What differences do you note? Consider how your own responses to the music are similar or different.

2. Listen to the beginning of the singing in *Shango* (0:13–1:00) and compare it with the opening of *Grand Entry Song* (0:09–0:15). Do you hear a similarity? What is the name for this phenomenon? How are the two pieces different?

3. Listen again to *Simple Gifts* [CD 1, track 2]. *Shango* and *Simple Gifts* are both religious music. What do these two pieces of music suggest to you about the cultures in which they developed?

4. Polyrhythm is not a common texture in most Western music, but it does occur occasionally, particularly in soul

Soul is an African American popular music from the 1960s. Its roots were in African American church music, but it incorporated elements of rock.

music. James Brown often described polyrhythm as "everyone coming together on the *one*" with freedom on the beats between. Does this description apply to how the playing of African drummers in *Shango* fits together? If not, how does their playing differ from James Brown's description?

5. Would experiencing *Shango* in its original setting enhance your appreciation? Why or why not?

6. *Shango* is music to be danced to. Which other pieces that you have listened to on CD 1 are also dance music? What do they have in common? Describe the style of dances you imagine that these pieces of music would generate.

Important Terms

polyrhythm 87
percussion 90
idiophone 90
membranophone 91

agogo (*gong-gong*) 91
xylophone 91
rattle 91

shakere 91
drum 91
talking drum 91

Names preceded by * have short biographies in Appendix B, page 346.

Musicians Mentioned

*Babatunde Olatunji
*Mickey Hart
*James Brown

Further Listening Resources

Planet Drum (Ryko). This album, produced by Mickey Hart, includes the musicians Zakir Hussain, Airto Moriera, Flora Purim, and Babatunde Olatunji.

Love Drum Talk (Chesky Jazz). This recording by Babatunde Olatunji was nominated for a Grammy award in 1998.

Denké-denké (daqui 332-006). Mamar Kassey, a West African band from Niamey, combines African pop with traditional music from the Fulani, Songhai, Zerma, and Hausa.

PART III

Melody

in Music

The song is ended, but the melody lingers on.

*IRVING BERLIN
AMERICAN SONGWRITER

In the following chapters we will concentrate on another important part of music—melody. Our response to music is strongly influenced by the power of melody to evoke strong emotions. Often when we hear a piece of music, it is the melody that remains in our memory. You may know melodies that remind you of particular places or people who are significant to you.

In this part of the book you will learn the differences between vocal melody and instrumental melody. These differences are related to the technical capabilities of instruments and voices, but, as you will learn in Chapter 8, the human voice is capable, with extensive training, of becoming much more like an instrument.

You will also learn how melodies are structured into phrases and longer units. Melody is an important element in creating coherence in music.

Art Resource

CHAPTER 6 Vocal Melody **100**
De sancta Maria, Hildegard of Bingen

CHAPTER 7 Instrumental Melody **122**
Máru Bihág, Ravi Shankar

CHAPTER 8 Vocal Melody in Opera **140**
La Bohème, Act II, Giacomo Puccini

Vocal Melody

De sancta Maria, Hildegard of Bingen

Otto Muller Verlag

S*ymphony is the harmony of the whole created world,*
united in the praise of God.

HILDEGARD OF BINGEN (1098–1179)

BENEDICTINE ABBESS, COMPOSER, HEALER, NATURALIST, AND MYSTIC

I n Part II we learned about rhythm in music, but music is much more than beat and rhythm. It is also **melody**—an organized succession of pitches that form a coherent whole (see page 103). Melody is all around us—in the songs we sing, in the music we listen to, and on radio and television. In this part of the book, we will learn how melody is structured; but first we need to become more aware of certain properties of sound.

Sound and Pitch

The sensations we perceive as sound are a result of disturbances in the air around us. These disturbances are called **vibration.** We perceive differences in the speed, or **frequency,** of vibration as changes in pitch. The term **pitch** refers to the relative "highness" or "lowness" of a musical tone. "Highness" and "lowness" are how we perceived faster and slower frequencies. Faster frequencies are perceived as higher in pitch; slower frequencies are perceived as lower in pitch.

Sounds in music can be categorized into two classes: pitched and unpitched. A **pitched sound** has a clearly defined **fundamental frequency.** Most sounds contain more than one frequency, but in a pitched sound the fundamental frequency is the lowest, and the other frequencies are integer multiples of it. For example, if the fundamental frequency of a tone is 100 Hz, the other frequencies might be 200 Hz, 300 Hz, 400 Hz, etc. Examples of pitched sounds are those produced by such musical instruments as the guitar, flute, and trumpet.

An **unpitched sound** is a mixture of many frequencies without a clear relationship among them. The static you sometimes hear on a radio during a storm is a good example of unpitched sound, as is the "static" sound of digital data being transmitted over a modem. The sounds of some musical instruments—for example, the snare drum and the cymbal—are also unpitched. Music is often made from a combination of pitched sounds and unpitched sounds, and both are important ingredients of music.

There is no universal standard for musical pitches. Every culture has its own preferred set of pitches, and much of the flavor of different styles of music comes from the different pitches to which instruments are tuned. In the West, a system called **equal temperament** has been used as a standard tuning system since the late eighteenth century. In equal temperament, all the relationships between adjacent pitches are the same. They are perceived as being "equidistant" from each other.

Hz is an abbreviation for hertz, the standard measurement for frequencies in vibrations per second.

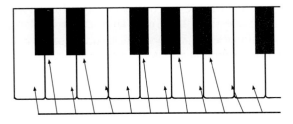

Western tuning (equal temperament)

Scales

The pitches used in Western music are those found on the piano keyboard. We will use the piano keyboard for demonstration because it provides a clear visual representation of pitches.

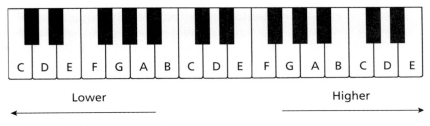

Lower   Higher

Piano keyboard

    Musicians select certain sets of pitches to create scales. A **scale** is a collection of pitches arranged in order from lowest to highest. The term *scale* comes from the Italian word *scala,* which means "ladder." You can think of each tone of a scale as a rung on a musical ladder. There are thousands of scales in the various musics of the world, and these scales vary in the number of pitches and the specific pitches they include.

    The most common scale in Western music is the **major scale.**

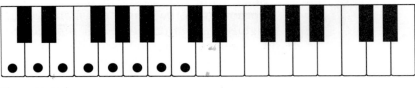

The major scale

As shown on the previous page, a major scale can be played on the white keys of the piano beginning on the key shown at the far left (C). This scale is called the C major scale because it begins and ends on the note named C and includes only the white keys. It can be played by beginning on any C on the piano keyboard. The tone C is said to be the **tonic** of the C major scale. The tonic of any scale is the beginning and end tone.

Another scale that is common in Western music is the **minor scale.**

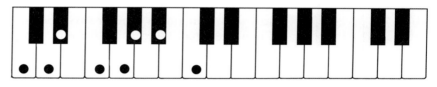

The minor scale

This scale is called the C minor scale. It also begins and ends on C, but it includes three black keys instead of three of the white keys of the C major scale. Only three tones of the minor scale are different from the major scale, but this is enough to completely change the character and sound of the scale. If you have a keyboard available, you can play these scales for yourself. You will hear the difference.

There are many other scales in the musics of the world, and many bear no resemblance to the scales selected from the eighty-eight pitches on the piano keyboard. Other musical cultures have selected an entirely different set of pitches from the infinite number available. In Chapter 7, for example, you will learn about the Indian *raga*, which is based on a set of scales different from those of Western music. In Chapter 16 you will learn about the Turkish system called *makam*, which is based on yet a different set of pitches.

Melody

A *leap* is a point where a melody skips over several tones in the scale. Melodies that follow the scale in order are called step-wise or smooth melodies.

A **melody** is an organized succession of pitches that form a coherent whole. Some melodies consist of only a few tones, while others cover the entire piano keyboard. The interval between the highest and lowest tones of a melody is the **range** of the melody. Some melodies are smooth and flowing, while others consist of many large leaps. Smooth melodies are said to be **conjunct;** more jagged melodies (containing many leaps) are called **disjunct.**

Phrase

Melodies are divided into phrases, much like sentences in a language. A **phrase** is the smallest complete musical thought. Phrases are identified by the pauses you sense in a melody. If you are singing, you will naturally take a breath at such a point. If there is a text with a melody, the musical phrases normally coincide with punctuation marks in the text.

Vocal Melody

Most of us can sing a tune or two, and some of us know hundreds of melodies that we can sing from memory. Vocal melody is usually associated with a text, and text is a prime force shaping such melodies. In fact, a line of the text of a song will often bring the melody to mind. The style of vocal melody varies from simple folk songs, which are usually conjunct, to the virtuoso melodies that characterize operatic singing, which are often quite disjunct.

Introduction to *De sancta Maria*

The music we will encounter in this chapter is more than 800 years old. However, it is also as contemporary as the latest rock music. In the last decade, the musical works of Hildegard of Bingen, a twelfth-century German abbess and mystic, have become extremely popular. A number of recordings of her works are available. Some attempt to duplicate the original style of the music; others are popularized New Age adaptations. What makes the music of this composer, poet, naturalist, and social critic appeal to modern listeners? For one thing, its passion and vitality are immediately apparent. For another, the soaring melodic lines create a timeless musical experience that is at once intellectually intriguing and emotionally appealing.

Who was this "Renaissance" woman who lived in the Middle Ages, and what was the context in which she composed her innovative music? We will examine her life, the culture in which she lived and worked, the place of music in that culture, and one common form of music of the time: the **sequence** (see page 115).

Hildegard of Bingen

Hildegard (1098–1179), who became one of the most celebrated women of her age, was born in a period of great religious and cultural development. This was the time of the Crusades to the Holy Land as well as a time of monastic reform and educational development. During this century, the Cathedral School of Paris was evolving into the University of Paris. The brilliant priest Abelard and his beautiful student Heloise fell in love; Frederick Barbarossa became the Holy Roman Emperor; Bernard of Clairvaux instituted major monastic reforms; Eleanor of Aquitaine was a patron of troubadours and courtly literature; and Thomas à Becket struggled with Henry II over the relative power of the English court and church.

Hildegard was born in the summer of 1098 at Bickelheim in the west German Rhine country. Her parents were nobles, and she was the youngest of ten children. She was a frail child, subject to severe illnesses. As a child, she was educated by a holy anchoress named Jutta, who lived in several rooms connected with the Benedictine monastery of Mount Saint Disibode near Bingen, a monastery founded by a seventh-century Celtic monk.

> An *anchoress* was a holy woman who withdrew from the world and chose to live in a restricted dwelling place.

When she was eight years old, Hildegard joined Jutta and another woman in their monastic cell. This monastery, unlike many others of the time, housed men and women in one community, although under different roofs. Here Hildegard studied music and spinning, and she followed the three fundamental Benedictine practices: prayer, Bible study, and work. During this time she became familiar with the music of the medieval church—the cycle of prayer and chanting that formed an integral part of monastic life. Seven times a day, the nuns would express their faith in heartfelt song.

The monastic life was deeply satisfying to Hildegard. When she was eighteen, she took formal vows and became a Benedictine nun.

Volmar recording Hildegard's awakening
Otto Muller Verlag

By 1136, when Hildegard was thirty-eight, a dozen women were living in the Benedictine community at Saint Disibode. Jutta died that year, and Hildegard succeeded her as abbess. Within four years Hildegard had a mystical experience that changed the rest of her life as well as the history of Western music. She describes it this way: "When I was forty-two years and seven months old, a burning light of tremendous brightness coming from heaven poured into my entire mind."

Although Hildegard had had visions since she was a young child, she had kept most of them to herself. Now, however, the voice in her visions commanded her to overcome her fear and self-doubt and to share these visions with the world. Rising from her sickbed with new determination, she began to share her powerful visions. Her secretary, Volmar, recorded her words in proper, grammatical Latin.

During the ten-year period between ages forty-two and fifty-two, Hildegard recorded a series of illuminated visions and text called *Scivias* (Know the Ways). Hildegard supervised the production of the paintings based on her visions. These illuminations were innovative in content and form, and they had a significant impact on medieval iconography.

As a result of her visionary experiences, Hildegard came to see herself—and to be seen—as a prophet. She was not a prophet who foretold the future but rather one who criticized "the present in such depth that the future might affect a deeper commitment to bringing about the Kingdom of God in the here and now." She became the voice of social conscience.

Hildegard's fame spread, and in 1148, after sending a committee to investigate her competence, Pope Eugenius III gave his approval to her work. This ecclesiastic "pat on the back" was extremely important because Hildegard was violating many social norms by teaching, preaching, and writing. At that time, it was most unusual for a woman to write. The pope's approval gave Hildegard the permission she needed as a Benedictine abbess to speak, write, and disseminate her visionary work. It provided the social and religious affirmation she desperately needed. The pope also encouraged Hildegard to keep writing. She, in turn, in a fashion typical of her courage and spirit, urged the pope to try harder to reform the church and its monasteries.

Hildegard's fame grew, and so did the size of the women's community at Mount Saint Disibode. The women decided to move to a new establishment, despite the vehement protests of the monks of Saint Disibode, who objected to losing their famous resident and the income that this "superstar" of the Rhine had brought to the monastery.

In 1151 Hildegard and her religious sisters moved to Rupertsburg (named after another Celtic monk) and established a new abbey there. They took with them the dowries (financial endowments) they had brought to Mount Saint Disibode. At Rupertsburg, Hildegard was consecrated abbess, and she secured the protection of the emperor, Frederick Barbarossa. She refused to acknowledge any religious superior except the archbishop of Mainz, thus freeing herself and her sisters from the control of their disgruntled former abbot.

Once established in the new monastery, Hildegard continued to develop the creative and spiritual life of her community. She founded

Iconography refers to the conventional images or symbols associated with religious subjects. These vary from one religion to another.

The Abbey of St. Hildegard in Eibingen, Germany, rebuilt in the nineteenth century
Robert Ferré

a second monastery at Eibingen in 1165, providing it with enough resources to support thirty sisters. Along with providing leadership for her own community of fifty sisters, Hildegard found time to write numerous letters to emperors, popes, archbishops, and abbots. She also wrote poems, composed many musical settings of her poetry (including the work we will listen to later), and wrote nine books. These books include three major theological works: *Scivias*, *Liber Vitae Meritorium* (on ethics), and *De Operatione Dei* (like *Scivias*, this includes both text and illuminations of her visions).

She also wrote a book (*Physica*) on physiology, which combines botanical and biological observations with pharmaceutical advice; and a medical book about illnesses (*Causae et Curae*) that describes symptoms, causes, and cures. For Hildegard, the garden, the field, the monastery, and the hospital were all intimately interrelated. In addition, she wrote biographies of saints and commentaries on the gospel. She was the first major medieval figure to talk about religious experience in terms of the divine feminine archetypes (Eve, Wisdom, Mary, Lady Caritas, etc.), providing a feminine counterbalance to the dominant masculine image of divinity.

In the Middle Ages, women were often highly constrained—for example, there were limits on their ownership of property, and marriage was often very restricting. Ironically, women had much more opportunity for self-determination and self-expression within one particular social context: the monastery. Here, in a "women only" environment, it was possible for a woman to have both power and independence—within, of course, the constraints of obedience to higher religious authorities, who were always male.

Called the "Sibyl of the Rhine," Hildegard found time to be involved in politics and diplomacy, and to preach in cathedrals and monasteries all over the land. She felt compelled to preach because of her sense of herself as a prophet calling for reform. She spoke out against the corruption of the church—a practice that did not, of course, make her uniformly loved. But that didn't stop her. In her middle seventies, she traveled to Paris and had the faculty of the influential University of Paris approve her writings.

Even when she was in her eighties, she continued to be embroiled in controversy because of her outspokenness. Hildegard and the sisters of Rupertsburg were interdicted (a serious punishment prohibiting them from participation in sacred rituals and silencing their singing) by the archbishop of Mainz because they had buried an excommunicated revolutionary youth in their cemetery. The archbishop demanded that they dig up the body, but Hildegard insisted that the youth had confessed and died after the proper Christian rituals were performed.

In an effort to remove the interdiction, Hildegard wrote to the archbishop that "he had silenced the most wonderful music on the Rhine." She concluded, "Those who choose to silence music in this lifetime will go to a place where they will be 'without the company of the angelic songs of praises in heaven.'" The interdict was lifted.

Hildegard died on 17 September 1179. Although she was never formally canonized, since the fifteenth century she has been listed as a saint in the Catholic *Martyrologies*.

This gifted and energetic woman left us an incredibly varied treasure of creative works. Not least among these is her music, which for centuries was ignored, as were her visions. This was not because of an interdict but because of a failure to recognize the value of women's creative contributions. For many years, little mention was made of her work in the standard music history references. Fortunately for us, her work was preserved in her monastery and has recently been rediscovered, as a result of painstaking work by the nuns at Eibingen. Her work has begun to be appreciated once again and is achieving considerable acclaim for its originality.

Music in the Middle Ages

Relatively little is known about the music of Hildegard's time, the period of Western European history known as the Middle Ages or the medieval period. Musical notation had developed by 900 C.E., but it was not in common use until the eleventh century. Since the majority of literate people were inside the church, the majority of notated music was church music. There is very little record of secular music, but we know from anecdotal accounts that music flourished in the courts of Europe as well as along the network of roads that carried pilgrims to sacred shrines spread across the continent.

Gregorian Chant

The largest repertoire of music from the Middle Ages is the liturgical chant of the Christian church. This is what Hildegard grew up singing in the monastery. In the Roman Catholic Church, liturgical chant is known as **Gregorian chant** in honor of Pope Gregory the Great (c. 560–604), although he was not the originator of the style. The texts for these chants are drawn mostly from the Book of Psalms in the Hebrew Bible (Old Testament) and from the Catholic mass. Gregorian chant is also known as **plainsong** or **plainchant.**

Monophonic Texture. Gregorian chant, like other liturgical music of this time, consists of a single melody that is sung by one or more persons, usually priests, monks, or nuns. Music that consists of only a single melodic line is said to be in **monophonic texture.** *Texture* refers to the way melodic, rhythmic, and harmonic materials are woven together in a composition. The word *monophonic* comes from the Greek *mono*, meaning "one," and *phono*, meaning "sound"—thus, "one sound."

The Cosmic Symphony

Who are the persons pictured in the illumination shown on the following page, and what are they doing? Hildegard described her vision as follows: "I saw a very bright sky in which I heard . . . in a wonderful way various kinds of music carrying on in praises of cities of celestial joys." It is clear from Hildegard's words that the entire company is singing. You can see that by carefully examining the illumination. The seven groups shown in the rings are distinct groups of holy personages. At the top is the Virgin Mary, Queen of Heaven, sitting on her throne; below her are the angels, who are protectors of the people. In the five groups below that, the virgins are pictured in the center, surrounded by the patriarchs and prophets, the apostles, the martyrs, and the confessors. "The goal of creation for Hildegard was that all creatures sing with one voice the same praises. We wake up to an awareness of eternity, a revelation of the inexhaustibility of feeling, through song."

"The Communion of Saints in Cosmic Symphony," from *Scivias*
Otto Muller Verlag

The Medieval Period

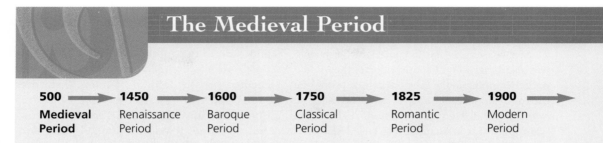

500 →	1450 →	1600 →	1750 →	1825 →	1900 →
Medieval Period	Renaissance Period	Baroque Period	Classical Period	Romantic Period	Modern Period

In the history of Western civilization, the medieval period (the Middle Ages) is thought of as roughly the time following the fall of Rome in 410 C.E. until the Renaissance (c. 1450). "Middle Ages" was a misleading term coined by Renaissance humanist scholars who believed that this thousand-year period was nothing but a gap between ancient Greece and Rome and their own great civilization.

In the medieval period there were many forces at work destroying old cultures and building the foundations of new cultures. Europe was marked by invasions of Huns, Visigoths, Vandals, and Ostrogoths. Christianity, followed by Islam, spread throughout Asia, Europe, and Africa.

In Western Europe the powerful Christian church and a few strong feudal lords dominated medieval life. After the fall of Rome, the church took charge of many essential aspects of human life, establishing and maintaining a system of laws, education, and social welfare for the poor and sick. The church grew wealthy and lavishly patronized the arts for the greater glory of God. The church's influence on music was enormous. Musicians of that time received their training as choirboys; all composers took holy orders; and all sacred music was sung in Latin, the official language of the Roman Catholic Church. Vocal music was preferred, and instruments, for the most part, were used to supplement the singers.

The life of the church and all its worshipers centered on religious services, and the role of music was to enhance these services. Monophonic chant (called *plainsong* or *plainchant*) was sung from choir stalls and in processions. This early Christian melody is often called Gregorian chant because of its close association with Pope Gregory I (c. 540–604). He collected and codified the large and disparate body of chant, and he decided what would be sung throughout Christendom.

Musical style changed radically from the beginning to the end of the medieval period. Single-line (monophonic) vocal music was the predominant musical texture until around the ninth century. The appearance of polyphony in the ninth century is perhaps the most important development in the history of music in the West. In its earliest form, polyphony consisted of a second voice added to plainsong melodies. Gradually, greater independence developed between the voices.

The earliest music notation developed around 900. Until the thirteenth century, two-part writing was still the rule, but three and even four parts were not uncommon. During the fourteenth century, music was characterized by increasing rhythmic complexity, and a more precise system for notating rhythm was developed. Instruments and voices were not generally specified in written music, however, and ensembles were put together from the available resources.

Secular song in the languages of the people was also an important contribution of the Middle Ages. Beginning in the eleventh century, songs by the troubadours and *trouvères* of France and the *Minnesinger* of Germany, Bavaria, and Austria were preserved in manuscripts called *chansonniers*. The texts of these songs were concerned primarily with courtly love, although politics and religion were sometimes included.

Most of Chartres Cathedral, shown in the photo below, was constructed between 1194 and 1260 in the gothic style. With its soaring lines, gothic architecture evoked awe and encouraged the faithful to raise their eyes (and spirits) toward heaven. Chartres Cathedral's upward-reaching arches and towers surround jewel-like stained-glass windows, which fill the interior with light as well as with a detailed visual retelling of biblical stories.

Notre Dame de Chartres, Chartres, France
B. Yarvin/The Image Works

Melodic Style. The melodic lines in Gregorian chant are generally of limited range, often spanning only five or six pitches. There are very few leaps, so the effect is a smooth, almost speechlike setting of a text. Indeed, the purpose of the musical setting is to make the text clear and audible, not to create drama. Some syllables of the text are sung on only one note; others are given several notes. When there is one note per syllable of text, the melody is said to be **syllabic.** When there are several notes per syllable, the melody is said to be **melismatic.**

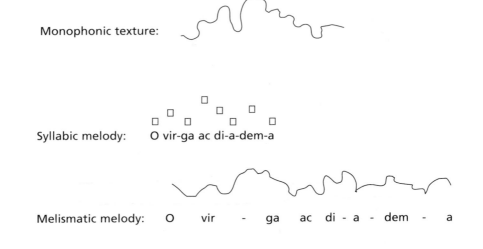

Monophonic texture:

Syllabic melody: O vir-ga ac di-a-dem-a

Melismatic melody: O vir - ga ac di - a - dem - a

Hildegard's Music

Hildegard's music and poetry were much admired in her own time. In 1148 Master Odo of Paris wrote, "It is said that you are raised to Heaven, that much is revealed to you, and that you bring forth great writings, and discover new manners of song."

For Hildegard, music was intensely spiritual—a "leaping up" to God by a human being. When Hildegard speaks of "harmony," she means not only the harmony of voices and instruments but, more importantly, celestial harmony and the internal harmony within a person and within the human soul. To act harmoniously is to live virtuously, to fully integrate body and soul, the divine and the human.

Hildegard says, "Through the power of hearing, God opens to human beings all the glorious sounds of the hidden mysteries and of the choirs of angels by whom God is praised over and over again."

Symphonia Harmonie Caelestium Revelationum

The title of Hildegard's collection of music and poetry, *Symphonia Harmonie Caelestium Revelationum* (The Symphony of the Harmony of Celestial Revelations), refers to her fundamental belief that music is both earthly and heavenly, produced by human means but evoking heavenly harmony.

Hildegard's songs and compositions grew out of her intense devotional life and her belief in the deep connection between music and the spirit. She wrote that "all sacred music—instrumental as well as vocal—functions as the bridge for humanity to life before the Fall." Her compositions include songs of praise to saints, martyrs, apostles, and Virtues (such as Wisdom), among others, as well as pieces praising the glory of those in Heaven. Feminine figures predominate in the *Symphonia:* fifteen songs are addressed to the Virgin Mary and thirteen to Saint Ursula.

In its first version, gathered together in 1150, the *Symphonia* contained some sixty pieces suited to the feasts of the liturgical year. It is impressive both for the quality of its content and for its size: it was one of the first large cycles of music composed for worship services. A subsequent enlarged version had several outstanding additions devoted to more philosophical themes.

The compositions in the *Symphonia* are considered to be among the finest compositions of the Middle Ages. They are grandly conceived, as if the intensity of Hildegard's visions flowed forth into her music. Her musical range is immense, from tranquil melodies to dramatic declamation. The poetic language of the songs is unusual, including a very innovative and daring use of mixed metaphors and superlatives, a great deal of poetic freedom, and an elaborately developed allegorical world.

The compositions in *Symphonia* were composed for the nuns to sing in the convent at liturgical and other functions. Their intent was spiritual. The text was important, filled with spiritual meaning that the singer was supposed to internalize before finally releasing the essence in sound. The music was sung and played in interaction with

> The *liturgical year* is the body of rites used in public worship in Christian churches.

"All Beings Celebrate Creation"
Otto Muller Verlag

the spiritual life that both produced it and gave it voice. To Hildegard, music was all of creation "rebounding to the celestial Creator with a single voice of exultation and joy and the giving of thanks."

Listening to *De sancta Maria* (For the Virgin Mary)

De sancta Maria is one of seventy-seven musical compositions in the *Symphonia Harmonie Caelestium Revelationum.* The music in this monumental work is monophonic, consisting of a single melodic line.

The melodies in *De sancta Maria,* like all melodies, are divided into phrases, which are identified by natural pauses or breathing places. The phrases correspond to logical divisions of the text. In the listening guide below, an asterisk (*) indicates the end of each musical phrase. Notice that the phrases are not of equal length. When phrases are of different lengths, they are called **irregular phrases,** as opposed to **regular phrases,** which are of the same length. The melodies in *De sancta Maria* combine syllabic and melismatic styles. Such melodies are sometimes called **neumatic.** This is a reference to the medieval method of notating more than one note per syllable by using symbols called *neumes.*

De sancta Maria is an example of Hildegard's treatment of the **sequence,** an important form of sacred music in the Middle Ages. In a sequence, each melody is repeated once with different text before the introduction of a new melodic idea. Notice that Hildegard is quite free in her use of the sequence form. The repeated sections near the beginning are nearly exact, but later in the work there is considerable freedom, and in some cases the number of phrases per section is not even the same.

Hildegard wrote the text for *De sancta Maria.* It sets forth her belief that the Virgin Mary was chosen by God to redeem her gender from the sin of Eve—tempting Adam to eat from the tree of knowledge, which God had specifically forbidden him to do. Through the virgin birth of Jesus, Mary "brought a blessing greater than the harm Eve did to mankind." In the final verse, there is an abrupt change from poetic imagery to realism, presenting a more feminine, human image of Mary as a mother holding her crucified child.

The melodic line Hildegard composed for this poetry is characterized by a soaring quality that is quite unlike Gregorian chant. According to one scholar, "her poetic effects are often strange and violent, and never (as in the hymnody of most of her contemporaries) smooth." There is a passionate quality to this music that keeps us intensely involved to the end.

The melody for *De sancta Maria* uses the minor scale (see page 103), which was relatively new in Hildegard's time. In this way as well, Hildegard's music is quite revolutionary and foreshadows the music of later periods.

As you listen to this recording of *De sancta Maria,* imagine the sisters of the Rupertsburg cloister singing these melodies more than 800 years ago. This performance was recorded by the Schola der Benediktinerinnenabtei at the abbey of Saint Hildegard Rüdesheim-Eibingen.

LISTENING ACTIVITY

De sancta Maria (For the Virgin Mary) (Hildegard of Bingen) [CD 1, track 10]
[Asterisks (*) indicate the end of each musical phrase.]

Time	Music	Text	Translation
00:00	Melody I	O virga ac diadema purpurae regis*	O branch and diadem of the king's purple,
		quae es in clausura tua sicut lorica*	you who are in your enclosure like a breastplate:
00:22	Melody I (repeated)	Tu frondens floruisti in alia vicissitudine*	Burgeoning, you blossomed after another fashion
		quam Adam omne genus humanum produceret*	than Adam gave rise to the whole human race.
00:45	Melody II	Ave, Ave de tuo ventre alia processit*	Hail, hail! from your womb came another life
		qua Adam filios suos denudaverat*	of which Adam had stripped his sons.
01:16	Melody II	O flos, tu non germinasti de rore nec de guttis pluviae,*	O flower, you did not spring from dew nor from drops of rain,
		nec aer desuper te volavitor*	nor did the air fly over you,

		sed divina claritas in nobilissima virga te produxit*	but the divine radiance brought you forth on a most noble branch.
02:00	Melody III	O virga, floriditatem tuam*	O branch, God had foreseen
		Deus in prima die creaturae suae praeviderat*	your flowering on the first day of his creation.
02:28	Melody III	Et de verbo suo auream materiam*	And he made you for his Word as a golden matrix
		o laudebilis Virgo, fecit.*	O praiseworthy Virgin.
02:56	Melody IV	O quam magnum est in viribus suis latus viri,*	O how great in its powers is the side of man
		de quo Deus formam mulieris produxit*	from which God brought forth the form of woman,
		quam fecit speculum omnis ornamenti sui*	which he made the mirror of all his beauty
		et amplexionem omnis creaturae suae.*	and the embrace of his whole creation.
03:52	Melody IV	Inde concinunt caelestia organa.*	Thence celestial voices chime in harmony
		et miratur omnis terra,*	and the whole earth marvels,
		o laudabilis Maria,*	O praiseworthy Mary,
		quia Deus te valde amavit.*	for God has greatly loved you.
04:29	Melody V	O quam valde plan-gendum et lungen-dum est*	Oh how greatly we must lament and mourn
		quod trisitia in crimine per	because sadness flowed in guilt through

		consilium serpentis*	the serpent's counsel
		in mulierem fluxit.*	into woman.
05:02	Melody V	Nam ipsa mulier, quam Deus matrem omnium posiut*	For the very woman whom God made to be mother of all
		viscerasua cum vulneribus ignorantiae decerpsit*	plucked at her womb with the wounds of ignorance,
		et plenum dolorem generi suo protulit.*	and brought forth consummate pain for her kind.
05:45	Melody VI	Sed, o aurora, de ventre tuo novus sol processit*	But O dawn, from your womb a new sun has come forth
		qui omnia crimina Evae avstersit*	which has cleansed all the guilt of Eve
		et majorem bene-dictionnem per protulit*	and through you brought a blessing greater
		quam Eva hominibus nocuisset.*	than the harm Eve did to mankind.
06:26	Melody VI	Unde, o Salvatrix, quae novum lumen humano generi protulisti*	Hence, O saving Lady, you who bore a new light for humankind:
		collige membra Filii tui	gather the members of your Son
		ad caelestem harmoniam.*	into celestial harmony.

Source: Translation of "O virga ac diadema" in St. Hildegard of Bingen, *Symphonia: A Critical Edition of the Symphonia Harmonie Celestium Revelationum,* trans. Barbara Newman, no. 20, pp. 128–131.

Response to the Music

After listening to *De sancta Maria,* reflect on your own responses to the music. Can you identify a physical response? An emotional response? A cognitive response? A spiritual response? This music comes from a distant time and place. Can you imagine how the nuns who sang it in the Rupertsburg cloister might have responded to it? When and where would you listen to this kind of music? In a religious setting? As background music while studying? For relaxation? As an aid for meditation?

Your religious background and experience are undoubtedly different from Hildegard's (you're not a medieval nun, for one thing), but you may still find this music spiritually moving. Why might this be? What does this say about the nature of the music?

Summary

In this chapter we have learned about the nature of sound and pitch, as well as about the difference between pitched and unpitched sounds. We have learned about scales and how important vocal melody is in music. Melodies are divided into logical units called phrases, which may be regular or irregular in length. We have also learned about a popular medieval musical form called the sequence. By listening to the medieval composition by Hildegard of Bingen, we have learned about the deeply spiritual purpose of her music.

Applying What You Have Learned

1. One way to appreciate the contour of a melody is to make a simple graph of it. You can show pitches as dots, with higher pitches above lower pitches. Connecting the dots gives you a graph of the contour. For example, the first phrase of Bob Marley's *Redemption Song* (CD 1, track 5) might be graphed as follows:

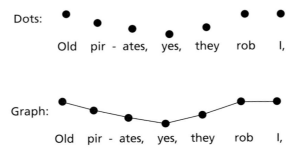

Copy the lyrics for the next eight lines of *Redemption Song* (through "Redemption songs," page 48) and graph the melody as shown above.

2. Copy the first two lines of the text for *De sancta Maria* and graph the melody using the technique suggested above. How does this melodic contour differ from that of *Redemption Song?*

3. Listen again to *Grand Entry Song* (CD 1, track 6), paying particular attention to the melodies. Most Native American melodies in powwows and other social settings are vocal melodies with a limited number of pitches. The typical phrase begins with the highest note in the melody and descends to the lowest note at the end. Phrases are fairly short, and the melodies are repeated with slight variations.
    If you are not familiar with Native American music, when you first hear these melodies you may find them very repetitive. The beauty of these melodies reveals itself only when you accept the repetitiveness as a given and listen to the subtle variations from one melodic statement to the next. Graph a phrase of *Grand Entry Song* and compare its contour with the melodies in *De sancta Maria.*

4. Listen again to *Simple Gifts* [CD 1, track 2]. Are the phrases of this song regular or irregular? (To answer this question, try counting the number of measures or beats in each phrase.) Is this melody melismatic, syllabic, or neumatic? Notice that *Simple Gifts* has a monophonic texture, like *De sancta Maria.*

5. Listen again to the melodies of Bob Marley's songs (CD 1, track 4, and CD 1, track 5). Are the phrases regular or irregular in length? Would you call the melodies in *Redemption Song* melismatic, syllabic, or neumatic?

6. Can you think of any music you have listened to in the past week that has no melody? If so, what was it?

7. *De sancta Maria* was composed to be sung in contemplation by nuns. How do you think the change of setting—a recorded performance on a CD—might affect your responses to this music? Has the song's purpose changed? How?

8. Listen to a piece of Gregorian chant (see Further Listening Resources on page 121). How is it different from and similar to *De sancta Maria?*

Important Terms

melody 101	pitch 101	fundamental
vibration 101	pitched sound 101	frequency 101
frequency 101		

unpitched sound
    101
equal temperament
    101
scale 102
major scale 102
tonic 103
minor scale 103
melody 103
range 103

conjunct 103
disjunct 103
phrase 104
Gregorian chant
    109
plainsong or plain-
    chant 109
monophonic texture
    109

syllabic style 113
melismatic style
    113
regular phrase 115
irregular phrase
    115
neumatic style 115
sequence 115

Names preceded by
"*" have short
biographies in
Appendix B, p. 346

Musicians and Ensembles Mentioned

*Hildegard of Bingen
*Pope Gregory the Great
Schola der Benediktinerinnenabtei

Further Listening Resources

Hildegard of Bingen, *Gothic Voices*, Hyperion 66039.

Hildegard of Bingen, *Vision, The Music of Hildegard of Bingen*,
    Angel CDC7243 5 55246 21.

Hildegard of Bingen, *Symphoniae*, Sequentia, DHM 77020-2-RG.

Hildegard of Bingen, *Voice of the Blood*, Sequentia, DHM 05472
    773462.

Hildegard of Bingen, *Feather on the Breath of God*, Hyperion, 2/88
    HYP 66039.

Hildegard of Bingen, *11,000 Virgins*, Anonymous 4, Harmonia
    Mundi (Fra).

Gregorian chant: *Chant*, Benedictine Monks of Santo Domingo de
    Silos, EMD/Angel 55138.

Instrumental Melody

💿 *Máru-Bihág,* Ravi Shankar

Henry Diltz/Corbis

R*avi Shankar has gone all his life touring. I did tours for two years and that was enough for me, but he's been touring for thirty years and still doing it to this day.*

GEORGE HARRISON (B. 1943)
MEMBER OF THE BEATLES

I n Chapter 6 you learned some fundamentals about pitch, scales, and melody. A work by Hildegard of Bingen was used as an example of vocal melody. In this chapter you will listen to an example of instrumental melody played on an Indian string instrument, the *sitar.*

Instrumental Melody

One obvious distinction between vocal and instrumental melody is the absence of text in instrumental melodies. Of course, an instrument can perform a melody that was originally vocal, but there is a body of melodies that are purely instrumental in nature, and these melodies are often composed to take advantage of the unique qualities of individual instruments. Many instruments have a wider range of pitches than the voice and are more agile in navigating leaps and complicated rhythmic patterns. In addition, some instruments are capable of playing several pitches at the same time.

The Indian Subcontinent

The Indian subcontinent, which today includes the nations of India, Pakistan, Bangladesh, Nepal, and Sri Lanka, has one of the most ancient and distinguished musical cultures of the world. In this chapter we will concentrate on the republic of India, which is the largest and most populated country in this region.

India is approximately one-third the size of the United States and has a population of approximately 900,000,000 people—over three times more than the United States. Nearly one-sixth of the people of the earth live in India, most in conditions of extreme material poverty.

The valley of the Indus river, now a part of western Pakistan, is thought to have been the birthplace of Indian civilization. Remains of a farming culture dating from 4000 B.C.E. have been found in this valley, and there is evidence that there were numerous cities and towns all over India by 2700 B.C.E. From archaeological evidence it appears that the Indus civilization was extremely advanced, with such modern conveniences as community bathhouses, underground sewers, and a centralized government, all based on a stable agricultural society.

This civilization had begun to deteriorate by 1500 B.C.E., and the *Rig Veda,* a scripture composed around that time, speaks of an invasion by the Aryans, a people from central Asia who conquered the Indus people and imposed the caste system that has continued into the twentieth century. The caste system is a rigid division into social

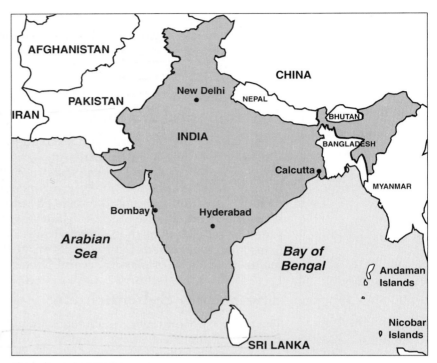

The Indian subcontinent

classes along occupational lines, with a fixed hierarchy and caste-specific duties and obligations. Although legally abolished in recent times, the caste system continues, especially in rural areas of the country.

From 1500 B.C.E. until the nineteenth century, numerous other groups invaded northern India, including the Persians, Arabs, Turks, Mongols, Afghans, Greeks, and English. Each group brought its own culture and music, creating a highly complex mixture. In the nineteenth century, the region became a part of the British Empire; during this period Western European culture made many inroads into traditional Indian culture. Among the religions that flourish in modern India are Hinduism, Islam, Sikhism, Jainism, Christianity, and Buddhism.

The Music of India

The music of India is as multidimensional as the culture. Every religious and cultural group has its own body of music. The American scholar Milton Singer has categorized music that appears only within a limited geographical or cultural region of India as the

Mohenjo-daro (2500 B.C.E.), the most famous ancient city in India
Diego Lezama Orezzali/Corbis

"Little Tradition." Included in the Little Tradition are the folk music and the religious music of the various cultural groups. There is another body of music, called the **"Great Tradition,"** which has spread over extensive parts of India and forms a common musical language among various peoples. In this chapter we will concentrate on the Great Tradition.

The music of the Great Tradition, also called Indian classical music, has a number of distinctive characteristics. Melody plays the primary role. Rhythm is second in importance, becoming the center of attention only later in a performance, when the drummers begin to play. A constant background **drone** consisting of three or more sustained pitches accompanies the performance.

Traditional Indian music is very ancient, passed down orally for thousands of years. Indian musicians are taught that music

Man playing tambura—the most important drone instrument
Sheldon Collins/Corbis

was created by a three-part godhead: Brahma (the creator), Vishnu (the preserver), and Shiva (the destroyer). The goddess Sarasvati, originally a mighty river goddess, is patroness of learning and the fine arts, including art, music, poetry, and literature. She is said to have created Sanskrit, the ancient classical Indo-Aryan language of India.

In India, music and dance are considered part of the same art.

It is believed that the great saints and sages taught the art of music and dance to humans. This art was taught alongside the arts of medicine, astrology, astronomy, science, and yoga as a means to attain self-realization. The most famous ancient description of music is found in the *Natya Shastra,* a treatise on drama that was compiled from the second century B.C.E. to the fifth century C.E.

Sacred Dance

The antiquity of sacred dance in India is attested to by ancient sculptures of Hindu dancers. Traditional Indian dance is a beautiful blend of sophisticated movement, colorful costumes, and a sense of drama. The posture and gestures of the dancer communicate a feeling, an idea, or a story to the knowledgeable audience.

Modern Indian dancer, Tamil Nadu, India
The Viesti Collection

Carved dancing figures, thirteenth century, Rajasthan, India
Scala/Art Resource

The training of musicians proceeds along very traditional lines that are summarized in three words: **guru,** *vinaya,* and **sadhana.** Ravi Shankar, one of the most famous Indian musicians of this century, describes the guru as follows: "Guru, as many people now know, means master, spiritual teacher, or preceptor. We give a very important place to the guru, for we consider him to be the representation of the divine." About *vinaya* he says: "*Vinaya* means humility; it is the complete surrendering of self on the part of the *shishya* (student) to the guru. The ideal disciple feels love, adoration, reverence, and even fear toward his guru, and he accepts equally praise or scoldings." The final part of the tradition is *sadhana.* Of this Shankar says: "The third principal term associated with our music is *sadhana,* which means practice and discipline, eventually leading to self-realization. It means practicing with a fanatic zeal and ardent dedication to the guru and the music."

In the past there were families of professional musicians going back many generations, and the musicians were themselves part of the caste system. The traditional system is breaking up in the twentieth century, and now there are schools, both in India and in the West, where one can learn the classical music of India.

Northern and Southern Styles

The music of the Great Tradition is divided into two basic styles, **northern** and **southern.** The music of southern India, called the *Karnataka* style, is thought to be less influenced than the northern style by the music of other cultures because many of the invasions mentioned earlier in this chapter did not reach the southern tip of the Indian peninsula. However, the influence of two centuries of British rule was felt throughout the country. In particular, the development of the public concert hall (as opposed to court or religious settings) came with British rule.

Karnataka (sometimes spelled **Carnatic**) music is characterized by both improvisation and composition. The music of north India, called the **Hindustani** style, is almost exclusively improvisational. Hindustani music has clearly been influenced by the music of the invading cultures, and scholars feel that it is less purely Indian. In the *Karnataka* style no distinction is made between vocal and instrumental music, whereas in the Hindustani style the two are seen as separate though similar traditions.

Raga and *Tala*

Rhythm and melody in classical Indian music are controlled by a system of melodic formulas called **raga** or **rag** and a system of

Improvisation

Improvised music is created by the performer while it is being performed. In the West much of our music is written in music notation, and the performer's role is to perform the music as written. That is not true for most of the world's music. In fact, written music notation is not considered a necessity in many parts of the world. In improvisation, performers have a framework to follow while they improvise. In the music of India, that framework is provided by the *raga*.

rhythmic patterns called **tala** or **tal.** While thousands of *ragas* have been identified in theoretical writings, less than one hundred are in practical use. The number of *talas* is not more than a few dozen, with only a few in common use. The northern (Hindustani) and southern (*Karnataka*) styles have *ragas* and *talas* that are related, but most are named differently. This is another way in which the two styles are distinct from each other.

The *raga* provides a basic melodic framework for improvisation. It is somewhat like the scale in Western music, but it also contains the basic patterns for the melodies that will be improvised upon it. The **vadi svara** or main melodic tone is the most important tone in a *raga*. Melodies continually return to it, as Western melodies return to the tonic (see page 103).

Each *raga* has an ascending and a descending form, just as in a Western scale. However, the descending form is often quite different from the ascending form. Indian musicians always know exactly which tones of the raga they are improvising on. Many listeners can also tell by the general melodic trend (upward or downward) where the performer is in the *raga*. Each *raga* is associated with a specific mood, color, deity, and time of day during which it traditionally has been performed.

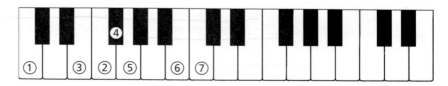

Raga *Máru-Bihág*—ascending form

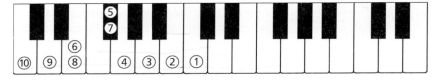

Raga *Máru-Bihág*—descending form

The *raga* provides a basic shape for the melodic material that is improvised. The purpose of the improvisation is to gradually unfold all the beauty inherent in the *raga* and bring the audience to an awareness of the mood the *raga* invokes. A comparison can be made to the melodies that Western jazz musicians use as a basis for improvisation, but it must be stressed that Indian classical music is not simply "Indian jazz," nor is jazz "Western *raga*."

The *tala* generally enters only in the latter part of an improvisation, after the melodic material is first thoroughly explored, beginning without any beat. The beat emerges gradually as the improvisation progresses. The point where the *tala* enters can be easily recognized, because it coincides with the entry of the drum. Since *talas* in Indian classical music are generally much longer (six to sixteen beats) than measures in Western music (two to six beats), and the tempos may be slower, the music seems to unfold over a longer time. This accounts for some of the "floating" quality one may feel

History of *Raga*

The origin of the system of *ragas* goes back to the early centuries of the Common Era, but the system was standardized in 800 C.E. in a treatise called *Brhaddeshi,* by Matanga. All later writers on the subject refer back to him.

The number of *ragas* is said to be infinite. King Nayadeva of Mithila (1097–1147) said, "The profoundly learned in *raga*, even Matanga and his followers, have not crossed the ocean of *raga*." *Ragas* have been created, become popular, and dropped out of the repertoire at various times. Some *ragas* are known to be ancient and others to be modern.

These historical distinctions, however, are of less importance to Indian musicians than placing the *ragas* in the proper time of day and, in some cases, the proper season of the year. Each *raga* evokes a particular mood or emotion that is thought to be appropriate for a particular time. For purposes of classification, the day is divided into three-hour intervals. *Ragas* may be placed in one of these times or be designated by a particular time or season, such as "at daybreak" or "any time in the spring of the year."

in listening to the latter part of a performance of Indian classical music. A single *tala* is chosen for each performance. There is usually a gradual increase in tempo as the composition progresses, leading to a climax near the end of the piece.

Instruments of Indian Classical Music

The ancient treatise *Natya Shastra,* mentioned earlier in this chapter, divided the instruments of Indian classical music into four groups: *tata* (string instruments), *avanaddha* (drums), *ghana* (wood and metal percussion), and *sushira* (wind instruments). This system of classification became the basis for the Hornbostel and Sachs instrument classification system, which is widely used in the West. In other words, our present-day Western system for classifying instruments comes from India and dates from as early as the second century B.C.E.

String Instruments. In most Indian classical music ensembles the drone is provided by a long-necked string instrument called the **tambura** (page 125). This instrument has four to six strings. The strings are caressed softly in the background throughout a performance.

A number of plucked-string instruments are used as melodic instruments in Indian classical music. The best known in the West is the north Indian **sitar.** The **sarod** is another important north Indian plucked string instrument. The **Saraswati vina,** an instrument similar to the *sitar,* is characteristic of south Indian music.

Among the bowed-string instruments, the Western violin has become very important in south India since its introduction during British colonial times. However, Indian musicians generally hold the violin differently from Europeans and they play it while sitting cross-legged on the floor.

Drums. In the north the most important percussion instrument is the **tabla,** a pair of tuned drums played with the hands (rather than drumsticks). In the south a number of drums and wood or metal percussion instruments often appear in ensembles. These instruments include the double-headed **mridangam,** a tambourine-like instrument

Boy playing *vina*
Hulton Deutsch/Corbis

The Hornbostel and Sachs system (1914) classifies musical instruments into four groups—chordophones (strings), membranophones (drums), idiophones (wood and metal percussion), and aerophones (wind instruments).

Indian musician playing the violin
DPA/The Image Works

called the **kanjira,** and the **ghatam,** which is a large clay pot.

Wood and Metal Percussion Instruments. Wood and metal percussion instruments (idiophones) are also present in Indian classical music. Two of these are the **marsang,** a metal jew's harp, and the **talam,** hand or finger cymbals.

Wind Instruments. Wind instruments that are native to the Indian subcontinent include a bamboo flute and the large **nagaswaram** and small **shahnai,** which are double-reed instruments similar to the Western oboe.

The marriage of Rama and his brothers from the Sangi Ramayana, Kulu-Mandi, Pradesh, Pahari School 1760–65 National Museum, New Delhi, India
Art Resource

Tabla player
DPA/The Image Works

During the British occupation of the nineteenth and early twentieth centuries, a number of Western wind instruments began to be used in India. Today small street bands of Western-style brass, woodwind, and percussion instruments playing Indian music are a common sight in India, particularly in wedding processions.

Ravi Shankar

Ravi Shankar was born in Benares, India, on 7 April 1920. He studied *ragas* on the *sitar* with Ustad Allaudin Khan, the most distinguished Indian instrumentalist of the twentieth century. When India became independent of British rule in 1947, Ravi Shankar became the director of All India Radio, where he did much to restore interest in Indian classical music after years of neglect. He also established a music school in Bombay to train young musicians in the art, which had nearly died out.

Ravi Shankar is credited with making north Indian classical music popular in the West. He has produced albums in collaboration with a variety of Western musicians, including the classical musicians Yehudi Menuhin, Jean Pierre Rampal, and André Previn, and the jazz musicians Bud Shank, John Coltrane, Don Ellis, and Buddy Rich. Ravi Shankar has written music for several outstanding Indian films, two concertos for sitar and orchestra, and numerous chamber works that combine the resources of Indian classical music and instruments with Western instruments and musicians. He has been awarded eleven honorary doctoral degrees.

The Impact of Indian Classical Music in the West

Ravi Shankar's best-known collaboration was with George Harrison of the Beatles in the late 1960s. This was a period when many rock musi-

The bamboo flute
Mary Grace Long, photographer

Street band in Bombay
Viesti Assoc., Inc.

cians were interested in Indian classical music, playing the *sitar*, and even dabbling in Indian philosophy and religion. While the pop fad of incorporating the *sitar* into Western rock music was short-lived, it did bring Indian classical music to the attention of the younger generation. There is now considerable Western interest in the classical music of India, and a number of schools have been established.

The culture shock that was felt on both sides when Western rock musicians encountered Eastern musicians and Eastern values is evident in several comments by Ravi Shankar in his autobiography, *My Music, My Life*. "Sadly, this feeling of *vinaya* (surrender) is lacking today in many young people, in the East and West alike. The Western student, especially, seems to have an excessively casual attitude toward his teachers and toward the process of learning. The teacher–student association is no longer patterned after the old father–son relationship, and the two are encouraged by prevailing attitudes to act as friends and to consider each other on an equal level. This system, of course, has its benefits, but it is far from ideal for studying Indian music and understanding our traditions. The Indian teacher finds this casualness disturbing, even in so small a thing as the position the student takes when he sits."

Since the 1960s, many people in the West have come to a greater understanding of Indian classical music, but considerable preparation is still necessary

Ravi Shankar playing the *sitar*
Henry Diltz

for Westerners to approach this complex music. They need to understand its structure and organization, as well as its rich history.

The Impact of Western Music in India

During the British colonial period the traditional music of India was nearly in eclipse. Indian aristocrats ceased their traditional support for the music, and the British showed little interest in cultures other than their own. During this period Western European music prevailed in India. This influence is still felt. A second invasion from the West has been the worldwide spread of Western popular music. That influence is very apparent in Indian films.

The Indian film industry is the largest in the world, turning out thousands of films, mostly musicals. Bombay is the largest center of film production outside Hollywood; in fact, it is referred to as **"Bollywood"** (as in the "Bollywood Division" of the Edinburgh Film Festival). These musicals are the primary source of popular music, and each film has several songs, many of which become popular hits. Western musical influences have entered film music, and one now hears rock, bluegrass, and Hollywood-style instrumentation and harmony accompanying a blend of local music sung by high-pitched, nasal voices—a mix that may sound quite strange to Western ears.

Film singers are called **playback singers.** They record the songs, which are played back in the studio, and the actors mime and mouth the words in a technique called **song picturization.** One male and one female singer will be the onscreen singing voice for all the characters in a film. In the last decade of the twentieth century, film music was increasingly influenced by MTV-style production techniques, with rapid cuts, special effects, and frenetic pace.

The steady stream of ephemeral film music (called cine-music or *filmi*) coexists with traditional Indian classical music. Both forms are now quite popular with Indian audiences.

Listening to *Máru-Bihág*

It is important to realize at the outset that this recorded performance of north Indian classical music is extremely abbreviated. The process that is demonstrated in slightly over eleven minutes in this recording might take over an hour in an actual performance. The opening unmeasured section, in particular, is only a fraction of its normal length.

In listening to *Máru-Bihág* (this particular *raga* is called **máru-bihág**) you will notice that there are very few internal divisions. Indeed, the only division that is unequivocal is the point where the *tabla* enters (2:34). The other noted division is much less clear. The

Movie billboard, Calcutta, India
Charles Steiner/The Image Works

beginning and the end of the composition are also not marked as definitely as in most Western music.

The first sound you hear is the sound of the *tambura* playing the background drone that will continue throughout the performance. Almost immediately the *sitar* enters and begins developing the melodic potential of the *raga máru-bihág.* This section, which is called **alap,** infuses the listener with the essence of this particular *raga.* The *alap* is considered the most important section of the improvisation. A little later the *sitar* player begins to establish a beat and the improvisation moves into its second section, called **jor.** With the entry of the *tabla* we know that the third section of the composition, called **gat,** has begun. From this point on, you can enjoy the interaction of the *tabla* and *sitar* as they perform with increasing virtuosity. This interaction between the *sitar* and the *tabla* is similar in character to what is called call and response in Western music (see page 18).

LISTENING ACTIVITY

Máru-Bihág (Ravi Shankar) [CD 1, track 11]

The form of this work is typical of the northern Indian style: an opening section (*alap*) without discernible pulse; a middle section (*jor*) where a pulse is gradually established; and a final section (*gat*) that introduces the *tala.* The musical content of the work, as with most classical northern Indian music, is improvised, with the *raga* and *tala* forming a framework. In this performance the *tala* is ***jhaptal,*** which has ten beats divided into four groups: 2 + 3 + 2 + 3. The overall effect of this improvised composition is a gradual increase in tempo and activity, leading to a climax near the end.

Time	Musical Event	Description
0:00		Ravi Shankar introduces the *raga* and *tala.*
0:36	*alap*	The melodic material of the *raga márubihág* is developed over the constant drone of the *tambura.* In this section there is little, if any, sense of beat.
1:24	*jor*	The beat begins to emerge in this section, becoming quite clear by 2:00.
1:34	*gat*	The *tabla* enters for the first time and the pattern of the *jhaptal tala* is set. (See if you can count along with the *tala:* "one, two, one, two, three, one, two, one, two, three.") From this point until the end of the piece there is a gradual increase in complexity and tempo. The *tabla* begins by emphasizing each beat but gradually introduces counterrhythms that go against, and seem to obscure, the *tala.* The sitarist plays more and more virtuosic patterns, introducing further rhythmic complexities, often creating a dialogue with the *tabla.* All complexities of rhythm are resolved, however, on the first beat (called the *sam*) of the *tala.*

(handwritten margin note: up to hour)

Response to the Music

Think about your physical, emotional, cognitive, and spiritual responses to this music. How did you respond to each section of the work? Were you able to follow the development of the *raga* in the *alap* section? How did your understanding of the underlying concepts of *raga* and *tala* influence your listening experience? Consider how an Indian listener, well versed in *raga,* might have responded to the *alap.* Could you follow the *tala* in the *gat* section? One of the authors has seen members of an Indian audience marking the rhythm of the *tala* with stylized hand gestures during a perform-ance of north Indian classical music. Think about how their response might be different from yours.

Summary

This chapter has discussed the historical and cultural background of Indian classical music. We have also examined the interaction of Indian and Western cultures in both classical and popular music. We have examined a single piece of northern Indian classical music to demonstrate the essential features of this music. Indian classical music is based on a set of melodic materials called *raga* and stan-dard rhythmic patterns called *tala*. These preexisting patterns are used as a background for improvisation. The overall shape of Indian classical music is a process that moves from an extended melodic improvisation (*alap*) on the melodic characteristics of a given *raga,* through a gradual introduction of a definite beat (*jor*), to a concluding extended improvisation (*gat*) based on both a *raga* and a *tala*. The beginning of the *gat* is clearly marked by the entry of the *tabla*.

Applying What You Have Learned

1. During the *gat* section of *Máru-Bihág,* the rhythmic rela-tionship between the *sitar* and the *tabla* becomes more and more complex. Would you describe the rhythm in this com-position as polyrhythm? Why or why not?

2. Indian music and philosophy have become increasingly important in the West. What might be the appeal of Indian classical music for Western listeners? Are you familiar with any pieces of music from the West that are influenced by Indian classical music? When might you want to listen to this kind of music?

3. Indian *filmi* music is very much influenced by Western pop-ular music. What do you think is the appeal of Western popular music to people in India?

4. Listen again to *Oy, Abram!* [CD 1, track 8]. Notice the dif-ference in style between the melody played by the violin in the introduction and the vocal melody of the song itself. This is a good example of the difference between vocal and instrumental melody. How are the two melodies different? Are the phrases regular or irregular in length? Is the vocal melody syllabic, melismatic, or a combination?

5. Listen again to *Bay a Glezele Mashke* [CD 1, track 7]. Pay particular attention to how the instruments occasionally embellish the melody to show off their individual capabilities. What have you learned about the capability of these instruments by listening to *Bay a Glezele Mashke?*

6. Listen again to *Shango* [CD 1, track 9]. Notice the pattern: an introductory section, with no beat, followed by the body of the work, with a beat. This pattern is quite similar to the pattern in Indian classical music. Are there other similarities? How do these two works differ from each other?

7. Compare the way Pete Gahbow learned to play and sing powwow music with the classical Indian system of apprenticeship. If you have studied a musical instrument, how did you learn? What are some of the advantages and disadvantages of the different ways of transmitting music?

Important Terms

"Little Tradition" 125
"Great Tradition" 125
drone 125
guru 127
vinaya 127
sadhana 127
southern Indian style 127
Karnataka (*Carnatic*) style 127
northern Indian style 127

Hindustani style 127
raga 127
tala 128
vadi svara 128
tambura 130
sitar 130
sarod 130
vina 130
tabla 130
mridangam 130
kanjira 131
ghatam 131
marsang 131

talam 131
nagaswaram 131
shahnai 131
playback singer 134
song picturization 134
Bollywood 134
filmi 134
máru-bihág 134
alap 135
jor 135
gat 135

Names preceded by "*" have short biographies in Appendix B, p. 346

Musicians Mentioned

*Ravi Shankar
Ustad Allaudin Khan
*Yehudi Menuhin
*Jean Pierre Rampal
*André Previn
*John Coltrane
*Buddy Rich
*George Harrison

Further Listening Resources

Ustad Ali Akbar Khan, Signature Series, volume I (AMMP, U.S.).

George Harrison. *Within You and Without You* from *Sgt. Pepper's Lonely Hearts Club Band* (1967).

An excellent source of tapes and CDs of Indian music is Shri Mati's Records in Berkeley, California.

CHAPTER 8

Vocal Melody in Opera

🌐 *La Bohème, Act II,* Giacomo Puccini

Vittoriano Rastelli/Corbis

M en die and governments change, but the songs of La Bohème *will live forever.*

THOMAS A. EDISON
INVENTOR OF THE PHONOGRAPH

Drama and Music

Throughout history almost every society has had some sort of drama associated with music. Many of the earliest dramas were religious festivals in which dancing and singing played an integral part. In many traditional cultures, the aim of music has been to put the participants in touch with the supernatural. *Incantation, charm,* and *enchant* are all derived from words having to do with singing. The combination of music and words has the ability to lift us to a higher emotional plane than either can do alone.

Noh drama, Kyogen, Japan
The Image Works

In Asia, music continues to be an integral element in both religious and secular drama. For example, it is a vital part of the puppet theater of Indonesia (see Chapter 12); China, India, and Japan also have ancient traditions of theatrical performances in which music is important. **Kabuki** theater and **Noh** drama in Japan are two examples. *Noh* is said to be "high art, the ultimate synthesis of literature, theater, dancing, and music," whereas *Kabuki* is "more energetic and popular."

The aristocratic *Noh* theater is over 600 years old and is highly ritualistic, stylized, and deeply influenced by Zen Buddhism. Performers wear masks as they move and dance slowly over a bare stage. The male actors and chorus sing, accompanied by a flute and three drums of different sizes. In contrast, *Kabuki* theater is about 400 years old and is a much more "popular" folk production. It combines dancing and lots of melodrama with elaborate costumes and scenery to create a kind of "dance theater." Music is provided by

Kabuki theater
Charles and Josette Lenars

flutes, drums, *shamisans* (three-string banjos), gongs, bell ensembles, and choruses. *Kabuki* is Japan's most popular theater.

Opera is a drama set to music. The characters sing their lines rather than speaking them (as in a play). In this chapter we will learn about Western-style opera, but opera also appears elsewhere in the world. For example, Chinese opera has existed for hundreds of years and is widely regarded as the highest expression of Chinese culture. Almost every province of China has more than one Chinese opera troupe. These operas feature both tragic and comic elements, and they dramatize historical events and popular legends.

Western Opera

With the recent enormous success of recordings like *The Three Tenors* (Luciano Pavarotti, José Carreras, and Plácido Domingo) and the work of Andrea Bocelli, a tenor who alternates between operatic singing and a pop-music style (see "Further Listening Resources," pages 166–167), opera has once again become popular with the Western public. This art form, which combines music, theater, and the visual arts, is beginning to appeal as much to audiences today as it did during its heyday in the eighteenth and nineteenth centuries.

In Western opera, the singers are accompanied by an orchestra, which is placed in an orchestra pit below the stage. A typical opera production has elaborate costumes, scenery, and lighting, and may even include a ballet or some other form of dance. True to the vision of the nineteenth-century opera composer, Richard Wagner, modern opera is a **_Gesamtkunstwerk_** ("total work of art") that unites all the art forms—music, poetry, dance, painting, and drama—into a single whole.

The text for an opera is called the **_libretto_,** and the person who writes it is the **_librettist._** Since continental European opera librettos are in languages other than English, most American opera houses provide translations on a screen above the stage and a synopsis of the action in a printed program.

Brief History of Western Opera

Western opera was invented in the late sixteenth century by the **Florentine Camerata,** a small group of Italian nobles, poets, and composers. Its members sought to create an art form that would have the emotional impact of ancient Greek drama. Their experiments—the first operas—were produced in court for a small aristocratic audience. It was only in the latter part of the seventeenth century that opera became a form of popular entertainment. Public opera houses sprang up all over Italy and in Hamburg, Paris, and London. The popular taste in opera ran to comedy, spectacle, and drama, and opera composers supplied the public with what it wanted. Outstanding singers became stars who were adulated much like film and rock stars in the twentieth century. Often operas were created as much to show off the capabilities of particular star performers as to present a drama.

By the nineteenth century—known as the romantic period in Western European art music—opera was the most important form of music in many cities in Europe. Major centers of opera were established in Vienna, Paris, London, Milan, Rome, and New York; and opera stars would travel the opera circuit, demanding ever-higher fees for their performances, which sold out wherever they

Major Opera Composers

Sixteenth Century	**Representative Works**
Jacopo Peri (1561–1633; Italy)	*La Dafne* (1597)
Seventeenth Century	
Claudio Monteverdi (1567–1643; Italy)	*Orfeo* (1607)
Jean-Baptiste Lully (1632–1687; France)	*Alceste* (1674)
Eighteenth Century	
Jean-Philippe Rameau (1683–1764; France)	*Les Indes Galantes* (1735)
Christoph Willibald Gluck (1714–1787; Bohemia)	*Iphigénie en Aulide* (1774)
*Wolfgang Amadeus Mozart (1756–1791; Austria)	*Don Giovanni* (1787)
Nineteenth Century	
Carl Maria von Weber (1786–1826; Germany)	*Der Freischütz* (1821)
Giacomo Meyerbeer (1791–1864; Germany)	*Les Huguenots* (1836)
*Giuseppe Verdi (1813–1901; Italy)	*Aida* (1871)
*Richard Wagner (1813–1883; Germany)	*Der Ring des Nibelungen* (1876)
*Giacomo Puccini (1858–1924; Italy)	*La Bohème* (1896)
Twentieth Century	
Richard Strauss (1864–1949; Germany)	*Der Rosenkavalier* (1911)
Kurt Weill (1900–1950; Germany)	*The Threepenny Opera* (1928)
Alban Berg (1885–1935; Austria)	*Wozzeck* (1925)
*Benjamin Britten (1913–1976; England)	*Peter Grimes* (1945)
*George Gershwin (1898–1937; United States)	*Porgy and Bess* (1935)
*Gian Carlo Menotti (b. 1911; United States)	*Amahl and the Night Visitors* (1951)
*Andrew Lloyd Webber (b. 1948; England)	*Evita* (1976)

went. Cities throughout the United States were visited by traveling opera companies, performing to great acclaim. The Swedish opera star Jenny Lind toured all over the United States, performing in sold-out theaters to huge crowds.

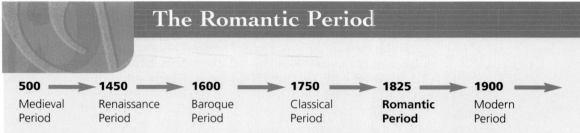

The Romantic Period

500 →	1450 →	1600 →	1750 →	1825 →	1900 →
Medieval Period	Renaissance Period	Baroque Period	Classical Period	**Romantic Period**	Modern Period

The romantic era in Western music is, roughly, from 1825 to 1900, although aspects of romanticism appeared before 1800 and lingered well into the twentieth century. "Romanticism" is often associated with heightened interest in nature, emphasis on emotions, subjectivity, and rebellion against rules and conventions. These traits are the antitheses of the classical ideals of organization, symmetry, and control.

Both nationalism and individualism characterized the nineteenth century. The American and French Revolutions spread the ideals of "liberty, fraternity, and equality" throughout the Western world. After the French Revolution (1789), individuality became a desirable character trait, and all artists developed a more individual style. Romantic poets suggested that all the arts should "aspire to the mysterious condition of music." The other arts were attractive to composers as well, and many romantic composers undertook literary works. Blending the arts in this way was an outgrowth of romantic attempts to provide a vision of the emotional interior of the human being. Form, objectivity, and restraint were felt to be inhibiting, and composers—indeed all artists—sought the strange, mysterious, and supernatural.

Many important and influential movements in art and literature were associated with the romantic period, including French Im-

pressionism, French symbolist poetry, German romantic philosophy, and European and American romantic literature.

Continuing strides in engineering and science resulted in the Industrial Revolution, which affected the social, cultural, and economic order of the nineteenth century. Innovations of this era, such as photography, the railway, the steamboat, steel production, electricity, the telephone, and canned foods, are taken for granted throughout much of the world today.

Music in the Romantic Era

Composers became more independent, both socially and economically, during the romantic era. Public concerts were routinely held, both in very large halls and in small, intimate salons. Philharmonic orchestra societies, opera and ballet companies, and public concert associations were established throughout Europe and the United States. Program music—instrumental music that is connected with, or inspired by, something nonmusical, such as a poem, painting, a character, or a scene from nature—flourished. Virtuosity, from both composer and performer, was also important.

Romanticism exalted the feelings of the individual and the inherent goodness of humankind. The rise in patriotism was not lost

on composers—who quickly took up the banner of nationalism by using the folklore of their native lands in their works. Many composers and artists wanted to develop art that was characteristic of a particular country or region and its people. Folk melodies sometimes appeared intact within larger compositions. Folk characters, dances, national heroes, legends, epics, and myths were glorified in songs, symphonic works, and operas.

Richard Wagner had the Bayreuth opera theater constructed in 1872 for the performance of his series of operas, *Der Ring des Nibelungen* (The Ring of the Nibelungs). The theater stands today as one of the most prominent monuments to the ideals of romanticism.

The Wagner Theater, interior, Bayreuth, Germany
Massimo Listri/Corbis

The devastation wrought by World War I (1914–1918) brought opera to a standstill in Europe. When Europe emerged from the war, a new art form began to capture the imagination of the public—the motion picture. The development of recordings and the emergence of the popular music industry meant that there was further competition for opera. In fact, opera lost its broad appeal and became the entertainment of a cultural elite. The new popular stars were performers on the silver screen and on recordings of light music, not on the opera stage. "Grand opera" was displaced by Broadway and film musicals.

In the latter part of the twentieth century the success of musicals such as *Cats*, *Evita*, *Les Misérables*, and *Phantom of the Opera*—which are more like traditional operas—has led the public back into the opera house to experience what "grand opera" could offer. Now opera is well established in most cities in the United States, and summer opera companies—such as those in Santa Fe, New Mexico, and Central City, Colorado, to name just two—are highly successful.

Madonna, scene from *Evita*
Bill Kaye/Everett Collection

The Operatic Singer

Although opera requires the talents of many artists—composers, librettists, stage designers, musicians, and costumers—the central figure in opera is the highly trained operatic singer. Operatic singers are vocal virtuosos. They are trained to project clearly—without amplifica-

Operatic Voices

The focus on vocal technique and the demanding requirements of operatic singing have resulted in considerable specialization. The following list details the subcategories of female and male voices in opera. The verbal descriptions are an attempt to describe the sound of these voices, but it is only by hearing a voice that you can form an exact impression of what the words mean.

Female Voices

Sopranos
   Coloratura   Highest human voice—light, flexible
   Lyric   Fuller, high voice with good flexibility
   Dramatic   Darker and less agile, but very powerful
Mezzo-sopranos
   Lyric   Good flexibility, dark quality
   Dramatic   Powerful, dark, strong low register
Contralto   Very dark, strong and heavy—not agile

Male Voices

Tenors
   Countertenor   Highest male voice, light in quality
   Lyric   Light and supple, not too powerful
   Dramatic (*Heldentenor*)   Distinct heavier quality, very powerful
Baritones
   Lyric   Darker and richer than tenor, less agile
   Bass baritone   Heavy, dark tone quality
Basses
   Basso cantante   Dark with heavy tone quality, good low register
   Basso profundo   Lowest voice—powerful but inflexible

tion—to the last row of a large hall and to compete with the sounds of large instrumental ensembles. They must sing melodies that far exceed the range and capabilities of an untrained voice. The years of training undertaken to achieve these ends usually produce a vocal quality that is somewhat darker and fuller than that of the untrained voice.

Melody in Opera

Operatic singers learn vocal techniques that enable them to perform the highly demanding melodic style of opera. The range of operatic melody is much greater than that of other vocal melody, and trained operatic sopranos can sing rapidly moving, highly ornamented melodies. The style of melody in opera somewhat resembles instrumental melody in that it takes advantage of the unique characteristics of each type of voice, just as instrumental melodies take advantage of the unique characteristics of different instruments.

In the remainder of this chapter we will present an excerpt from one of the best-known operas, *La Bohème,* by the Italian composer Giacomo Puccini. This opera is written in the romantic style. You can gain some sense of the dramatic power of grand opera from the recording, but to fully appreciate what an opera has to offer, you must actually experience it in a live performance.

Giacomo Puccini

Giacomo Puccini (1858–1924) was born on 22 December 1858 in Lucca, Italy, the oldest son in his family. He was encouraged by his mother to become a musician—not surprisingly, since the preceding four generations of Puccinis had all been composers.

At the age of fourteen, after studying with his uncle Fortunato Magi and Carlo Angeloni, the director of the Istituto Musicale Pacini, Puccini became organist at San Martino and San Michele, two churches in Lucca. Through Angeloni's tutelage, Puccini became acquainted with many of Giuseppi Verdi's opera scores.

Puccini helped to supplement the family income not only by playing the organ in churches but also by singing as a choirboy and by playing the piano in bars. It was in these bars that he acquired his lifetime habit of heavy cigarette smoking, which may have ultimately contributed to his death from throat cancer.

By his sixteenth birthday Puccini was already writing music for the church, and one composition—*Messa di Gloria,* written as a graduation exercise at the Istituto Pacini—helped earn him a scholarship to the Royal Music Conservatory of Milan. Puccini's poverty-stricken student days later exerted a profound influence on the creation of *La Bohème.*

Young Puccini, 1874
Metropolitan Opera Archives

After graduation, Puccini went to stay with friends in Caprino Bergamasco. There he met Ferdinando Fontana, a famous poet and dramatist. At the urging of one of his friends, the two began work on a one-act opera called *Le Villi* (The Witches). It was entered in an opera competition. Although the work did not receive even an honorable mention, the composer Arrigo Boito (1842–1918) heard Puccini playing some of it on the piano and used his influence to bring it to the stage. *Le Villi* received its first performance on 31 May 1884 and was a success.

In the summer immediately following the initial success of *Le Villi* the Milanese publishing house of Giulio Ricordi contracted Puccini for a second opera and paid him a monthly salary. The result was *Edgar,* a full-length opera, which failed miserably in its Milan premiere in 1889.

Ricordi's faith in Puccini's dramatic sense persisted, and he encouraged the young composer to continue. *Manon Lescaut,* a story by Abbé Prévost, served as the basis for Puccini's next opera, also called *Manon Lescaut.* This was well received by the public and critics alike, and it had numerous successful performances in and out of Italy, establishing Puccini's international reputation.

For his next opera, Puccini turned to the French author Henri Mürger's *La Bohème* (Bohemian Life, or The Bohemians). The critics' lukewarm response to *La Bohème*'s premiere in 1896 was overshadowed by the popularity of the opera with audiences. The year following its premiere in Turin, it was presented in Alexandria, Vienna, Moscow, Berlin, Mexico City, Rio de Janeiro, and Los Angeles.

In Puccini's next opera, *Tosca,* the story takes place in Rome. The opera had its premiere there in 1900, amid great tension—the queen of Italy was supposed to attend, but a bomb scare kept her away. Nevertheless, the performance was greeted with cheers and accolades by both audience and critics. *Tosca,* like *Manon Lescaut* and *La Bohème* before it, was highly successful both in and outside of Italy.

Puccini's next opera, *Madama Butterfly,* began as one of the worst fiascoes in operatic history but ended as an unparalleled success. In 1900, during a visit to London to help prepare the English premiere of *Tosca,* Puccini saw a one-act play called *Madame Butterfly.* So touched was he by the tale that he went backstage immediately following the performance to secure permission to turn it into an opera.

Madama Butterfly premiered at the famous La Scala Opera House in Milan, Italy, in February 1904. The performance was marred by noisy interruptions and catcalls from a **claque**—a group of audience members paid to loudly support or denigrate a production or a player. At the work's conclusion, there was no cheering or applause but only icy silence. Puccini immediately withdrew the work and, with his librettist's help, made some alterations. He brought it out again in May 1904, and this time it met with immediate success.

Another play, *The Girl of the Golden West (La fanciulla del West)*, written by David Belasco, served as the subject for Puccini's next opera. He discovered this play when he visited New York early in 1907 to supervise productions of *Manon Lescaut* and *Madama Butterfly* at the Metropolitan Opera. He had been searching for a subject and was fascinated with the American West, although he knew little about it. The premiere took place at the Metropolitan Opera in New York; it starred the famous tenor Enrico Caruso (1873–1921) and was conducted by Arturo Toscanini (1867–1957). This opera too was a popular and a critical success.

Belasco, Toscanini, Puccini
Metropolitan Opera Archives

By 1914 World War I had broken out across Europe, and Italy entered the war in 1915, joining an alliance with France, Russia, and England against Austria-Hungary. Puccini was genuinely worried about his son, Tonio, who was at the front, but he remained indifferent to the war itself. He liked Austria—the Viennese had long championed his operas—and was not fond of the French—whose reception of his works had been lukewarm at best. Puccini's opera *La Rondine* was given its premiere in 1917 in Monte Carlo, Monaco, one of the last neutral spots on the European continent.

The idea of a series of three separate one-act operas performed in one evening had long intrigued Puccini. He began composing music for a one-act opera based on the gruesome French tragedy *La Houppelande* (The Cloak), by Didier Gold. This opera, *Il Tabarro* (which also translates as The Cloak), became the first of three parts of Puccini's *Il Trittico*. Another play, *Suor Angelica* (Sister Angelica), by Puccini's new librettist, Giuseppi Adami, served as the melodramatic second part. *Gianni Schicchi*, the final part, was based on a few lines in Dante's *Inferno*, and it fulfilled Puccini's lifelong dream of writing a comic opera. The war made it impossible to find first-rate singers in Rome, where Puccini had planned the premiere of *Il Trittico*, so he accepted an offer to hold it at the Metropolitan Opera House in New York. The performance, on 14 December 1918, came so soon after the Armistice (11 November) that Puccini could not get to New York in time for the premiere.

As Puccini neared his sixties, he became more contemplative. His troubled marriage to his wife, Elvira, became more serene and more affectionate. They moved to a villa on the outskirts of Viareggio at the end of 1921, and there he began work on his final opera. Always impatient for a new libretto, he settled on the play *Turandot*, by Count Carlo Gozzi.

By 1923 Puccini had begun having severe throat pains, and he consulted several specialists, who found nothing out of the ordinary. In March 1924, when Puccini had completed all the orchestration of *Turandot* except the final duet, continued throat pain led him to visit another physician, in Florence, who found a cancerous growth. It was recommended that Puccini travel to the Ledoux cancer clinic in Brussels for treatment. He whispered to Toscanini, who visited him shortly before his departure: "If anything happens to me, don't abandon *Turandot*."

The treatments went well at first, but Puccini soon took a turn for the worse. He lost his voice following painful treatments with radioactive needles and was forced to write his directions for *Turandot* on a pad of paper. The severity of the treatments was too much for Puccini's heart, and he died on 29 November 1924. All Italy went into mourning. The composer Franco Alfano finished

Puccini's funeral procession in Brussels, Belgium
Metropolitan Opera Archives

Turandot, relying on musical sketches left by Puccini, and the opera was premiered at La Scala Opera House on 26 April 1926.

Listening to *La Bohème*

Puccini's Music

For more than 100 years *La Bohème* has been one of the three or four most frequently performed operas in the repertoire. Puccini's gift for beautiful melody and his consummate skill as an orchestrator make it a favorite with audiences. Its principal characters are young, and their joys, sorrows, and problems are universal. *La Bohème* is an animated and cheerful opera, although it ends sadly. The music develops in a natural, conversational style. The action in *La Bohème* is so compelling that it would be dramatically inappropriate for a singer to stand and proclaim long-held high notes for the sake of display, as often happens in other operas. Puccini, the supreme dramatist, insisted that a pause over a note should be sustained no more than twice its written value. The romantic appeal of Rodolfo and Mimi's "love at first sight" is enhanced by *La Bohème*'s dramatic intensity. It also makes the melancholy of Mimi's illness and eventual death from tuberculosis all the more poignant.

Plot Synopsis of *La Bohème*

Act I. Rodolfo, a poet, and his friend Marcello, a painter, are trying to work in their garret in Paris. It is Christmas Eve and they are cold and hungry—and without money. Colline, another bohemian, comes in, equally discouraged. But then Schaunard, the fourth and luckiest of the group, enters with money and provisions. The friends decide to celebrate by dining out. After a successful skirmish with their landlord, Benoit, they set out for the Café Momus. Only Rodolfo stays behind, to finish an article he is writing. There is a knock at the door. To his surprise, he finds a beautiful young girl on

Rent

On 1 February 1996, exactly 100 years after the premiere of *La Bohème*, the American musical *Rent*, loosely based on its story and characters, opened off-Broadway. In *Jonathan Larson's musical, *La Bohème*'s off-again, on-again love affairs, the poverty of bohemian life, and death at an early age from consumption (tuberculosis) are newly experienced in Manhattan's East Village in the 1990s by rock musicians, filmmakers, and other artisans who live in the shadow of AIDS.

This off-Broadway musical took the New York theater scene by storm in 1996. It won four Tony Awards, including Best Musical; awards for Best Musical from the New York Drama Critics Circle, Drama League, Drama Desk, and Outer Critics Circle; and the 1996 Pulitzer prize for Best American Drama.

Rent
Joan Marcus

the landing. It is his neighbor, Mimi, who has knocked to ask for a light. Her candle has gone out. Rodolfo relights it for her, but it goes out again, and in the confusion, she loses her key. In the darkness she and Rodolfo search for it. Their hands touch. Rodolfo and Mimi exchange confidences and, finally, declarations of love. Then they are off to join his friends.

Nellie Melba as Mimi
Culver Pictures

Enrico Caruso as Rodolfo
Culver Pictures

Act II. Christmas Eve in the Latin Quarter. The friends are separated in the bustling of merrymakers and vendors of every kind. Rodolfo and Mimi go into a milliner's, and he buys her a pink bonnet. Later all are reunited at the Café Momus, where they order a sumptuous supper. As they are enjoying themselves, Musetta—Marcello's beautiful but fickle beloved—enters with Alcindoro, an elderly and straitlaced admirer. Seeing Marcello, Musetta contrives to get rid of her escort. She and Marcello are again in each other's arms. The friends all go off, leaving their bill to the hapless Alcindoro.

Act III. A cold February dawn. Outside a tavern near one of the gates of Paris, Mimi appears and sends for Marcello, who is working in the tavern with Musetta. When he comes out, Mimi tells how Rodolfo's insane jealousy is forcing them apart. Their conversation is cut short when Rodolfo, who was sleeping in the tavern, wakes and comes out. Mimi hides behind a tree. Taxed by Marcello with his fickleness, Rodolfo reveals that he is really concerned for Mimi's health and thinks that another person, less poor than he, could take better care of her. Mimi's presence is discovered, and though she first bids Rodolfo good-bye, in the end they agree to stay together at least until spring comes. As Marcello and Musetta quarrel in the background and finally separate, Rodolfo and Mimi go off reconciled, arm in arm.

Act IV. The garret, months later. Rodolfo and Marcello are again trying to work, but this time each is distracted and tormented by the memory of his lost love. Schaunard and Colline come in, and the four friends clown, making light of their poverty, until Musetta interrupts them, bursting in with the news that Mimi is outside, too ill to climb the last stairs. Rodolfo helps her into the room, where she is settled on the bed. Musetta sacrifices her earrings and Colline his coat to buy medicine and a muff for the dying girl. Marcello goes for a doctor. Left alone, the two lovers renew their vows of love and recall their first meeting. Soon the others return. As Musetta prays, Mimi quietly dies, with Rodolfo calling her name in despair.

LISTENING ACTIVITY

La Bohème, **End of Act II** (Giacomo Puccini)
[CD 1, tracks 12–13]

In this excerpt from the end of Act II, the friends have gathered in Café Momus and ordered their meal. Rodolfo has introduced them to his new love, Mimi. Musetta has entered with her elderly admirer. She sings her famous waltz to entice Marcello to pay attention to her.

The end of this act includes almost every aspect of the grand spectacle of opera—beautiful **arias,** crowd scenes, marching bands, children's choruses, and people talking and singing at the same time. The music allows the audience to experience these different levels of activity simultaneously.

The performance you will be listening to was recorded at Jesus-Christus-Kirche, Berlin, in 1972 with Herbert von Karajan conducting the Berlin Philharmonic. The singers are Mirella Freni (soprano) as Mimi, Elizabeth Harwood (soprano) as Musetta, Luciano Pavarotti (tenor) as Rodolfo, Rolando Panerai (baritone) as Marcello, Gianni Maffeo (baritone) as Schaunard, Nicolai Ghiaurov (bass) as Colline, and Michel Sénéchal (bass) as Alcindoro.

An *aria* is a song for solo voice within an opera.

La Bohème
Vittoriano Rastelli/Corbis

Track 12

0:00   Musetta [seated at a cafe table and deliberately addressing Marcello, who shows signs of agitation]:

   [Musetta's Waltz]
   Quando me'n vo'   When I saunter alone down
                                the street

soletta per la via   they all stop to stare at me.
la gente sosta e mira . . .   People turn and look
e la bellezza mia   to see my beauty
tutta ricerca in me   and survey me from
da capo a piè . . .   head to toe.

Marcello [to his friends]:
Legatemi alla seggiola!   Tie me to a chair!

Alcindoro [with embarrassment]:
Quella gente che dirà?   What will people say?

Musetta:
. . . Ed assaporo allor   . . . then I savour the hidden
bramosia sotti!   longing
che da gl'occhi traspira   that gleams in their eyes
e dai palesi vezzi   and from visible attractions
intender sa   can deduce my concealed
alle occulte beltà   charms.

[stands up]

Cosi l'effluvio del desio   Surrounded by this sense of
tutta m'aggira;   desire,
felice mi fa!   How happy I am!

1:49 Alcindoro:
Quel canto scurrile   This scandalous song
mi muove la bile!   infuriates me!

Musetta:
E tu che sai . . . che memori   And you who know this,
  e ti struggi,   who remember and yearn,
da me tanto rifuggi?   why do you ignore me?
So ben: le angoscie tue   I know full well
non le vuoi dir,   that you would rather die
non le vuoi dir,   than speak
so ben, ma ti senti morir!   of your torment!

Mimi [to Rodolfo]:
Lo vedo ben che quella   It's plain to see that the
 poveretta   poor girl's
tutta invaghita ell'è,   very much in love,
tutta invaghita di Marcel!   very much in love with
                                      Marcello.

Alcindoro:
Quella gente che dirà?   What will the people say?

Schaunard and Colline get up and watch the scene from one side of the stage while Rodolfo and Mimi remain seated talking only to each other. Marcello becomes increasingly agitated, leaves his seat, and would like to escape, but he cannot seem to resist Musetta's voice. Alcindoro tries in vain to persuade Musetta to sit down again at his table, where supper has been served.

Rodolfo [to Mimi]: Marcello un di l'amò.	Marcello was once her lover.
Schaunard: Ah! Marcello cederà!	Ah! Marcello will give in!
Rodolfo: La fraschetta l'abbandonò . . .	. . . she heartlessly left him . . .
Colline: Chi sa mai quel ce avverrà!	Who knows what will happen?
Rodolfo: . . . per poi darsi a miglior vita.	. . . to lead a more luxurious life.
Schaunard: Trovan dolce al pari il laccio . . .	The trap is found equally pleasant . . .
Colline: Santi numi, in simil briga . . .	Heavens above, in such a trap . . .
Schaunard: . . . chi lo tende e chi ci dà.	. . . by the hunter and the quarry!
Colline: . . . mai Colline intopperà!	. . . Colline will never fail!

3:01
Musetta: (Ah! Marcello smania . . .)	(Ah, Marcello is restless . . .)
Alcindoro: Parla pian!	Not so loud!
Mimi: Quell'infelice mi muove a pietà!	Such unhappiness touches my heart!
Musetta: (Marcello è vinto!)	(. . . Marcello is defeated!)

Alcindoro:
  Zitta, zitta!   Do be quiet!

Colline:
  Essa è bella, io non son   She's pretty, I can't deny . . .
  cieco . . .
  ma piaccionmi assai più   . . . but I'd rather
  una pipa e un testo greco,   have a pipe,
  mi piaccion assai più.   and a Greek text!

Mimi [warmly to Rodolfo]:
  T'amo!   I love you!

Rodolfo [arms around Mimi's waist]:
  Mimi!   Mimi!

Schaunard:
  Quel bravaccio a momenti   His stubborn heart will yield
  cederà!   in a moment!

Mimi:
  Quell'infelice mi muove   Such unhappiness touches
  a pietà!   my heart!
  L'amor ingeneroso è   Unworthy love is sad love.
  tristo amor!

Rodolfo:
  È fiacco amor quel che   It's a feeble love that,
  le offese
  vendicar non sa! . . .   when wounded,
  Non risorge spento morir!   can't avenge itself!

Schaunard:
  Stupenda è la commedia!   The comedy is stupendous!

Musetta:
  So ben, le angoscie tue   I know full well,
  non le vuoi dir,   you like to conceal your
                                         torment
  ah! ma ti sento morir!   but you'd rather die than
                                         admit it!

Alcindoro:
  Modi, garbo!   Your behavior! Be quiet!

Schaunard:
  Marcello cederà!   Marcello will surrender!

Alcindoro:
  Zitta, zitta!   Be quiet, be quiet!

Schaunard [to Colline]:
Se tal vagga persona   If such a frivolous woman
ti tratasse al tu per tu,   were on confidential terms
                              with you,
la tua scienza brontolana   you'd send to the devil
manderesti a Belzebù!   your grumbling wisdom!

Musetta [rebelling against Alcindoro]:
Io voglio fare il mio piacere! I'll do what I like!
Voglio far quel che mi par!   I'll do as I think fit!
Non seccar, non seccar!   Don't be such a bore!

Colline:
Essa è bella, io non son   (She's pretty, I can't deny,
    cieco . . .
ma piaccionmi assai più   but I'd far rather have a
                               pipe
una pipa e un testo greco!   and a Greek text!)

Musetta:
Non seccar!   Don't interfere!
(Or convien liberarsi del   (I must get rid of this old
vecchio!)   coot!)

[She sits down again, pretending to have a pain in her foot.]

3:53   Ahi!!   Ah!!

Alcindoro:
Che c'è?   What's the matter?

Musetta:
Qual dolore, qual bruciore!   What pain, what agony!

Alcindoro:
Dove?   Where?

Musetta [coquettishly showing her foot]:
Al piè!   My foot!

Marcello [deeply moved, approaching]:
Gioventù mia, tu non sei   Youthful dreams of mine,
    morta,   you are not dead,
nè di te morto è il souvenir! nor is your memory!

Musetta:
Sciogli, slaccia, rompi,   Undo it, untie it! Break it,
    straccia!   tear it!
te ne imploro . . .   Oh, please . . .
Laggiù c'è un calzolaio.   There's a cobbler over there!

Alcindoro:
  Imprudente!   Be more discreet!

Musetta:
  Corri presto!   Go quickly!
  Ne voglio un altro piao.   I must have another pair!
  Ahi! che fitta, maledetta   Oh, what torture!
  scarpa stretta! Or la levo!   Take them off!

Alcindoro:
  Quella gente che dirà?   What will people say?

Schaunard and Colline:
  La commedia è stupenda!   The comedy is stupendous!

Marcello:
  Se tu batessi alla mia porta   If you were to knock at my door

  t'andrebbe il mio core as   my heart would fly to open
    aprir!   it!

Alcindoro:
  Ma il mio grado!   Think of my position!

Musetta [taking off her shoe; putting it on the table]:
  Eccola quà.   There it is!

Mimi:
  Io vedo be, ell'è invaghita   It's plain to see that she's in
    di Marcello.   love with Marcello!

Rodolfo:
  Il vedo ben, la commedia   It's plain to see that the
    è stupenda!   comedy is stupendous!

Alcindoro [hides Musetta's shoe under his vest and does up
the buttons of his coat]:
  Vuoi ch'io compormetta?   Do you want to make me a
                                       laughingstock?

Musetta:
  Corri, va corri!   Run, get going!

Alcindoro:
  Aspetta!   Wait!

Musetta:
  Presto, va, va!   Hurry, go, go!

Alcindoro:
  Vo!   I'm going!

[He hurries off while Musetta and Marcello embrace passionately.]

4:58   Musetta:
  Marcello!   Marcello!

  Marcello:
  Sirena!   Enchantress!

  Schaunard:
  Siam all'ultima scena!   Here's the final scene!

A waiter enters and presents the bill.

  Rodolfo, Schaunard, Colline:
  Il conto?   The bill?

  Schaunard:
  Così presto?   So soon?

Track 13

0:00   Colline:
  Chi l'ha richiesto?   Who asked for it?

  Schaunard [to the waiter]:
  Vediam.   Let's see it.

  Rodolfo and Colline [examining the bill]:
  Caro!   How expensive!

  Rodolfo, Schaunard, Colline:
  Fuori il danaro!   Empty your pockets!

  Schaunard:
  Colline, Rodolfo, e tu   Colline, Rodolfo, and you,
   Marcello?   Marcello?

  Street children [coming from the right]:
  La Ritirata!   The parade!

  Marcello:
  Siamo all'asciutto!   We're broke!

  Schaunard:
  Come?   What?

  Seamstresses and students [coming out of the Café Momus]:
  La Ritirata!   The parade!

In the distance, marching soldiers are heard coming closer. As the parade is still a long way off, people run from one side to the other, trying to see where the soldiers are coming from.

Rodolfo, Schaunard, Colline:
 Come? Non ce n'è più?   What? Is that all we have?

Schaunard:
 Ma il mio tesoro ov'è?   What happened to all my
             money?

They all feel in their pockets, which are empty; no one can explain the rapid disappearance of Schaunard's money. They look at each other in amazement.

0:30   Street children [trying to discover the direction]:
      S'avvicinan per di quà?   Will they come along this
             way?

Musetta [to the waiter]:
 Il mio conto date a me.   Please bring me my bill.

Seamstresses and students:
 No! di là!   No! That way!

Street children:
 S'avvicinan per di là!   They're coming this way!

Seamstresses and students:
 Vien di quà!   No! They're coming this way!

Street children:
 No! vien di là!   No! That way!

Windows are opened, and at them and on balconies appear mothers with their children, eagerly looking to see where the parade is coming from.

Musetta [to the waiter who brings the bill]:
 Bene!   Thank you!

Townspeople and vendors:
 Largo! Largo!   Make way!

Boys (from the windows]:
 Voglio veder! voglio sentir!   Let me see! Let me hear!

Musetta:
 Presto sommate quello   Put both these bills
 con questo!   together!

[The waiter does so.]

Mothers [from the windows]:
 Lisette, vuoi tacer!   Lisette, will you be quiet!

0:48   Boys:
   Mamma, voglia veder!   Mother, let me see!
   Papà, voglio sentir!   Daddy, let me hear!

   Musetta:
   Paga il signor   The gentleman
   che stava qui con me!   who was with me will pay.

   Mothers:
   Tonio, la vuoi finir!   Tony! Stop that!

   Rodolfo, Marcello, Schaunard, Colline [pointing in the
   direction taken by Alcindoro]:
   Paga il signor!   That gentleman will pay!

   Mothers:
   Vuoi tacer, la vuoi finir!   Be quiet! Stop that!

   Boys:
   Vuò veder la Ritirata!   Let me see the parade.

   Seamstresses and townspeople:
   S'avvicinano di là!   They're coming this way!

   Seamstresses, students, townspeople, vendors:
   Si, di qua!   Yes, that way!

   Street children:
   Come sarà arrivata   When they get here,
   la seguiremo al passo!   let's fall in behind!

   Colline, then Schaunard:
   Paga il signor   The gentleman will pay!

   Marcello:
   Il signor!   The gentleman!

1:02   Musetta [putting the two bills together and placing them
   on the table where Alcindoro sat]:
   E dove s'è seduto   When he sits down, he'll
                                 find
   ritrovi il mio saluto!   this greeting from me!

   Shopkeepers and street vendors close their shops and stalls
and come out into the street.

   Vendors [to a group of townspeople they meet]:
   In quel rullio tu senti   In these drumrolls you feel
   la patria maestà!   the majesty of our country!

   Rodolfo, Marcello, Schaunard, Colline:
   E dove s'è seduto   And where he was sitting

ritrovi il suo saluto!	he'll find this greeting from her!

Seamstresses, students, townspeople:

Largo, largo, eccoli qua!	Make way! Make way! Here they come!

Street children:

Ohè! attenti, eccoli qua!	Attention! here they come!

Marcello:

Giunge la Ritirata!	Here's the parade!

The crowd:

In fila!	All in line!

Marcello and Colline:

Che il vecchio non ci veda	Mind the old coot doesn't see us,
fuggir colla sua preda!	running off with his booty!

Rodolfo:

Giunge la Ritirata!	Here's the parade!

Marcello, Schaunard, Colline:

Quella folla serrata	This dense crowd
il nascondiglio appresti!	will give us cover!

1:24 The parade enters from the left, headed by a drum major twirling his baton, leading the way.

The crowd:

Ecco il tambur maggiore!	Here's the drum major!
Più fier d'un antico guerrier!	Prouder than a warrior of old!

Mimi, Musetta, Rodolfo, Marcello, Schaunard, Colline:

Lesti, lesti, lesti!	Quickly, quickly, quickly!

The crowd:

I Zappatori olà!	And here comes the band!
Ecco il tambur maggior!	Here comes the drum major!
La ritirata è qua!	The parade is here!
Il tambur maggior!	See the drum major,
Pare un general!	He looks like a general!
Ecco là!	See, there he goes,
Il bel tambur maggior!	the handsome drum major!
La canna d'or,	The splendid,
tutto splendor!	golden baton!
Che guarda, passa, va!	See, there he goes!

Musetta, who cannot walk with only one shoe, is carried off in the arms of Marcello and Colline, who break through the bystanders and follow the parade. The crowd, seeing her carried in triumph, take the opportunity of giving her a loud ovation. Rodolfo and Mimi follow arm in arm, as does Schaunard, with his horn to his lips. The whole crowd—students, children, women, seamstresses, men—falls in behind the parade and goes marching off into the distance.

The crowd:

Tutto splendor!	Such splendor!
Di Francia è il più bell'uom!	The greatest beau in France!
Il bel tambur maggior!	The handsome drum major!
Eccolo là!	Look at him!
Che guarda, passa, va!	See, there he goes!

Rodolfo, Marcello, Schaunard, Colline:

Viva Musetta!	Hurrah for Musetta,
Cuor biricchin!	fickle heart!
Gloria ed onor	Glory and honor
del Quartier Latin!	of the Latin Quarter!

Meanwhile, Alcindoro, with a pair of shoes well wrapped up, has returned to the Café Momus and is looking for Musetta. The waiter takes the bills she left and with a bow presents them to Alcindoro, who—seeing the amount and finding himself deserted—sinks into a chair, flabbergasted.

Source: "La Bohème" summary and libretto from *Seven Puccini Librettos* by William Weaver, pages 4–5, 36–61. Copyright © 1981. Published by W. W. Norton. Reprinted by permission of William Morris Agency, Inc.

Response to the Music

Were you able to follow the libretto as you listened to the recording? You will have noted that sometimes the singers' words overlap each other, and occasionally they are all singing at the same time. If you are following the libretto, you can see that it is not necessary for the audience to understand everything that is sung in such situations. The text is usually repetitive enough to allow comprehension of the gist of the libretto. Were you able to hear the differences among the various operatic voices on the recording? What were your physical, emotional, cognitive, and spiritual responses to the music? How did you react to the singing styles? Have you gained a new appreciation of the skills required to sing opera? Did this excerpt make you want to see a performance of the opera?

Summary

The combination of music and drama is found throughout the world. Japanese *Noh* and *Kabuki* and Chinese opera are three kinds of popular musical dramas. The history of Western European opera began in Florence, Italy, at the end of the sixteenth century. Although this form of entertainment originated as an attempt to rival classical Greek drama, it soon became a popular entertainment. As opera became even more popular during the seventeenth and eighteenth centuries, public opera houses were built and the subject matter of operas was changed to have wider appeal. Nineteenth-century composers such as Richard Wagner developed the musical drama and moved opera toward a total art form, encompassing all the arts in a single work.

Melody in opera is designed to show off the capabilities of highly trained singers, whose specialized voices have particular qualities. The singers are the stars of an opera performance. In fact, the star system that was later to become a part of films and popular music first arose in opera. The text of an opera is called the libretto and is written by a librettist.

We have listened to an excerpt from one of the most popular operas of all times, Puccini's *La Bohème*.

Applying What You Have Learned

1. Which of the voices you heard in *La Bohème* was most surprising to you? Which type did you like most? Why?

2. If you sing, how did you learn the style of vocal production that seems most natural to you? Did you have any formal voice training? Did you mimic sounds on recordings? Did you learn from friends or family members?

3. How do you think a live opera performance would differ from a recording? What would you experience that you could not experience listening to the CD? Which would you prefer?

4. What were your impressions of the sections where several characters are singing different lyrics at the same time? Did those sections confuse you? Increase the excitement? Propel the drama forward? Seem silly? Why do you think Puccini would write sections with overlapping voices?

5. The style of singing in opera was developed to enable the performers to project their voices over an orchestra without amplification. In modern musicals the singers are "wired for sound," and a sound engineer makes sure their voices

are heard at all times. Would opera be better if the singers were amplified? What would be gained? What would be lost? Do you think that if they were amplified, singers could perform opera more in the style of popular music?

6. Andrea Bocelli and Sarah Brightman are two performers who have become opera and popular singers. Listen to each of them singing a song in operatic style and a different song in pop style. Comment on the vocal differences. In their duet "Time to Say Goodbye" (on *Romanza*, Polydor 533 991-2), they combine a bit of both styles. Which style do you prefer? Why?

Important Terms

Kabuki 141   libretto 142   claque 149
Noh 141   librettist 142   aria 154
opera 142   Florentine
Gesamtkunstwerk 142   Camerata 142

Names preceded by "*" have short biographies in Appendix B, p. 346

Musicians Mentioned

*Luciano Pavarotti
*José Carreras
*Plácido Domingo
*Andrea Bocelli
*Richard Wagner
*Jenny Lind
*Giacomo Puccini
*Arrigo Boito
*Enrico Caruso
*Arturo Toscanini
*Franco Alfano
*Herbert von Karajan
Mirella Freni
Elizabeth Harwood
Rolando Panerai
Gianni Maffeo
Nicolai Ghiaurov
Michel Sénéchal
*Sarah Brightman

Further Listening Resources

La Bohème, Angel 2 CDCB-47235.
Tosca, London 2414597-2 LH2.

The Three Tenors (Carreras, Domingo, and Pavarotti), London 30433.

Three Tenors (Caruso, Crooks, and Widdop), Claremont 785052 (historic recordings from early in the twentieth century).

The Opera Album (Andrea Bocelli), Philips 462033.

Romanza (Andrea Bocelli), Polydor 533 991-2.

Harmony

in Music

If only the world could feel the power of harmony.

*WOLFGANG AMADEUS MOZART (1756–1791)
AUSTRIAN COMPOSER

Chances are good that if you are not a musician you will seldom have been consciously aware of harmony (see page 171). You may, however, have been aware of someone strumming a guitar behind a folksinger, or you may have noticed that several musicians in a rock band are playing keyboard instruments or guitars. These musicians are providing harmonic background for the vocalist.

The quotation from Mozart above is the wistful statement of a professional musician who knows full well the power of this musical element but also knows that it is unnoticed by the general listener. If you have musical training or have played a musical instrument like the guitar, however, you will be much more aware of harmony, since this element would have been brought to your attention early in your study.

In this part of the book, you will learn about diatonic and chromatic harmony as well as about the practice of harmonizing.

Neal Preston/Corbis

CHAPTER 9   Harmony **170**
The Four Seasons—Spring, Antonio Vivaldi

CHAPTER 10   Harmonizing **189**
This Land Is Your Land, Woodie Guthrie
Bring Me Little Water Silvy, Leadbelly: Huddie Ledbetter

Harmony

The Four Seasons—Spring, Antonio Vivaldi

Amanda Merullo/Viesti Assoc. Inc.

Sentimentally I am disposed to harmony; but organically
I am incapable of a tune.

CHARLES LAMB (1775–1834)
BRITISH ESSAYIST AND CRITIC

Harmony is a musical term that is used to describe simultaneous pitches. Sometimes the result is simple and pleasant to our ears; at other times it sounds complex and challenging. Nevertheless, all simultaneous pitches—by voices, by instruments, and by combinations of the two—are considered to be harmony. The study of harmony is a study of how pitches are combined in various musical styles.

Tonal Harmony

The music of other cultures tends to place much less emphasis on harmony than Western European music does. In the music of India, for example, harmony consists of the relationship between a melody and a static drone that is unchanging throughout a composition (see CD 1, track 11). However, with the rapid assimilation of Western popular music throughout the world, Western-style harmony is now heard nearly everywhere. Western-style harmony is generally known as **tonal harmony** because it creates a sense of a tonal center or key (see "Scales," page 102).

Chords

A Western system of harmony based on chords began to develop during the latter part of the Renaissance and has continued to evolve ever since. By the close of the baroque period (1600–1750; see page 177), a system of tonal harmony based on chords had been established, and the harmony of later periods can be seen as an extension of these principles.

A **chord** is a group of three or more pitches sounding together. Any combination of tones might be considered a chord, but certain combinations of three tones, called **triads,** predominate in the tonal harmony of Western music. We'll demonstrate these concepts using a drawing of the piano keyboard. (Remember that we are using the piano keyboard because it provides a clear visual representation of the pitches used in most Western music; however, these pitches may be played on most Western pitched musical instruments.)

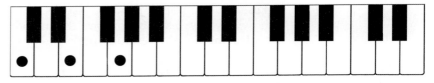

A triad on the piano keyboard

Simple Gifts

Shaker hymn

'Tis the gift to be sim-ple, 'Tis the gift to be free, 'Tis the gift to come down where we ought to be, And when we find our-selves in the place just right, 'Twill be in the val - ley of love and de-light. When true sim - pli - ci - ty is gained, To bow and to bend we shan't be a-shamed, To turn, turn, will be our de-light, Till by turn - ing, turn - ing we come 'round right.

Chord symbols

Harmonic Progression

The motion from one chord to another is called **harmonic progression.** In popular music scores, harmonic progressions are shown by chord symbols above the melody.

Harmonic progressions make a contribution to the rhythmic life of a piece of tonal music. The duration of chords (the length of time between chord changes) creates a rhythm called **harmonic rhythm.** Harmonic rhythm helps establish the sense of meter since there is a strong tendency for chords to change on the first beat of a measure.

Harmonic Tension and Release

The succession of chords in tonal harmony creates a sense of rising and falling tension, which your body may experience as slight increases and decreases in muscular tension. Chords of greater complexity tend to increase tension; simpler chords decrease it. In tonal harmony there is a single chord, called the **tonic triad,** which acts as a point of rest or lowest tension. The piano keyboard on page 171 shows the tonic triad for the key of C major (see the C major scale on page 102). As the harmony moves away from the tonic chord through chord changes, the tension rises; when the tonic chord returns, that tension is released. Another important common chord is the **dominant triad,** which creates tension that is resolved by the reappearance of the tonic chord. You will experience this rising and falling tension in the concerto by Antonio Vivaldi that we will be listening to later in this chapter.

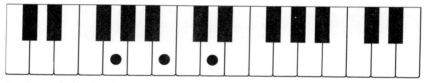

Dominant triad in C major

Diatonic Scales

The most common scales in Western music are the **diatonic scales,** which can be found by playing the white keys of the piano in succession. There are two common diatonic scales, the **major scale** and the **minor scale** (see pages 102–103). The major scale is by far the more common of these two. It is so pervasive that most people can identify it when they hear it played. Music based on the major scale is said to be in a **major key;** music based on the minor scale is said to be in a **minor key.**

Diatonic and Chromatic Harmony

Harmony based on the diatonic scales is called **diatonic harmony**. Diatonic harmony tends to seem "natural" or expected. If tones outside the diatonic scale appear in harmony, the result is called **chromatic harmony.** The term *chromatic* comes from the **chromatic**

scale, which can be found by playing all the white and the black keys on the piano keyboard in succession.

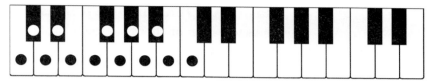

Chromatic scale

Chromatic harmony tends to increase tension in music. When you listen to the concerto by Vivaldi, you will have an opportunity to hear the difference between diatonic and chromatic harmony.

Antonio Vivaldi

Antonio Vivaldi (1678–1741) was born in Venice on 4 March 1678, in the middle of the baroque period of Western European art music (see page 177). He learned to play the violin from his father—who was a professional violinist and opera manager—and quickly developed into a virtuoso performer. Vivaldi was trained for the priesthood and ordained in 1703. Although he soon left the priesthood to pursue a career in music, he was known throughout his life as *il Prete Rosso* (the Red Priest), a reference to his red hair and his religious training. In the same year as his ordination Vivaldi became *maestro di violin* (violin teacher) at the Ospedale della Pietà, one of four girls' orphanages in Venice, and he remained associated with this institution for much of his professional career. It was for its very unusual all-female orchestra that Vivaldi wrote many of his concertos.

In Vivaldi's time, Venice was a decaying city known for revelry and high living. Young travelers from all over Europe came to Venice, ostensibly to study its art and architecture but often to partake of its exuberant nightlife and its many festivals. Venice was then known as the "brothel of Europe"; approximately 66 percent of its citizens remained unmarried—a situation that accounts for the large number of prostitutes and also for the large number of orphans. Historian John Julius Norwich explains this peculiar phenomenon as follows: "The family must continue; and it must continue rich. One son—often the youngest—was therefore required to marry, and to beget enough legitimate heirs to ensure the first of these requirements; the other sons would remain single—or at least [legally] childless—thus, by preventing the dispersal

A *concerto* is a composition, consisting of several movements, for one or more soloists and orchestra. See page 178.

The Ospedale della Pietà

How was it that Vivaldi, one of the most renowned composers of the baroque period, was employed at an orphanage? The Ospedale della Pietà, which was established in 1346–1348 as a foundling hospital for girls, had by the eighteenth century become the premier music school in northern Italy. While the Pietà continued to serve its original purposes (a contemporary source claims that it housed as many as six thousand orphans), the center of activity gradually shifted to the conservatory that was attached to it. Indeed, the reputation of the school was such that a bronze plaque was affixed to the outside wall threatening that fulmination (being struck by lightning) would befall any man who attempted to pass off his legitimate daughter as illegitimate in order to get her accepted in the music school.

The female orphanages were the primary centers of musical activity in Venice. The religious services at the Pietà really amounted to public concerts and were the focal point in the social calendar of the Venetian nobility and foreign visitors as well.

In 1730 the British traveler Edward Wright wrote the following description of concerts at the orphanages: "Every Sunday and holiday there is a performance of music in the chapels of these hospitals, vocal and instrumental, performed by the young women of the place, who are set in a gallery above and, though not professed, are hid from any distinct view of those below by a lattice of ironwork. The organ parts, as well as those of other instruments, are all performed by the young women. . . . Their performance is surprisingly good, and many excellent voices are among them." Of the orchestra of the Pietà, trained by Vivaldi, it was said: "Only there is heard that crisp orchestral

Concert at the Pietà
Scala/Art Resource

attack so falsely boasted of at the Paris Opera."

As these quotations indicate, the young women of the Pietà orchestra were thorough professionals in every way—by no means the amateurs one might expect to hear in an orphans' home. They were a respected attraction in the musical life of the city.

A *sonata* is a composition, usually in several movements, for one or more solo instruments.

of wealth, fulfilling the second." One notable result was the founding of several orphanages, including the Ospedale della Pietà.

Vivaldi's reputation as a composer began to grow throughout Europe with the publication of a set of trio sonatas in 1705 and twelve concertos in 1711. In 1713 an opera by Vivaldi was premiered in Vicenza and he began a career as an opera impresario (producer), which led to considerable travel all over Europe. Even while traveling, Vivaldi continued his association with the Pietà, which contracted with him to supply two concertos every month, sending them by post if necessary. Vivaldi's output as a composer was astounding—about 550 concertos, 90 sonatas, 50 operas, and a considerable amount of sacred vocal music. But Vivaldi was given to exaggeration: he once claimed that he could compose a concerto more quickly than it could be copied, and he claimed to have composed 94 operas, nearly double the actual number.

Vivaldi's personal life has been the subject of much rumor. He traveled with a considerable entourage, including two sisters, Anna and Paolina Giraud. There was considerable speculation that both sisters were his mistresses, a charge that Vivaldi vehemently denied. Anna Giraud was one of Vivaldi's voice students, possibly from the Pietà, since she was sometimes referred to as "Annina della Pietà," and Vivaldi claimed that Paolina was his nurse. What is certain is that Anna appeared in many performances of his operas, even though she was not known as a strong singer.

By 1739 Vivaldi's music was considered old-fashioned in Venice, and he decided to move to Vienna, perhaps hoping that Emperor Charles VI would become his patron. He arrived in Vienna

Antonio Vivaldi
Bettman/Corbis

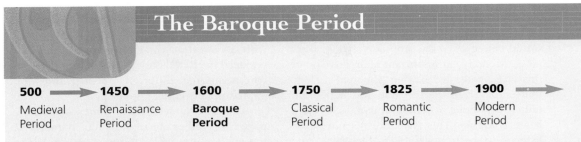

The Baroque Period

500 →	1450 →	1600 →	1750 →	1825 →	1900 →
Medieval Period	Renaissance Period	**Baroque Period**	Classical Period	Romantic Period	Modern Period

Music—indeed all art in the seventeenth century and the first half of the eighteenth century—was opulent, using contrast, grandiose concepts, and ornate designs, and with a definite theatrical quality. This era is known as the **baroque,** a word perhaps derived from the Portuguese *barroco,* an irregularly shaped pearl that was often used in extremely fanciful jewelry. Later writers used *baroque* negatively, to describe art forms that seemed to them to be distorted by an overabundance of unnatural ornamentation. Only in the late nineteenth century did people begin to see the baroque as a period of artistic value.

The great altar of Melk Abbey, Melk, Austria
Scala/Art Resource

The baroque period was a time of great change: there was much political upheaval in Europe, and Europeans established colonies in the Western hemisphere. It was also an era of important historical, scientific, and artistic achievements. The English playwright William Shakespeare (1564–1616) was alive when the baroque period began. Two important scientists were Galileo Galilei (1564–1642), the Italian pioneer of modern physics and telescopic astronomy; and Isaac Newton (1643–1727), the culminating figure of the seventeenth-century scientific revolution, who made significant contributions in every area of science and mathematics.

Music in the Baroque

During the baroque period, instrumental music came of age and, for the first time in Western history, began to rival vocal music in importance. Several new instrumental forms emerged during this time. Musical improvisation was also a common practice, especially in accompaniment (*basso continuo*). Collections of dances, called dance suites, became important concert works (see page 25). The fugue was an important instrumental and choral form. The *concerto grosso*, which featured a group of two or three solo instruments opposing the full orchestra, became quite popular. The solo concerto was similar to the *concerto grosso*, but with a single solo instrument opposing the full orchestra.

As mentioned in Chapter 8, opera was developed during the last decade of the sixteenth century by a group of Florentine noblemen. They developed a new singing style, which they called *stile rappresentativo*, which they believed would better serve the dramatic style of their plays. Monody, an important characteristic of this style, consisted of one principal melody that emphasized the text and was supported only by simple accompaniment, usually a *basso continuo*. This structure permitted the listener to both understand the words and appreciate the expressive beauty of the singing voice.

The ideal sound of baroque music was a melodic line in one voice, usually the highest, with an accompaniment supporting it. This replaced the Renaissance ideal of a number of voices singing different musical lines of approximately equal importance.

The great altar of Melk Abbey, shown on page 177, typifies one of the main characteristics of baroque style: it has a sturdy, clear structure, which is partly obscured by rich, elaborate ornamentation.

sometime in the spring of 1741 to find that Charles VI had just died. Vivaldi was left nearly penniless, old, and ill. On 28 July 1741 this once highly acclaimed violinist and composer died of "internal inflammation"; he was given a pauper's funeral and burial.

A contemporary Venetian memoir noted Vivaldi's passing as follows: "Antonio Vivaldi, the incomparable violin virtuoso, called the Red Priest, was very highly regarded for his compositions and had earned at one time more than 50,000 ducats, but his inordinate extravagance caused him to die poor, in Vienna."

The Music of Vivaldi in Recent Times

Vivaldi, like Venice, fell upon hard times. By the end of his life, Vivaldi's music was nearly forgotten. He was remembered, if at all, as a violin virtuoso who had written some music.

Interestingly, a rising interest in the music of Johann Sebastian Bach (1685–1750) during the nineteenth century brought Vivaldi's name to light again. Bach had transcribed a number of Vivaldi's concertos for keyboard instruments. When these manuscripts were discovered and subsequently published as a part of the complete works of Bach, Vivaldi's name began to be known again. However, it was not until the discovery in the 1920s of what must have been Vivaldi's personal collection of scores that his music began to be performed with its original instrumentation. A collected edition of Vivaldi's instrumental music was begun in 1947, and the number of recordings of his concertos has increased steadily in recent years.

Vivaldi's *Four Seasons*

A **concerto** in the baroque period (1600–1750) was a multimovement work for orchestra and one or more soloists. The usual pattern was three movements: the first and final movements were in a fast tempo, and the middle movement was slower and often fairly short. If several soloists performed as a smaller ensemble, alternat-

The "Early Music" Movement

In Vivaldi's day and throughout much of the history of Western music, audiences were interested primarily in new music—music created for an occasion or commissioned to celebrate a specific event such as a wedding, a funeral, or an annual festival. Vivaldi, for example, spent his entire career creating and performing new music. There was little interest in the music of the past. This gradually began to change in the nineteenth century, when music historians (musicologists) began to collect and study the huge quantities of music stored in libraries and private collections. When this music was performed, however, it was with nineteenth-century instruments in arrangements and adaptations that conformed to current musical taste.

Re-creating "authentic" performances using original instruments is a distinctly twentieth-century phenomenon. Such performances require understanding the performance practices and musical notation of earlier times as well as using authentic or re-created instruments. In England in the early years of the twentieth century, Arnold Dolmetsch (1858–1940) set up a shop to re-create ancient musical instruments such as the lute and the baroque recorder, and to encourage performances of early music on authentic instruments. In 1952 the New York Pro Musica, an ensemble dedicated to performing early music on authentic instruments, began a series of concerts and recordings that led to the "early music" movement. More recently the movement has included ensembles such as His Majesties Sacbutts and Cornetts, the Boston Camerata, the Academy of Ancient Music, and Sequentia. Recordings on authentic instruments, such as the recording we will be listening to, are now available for much of the music of the past. The actual performance practices of earlier times have long since died out, however, and it is an act of invention on the part of modern musicians to attempt to re-create them.

Other musical revivals include the rediscovery of klezmer music (see page 79) and the revitalization of certain Native American traditions (see page 56). Throughout Europe, traditional Celtic music is experiencing a resurgence of popularity, and contemporary Celtic music groups combine authentic folk songs with modern elements.

One might ask why people in the second half of the twentieth century felt the need to reinvent the past and make it part of their musical present. The "early music" movement is certainly an example of an "invented tradition," as defined by cultural anthropologists. Many factors have contributed to this phenomenon, including the desire of modern urbanized people, cut off from any connection to their own "roots," to feel part of some tradition.

ing with a full orchestra, the work was called a ***concerto grosso.*** Approximately 60 of Vivaldi's concertos are concerti grossi; the remaining 425 are for one or two soloists. Most are for one or two violins and orchestra, but Vivaldi also wrote concertos for a wide variety of other instruments, including guitar, piccolo, bassoon, cello, oboe, and flute.

The Four Seasons—without doubt the best known of Vivaldi's many works—is a set of four violin concertos, one for each season, beginning with spring. These works were published together around 1725 as the first four of a series of twelve violin concertos.

Musical Materials of *Spring*

Spring is the first concerto in *The Four Seasons*. It follows a pattern typical of Vivaldi's other concertos: it is divided into three movements—an opening fast movement (**allegro**), a slow movement (**adagio**), and a closing fast movement (allegro). The solo violin part is much more complicated than the orchestral parts, and it can be assumed that Vivaldi himself would have played this solo part. The work has many characteristics that are common to all of baroque music (see *"Basso Continuo,"* below) but also a few that are unique (see "Programmatic References," page 182).

Rhythm in *Spring*. The rhythmic material in the first and third movements of *Spring* is very straightforward and repetitive in the orchestral parts. The solo sections sometimes contain greater rhythmic complexity, but the rhythms always make the meter clear and easy to follow. The first movement is in quadruple-simple meter; the second movement is in triple-simple meter; the third movement is in quadruple-compound meter.

Melody in *Spring*. The melodies for the string instruments in the first and third movements of this concerto are quite idiomatic. They are clearly instrumental rather than vocal in character. A single melodic idea dominates each movement, and this melody is stated at the outset. In the second movement, an extended lyric melody for the solo violin shows off the instrument's ability to produce expressive lines.

Harmony in *Spring*. The harmony in the first and second movements of *Spring* is quite conventional. A few simple chord progressions are repeated over and over, giving the music a sense of great stability. Details of some of the harmonic progressions will be given in the listening guides that follow. The third movement is much more chromatic than the first or second. The contrast between the first two movements and the third movement will give you a good chance to appreciate the effect of these two distinct harmonic styles.

Basso Continuo. One characteristic of nearly all ensemble music of the baroque period is the ***basso continuo*** or **figured bass.** The *basso continuo* was a shorthand method of composing. Instead of writing out a complete keyboard part (in this case, the harpsichord part), the composer supplied only the bass line with some figures—numbers placed above or below bass notes—to indicate the intended harmony. The keyboard performer was expected to improvise a complete part from this shorthand.

An apt comparison might be drawn between this practice and twentieth-century jazz and popular music, in which chord symbols are shown on the sheet music and the keyboard player or guitarist improvises an accompaniment from them. In our recording of *Spring*, the sound of the harpsichord is generally covered in the louder passages, but it is more apparent in softer orchestral passages and in the second movement. The keyboard part is being improvised by the harpsichordist, just as it would have been in Vivaldi's time.

Figured bass in *Spring*

A *sonnet* is a strict poetic form consisting of fourteen lines divided into two major sections of eight and six lines.

Programmatic References. A distinctive characteristic of each concerto in *The Four Seasons* is the programmatic element. **Program music** is music that has an external, nonmusical reference such as a story, a picture, or a poem. In addition to the general titles (the seasons), Vivaldi supplied a sonnet for each work, with lines carefully labeled to relate them to sections of the music. The poems were in all likelihood written by Vivaldi himself, but no author is mentioned. The sonnet for *Spring* is translated below:

First movement:
Spring has come and with it gaiety,
the birds salute it with joyous song,
and the brooks, caressed by Zephyr's breath,
flow meanwhile with sweet murmurings.
The sky is covered with dark clouds,
announced by lightning and thunder.
But when they are silenced, the little birds
return to fill the air with their song.

Second movement:
Then does the meadow, in full flower,
ripple with its leafy plants.
The goatherd dozes, guarded by his faithful dog.

Third movement:
Rejoicing in the pastoral bagpipes,
Nymphs and Shepherds dance in the glade
for the radiant onset of Springtime.

"Sonnet for Spring" by Vivaldi. Source: Antonio Vivaldi, sonnet for *Spring,* trans. H. C. Robbins Landon, in *The Four Seasons,* Sony Classical SK48251, p. 32. Reprinted by permission of H. C. Robbins Landon.

Vivaldi's Orchestra

The violins in an orchestra are divided into two groups: first (I) and second (II).

The instrumentation of this concerto is a string orchestra consisting of violins I and II, violas, violoncellos (cellos), and basses, plus a solo violin part. The cellos and basses are given a single part, as was the custom of the day. Figures are written above the line of the cellos and basses, indicating the presence of the *continuo* instrument, which was specified in the original manuscript as *Organo* (organ), but a harpsichord is used in most modern performances. In the baroque period, the choice of keyboard instruments was usually more a matter of availability than a requirement, and it is certain that Vivaldi himself would have substituted a harpsichord if an organ was not available in the performance space.

Listening to *Spring*

Imagine a Sunday afternoon in Venice with an audience gathering in the chapel of the Ospedale della Pietà to hear the young women perform a new concerto by Vivaldi. The performers are discreetly hidden from view by an ironwork lattice. The nobility of Venice are assembled in their finery, and other distinguished visitors are present as well. There is much moving about and conversation among the guests (see the illustration on page 175). The young women take their places in the gallery, and the performance begins.

The performance you will hear, which is in "early music" style, was recorded at Humbercrest United Church, Toronto, Ontario, on 1 December 1991. Jeanne Lamon is the solo violinist and conductor of Tafelmusik Baroque Orchestra, an internationally renowned chamber orchestra based in Toronto. Its musicians are specialists in historical performance practice. The performers have tuned their instruments to a pitch that Vivaldi may have used, and the instruments are of Vivaldi's time.

LISTENING ACTIVITY

The Four Seasons—Spring (Antonio Vivaldi) [CD 1, tracks 14–16]

Time   Description

First movement [CD 1, track 14]:

0:00   Primary theme of the movement, in a major key and in quadruple-simple meter. Program: "Spring has come." The opening phrase begins on the tonic chord and closes on the dominant chord. The second phrase (0:08) repeats the same harmonic pattern. The third phrase, beginning at 0:15, starts on the tonic and concludes with a dominant-to-tonic progression. The fourth phrase (0:24) repeats the previous phrase.

0:32   Solo violin enters. Notice the melody, which emphasizes some unique characteristics of the violin.

0:46   Solo passage continues. Program: "and with it gaiety, the birds salute it with joyous song."

1:06   One phrase of the primary theme.

1:14   New musical idea expressing the program: "and the brooks, caressed by Zephyr's breath, flow meanwhile with sweet murmurings."

1:38   One phrase of the primary theme.

1:46   New musical idea expressing the program: "The sky is covered with dark clouds, announced by lightning and thunder." A technique called bowed tremolo and some rapid scale passages create this stormy effect.

2:15   Primary theme in a minor key. Compare the sound with the opening statement.

2:24   Chromatic passage expressing the program: "But when they are silenced, the little birds return to fill the air with their song."

2:43   Part of the primary theme. Notice the progression of four chords, which occur every two beats.

2:55   Solo passage for the violin.

3:12   Part of the primary theme closes the movement.

Bowed tremolo is a string technique in which the player draws the bow very rapidly back and forth over a string to produce a rustling, agitated sound.

Second movement [CD 1, track 15]:

Slower tempo typical in baroque

0:00   Very soft background for the solo violin, which enters on the second measure. The meter is triple-simple and the key is minor. Program: "Then does the meadow, in full flower, ripple with its leafy plants. The goatherd dozes, guarded by his faithful dog."

1:09   Second statement of the theme in the solo violin. This time the violinist "decorates" the melody extensively.

Third movement [CD 1, track 16]:

harmony is chromatic

0:00   Pastoral dance in quadruple-compound meter and in a major key. Program: "Rejoicing in the pastoral bagpipes, Nymphs and Shepherds dance in the glade for the radiant onset of Springtime."

0:27   First solo passage for the violin. Notice the chromatic harmony around 0:39.

0:48   Opening theme in a minor key.

1:16   Solo passage for the violin.

1:47   New musical idea for the full ensemble.

2:08   Opening theme in major.

2:15   Passage in chromatic harmony. Notice particularly the chromatic passage around 2:30.

2:38   Solo passage for the violin.

3:01   Repeat of opening theme in a major key brings the work to a close.

Response to the Music

This concerto lets you hear the effect of chord progressions and the difference between chromatic and diatonic harmony. Now listen again without the listening guide and observe your response to the music. How does the harmony help to create your response? How does understanding the harmonic progressions change your experience of the music?

Summary

Tonal harmony is a Western invention that became fully developed by the baroque period (1600–1750). In this chapter we have identified two basic styles of harmony—diatonic and chromatic. Harmonic progressions contribute to the rhythmic life of music and also create cycles of tension and relaxation.

We have studied a single concerto, *Spring*, from *The Four Seasons* by the baroque composer Antonio Vivaldi. We have come to understand the society in which this music came into being and some of the characteristics of baroque music in general, such as the *basso continuo* (figured bass). We have presented the programmatic background of the work and looked at some of the harmony Vivaldi used. This information contributes to your intellectual understanding of the music, and hence to your enjoyment of it.

Applying What You Have Learned

1. Listen again to *Redemption Song* by Bob Marley (page 48; CD 1, track 5). You can hear the harmonic progressions in this song quite clearly. In the first verse, quoted below, syllables of the text are set in **boldface** to indicate each new chord.

    *Old **pirates**, yes, they rob **I**,*
    Sold** I to the **merchant ships
    *   **minutes** after they took **I** from the **bottomless pit**.*
    *But my **hand** was made **strong***

*by the hand **of** the Al**mighty**.
We **for**ward in this generation tri**umphant**ly.*

Source: *Redemption Song*—words and music by Bob Marley. Copyright © 1980 Fifty-Six Hop Road Music Ltd./Odnil Music Ltd./Blue Mountain Music Ltd. All rights controlled by Rykomusic, Inc. (ASCAP). International Copyright Secured. All rights reserved

Copy the rest of the words of *Redemption Song* and underline each syllable where you hear a chord change.

2. Listen to *Oy Abram!* (page 81; CD 1, track 8) and try to hear the chord progressions. (Remember to concentrate on the lower instruments.) In the introduction, the chords change on the first beat of a measure. Most chords are two measures in duration. In the first verse of the song, quoted below, syllables of the text are **boldface** to indicate each new chord. Notice how the band sometimes emphasizes the chord changes with percussion accents.

***Oy,** Abram! Ikh ken on dir nit zayn!*	*Oh, Abram! I can't live without you.*
*Ikh on dir un **du** on mir*	*I without you and you without me,*
***Kenen** mir beyde nit zayn.*	*That could never be.*
Gedenkstu, gedenkstu, bay bem toyer	*Do you remember when we stood at the gate*
***Hostu** mer gezogt a sod in oyer*	*How you whispered a secret in my ear?*
***Oy vey, Riv**kele*	*Oh, Rivkele!*
***Gib** zhe **mir** dayn **pis**kele!*	*Give me your lips! (repeat)*

Verse II of *Oy Abram* lyrics. Source: David Fishman, trans., "Oy, Abram!" in liner notes for the CD titled *Klez: The Klezmer Conservatory Band*, directed by Hankus Netsky, with Judy Bressler performing the vocal; Vanguard VCD-79449. Reprinted with permission of the Klezmer Conservatory Band.

Copy the lyrics of the second verse of *Oy Abram!* and underline each point where the chord changes.

3. As you listen to these works, concentrating on the harmony, can you identify how much of your previous response was due to the harmony? Were you aware of this before now? How do the different styles of harmony affect you? If you have not given much attention to harmony in the past, you can now make a conscious effort to include it in your active listening.

4. In which of the following works is harmony an important element?

La Bohème (CD 1, tracks 12–13)?
Máru-Bihág (CD 1, track 11)?
De sancta Maria (CD 1, track 10)?
Shango (CD 1, track 9)?
Bay a Glezele Mashke (CD 1, track 7)?
Grand Entry Song (CD 1, track 6)?

If harmony is not an important element in one of these works, what is the most important element?

5. When you listen to popular music, how can you listen for harmonic progressions? Which part of the musical texture will be most important to listen to: Melody? Bass? Keyboards and guitars?

6. In *Dolphin Dreams*, the "wordless lullaby" and the chanted "*om*" sound together as "simultaneous pitches." Do you think that this creates harmony? Why or why not?

Important Terms

tonal harmony 171
chord 171
triad 171
harmonic progression 172
harmonic rhythm 172
tonic triad 173
dominant triad 173
diatonic scale 173

major scale 173
minor scale 173
major key 173
minor key 173
diatonic harmony 173
chromatic harmony 173
chromatic scale 173
concerto 178

allegro 180
adagio 180
basso continuo (figured bass) 180
program music 182

Names preceded by "*" have short biographies in Appendix B, p. 346

Musicians and Ensembles Mentioned

*Antonio Vivaldi
Anna Giraud
*Johann Sebastian Bach
Jeanne Lamon
Tafelmusik Baroque Orchestra

Further Listening Resources

Other music by Vivaldi:

Concerto for Diverse Instruments, Amon Ra CD-SAR 47 (period
instruments).
L'Estro armonico, op. 3 (nos. 1–2), L'Oiseau-Lyre 414554-2 OH2
(concerto for violin and orchestra).
Gloria in D, R. 589, DGG (Archiv) 423386-2 AH.

Music that is part of the Celtic revival:

Chieftains, *The Best of the Chieftains,* Sony/Columbia.
Chieftains, *From the Beginning: The Chieftains 1 to 4,* Wea/Atlantic
(box set).
Maggie Sansone, *Mist & Stone,* Maggie's Music, MMCD 106.
Milladoiro, *Castellum honesti: Celtic Music from Spain,* Green
Linnet Records, GLCD 3055.

Harmonizing

🔵 *This Land Is Your Land,* Woody Guthrie

🔵 *Bring Me Little Water Silvy,* Leadbelly: Huddie Ledbetter

Culver Pictures

$\mathcal{W}$e sing our own kind of a harmony, and we ourselves don't know what to call it.

WOODY GUTHRIE
AMERICAN FOLKSINGER AND COMPOSER

189

Harmonizing

When people get together to sing traditional songs, hymns, or ballads, they often create a second or third part to sing along with the melody. This practice of adding extra parts is called **harmonizing.** In the West, harmonizing can be heard in folk music, country-and-western music, and gospel music. Harmonizing can be found in several other musics of the world, including group singing in sub-Saharan Africa and the folk traditions of Hungary and Bulgaria.

A basic strategy for harmonizing is to find a pitch in the tonic chord that fits with the melody note at the beginning of the song and then to sing a melody, beginning on that pitch, parallel to the melody of the song. The singer will continue in this way until the harmonizing part doesn't fit the chord; then he or she will seek another tone that does. A second technique is to create a bass part using the chords that accompany a song. A third technique is to sing the words of the song on one pitch in the chord until the harmony changes and then to move to the nearest pitch in the new chord. Several singers using this third technique and choosing different pitches in the first chord can produce a full harmonic background for a song. This third technique has been used a great deal by barbershop quartets and popular singing groups of the 1960s.

Harmonizers also may create short melodies called **fills** in between phrases of a song. These fills add melodic interest as well as adding to the harmony. Instrumentalists may also harmonize and add melodic fills between phrases.

Most songs that are used as a basis for harmonizing are diatonic (based on the major and minor scales) and have a very simple harmonic background, similar to those discussed in Chapter 9. The harmonies are often played on a guitar or keyboard instrument, providing a supporting framework for the harmonizers. In live concerts, the performers may encourage audience participation, and it is common to hear harmonizing from audience members.

Barbershop quartet
Corbis

Performers may even encourage harmonizing by teaching harmonizing parts to the audience.

In this chapter we will listen to two songs with extensive harmonizing. The first example, *This Land Is Your Land*, is by the American folksinger Woody Guthrie. It has an accompaniment provided by guitars, banjos, and harmonica, as well as by a sizable group of singers. The second song, *Bring Me Little Water Silvy*, is by Leadbelly (Huddie Ledbetter), a Texan who was a country blues singer and guitar player. This arrangement is sung by the *a cappella* ensemble Sweet Honey in the Rock. Both Guthrie and Leadbelly are musical figures from the first half of the twentieth century.

Woody Guthrie

Woodrow Wilson (Woody) Guthrie was born in 1912 in Okemah, Oklahoma. His parents, Charley and Nora Guthrie, named him after Woodrow Wilson, who was elected president that same year.

American Vernacular Music

Vernacular music is a general designation for music other than art music. The term *vernacular* refers to the native language or architectural style of a place. The vernacular music of the United States grew out of a rich blend of musical elements that various ethnic groups brought with them to the "New World" from the early sixteenth century through the nineteenth century. The folk musics of England, Ireland, Wales, and Scotland were early imports to the colonies, along with West African music brought by slaves. The songs of Woody Guthrie, for example, are clearly linked in style to English and Irish folk music that was sung in the hills of Arkansas and Oklahoma, and the country blues of Leadbelly comes out of an African American tradition of southern Mississippi and eastern Texas.

Vernacular music was performed by groups of relatively isolated people until the twentieth century brought recordings, radio, and television. The power of these media to spread all aspects of culture has drawn national attention to various types of vernacular music. For example, the so-called "race records" of the 1920s brought the music of African Americans to the attention of the general public. "Race records" were recordings of African American artists performing for a largely African American audience. In the 1930s, gospel music gained a national audience through radio programs like the popular "Wings Over Jordan," which CBS broadcast nationally. In the 1960s, a commercial style broadly known as country-and-western music became very popular. Television programs such as *Grand Ole Opry, Shindig*, and *Hullabaloo* generated wide interest in this music. As the mass media became the dominant force for the promulgation of music, the music industry arose. This industry is responsible, to a great extent, for determining which vernacular music will be popular at any given time.

Charley Guthrie was an entrepreneur and politician who dealt in real estate. Hard economic times and the burning of the family home left the family in difficult circumstances. Nora Guthrie developed Huntington's chorea, a hereditary nervous system disorder that leaves its victims totally incapacitated. She spent her final years in a mental institution in Oklahoma.

In 1933 Woody married Mary Jennings, the sister of a friend and fellow musician. The couple had three children. When the devastating dust storms of the "dirty thirties" hit in 1935, Woody went on the road to California. The plight of the migrants moved him deeply, setting the course of his life—a crusade for justice and equality and a strong belief in trade unionism as the solution to capitalistic exploitation.

Woody wrote over a thousand songs, many about the difficult lives of migrant workers. While he was in California, he began performing at union organizing events, and this put him on the stage with members of the Communist Party. He was later to sing for Party gatherings, though he never actually joined the Party. These activities would come back to haunt him in the 1950s, during the height of anticommunist hysteria in the United States.

Advertising board for Woody Guthrie's Skid Road Show
The Woody Guthrie Archives and the Woody Guthrie Foundation

Woody moved to New York in the late 1930s, where he met Leadbelly, Pete Seeger, and other musicians who would figure prominently in his career from then on. When he was hired for a CBS radio program in New York called "Back Where I Come From," Woody asked Mary and their children to move there from Oklahoma. After sudden moves to California and the Pacific Northwest, Mary decided she and the children needed a more stable situation. She divorced Woody and moved back to Oklahoma. (Two of their

The Almanac Singers
The Woody Guthrie Archives and the Woody Guthrie Foundation

children were later to die of Huntington's chorea, the disease that killed Woody's mother.)

With the outbreak of World War II, Woody joined Pete Seeger's Almanac Singers, and they toured together in support of left-wing causes. During this time Woody wrote his autobiography, *Bound for Glory*. He also wrote antifascist songs in support of the Allies' war against Hitler. For a time his guitar carried a sign that said: "This Machine Kills Fascists."

In 1942 Woody met a young dancer, Marjorie Greenblatt. They married and had four children, the first of whom died in a fire in their apartment. Arlo Guthrie, the couple's second child, became a well-known singer and songwriter.

In the early 1950s Woody began to show the first signs of Huntington's chorea. As the disease progressed, he could no longer work and gradually withdrew from public life. Woody Guthrie spent his final years in and out of hospitals and died totally incapacitated in 1967. His son Arlo and Pete Seeger have kept alive the creative output of one of America's premier balladeers. In 1988 Woody Guthrie was inducted into the Rock 'n' Roll Hall of Fame.

This Land Is Your Land was written by Woody Guthrie in 1940 as a working-class "national anthem." The original title and the final line of each verse was "God blessed America for me." This has prompted some to view the song as Guthrie's reaction to Irving Berlin's popular patriotic hymn, *God Bless America*.

Two of the original verses were omitted when the song became popular because of their somewhat controversial nature. One verse described a line of hungry people waiting to get assistance from the relief office. Another verse described a high wall dividing private property on one side from the other side "made for you and me."

Guthrie's criticism of private property seems to have extended to his own songs. In 1940 he wrote the following as part of the introduction to the release of some of his other songs on *Dust Bowl Ballads* by RCA Victor:

> These songs here ain't mine. The government says so, and so does Victor Records, but they really ain't, and I hope that when they are played on your loud speakers in these U.S. camps and over Radios, that you say, well, you made 'em up yourself. . . . This bunch of songs is really just one song, cause I used the same notes. Just fixed 'em up a little different, that's all. Same old notes as ever.

Whatever Woody might have believed about owning his songs, his publisher was careful about protecting them through copyright.

LISTENING ACTIVITY

This Land Is Your Land (Woody Guthrie) [CD 1, track 17]

This recording of *This Land Is Your Land* is performed by a large group of musicians, including Pete Seeger, banjo and vocals; Sweet Honey in the Rock (see page 197), vocals; Doc Watson, guitar and vocals; Little Red School House Chorus (a children's chorus); and several other guest instrumentalists on harmonicas, guitars, and vocals.

Time   Description

0:00   Chorus: "This land is your land, this land is my land, from California, to the New York Island, from the Redwood Forest, to the Gulf Stream waters, this land was made for you and me." The leader (Pete Seeger) and Sweet Honey in the Rock start the song. The full texture begins at the words "your land." The harmonica (Charlie Sayles or Phil Wiggins) begins to play fills at every pause in the melody and continues for the rest of the chorus. The guitars and banjo (Doc Watson, John Cephas, and Pete Seeger) begin to provide rhythmic and harmonic background, and the other singers (Sweet Honey in the Rock and the children in the Little Red School House Chorus) begin harmonizing by singing chord tones and moving with the chord progressions.

0:23   First verse: "As I went walking that ribbon of highway, I saw above me that endless skyway, I saw below me the golden valley, this land was made for you and me." Sung by Pete Seeger and one member of Sweet Honey in the Rock. The words here differ from Woody Guthrie's original lyrics. Taking liberties with lyrics is typical of the folk idiom. Singers make a song their own, both in lyrics and in melodic details. Harmonizing returns at "This land was made for you and me."

0:45   Chorus, repeated by full ensemble.

1:08   Instrumental chorus for guitars and banjo.

1:29   Second verse: Solo by Pete Seeger. "Well, I roamed and I rambled, yes, I followed my footsteps, to the sparkling sands of her diamond deserts, but all around me a voice was sounding, this land was made for you and me." Again there are differences in the lyrics and the liberties taken with the melody.

1:50   Chorus, repeated. Full ensemble harmonizing.

2:12   Solo chorus by harmonica with background on guitars and banjo. (Pete Seeger makes comments.)

2:32   Third verse: Solo by Pete Seeger. "Well, the sun is shining, I was strolling, and the wheat fields waving, and the dust clouds rolling, and the fog was lifting, and a voice was chanting, saying This land was made for you and me." A member of Sweet Honey in the Rock joins at "and the fog was lifting," and the full ensemble enters harmonizing at "This land was made . . ." There are major differences in the lyrics and melody from the published version. Pete Seeger is actually singing a harmonizing line at the beginning of the verse. We supply the original melody in our minds.

2:53   Chorus, repeated. Pete Seeger begins harmonizing over the melody at this point.

3:14   Final chorus. Note Pete Seeger harmonizing over the melody.

Leadbelly (Huddie Ledbetter)

In the 1930s the Library of Congress sent folklorists out to record blues and jazz "in the field." Huddie Ledbetter (better known as "Leadbelly"), who later became one of the most popular American blues singers, was the first blues singer to record for the Archives of Folk Song. He provided a vital link between "the rich tradition of nineteenth-century black southern folk music and the age of radio and television."

Huddie Ledbetter was born around 1888 in a rural area of Louisiana near Shreveport. His parents were farmers, and he worked the cotton farms with his father. He learned to play several instruments early in life and began a career as a part-time musician, playing and singing in bars and bordellos in the notorious Fannin Street section of Shreveport. In 1915, while he was serving a thirty-day prison term for carrying a concealed weapon, he escaped from a chain gang. Moving with his wife to Texas, he took an assumed name—Walter Boyd.

In 1918, under his new name, Ledbetter was convicted of murder and began serving a twenty-year term at the Shaw State Prison Farm, better known as "Sugarland." It was at Sugarland that he acquired the name Leadbelly. In 1925 the governor of Texas, Pat Neff, pardoned Leadbelly after he had composed a ballad as a plea for mercy and sang it for the governor during a visit to the prison—or so the legend goes. In fact, Ledbetter was due for early release for good behavior. During his apprenticeship in Fannin Street and his prison sentence in Sugarland, Leadbelly collected and composed many songs and ballads, adopting the twelve-string guitar as his instrument of preference. He learned to sing country blues and was much in demand as a blues singer.

In 1933 John A. Lomax, collector of American folk songs for the Library of Congress, discovered Leadbelly in Louisiana, where he had returned after his pardon from prison. Lomax brought Leadbelly to the attention of a wider public through a series of recordings and appearances in New York and elsewhere. Leadbelly quickly became a widely known blues singer. He recorded for several national record labels, sang on network radio, and toured all over the country.

During his career he was associated with a number of famous blues and folk singers, including Blind Lemon Jefferson, Woody Guth-

Leadbelly

Weegee (Arthur Fellig), ICP, Hulton Getty/Liaison

rie, and Pete Seeger. Leadbelly died in 1949 of amyotrophic lateral sclerosis ("Lou Gehrig's disease") in New York City, leaving a legacy of hundreds of songs. His best-known song, "Goodnight Irene," sold over two million copies just six months after his death, making Hit Parade history.

In this chapter, we will be listening to Sweet Honey in the Rock's harmonizing version of Leadbelly's song *Bring Me Little Water Silvy*.

Sweet Honey in the Rock

Sweet Honey in the Rock, a Grammy-Award-winning African American female vocal ensemble, has been an important force in American music for over twenty-five years. Expanding from their roots in the gospel music of the American South, Sweet Honey in the Rock has grown to incorporate elements of traditional African music. Never afraid to speak out on controversial topics, the group has produced music dealing with the **AIDS** crisis, domestic violence against women, and inhumanity and injustice in all forms. The ensemble's name came from a song based on a religious parable about a promised land so rich that when rocks were cracked open, honey flowed from inside.

Sweet Honey in the Rock
Michael Ochs Archives

Members of the group have composed many of the works they perform. The group occasionally uses the accompaniment of African percussion instruments. This *a cappella* (unaccompanied) style of singing has roots in the sacred vocal harmony quartets that have been popular in African American churches in the South for over one hundred years. Sweet Honey in the Rock's arrangement of *Bring Me Little Water Silvy* is typical of this style.

Bernice Johnson Reagon, leader of Sweet Honey in the Rock, offers the following insight into the workings of a harmonizing group: "For a singer in Sweet Honey, knowing the composition and the harmony system allows her flexibility—if the key of a song throws her line too low or too high, she can restructure her lines for comfort in delivery. This is possible only if you know the entire composition, a lot more than your part."

LISTENING ACTIVITY

Bring Me Little Water Silvy (Ledbetter) [CD 1, track 18]

Bring Me Little Water Silvy is a work song (see page 17). Farmworkers in the fields would call out for water to quench their thirst in the hot Louisiana summer. Perhaps Leadbelly's own introduction says it best: "July and August is hot and this man's wife—he call her Sylvy (sic)—and the only way he gets his cool water, he got to call Silvy to get his water down there 'cause he's burnin' down." Although Silvy may have been a real woman, the name might also be a symbol for respite, relief, and comfort. The use of a name to stand for (or signify) a more abstract concept is not unusual in African American music.

Time   **Description**

0:00   First statement of chorus: "Bring me little water, Silvy, Bring me little water now. Bring me little water, Silvy, Every li'l once in a while." The opening line begins with only the melody and splits into harmonizing with the word "water." Sweet Honey in the Rock harmonizers are singing chord tones and moving with the harmonic progressions (the third technique discussed above).

0:15   First verse: "Don't you see me comin', Don't you see me now, Don't you see me comin', Every li'l once in a while?" A bass part is now added.

0:30   Chorus restated.

0:45   Second verse: "Bring it in a bucket, Silvy, Bring it in a bucket now, Bring it in a bucket, Silvy, Every li'l once in a while."

1:00   Chorus restated.

1:16   Third verse of the song: "See me come a-runnin', See me comin' now, See me come a-runnin', Every li'l once in a while." Solo by one of the singers. The other singers produce a harmonic background by humming in harmony. Notice that the original melody is now replaced by a new melody that would fit as a harmonizing part with the original melody. The original melody is present only in our minds, but this harmonizing part fits with it perfectly. Full ensemble returns for the final line of this verse.

1:30   Fourth verse of the song: "Silvy come a-runnin', Silvy comin' now, Silvy come a-runnin', Every li'l once in a while." Similar treatment to the third verse.

1:45   Chorus restated.

Source: Words and music by Huddie Ledbetter. Collected and adapted by John A. Lomax and Alan Lomax. TRO © Copyright 1936 (Renewed) Folkways Music Publishers, Inc., New York, NY. Used by permission.

The melody of *Bring Me Little Water Silvy* as sung by Sweet Honey in the Rock differs slightly from the melody transcribed from Leadbelly's recordings. In the folk tradition, as we have noted earlier, music is not static. Every singer brings his or her own creativity to bear on a song, and variations are to be expected. Indeed, it is likely that Leadbelly himself sang the song differently from performance to performance.

Response to the Music

Does knowing their social and political background increase or decrease your enjoyment of these two songs? What are your physical, emotional, cognitive, and spiritual responses to these songs? Did you sing along with them? Did you appreciate Pete Seeger's comments to the other performers? This informality is very much a part of the folk music genre.

Summary

In this chapter we have listened to two examples of harmonizing, a technique for creating melodic lines that harmonize a melody. This technique is common in folk singing, gospel, and country-and-western music. We have learned about two of America's most famous folk artists, Leadbelly and Woody Guthrie, and about a very successful modern African American vocal ensemble. We have seen how folk artists take many liberties with both lyrics and melody to make a song their own.

Applying What You Have Learned

1. Listen to another example of folk, gospel, or country-and-western music and make a listening guide like those in this chapter. Do you find that you listen more actively to the music after this exercise?

2. The last decade of the twentieth century saw a revival of the styles and songs of *a cappella* pop groups similar to those of the 1950s and 1960s. Do you think the harmonies these groups sang were written out or improvised? Why?

3. Listen again to *Bay a Glezele Mashke* (page 80; CD 1, track 7). Do you think the harmony parts were written out or created through harmonizing? Why?

4. Bernice Johnson Reagon stated that to harmonize well "is possible only if you know the entire composition, a lot more than your part." Do you agree with her? Why or why not?

5. We noted that for the songs in this chapter, the melody varies slightly compared with the printed music and recordings by the composers themselves. Cite an example of music you know in which similar alterations of an original song occur.

6. Woody Guthrie's belief in the public ownership of all property made it easy for him to appropriate other people's melodies for his own use. He did not believe in copyright. Compare his attitude with that of rap and hip-hop recording artists. Also, refer back to the discussion of the *Grand Entry Song* in Chapter 3. Both folk music and powwow music have traditionally been transmitted orally rather than through written texts. How might this means of transmission influence both Pete Gahbow's and Woody Guthrie's views about copyright?

7. Listen to a recording of the South African group Ladysmith Black Mambazo and a recording of the Bulgarian Women's Chorus (see Further Listening Resources). Compare their harmonizing with that of Sweet Honey in the Rock. How are they similar and how are they different?

Important Terms

harmonizing 190   fills 190   *a cappella* 197

Names preceded by
"*" have short
biographies in
Appendix B, p. 346

Musicians and Ensembles Mentioned

*Woody Guthrie
*Leadbelly (Huddie Ledbetter)
*Sweet Honey in the Rock
*Pete Seeger
*Almanac Singers
Arlo Guthrie
Doc Watson
Little Red School House Chorus
*Blind Lemon Jefferson
*Bernice Johnson Reagon

Further Listening Resources

Recordings of Leadbelly in performance:

Gwine Dig a Hole to Put the Devil In (PGD/Rounder). Contains *Governor Pat Neff,* which describes Leadbelly's musical plea for a pardon.
Bourgeois Blues (Collectables Records). Contains Leadbelly's original recording of *Bring Me Little Water Silvy.*

Recordings of Woody Guthrie in performance:

Library of Congress Recordings (PGD/Rounder). Original recordings made by Alan Lomax for the Library of Congress.
This Land Is Your Land (PGD/Rounder). A mixture of original Guthrie recordings along with tracks by Arlo Guthrie and other later artists.

Recordings by Sweet Honey in the Rock:

Twenty Five (RYKO). An enhanced CD with files that can be accessed using a CD-ROM drive. Also contains a wonderful *a cappella* arrangement of Bob Marley's *Redemption Song.* Not to be missed.
Selections (Flying Fish). A two-disc retrospective of earlier recordings by the group.

Recording by Pete Seeger:

Greatest Hits (SONY Music). A selection of Seeger's best-known songs, including *Little Boxes* and *Turn! Turn! Turn!*

International harmonizing groups:

Best of Ladysmith Black Mambazo (Shanachie).
Le Mystère Des Voix Bulgares (Wea/Atlantic/Nonesuch).

Dynamics,

Timbre, and Texture in Music

W*e're working with dynamics now. We've spent two years with loud, and we've spent six months with deafening.*

*JERRY GARCIA (1942–1995)
LEADER OF THE GRATEFUL DEAD

I n Chapters 3–10 we considered three important musical elements: rhythm, melody, and harmony. In this part of the book,
we introduce three more musical elements—dynamics, timbre
(pronounced "TAM-burr"), and texture. These three elements main-
ly determine how music sounds to our ears.

The term dynamics refers to the relative loudness of various
sounds in music. There are several common dynamic patterns in
music. Dynamics may be constant and unchanging, may gradually
increase and decrease, or may change suddenly.

If two instruments—for example, a piano and a guitar—play the
same pitch at the same dynamic level, you can tell quite easily which
instrument is playing. The quality of sound that distinguishes the two
instruments is called timbre or tone color. We normally describe timbre using terms like *bright, dark, thin, mellow,* or *brilliant.*

The term texture refers to the way the melodic, rhythmic, and
harmonic materials are woven together in a composition. At one
moment you may hear a single melodic line; at another moment, you
may hear several melodies combined. Sometimes the music seems to
be organized into large blocks of sound; at other times it is only a
melody with a simple accompaniment. Texture is an important element of music, as will become even clearer in Part VI, when we begin
discussing musical form.

Platt Collection/Archive Photos

CHAPTER 11   A Western Ensemble: The Symphony Orchestra **206**
              The Young Person's Guide to the Orchestra, Benjamin Britten

CHAPTER 12   A Non-Western Ensemble: The Balinese *Gamelan* **227**
              Gending Petegak, Sekehe Gender Bharata Muni, Sading

CHAPTER 13   In the Recording Studio **240**
              Animal Crackers, Matt Ryan

A Western Ensemble: The Symphony Orchestra

The Young Person's Guide to the Orchestra, Benjamin Britten

Steve Kagan/Gamma Liaison

It is cruel, you know, that music should be so beautiful. It has the beauty of loneliness & pain; of strength & freedom. The beauty of disappointment & never-satisfied love. The cruel beauty of nature, & the everlasting beauty of monotony.

BENJAMIN BRITTEN
(LETTER, 29 JUNE 1937)

Ensembles

Whether its function is ceremonial, utilitarian, or purely aesthetic, music is often made by groups of people, either for each other or for an audience. Making music together is an important part of the social experience of people around the world. Apart from the enjoyment that people can have by playing music together, there are musical reasons for ensemble performance. Since ensembles can have a variety of instruments, the resulting music can be richer in timbre and tonal variety. Also, an ensemble can produce more varied sounds than a single performer. Consider, for example, what would happen if the marching band at a football game was replaced by a single performer. Even with digital technology and electronic amplification, a single performer could hardly produce anything like the musical effect of several hundred musicians playing a variety of instruments.

Small Ensembles

Small ensembles are generally defined as having no more than nine performers. Musical groups of this size are quite common throughout the world. In the West, small ensembles consisting of approximately two to nine players are often named for the number of performers:

Ensemble	Number of performers
Duo	2
Trio	3
Quartet	4
Quintet	5
Sextet	6
Septet	7
Octet	8
Nonet	9

Large Ensembles

A band is a large instrumental ensemble, and a chorus is a large vocal ensemble.

Large ensembles—those with more than nine performers—are found in many cultures. A very large ensemble may have several hundred musicians. In the West, **bands** and **choruses** of several hundred performers are not uncommon. Some large ensembles, like the symphony orchestra, have fairly standard instrumentation.

The Symphony Orchestra

The symphony orchestra is a uniquely European ensemble. Although other cultures have similar ensembles, they do not consist of Western instruments. However, symphony orchestras have been

Ensembles Around the World

The standard ensemble in northern and southern Indian classical music is a trio consisting of a melodic instrument (*sitar*, *sarod*, violin, etc.), a drone instrument (normally the *tambura*), and a percussion instrument (normally the *tabla*). (See Chapter 7, pages 130–131.) The Indonesian *gender wayang* is an ensemble consisting of two or four similar instruments called *gender* (see Chapter 12, page 234). The *koto* ensemble in Japan usually consists of two to six *kotos*.

Flute and *Koto* Ensemble
Corbis

The Dave Brubeck Quartet
Culver Pictures

A trio or quartet, consisting of piano, bass, drums, and an optional solo instrument, is a standard small ensemble in jazz.

The Grateful Dead
Matthew Mendelsohn/Corbis

Country music band
Dean Abramson/Stock Boston

The standard ensembles for popular music in the West are bands of three to seven performers. The country-and-western band, the rhythm-and-blues band, and the rock band are examples.

Chinese classical orchestra
Dean Conger/Corbis

Turkish military band
Douglas Miller/Hulton Getty/Liaison

Large ensembles are less common worldwide than smaller ensembles. The Chinese classical orchestra is one example of a larger ensemble, as is the Western symphony orchestra.

The Turkish military band has seven different wind and percussion instruments. An interesting feature of this ensemble is a preference for having nine of each different instrument. This use of groups of nine is related to the fact that nine was considered a lucky number in Turkey.

imported from Western Europe into many other regions of the world.

The symphony orchestra developed gradually during the baroque period (1600–1750; see page 177) and became a standard ensemble during the classical period (1750–1825; see page 284). Later, the ensemble grew considerably in size, and the modern symphony orchestra has about one hundred players. This orchestra consists of four large families of instruments: **strings, woodwinds, brass,** and **percussion.**

String Section

The string family consists of the **violin, viola, violoncello (cello),** and **double bass (string bass).** It developed in Europe during the seventeenth century. The antecedents of these string instruments include the medieval fiddle and the *rebec*. The violin has the highest pitch; the viola is somewhat lower; the cello is below the viola; and the double bass is lowest. In a symphony orchestra, the strings are the most numerous instruments. There may be twenty or more violinists, divided into two groups called the first and second violins.

There may also be ten viola players, ten cellos, and eight double basses.

Modern orchestral strings are played with a **bow** made of horse-hair stretched over a slightly curved stick. Over the centuries, bows

Symphony Orchestra, Vienna, 1997
Reuters/Dieter Nagl/Archive Photos

String section of a symphony orchestra
Steve Kagan

developed from simple archery-type bows to their present form, which they reached in the late eighteenth century. Fine string instruments are highly valued. The masterpieces of the violinmakers Andrea Guarneri (ca. 1626–1698) and Antonio Stradivari (1644–1737), for example, have never been surpassed. Violinists dream of being able to play one of these instruments, and they bring fabulous prices whenever they are sold.

Woodwind Section

Woodwind section of the orchestra
Stephanie Mare/Corbis

The woodwind family consists of a number of instruments differing in design and in playing techniques. The name **woodwinds** was chosen when nearly all of these instruments were actually made of wood; but many modern instruments, such as the flute and saxophone, are made of metal, so the term is no longer accurate. However, tradition dies hard, and the name *woodwinds* persists.

In the modern symphony orchestra the standard woodwind section consists of two or three **flutes,** two or three **oboes,** two or three **clarinets,** and two or three **bassoons.** Additional instruments such as the **piccolo, English horn, bass clarinet,** and **contrabassoon** sometimes augment this section. On rare occasions, the **saxophone** is also added to the section.

Brass Section

Trumpet player
Richard Pasley/Stock Boston

The instruments of the **brass** section are so named because they are usually made of brass. These instruments are capable of louder sounds than the strings or woodwinds. Only the percussion section can overpower the brasses.

Brasses provide much of the weight in orchestral climaxes, but they are also capable of playing soft and lyrical melodies. In the modern symphony orchestra the standard brass section consists of two or three **trumpets,** four or five **horns,** two or three **trombones,** and one **tuba.**

Percussion Section

Percussion section of the orchestra
Archive Photos

The **percussion** family includes thousands of instruments, and percussion performance techniques include almost every imaginable kind of tone production. Percussion instruments can be classified in two general groups: those of **definite pitch** and those of **indefinite pitch.** Definite-pitch percussion instruments are sometimes referred to as "melodic" because they are normally used for melody. Indefinite-pitch percussion instruments are used primarily for rhythmic effects, but they are also sometimes used to express simple melodic ideas.

Modern symphony orchestras use a variety of pitched and indefinite-pitch percussion instruments. Pitched instruments include **timpani, xylophone, marimba,** and **chimes.** The most prevalent indefinite-pitch instruments are **snare drum (side drum), tenor drum (field drum), bass drum, tambourine, cymbals, triangle, tam-tam, temple blocks,** and **woodblock.** A modern symphony orchestra has three or four percussionists who each play a variety of percussion instruments and a timpanist who plays only the timpani.

We will learn to identify the sounds of the instruments in the symphony orchestra by listening to *The Young Person's Guide to the Orchestra,* by Benjamin Britten.

Benjamin Britten

Edward Benjamin Britten was born in 1913 at Lowestoft, Suffolk, England. When he died in 1976 he was the most famous composer in the British Isles, the leading figure in the annual Aldeburgh Music Festival, and a conductor and pianist of world renown.

Britten's talents were recognized early by his mother, who brought him to the attention of Frank Bridge, a well-known British composer. When Britten was only fourteen, Bridge took him as a student. Britten's ability as a composer flowered under Bridge's guidance, and by 1932 his career was firmly launched. The next decade saw a flood of songs and orchestral, choral, and chamber music, which established Britten as an important musical figure in England and throughout the world.

Britten's music become quite popular, partly because of its accessibility. In a time when many composers were writing music that was incomprehensible to a general audience, Britten continued to produce music that was firmly in the tradition of earlier times.

The peak of Britten's creative output came during World War II, when England was under fairly constant air attack. Notable among the works of this time were *Sinfonia da Requiem* (1940); *Ceremony of Carols* (1942); *Serenade for Tenor, Horn, and Strings* (1943); *Festival Te Deum* (1944); and two operas, *Paul Bunyan* (1941) and *Peter Grimes* (1945). The *Sinfonia da Requiem* and *Paul Bunyan* were written in the United States, where Britten lived from 1939 through 1941.

Peter Grimes
Alex Bender/Hulton Getty Picture Library

In addition to concert music and operas, Britten composed music for the theater and films. He composed *The Young Person's Guide to the Orchestra* for the film *The Instruments of the Orchestra* (1945).

In 1948 the Aldeburgh Festival was established in the small Suffolk town that Britten called home. He devoted the rest of his life to the festival, which premiered many of his works. During these years Britten composed a number of operas including *The Little Sweep* (1949), *Billy Budd* (1951), *Gloriana* (1953), *The Turn of the Screw* (1954), *Noye's Fludde* (1958), *A Midsummer Night's Dream* (1960), *Owen Wingrave* (1971), and *Death in Venice* (1973). Britten served the festival as composer, conductor, pianist, and organizer, a huge task that he performed with vigor until 1973, when ill health forced him into semiretirement. He continued to compose until his death in 1976. Since Britten's death, Aldeburgh has become the home of the Britten-Pears Library and Archives and the Britten-Pears School for Advanced Musical Studies—important tributes to the genius of England's premiere composer in this, and perhaps any other, century.

Peter Pears was Britten's longtime partner and the leading tenor in many of his operas.

The Young Person's Guide to the Orchestra

The Young Person's Guide to the Orchestra, subtitled *Variations and a Fugue on a Theme of Purcell,* op. 34, is perhaps the most popular and most immediately appealing of Benjamin Britten's instrumental compositions. The British Ministry of Education commissioned the work in 1945 for a documentary film called *The Instruments of*

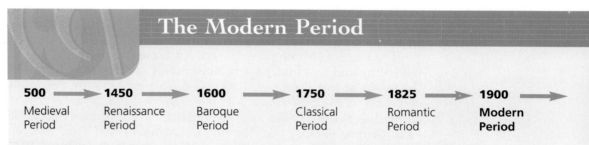

The Modern Period

500 ➡	1450 ➡	1600 ➡	1750 ➡	1825 ➡	1900 ➡
Medieval Period	Renaissance Period	Baroque Period	Classical Period	Romantic Period	**Modern Period**

Throughout the twentieth century, technological innovation brought changes unparalleled in any previous era. Technology has resulted in mass production of goods as well as in rapid global communication and travel. It has also resulted in weapons of mass destruction. In the first half of the century the world saw two global wars, World War I (1914–1918) and World War II (1939–1945). These global conflicts intensely affected all aspects of life. Other political, economic, and cultural changes further affected the order of world society. The Bolshevik Revolution of 1917 marked the emergence of communism and of Russia as a world power, along with China and Japan. The rise of independent states, particularly in Africa, India, and southeast Asia, followed the decline of European colonialism.

Composers and performers—indeed, all artists—struggled to find ways to express the alienation of the individual resulting from the impersonality of the "machine age" and from global political upheaval. Science seemed to change from a tool for improving the quality of life into something that existed for its own sake

and progressed unalterably on its own course. Twentieth-century artists were perplexed and ambivalent about this new era. They took advantage of developing materials and technologies, but they also wrestled with how best to represent their impact on the human condition.

Romantic, nationalistic, and impressionistic musical styles all coexisted in Europe by the beginning of the twentieth century. For many composers, however, the formal procedures for manipulating sound, melody, harmony, rhythm, and form—procedures established and perfected from 1600 to 1900—seemed inadequate to express the complexities of the machine age. These composers turned to extremes in texture and timbre as they searched for more innovative sonorities. Their explorations resulted in more angular melodies, harsher dissonances, irregular rhythms, and asymmetrical forms, which often made extreme technical demands on players and singers. Other artists turned away from complexity and technical demands, choosing instead light or trivial styles or abstraction to reflect disorientation and depersonalization.

The architect Frank Lloyd Wright developed his Prairie Style in the first decade of the twentieth century. He believed that buildings should blend into their natural surroundings and should be constructed of natural materials. Wright showed that modern materials and techniques, which many people considered cold and impersonal, could produce architecture integrated into nature.

Exterior of Falling Water (1936–1939) by Frank Lloyd Wright

Richard A. Cooke/Corbis

Today we live in a world where nuclear weapons of mass destruction exist alongside another, more insidious method of destruction: ecological disaster. We live in an era of "virtual reality," where computer interfaces have partially replaced face-to-face interactions. These technological revolutions have radically changed the way we live, including the way we make, listen to, and purchase music. Prospective buyers can now "dial up" the World Wide Web, listen to short musical excerpts, and buy music on-line. Some enterprising musicians are making their music available only on-line. Computer programs have also revolutionized the way people make music. Relatively untrained people can use computer software to compose, record, and play back music.

the Orchestra. Britten dedicated this work to four of his young friends, "for their edification and entertainment."

Since its premiere, *The Young Person's Guide to the Orchestra* has entertained and educated countless adults and children in many settings. The music makes its points so clearly and attractively that words are unnecessary, and most concert performances are now done without the narrative. The work has also been used at least three times as the score for a ballet. The most prominent setting was *Fanfare,* a ballet choreographed by Jerome Robbins for a gala honoring the coronation of Queen Elizabeth II in 1953.

It was obviously no coincidence that Britten chose a theme by England's most esteemed opera composer as the basis for *The Young Person's Guide to the Orchestra.* Using a theme from a work by Henry Purcell enabled Britten to introduce his audience to one of the most important and beloved figures in English music history as well as to the instruments of the orchestra.

The *Young Person's Guide* is a showcase of **orchestration:** the art of writing for the instruments of the orchestra singly and in various combinations. During this work, the symphony orchestra is taken apart and put back together twice, first in families of similar instruments and then as individual types of instruments.

Henry Purcell

Henry Purcell (1659–1695) is considered one of the greatest composers of the baroque period and among the finest of all English composers. His illustrious musical career included posts as keeper of the king's keyboard and wind instruments, organist at Westminster Abbey, and organist of the Chapel Royal. Purcell, like Benjamin Britten 300 years later, was musically precocious. He began his musical life as a chorister at the Chapel Royal, and Playford's 1667 publication *The Musical Companion* includes a three-part song, *Sweet tyranness*, written by the eight-year-old Purcell.

Henry Purcell
Culver Pictures

Many of London's theaters, which had been closed in 1642 by the Puritans, re-opened following the restoration of the monarchy in 1660 (this was the reign of Charles II), and plays became popular once again. Purcell, carrying on a tradition that encouraged well-known church musicians to provide lighter music for plays and operas, contributed incidental music to more than forty plays between 1690 and 1695.

Incidental music was usually in the form of overtures, entr'acts, dances, and songs, and Purcell provided incidental music of this sort for *Abdelazar, or The Moor's Revenge*, a play by Aphra Behn produced in 1695. Benjamin Britten chose the rondeau from this work by Purcell as the principal theme for *The Young Person's Guide to the Orchestra*. A *rondeau* is a baroque composition in rondo form (see page 281).

Benjamin Britten has often been compared to Purcell, and there are a number of interesting parallels: both Britten and Purcell showed musical gifts at an early age, both composed operas, and both wrote incidental music (Britten for films, Purcell for the stage). Britten's interest in Purcell continued throughout his life, and he edited a number of Purcell's dramatic and instrumental works.

In the opening portion of the work, Britten divides the orchestral forces into the four families—strings, woodwinds, brass, and percussion. After the families of the symphony orchestra are introduced, individual types of instruments are presented in a series of variations on the theme. Having systematically taken the orchestra apart into its constituent instruments, Britten now puts it back together, using a second theme. The instruments enter one by one, building to the full orchestra. At this point the lower brasses again proclaim Purcell's theme, while the strings and woodwinds continue the second theme. The work concludes in a blaze of orchestral color and percussive accents.

Benjamin Britten rehearses with the English Chamber Orchestra at the Elizabeth Hall, 1967
Express Newspapers/2367/Archive Photos

LISTENING ACTIVITY

The Young Person's Guide to the Orchestra
(Benjamin Britten) [CD 2, track 1]

In this listening guide (the first of two for this work), concentrate on listening to and remembering the timbres of the various instruments in the orchestra. This performance was recorded in 1964 by the London Symphony Orchestra, with Britten conducting.

Time	Musical Event
00:00	Purcell theme stated by the full symphony orchestra.
00:24	Theme stated by the woodwind section.
00:46	Theme stated by the brass section.
01:06	Theme stated by the full string section.
01:23	Theme stated by the percussion section, led by the timpani.

01:38	Theme repeated by the full orchestra.
01:58	Variation for piccolo and two flutes with harp accompaniment.
02:32	Variation for two oboes accompanied by strings.
03:33	Variation for two clarinets accompanied by tuba.
04:10	Variation for two bassoons accompanied by strings.
05:03	Variation for violins accompanied by brass.
05:39	Variation for violas accompanied by woodwinds and brass.
06:39	Variation for cellos accompanied by woodwinds and strings.
07:53	Variation for double basses accompanied by woodwinds and tambourine.
08:54	Variation for harp accompanied by percussion and strings.
09:41	Variation for four horns with harp and string accompaniment.
10:28	Variation for two trumpets accompanied by snare drum and strings.
10:59	Variation for three trombones, and, later, tuba (11:13) accompanied by woodwinds.
12:00	Variation for percussion accompanied by strings.
13:44	Piccolo enters with second theme.
13:50	Flutes enter.
13:59	Oboes enter.
14:04	Clarinets enter.
14:15	Bassoons enter.
14:25	Violins enter.
14:35	Violas enter.
14:41	Violoncellos enter.
14:45	Double basses enter.
14:57	Harp enters.
15:10	Horns enter.

15:14	Trumpets enter.
15:24	Trombones and tuba enter.
15:29	Percussion enters.
15:40	First theme returns—first in the low brass, then in the trumpet (15:53), while the woodwinds and strings continue the second theme.
16:10	Burst of brilliant orchestral color alternating with intense percussion closes the work.

Textures in *The Young Person's Guide to the Orchestra*

The Young Person's Guide to the Orchestra provides a good opportunity to learn about musical texture. In Chaper 6 (page 100) you learned about **monophonic texture,** which consists of a single melody played or sung by one or more musicians.

Melody

Monophonic texture

Now we will introduce additional textures and explore how they are used in *The Young Person's Guide to the Orchestra*.

Polyphonic Texture. In **polyphonic texture,** more than one melody can be heard at the same time. Polyphonic textures may consist of only two melodies or as many as a dozen. Of course, it becomes more and more difficult to follow each melody if others are competing for your attention, as you may have discovered while listening to *La Bohème*. If you have sung a **round** with a group of friends, you have been singing in polyphonic texture.

The melodic lines in polyphonic texture are said to be in **counterpoint** with each other. This is a reference to the Latin *punctus contra punctum* (note against note), which was how polyphonic textures were described in early Western music.

In *The Young Person's Guide to the Orchestra* there is an extended section in polyphonic texture from 13:50 until after 15:29. The overlapping entries of the instruments playing the second theme

> A *round* is a simple musical composition, in which different singers enter singing the same melody at different times.

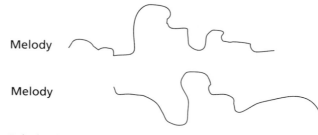

Melody

Melody

Polyphonic texture

can be clearly heard against other melodic lines in the instruments that are already playing.

Homophonic Texture. Perhaps the texture most familiar to you is **homophonic texture,** which consists of a melody and an accompaniment. Most popular music is homophonic: a melody is played or sung and an instrumental ensemble provides an accompaniment. In homophonic texture, the melody is clearly the most important element; in fact, melody may be the only part you have been aware of. However, the accompaniment is important in providing a harmonic and rhythmic setting for the melody. If the accompaniment were suddenly omitted, you would be aware of how much it had been contributing to the overall effect of the music.

Melody

Accompaniment

Homophonic texture

In *The Young Person's Guide to the Orchestra* the sections introducing the individual instruments (from 1:58 until around 12:00) provide many examples of homophonic texture. Sometimes two instruments are introduced (the two oboes, for instance), and in those cases the homophonic texture is expanded—that is, there are two melodies, one for each of the instruments, above the accompaniment. These two melodies are in counterpoint with each other. Combinations of homophonic and polyphonic texture are common in music.

Homorhythmic Texture. A homorhythmic texture consists of several parts with the same or very similar rhythm. A typical example is a church hymn, which has soprano, alto, tenor, and bass parts in the same rhythm. Homorhythmic textures are also referred to as *hymn style, chordal homophony, chordal texture,* and *familiar style.* In homorhythmic textures the soprano part is often the most important and is considered the melody. The other parts are considered to be the accompaniment.

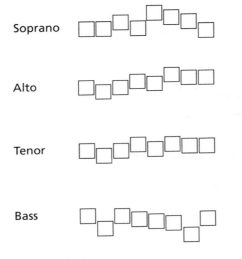

Homorhythmic texture

The opening section of *The Young Person's Guide to the Orchestra* is in homorhythmic texture. You can hear that all the instruments tend to play together, in hymn style, except for moments of activity in the melody.

Dynamics in *The Young Person's Guide to the Orchestra*

The Young Person's Guide to the Orchestra provides a good opportunity to become aware of how dynamic patterns contribute to the effect of a piece of music. The loudest point in the piece is near the end, when the full orchestra and all the percussion instruments are playing. The softest points come between the sections of the work. These soft passages are intended as a background to the narrative, if it is present. Between these two extremes you find a wide variety of dynamic patterns. For example, in the section that introduces each of the instruments (1:58 until after 12:00) there are many contrasts in dynamics. The variation for piccolo and flutes is at a medium dynamic level, whereas the variation for oboe begins softly and then each phrase builds in intensity. The variations for the clarinets and for the bassoons are at a medium dynamic level with louder moments. In contrast, the variation for violins is at a much higher dynamic level; the viola variation, on the other hand, is quite soft.

A very different dynamic pattern occurs in the second thematic section. Here the music begins quite softly. There is a sense of intensity accumulating to the end, with momentary breaks as softer instruments, such as the harp, play the theme. This dynamic pattern of increasing intensity generates the excitement that we feel at the end of the work.

LISTEN AGAIN

The Young Person's Guide to the Orchestra
(Benjamin Britten) [CD 2, track 1]

This second listening guide concentrates your attention on the textural and dynamic aspects of *The Young Person's Guide to the Orchestra.*

Time	Musical Event
00:00	Full orchestra in homorhythmic texture playing quite loudly.
00:24	Softer passage in homorhythmic texture.
00:46	Loud passage in homorhythmic texture.
01:06	Medium dynamic level, homorhythmic texture.
01:23	Medium dynamic level.
01:38	Full orchestra again in homorhythmic texture.
01:58	Soft passage in homophonic texture.
02:32	Soft passage in homophonic texture. Later there is counterpoint between the two oboes.
03:33	Soft to medium dynamic level, homophonic texture continues.
04:10	Medium dynamic level at the beginning, but softer later on.

Monophonic ✓
Polyphonic ✓
(Homophonic ✓

05:03	Much louder section in homophonic texture.
05:39	Soft passage with very light accompaniment in homophonic texture.
06:39	Soft passage in homophonic texture; dynamic level increases later.
07:53	Begins very softly but builds to a medium dynamic level; a good example of accompaniment above the melody—a reversal of the normal pattern.
08:54	Soft passage with a few sudden punctuations in the percussion.
09:41	Four horns begin in polyphonic texture but continue in homophonic texture; a louder passage than the previous one.
10:28	Medium dynamic level with louder moments.
10:59	Much louder section of homorhythmic texture with moments of polyphony and homophony.
12:00	Here the melody is suggested by the timpani and other percussion. As the melodic percussion enters, the homophonic texture is obvious.
13:44	Moment of monophonic texture at a medium-soft dynamic level.
13:50	Polyphonic texture gradually becomes more complex, and the dynamic level builds.
14:57	Softer moment.
15:10	Polyphonic texture continues, and the intensity builds to the end of the work.
15:40	Here we have homorhythmic texture in the brass with polyphonic texture in the rest of the orchestra. This is the point of maximum textural complexity in the work. It is also the climax, generated primarily by texture and dynamics.
16:10	Work ends with homorhythmic texture and a high dynamic level. It resolves the excitement of the climax.

Response to the Music

In the first listening guide for *The Young Person's Guide to the Orchestra* you concentrated on the timbre of the orchestral instruments. Do you feel that identifying the sounds of the individual instruments contributes to your enjoyment of the work? Will it enhance your listening experiences with other music?

In the second listening guide your attention was directed toward the textural and dynamic aspects of the work. Does knowledge of musical textures contribute to your enjoyment of this work? How do the changes in dynamics contribute to your physical and emotional response?

Summary

In this chapter we have concentrated on the instruments of the modern symphony orchestra and their timbre. In addition we have begun a systematic study of musical texture and dynamics and their contributions to music. *The Young Person's Guide to the Orchestra* by Benjamin Britten was our featured work.

Applying What You Have Learned

1. Listen again to *Redemption Song* [CD 1, track 5]. Can you identify the texture at the beginning? When Bob Marley begins singing, what is the texture? Notice that there is little contrast in dynamic levels throughout this work. This is typical of much popular music.

2. Listen again to *Bay a Glezele Mashke* [CD 1, track 7]. Can you now name the instruments in this ensemble? Notice that most of them are found in the symphony orchestra. Name an instrument in this ensemble that we did not hear in *The Young Person's Guide to the Orchestra*.

3. Listen again to the third movement of the Vivaldi concerto [CD 1, track 16]. Notice that the passage beginning at 0:07 is the opening material repeated exactly, but at a lower dynamic level, creating an echo effect. Listen to the rest of the movement and notice when musical materials are repeated at lower dynamic levels. This technique for providing contrast is often known as **terraced dynamics.** Notice that this work is written for a string orchestra. Can you estimate how the size of the string section for the Vivaldi concerto compares with the string section in *The Young Person's Guide to the Orchestra?* An orchestra of the size heard in the Vivaldi concerto is sometimes called a **chamber orchestra** because it originally performed in rooms—chambers—of private houses and palaces.

4. Listen again to *Bring Me Little Water Silvy* [CD 1, track 18]. Identify the texture of the chorus at the beginning. When does the texture type change? What is the new texture?

5. Does the first theme of *The Young Person's Guide to the Orchestra* (CD 2, track 1, 0:00) have the characteristics of vocal melody or instrumental melody? Explain.

6. Does the second theme of *The Young Person's Guide to the Orchestra* (CD 2, track 1, 13:44) have the characteristics of vocal melody or instrumental melody? Explain.

7. Can you find examples of homorhythmic texture in the excerpt from *La Bohème?* If so, give the track numbers and times.

Important Terms

duo 207
trio 207
quartet 207
quintet 207
sextet 207
septet 207
octet 207
nonet 207
band 207
chorus 207
strings 210
 violin, viola, violoncello (cello), double bass
bow 210
woodwinds 211
 flute, oboe, clarinet, bassoon, piccolo, English

horn, bass clarinet, contrabassoon, and sometimes the saxophone
brass 211
 trumpet, horn, trombone, tuba
percussion 212
 xylophone, marimba, chimes, timpani, snare drum (side drum), tenor drum (field drum), bass drum, tambourine, cymbals, triangle, tam-tam, temple blocks, woodblock

definite-pitch percussion 212
indefinite-pitch percussion 212
orchestration 215
monophonic texture 219
polyphonic texture (counterpoint) 219
round 219
homophonic texture 220
homorhythmic texture 221
terraced dynamics 224
chamber orchestra 224

Names preceded by * have short biographies in Appendix B, page 346.

Musicians and Ensembles Mentioned

*Benjamin Britten
*Frank Bridge
*Peter Pears
*Henry Purcell
London Symphony Orchestra

Further Listening Resources

Benjamin Britten:

The Young Person's Guide to the Orchestra (with narration), Angel
   CDM-63777.
Four Sea Interludes from Peter Grimes, Op. 33a, London 425659.
Peter Grimes (opera), London 414577-2 LH3.
The Holy Sonnets of John Donne, Op. 35, London 47428-2 LH3.

An excellent **CD-ROM** of *The Young Person's Guide to the
Orchestra,* with a complete audio performance as well as photos,
commentaries, diagrams, analysis, historical information, and a
musical glossary, is available from Warner New Media (10004).

Henry Purcell:

Dido and Aeneas (opera), Phillips 416299-2 PH.
Suite of Incidental Music from *Abdelazar,* Deutsche Harmoni Mundi
   77251-2.

CHAPTER 12

A Non-Western Ensemble: The Balinese *Gamelan*

Gending Petegak, Sekehe Gender Bharata Muni, Sading

Ernst Haas/Hulton Getty/Liaison

In 1893 oriental elements from the Javanese gamelan *took root in the Quartet. Then suddenly, under the impact of all the extraneous influences, there was to emerge, in* L'Après-midi d'un faune, *one of the most beautiful of all French creations.*

EDWARD LOCKSPEISER
BIOGRAPHER OF CLAUDE DEBUSSY, DESCRIBING HOW A *GAMELAN* PERFORMANCE AT THE 1889 PARIS WORLD EXPOSITION INFLUENCED DEBUSSY

In this chapter we consider a piece of music from a culture that is very distant from Western European culture—Bali. First, you will learn something about this culture and the place of music within it. Second, you will listen actively to the musical materials, rhythm, melody, timbres, textures, and dynamics of this music.

Place and Time: Bali

The island of Bali is one of over 13,000 islands that make up the republic of Indonesia, located in the middle of the Pacific Ocean off the coast of the southeast Asian mainland. Indonesia is the largest and most populous country in southeast Asia.

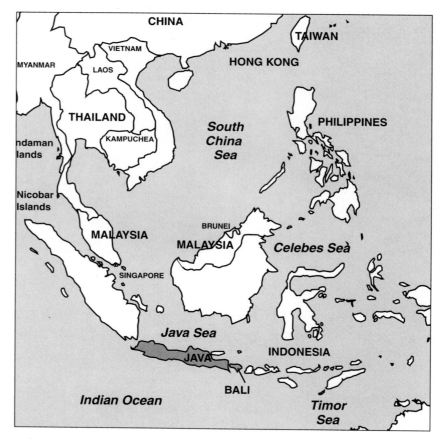

Indonesia

Indonesia's population is made up of 300 ethnic groups who speak 250 different languages. The cultural life of Indonesia is characterized by centuries of ethnic, cultural, and religious assimilation, resulting in a rich diversity.

Originally separate nations, the islands were grouped together to form the Dutch East Indies when the Netherlands colonized the area in the seventeenth century. A single national language (Bahasa Indonesia) was adopted early in the twentieth century, but most people continue to speak their indigenous languages as well. In the mid-1940s a revolution against the Dutch resulted in the formation of the independent nation of Indonesia.

History of Indonesia

The republic of Indonesia is a nation made up of 13,670 islands—including Java, Bali, Borneo, Sumatra, and Timor—off the coast of the southeast Asian mainland. It is the largest country in southeast Asia and has the largest population (190 million); because of its strategic location and its important exports—petroleum and tin—it plays a significant role in international political and trade groups.

Scientists have found bones in Java of early prehumans who lived there perhaps 1.5 million years ago. The ancestors of modern Indonesians were migrating from the southeast Asian mainland as early as 2500 B.C.E. They brought with them bronze age technology, which reached a peak in the third and second centuries B.C.E. This enabled native artisans to create the gongs and other metal percussion instruments that characterize the music of the islands.

Indian Buddhism and Hinduism began to influence Indonesian life during the 400s. Small kingdoms developed, and the influence of Indian architecture can be clearly seen in early Indonesian temples. Indian legends (the *Mahabharata* and *Ramayana*) became part of the local puppet plays. Muslim traders from India and Arabia brought Islam to Indonesia in the thirteenth century. Over the centuries, various powerful kingdoms with sophisticated aristocracies flourished and faded. They developed a highly advanced culture, including instrumental ensembles called *gamelans*, vocal music, and dance.

The Portuguese arrived in 1511, and they were soon followed by Spanish, Dutch, and British traders and colonizers, who were able to set local rulers against each other. In the 1620s, the Dutch gained control of almost all the islands. A modern nationalist movement began in the early 1900s. Japanese forces occupied the region during World War II (1942–1945). At the end of the war Indonesia declared its independence and elected a president.

Java is the dominant island, with over half the population, most of whom are "Hinduized" Muslims. Bali is one mile east of Java and has a population of about 3 million. When the Javanese Hindu rulers retreated from the Muslim invaders in the sixteenth century, many nobles, priests, and intellectuals fled to Bali. Today Bali remains the only stronghold of Hinduism in the archipelago.

Modern Balinese life is centered on a blend of Hinduism, Buddhism, Malay ancestor cults, and indigenous beliefs. Each family group has its temple, as does each village. The Balinese are famous for their arts and crafts, music, dance, puppet theaters, and colorful festivals. Elaborate dance performances, accompanied by the *gamelan* orchestra, are integral to Balinese life. Artistic expression of all kinds—painting, sculpture, dance, music—is so central to Balinese life that Bali has been called the "island of artists."

Gamelan

In Bahasa Indonesia **gamel** means "hammer" and *gamelan* means "struck with a hammer." A **gamelan** (sometimes called **gamelan orchestra**) is a collection of instruments (gongs and other tuned instruments) that are played by being struck with *gamels*. They have a common tuning system and similar painted and carved decorations. The instruments in a *gamelan* remain together and are not combined with instruments from other *gamelans*. They are the property of palaces, town governments, and religious organizations. This contrasts with the usual Western practice of private ownership of instruments by the individual performers.

Gamelans vary greatly in size and instrumentation, ranging from the large ensembles found in the courts of rulers to the tiny *gender wayang* that accompanies the Indonesian shadow-puppet theater (see page 233). *Gamelans* usually consist mostly of bronze instruments, but bamboo *gamelans* and iron *gamelans* also exist. Balinese *gamelans* are generally more brilliant in sound than Javanese *gamelans,* in part because they are played with harder wooden mallets. It has been said that there are more *gamelans* outside of Indonesia than inside, because they have become so popular in the rest of the world.

The Instruments

A typical large *gamelan* has a number of gongs. A **gong** is a tuned bronze instrument with a prominent knob on the face. It is played by striking the knob with a padded stick. Gongs vary in size from low-pitched instruments that are over three feet in diameter to higher-pitched instruments that are eight inches or less in diameter. The larger gongs are hung on elaborately decorated stands; the smaller instruments are in wooden frames that sit on the floor. A typical large *gamelan* has thirty or more gongs. After casting the largest gong, the instrument makers tune the other instruments to it. Since *gamelans* are not tuned to a standard pitch, it is impossible to share the instruments of one *gamelan* with another *gamelan*.

The **metal bar percussion instruments** are another large group of instruments found in the *gamelan*. These are tuned metal bars suspended over a trough resonator. They are played with a

Small gongs in a *gamelan*
Christine Osborne/Corbis

Metal-bar percussion instruments in a
gamelan
Jack Fields/Corbis

gamel held in the right hand while the left hand dampens the previous resonating bar. A typical large *gamelan* may have six or more of these instruments, each with six or more metal bars.

Other melodic instruments that may be present in a *gamelan* are wooden bar percussion instruments, similar in design to the metal bar instruments; plucked string instruments that have twenty or more strings stretched over wooden boxes; bamboo flutes; and two-string fiddles. Four or more double-headed cylindrical drums complete the ensemble, providing the only unpitched component in the music. There may also be separate male and female choruses.

Gamelan orchestra
Christine Osborne/Corbis

Gamelans are treated with great respect. They are often given proper names, like people. A particularly fine old Javanese *gamelan* that is used for important celebrations like Muhammad's birthday is called "Venerable Sir Torrent of Honey." It is thought to possess a spirit of its own, and devoted Muslims often give it offerings of food and flowers.

Performers and Instrument Makers

In general, men play together and women do most of the dancing, although there are *gamelans* with women instrumentalists. The *gamelan* performers are highly skilled and capable of great feats of virtuosity. In addition to their careers as performers, they typically hold other jobs to provide income. The instrument makers, on the other hand, are usually full-time professionals who devote their entire lives to creating the gongs and metal bar instruments for *gamelans*. Gongs are forged, beaten, and tuned entirely by hand. A large gong may take a month of full-time work to complete. The instruments themselves are considered sacred objects, since instrument makers are thought to have supernatural powers. The large hanging gongs are particularly venerated.

John Galm, an ethnomusicologist at the University of Colorado, relates the following story about his *gamelan* study in a town in Bali: "The *gamelan* was left out completely unguarded for anyone to use—there wasn't even a 'warning sign.' People felt it was so well protected by its sacred nature that no harm could come to it. I would go to the *gamelan* to practice, and different boys in the community would join me and help me practice by playing the interlocking parts with me. I would have preferred to practice alone, but the Balinese couldn't understand that, since playing the *gamelan* is always a community activity in Bali."

Gamelan Performances

Over the centuries a repertoire of *gamelan* music has developed that is performed at religious functions, ritual gatherings, and temple festivals all over the islands. *Gamelans* also accompany puppet plays, dance dramas, and social dancing. Nearly every village or ward of any size in Java and Bali has its own *gamelan* club. Regional differences in the music are disappearing, however, as a result of the centralized, standardizing education *gamelan* players are now receiving at Asti, the government music school.

Gamelan Music in the West

Gamelan music first came to the West in 1883, when an ensemble was brought to Amsterdam for an exposition. The French Impressionist composer Claude Debussy is said to have been enchanted by the sound of a *gamelan* at the *Exposition Universelle* in Paris in 1889. His orchestral piece *Prélude à L'après-midi d'un faune* shows some evidence of how the sound of the *gamelan* influenced his music. The first *gamelan* in the United States was brought to the Columbian Exposition in 1893. This *gamelan* is still in the collection of the Field Museum in Chicago. Today, *gamelan* ensembles can be found at a number of colleges and universities in the United States, reflecting the growing Western interest in the traditional music of Indonesia.

Wayang Kulit: **Shadow-Puppet Theater**

Shadow-puppet theater is a popular religious form in both Java and Bali. The theater gets its name, **wayang kulit,** from the name of the sacred flat leather puppets used in performances. *Wayang* means "puppet" and *kulit* means "leather" (in this case water buffalo hide), thus: leather puppets. The theater serves as an educational medium in a culture that retains its history largely as oral tradition. Most Balinese practice Hinduism, and the subject matter of *wayang kulit* is usually taken from the **Mahabharata,** the great, 2000-year-old Hindu epic of India. Religion is woven throughout the daily life of the Balinese. They do not separate the secular from the sacred in the same way as most Westerners do.

Wayang kulit is an all-night performance given by a **dalang**—a puppet-master and priest—who operates the puppets, speaks all the parts with appropriate changes in pitch and delivery for each character, and cues the performing musicians (*gender wayang*) to enter with appropriate music. The *dalang* sits between a cloth screen and

The *gender wayang* is the smallest *gamelan* ensemble. See page 234.

Dalang with shadow puppets
Reuters/Archive Photos

Balinese shadow puppet

*Luca Tettoni/The Viesti
Collection*

an oil lamp in such a way that his puppets cast a shadow on the screen, which is viewed by the audience on the opposite side. By moving the articulated arms of the puppets and by turning them from side to side, the *dalang* is able to create a three-dimensional performance that is full of movement and entertaining action.

Wayang kulit is a staged religious performance, similar in function to medieval passion plays in the West. Its purpose is to educate and entertain. Although the subject matter of the play may come from the *Mahabharata*, the *dalang* embroiders the story to bring in a discussion of contemporary events and to deliver moral and ethical instruction. (Currently, *wayang kulit* is often used as a medium to explain government social programs.)

Wayang kulit is far from being totally serious. A number of comic characters always appear, taking the role of clowns or jesters and providing both comic relief and good advice to the audience.

Gender Wayang: Instrumental Ensemble

The **gender wayang** is the smallest *gamelan*, consisting of a duo or quartet of similar instruments called **gender**. The *gender* is a two-octave metal bar percussion instrument with bar-shaped keys hung over bamboo resonators. A full-sized *gender wayang* consists of two lower-pitched (**gender gede**) and two higher-pitched (**gender barangan**) *genders*. When there are only two instruments in an ensemble, there will be one lower-pitched and one higher-pitched instrument.

Performers play the instruments with mallets. The playing technique is quite difficult because it often involves playing two separate parts simultaneously while muting some notes with the fingers and hands.

A *gender*

Wolfgang Kaehler/Corbis

The *gender* has a pentatonic (five-tone) **slendro** tuning, one of the two primary tuning systems in Balinese music. *Slendro* tuning is different from the Western musical scale as found on the piano keyboard. Since the pitches are probably different from what you are used to hearing, you may think at first that the ensemble is "out of tune." In addition, there is a purposeful mistuning among the instruments. The "male" instruments are tuned slightly higher than the "female" instruments to produce a

Vibrato is a slight fluctuation in pitch.

beating vibrato that is a characteristic sound in the music of Bali. The overall effect is resonant and shimmering.

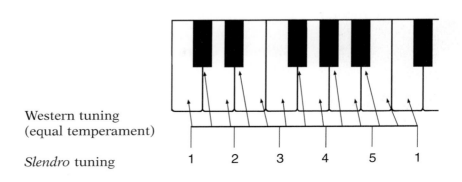

Western tuning (equal temperament)

Slendro tuning

During a shadow-puppet play the *gender wayang* performs whenever it is cued by the *dalang*. The ensemble has a repertoire of set pieces for different situations, including music for entrances and exits, walking, weeping, kissing, fighting, and the like. Its role is to provide a suitable background for each scene in the play. A comparison might be made with the pianist in early silent film theaters who had set musical pieces for various kinds of action, which the pianist creatively linked together to fit a given film. In the case of the *wayang kulit,* however, it is the *dalang,* not the musicians, who controls the use of music.

Musical Materials

The musical materials of the *gender wayang* (and *gamelans* in general) are primarily melodic. Musicians play a single nuclear melody with elaborating layers; how each instrument elaborates depends on its ability. This resembles what is known in the West as **heterophony.** In heterophonic texture, more than one version of a melody is being played simultaneously.

Melody

Heterophonic texture

At other times there are several simultaneous, independent melodic lines in the texture (polyphony), with the basic melody lower in pitch and a variety of secondary lines (called **kotekan**) above the melody. The basic melody is played by each player's left hand, while the right hand plays the *kotekan*.

Gamelan Compositions

Although there are many favorite compositions for the *gamelan*, pieces also go in and out of popularity, and new pieces are composed. A notation system exists, but only the nuclear melody is usually written down. First the ensemble learns the nuclear melody; then the players learn the various elaborating layers. In recent years some composers have become quite famous.

Listening to *Gending Petegak*

Gending Petegak is a piece played while the audience is waiting for a shadow-puppet performance to begin. During *Gending Petegak* the *dalang* takes his place and prepares an offering. This piece is followed by a lengthy overture, during which the *dalang* removes his puppets from their case and prepares to begin the performance. *Gending Petegak* is preliminary music, similar in function to the background music played in a movie house before a film begins. It establishes the mood and provides a transition between everyday life and the special world of shadow-puppet theater.

LISTENING ACTIVITY

Gending Petegak [CD 2, track 2]

This piece is performed by Sekehe Gender Bharata Muni, Sading, led by Pan Menga, one of the most celebrated *gender* players in Bali. Pan Menga and Pak Teri play the *gender gede;* Pan Sipon and I Nengah Senter play the *gender barangan.* The performance was recorded at Pura Dalem, Pembungan, Sading, Bali, in September 1989. Near the beginning there are several opportunities to hear the beating vibrato among the instruments and the difference between muted and unmuted sounds. As the piece progresses there is a general increase in complexity and virtuosity, culminating in highly syncopated patterns.

Time	Event	Description
0:00	Introduction (part 1)	Series of short sections, each beginning with a repeated tone, followed by melodic

		material. At first the melodies are short, but they gradually increase in length and complexity.
1:40	Introduction (part 2)	A large chord introduces this section, and the material begins to resemble the following sections.
1:54	Section 1	Four-note repeated figure is introduced with elaborating layers (*kotekan*) above.
2:22	Section 2	Single melody again. There is a gradual increase in complexity during this section. The material becomes more and more syncopated and builds in intensity. A clear quadruple meter emerges in this section. There is considerable decoration of the basic melody.
3:02	Section 3	Begins softly and gradually builds in complexity and intensity. Similar to previous material.
3:46	Section 4	The pattern established in section 3 (soft beginning, gradual increase in intensity) recurs here.
4:36	Section 5	Another similar section (considerable elaboration around 4:54).
5:12	Section 6	Another similar section.
5:33	Section 7	Another similar section.
5:54	Closing section	Set off by silence, this section brings the work to a close.

It is clear from this outline that the sections follow a similar pattern. The introductory sections open with repeated notes followed by melody. In the body of the work, sections are created by changes in dynamics (always beginning softly and building in intensity) and by changes in complexity of texture (the opening of a section is always less complex than the conclusion).

Response to the Music

What are your emotional, physical, intellectual, and spiritual responses to this music? How might your responses differ from those of a Balinese audience hearing the music while preparing to watch a puppet play? Remember that Balinese audiences are familiar with the story line but not necessarily with the social commentary and comic sections that have been added.

Summary

In this chapter you have studied a piece of music called *Gending Petegak*. If your frame of reference is Western music, this piece will sound different from the music you are familiar with because the instruments and pitch system are not Western. *Gending Petegak* is an introductory piece for *wayang kulit,* the shadow-puppet theater of Bali. These performances are staged religious dramas intended to educate and entertain the audience.

Applying What You Have Learned

1. Think back over the music you have heard in earlier chapters. Which piece strikes you as being most similar in sound to *Gending Petegak?* Listen again to that piece and compare it with *Gending Petegak,* considering various aspects of the music: rhythm, melody, harmony, timbre, texture, and dynamics. How similar are the two works? Are there more differences than similarities? Making comparisons between two pieces of music is a good way to clarify for yourself the distinctive characteristics of both works.

2. Do you know of other music that reminds you of *Gending Petegak?* If so, listen carefully to that music and make a similar comparison of rhythm, melody, harmony, and sound. How similar are the two pieces?

3. In which works presented so far in this textbook have you heard heterophony? Name three examples. Name three examples of heterophony in other music that you know.

4. Purposeful "mistuning" of instruments to produce a shimmering vibrato sound is a desired effect in Balinese *gamelan* music. In most music in the West this would be considered "out of tune." Why is it acceptable in Balinese music and not in the music of the West? Can you think of an example of Western music where purposeful mistuning is characteristic? Is the mistuning used for the same purpose in that music?

5. Is it easy for you to sense meter when you listen to *Gending Petegak?* Explain your answer.

6. *Gending Petegak* is music to prepare the audience for the ensuing puppet theater performance. Unlike the music that follows, it does not accompany anything. It is intended to be listened to for its own sake. Should it then be described as art music? Explain.

Important Terms

gamel 230
gamelan (*gamelan* orchestra) 230
gongs 230
metal bar percussion 230

wayang kulit 233
Mahabharata 233
dalang 233
gender 234
gender wayang 234
gender gede 234

gender barangan 234
slendro tuning 234
heterophony 235
kotekan 236

Names preceded by * have short biographies in Appendix B, page 346.

Musicians and Ensembles Mentioned

*Claude Debussy
Sekehe Gender Bharata Muni, Sading
Pan Menga
Pak Teri
Pan Sipon
I Nengah Senter

Further Listening Resources

Kecak from Bali, Bridge Records, BCD 9019.
Gamelan Music of Bali, ARC.
Music of Indonesia (Smithsonian Folkways Series) This is an ongoing series of recordings presenting a cross section of all of the various musics of Indonesia.

In the Recording Studio

💿 *Animal Crackers,* Matt Ryan

Culver Pictures

There is no doubt that I shall be able to store up and reproduce automatically at any future time the human voice perfectly.

THOMAS A. EDISON (1877)
INVENTOR OF THE PHONOGRAPH

The Impact of Recording Technology on Music

The ways that timbre, texture, and dynamics are controlled in music were greatly changed in the mid-twentieth century by the introduction of recording technology. Unlike the ensembles we considered in Chapters 11 and 12 (the symphony orchestra, the *gamelan*), the "ensembles" created in a recording studio are the creations of a recording engineer. The engineer selects, balances, and mixes the sounds of the various instruments to create a composite sound that could not exist in the natural world. Only in a recording studio, for example, can an "ensemble" be created that consists of several simultaneous performances by a single musician. Because of this technology, an "ensemble" can consist of musicians who are separated in space and time—and may never actually meet. Such paradoxes have become commonplace in the second half of the twentieth century and account for much of the recorded music we hear. In addition, the electronic processing of sound has considerably expanded the tonal palette. Most of the sounds we hear in commercial music have been processed extensively.

One outcome of obtaining most of our music through recordings has been the elimination of the immediacy of a live performance. The rise of MTV has come about in part from a desire to give back to music a visual as well as an aural dimension. Since recording technology is central to today's music, we will devote this chapter to a brief history of recording and to learning how two pieces of music are put together in the studio.

Early History of Recording

The development of the first practical **phonograph** in 1877 set in motion a process that has resulted in our mass entertainment industry, which transformed the nature of twentieth-century music. Thomas Edison (1847–1931) saw the phonograph primarily as a device "to record in permanent characters the human voice and other sounds, from which characters such sounds may be reproduced and rendered audible again" (from the patent application in 1878 for the first phonograph). In fact, the first recording made was Edison himself reciting the nursery rhyme "Mary had a little lamb." However, the potential for recording music was recognized almost immediately. An editorial in *Scientific American* in November 1877 stated, "Music may be crystallized as well. Imagine an opera or an oratorio sung by the greatest living vocalists, thus recorded, and capable of being repeated as we desire."

Mr. Edison's Phonograph

The earliest phonograph consisted of a cylinder turned by a crank. A piece of tinfoil was attached to the cylinder and a stylus inscribed a groove on the surface of the foil, recording the sound wave. A "reproducer" on the opposite side of the cylinder was used to play back the recorded sound, which could be heard from several feet away. The patent application stated that the piece of foil could be "detached from the machine and preserved for any length of time. . . . The record, if it be upon tin foil, may be stereotyped by means of the plaster of paris process, and from the stereotype multiple copies may be made expeditiously and cheaply." Modern methods of pressing records appear to have been anticipated by this statement.

Early phonograph recordings from the first years of the twentieth century preserved the performances of such illustrious opera singers as Enrico Caruso (whose first recording in 1902 was the opera aria *"Vesti la giubba"*) and of many singers of vernacular music as well. Most early recordings are of singers or brass bands, since recording the more delicate sounds of orchestral music was nearly impossible before the introduction of electrical recording methods in the 1920s.

Thomas Edison
Culver Pictures

Records to Compact Discs

The first records were made of tinfoil wrapped over a metal cylinder (1877–1886). These records were intended for home or office recording, and no commercial recordings of music were produced. In 1885 the Volta Graphophone Company introduced the first wax cylinder recordings. **Cylinder recordings** were sold commercially from 1887 until 1929. Many early recordings of music were made on cylinders. In 1893 the Berliner Gramophone Company began issuing **disk recordings.** The early disk records were single-sided (the reverse side was blank), but in 1904 the Odeon Company of Germany produced the first double-faced records, which quickly became the standard in the industry; and 78-rpm (revolutions per minute) records were sold commercially into the early 1960s. By then, however, they had been superseded by the 33⅓-rpm **long-playing record** (LP), introduced by Columbia Records in 1948; and by the 45-rpm record introduced by RCA Victor Company in 1949. The 33⅓-rpm and 45-rpm records were the industry standards for disk recordings until the introduction, in 1983, of the **digital**

compact disc (CD). In the meantime, **magnetic tape recording,** which was first introduced in the late 1940s for studio recording, began to invade the home market. The first magnetic tape media to have a wide popular appeal were the Phillips **four-track cassette,** introduced in 1963, and the Lear Jet **eight-track cartridge,** introduced in 1965. The eight-track cartridge is no longer available, but the four-track cassette remains one of the more popular media for recordings.

The Emergence of Recording Engineering

In the first part of the twentieth century most recordings attempted, with increasing success, to accurately reproduce the sounds of an original performance—to bring the listener "into the concert hall." With the advent in the 1920s of radio crooners, whose singing style was adapted to the microphone ("mike"), a more intimate recording style was created that attempted to bring the performer "into the living room." With this change of perspective, and the advances brought about by electrical recording, the recorded medium itself became a part of the creative process. The stage was set for the recording studio techniques of today.

The advent of magnetic tape recording in the late 1940s gave engineers greater flexibility by allowing cutting and splicing of various "takes" to create a final recording. Edward Tatnall Canby, writing in the *Saturday Review of Recordings* in 1950, bemoaned the advent of tape editing.

> A very well-known soprano of the Met [New York Metropolitan Opera Company]—so the story goes among the tape recording folk—recently hit a whale of a false high note in a broadcast opera performance. It was all over in an instant and nobody minded. The trouble was that the opera was to be rebroadcast later from tape. That, the lady couldn't take. The tape editors were called in, the squawk was snipped out; a search was made through the opera for another high note of the same pitch, which was patched into place—and a "perfect" performance went on the air.

Canby went on to ask what protection the public had against such "abuse of editorial privilege." His objection reflected the attitude that recordings should only be accurate representations of actual performances. At the same time, however, hundreds of popular recordings were being made with musical effects that could only have been created in a recording studio. Canby might have been shocked and surprised to learn that by the 1950s popular recordings were often made in several sessions, with the singers adding the vocals only after the instrumental accompaniment was completed. The **recording engineer** and the producer had final control over the balance of various elements, and engineering had become a creative art in itself.

Multitrack Recording and "Effects"

Popular musicians associated with radio broadcasting were the first to realize the potential of tape recording and its associated effects in creating a new musical medium. Les Paul (Lester William Polfuss), a multitalented musician responsible for many innovations in popular music, sums up his contribution as follows:

> I moved to Los Angeles in '43 and worked for Bing Crosby, who was interested in my work with electronics and sound. He encouraged me to build my own studio. . . . I've been experimenting with recording techniques and special effects all along—echo, reverb, overdubbing, speeded-up guitars, and so on. I was doing disk multiples in '46 and sound-on-sound with tape in '49. I built the first multitrack recorder, the kind that's used on just about every record you hear nowadays. On a lot of my hits with my wife, Mary Ford, I played all the parts myself. . . . And I was doing phase shifting with discs ten years before anyone tried it with tape.

Multitrack Tape Recorders

Multitrack recording, which allows separate recording of several layers of sound, broke through the boundaries of traditional ensembles. This technology made it possible to create "ensembles" that could not exist in live performance.

Multitrack tape recorders
Richard Pasley/The Viesti Collection

A **multitrack tape recorder** is a machine capable of recording several separate sounds on independent channels called *tracks*. Although there are a number of smaller recording studios with two- and four-track recorders, the standard in the recording industry is sixteen, twenty-four, and even thirty-two tracks. With these large recorders it is possible to record different instruments on separate tracks, either in the same session or at different times, and experiment with changing the relative loudness of the various tracks in producing the final result. Shifting the relative intensity of the various tracks is called **balancing,** and combining several tracks into a single track is called **mixing.**

Echo and Reverberation

The most common "effect" unit in a recording studio is a device for producing **reverberation** or **echo.** With reverberation, a sound recorded in a studio with padded walls can be made to sound as if it came from a large concert hall. In earlier times this was accomplished by playing back the sound in a room with hard, reverberant walls and recording the result, but all modern studios have electronic devices to create this effect. Tracks with no reverberation added are said to be **dry.** Most recording is done dry and reverberation is added in the mixing process. This gives the recording engineer more control of the final product.

Delay and Flanging

Another common unit in a recording studio is a device for storing a sound and replaying it with time **delay.** The delayed sound is normally mixed with the original sound, producing one or more overlapping "copies." If the delay is short, it can approximate reverberation. If the delay is longer, it can sound like several musicians performing simultaneously. If the amount of delay is changed constantly, an effect called **flanging** is produced. Ken Townsend, a recording engineer at the Abbey Road Studios in London, developed a system of using various pieces of equipment to record two sets of voices simultaneously, then spacing the second voice at any required time interval before or after the original. The device was called an ADT (artificial double tracking) unit, but John Lennon called it Ken's Flanger, and his term, flanging, has been used in studios all over the world ever since. This effect, while difficult to describe in words, is a common sound in much rock music.

Compressors, Expanders, and Limiters

A **compressor** is a device for decreasing the total dynamic range of a sound during recording. Some voices and instruments produce such a wide range of loudness that they exceed the limits of recorders, and compressors are used to remedy this situation. Also, some sounds (guitars and voices) can be made to have more "punch" if they are compressed.

An **expander** is the reverse of a compressor, in that it expands the total dynamic range of a sound. This can be useful in removing small background noises, since these low-level signals can be pushed below the level where they can be heard. If a compressor and expander are combined into a single unit, it is called a **compander.**

Limiters are devices that prevent the level of a sound from going above a predetermined limit. They are useful in keeping recorders from overloading without otherwise modifying the sound. Recording engineers use compressors, expanders, and limiters in recording individual tracks and in mixing. Much of the so-called "commercial" sound of pop recordings comes from the use of these devices, which make the consistently high-level sounds demanded by pop radio stations.

Effects modules in a recording studio
OGUST/The Image Works

History of Popular Music in the U. S.

1607 → **1850** → **1900** → **1920** → **1950** → **1960** → **1980** →

| Hymns and psalms | Minstrel show and vaudeville | Jazz, blues, recordings | Hillbilly, swing | Rock 'n' roll | Folk, soul | MTV |

Popular music, as distinct from art or folk music, is created as a commercial product. It has a long history in North America, going back to the published hymns and psalms of the colonial period (1607–1776). A number of music publishing companies were established in the late eighteenth century, producing mostly sheet music for voice and piano. This music was popular in North American homes, where it was usually played in the parlor (a room used for entertaining guests).

During the nineteenth century, minstrel shows became a popular form of entertainment in the United States. In these shows, white performers wore blackface to impersonate African Americans. *Camptown Races* (1850) and *Old Folks at Home* (1851) were among the popular songs associated with the minstrel shows. Stephen Foster (1826–1864), who composed those two songs, was the first American to make his living as a songwriter.

The Civil War (1861–1865) produced a large number of popular songs, including *Dixie* (1859) and *The Battle Hymn of the Republic* (1862). All these songs were published as sheet music for amateur parlor performance.

During the latter part of the nineteenth century, vaudeville replaced the minstrel show as the most popular form of entertainment. It was during this time that the music publishing industry was established in an area of New York City called Tin Pan Alley. Tin Pan Alley, which got its name from the innumerable pianos that were banging out popular tunes in various publishing houses, became the center

of popular music in the United States. The musical comedy, later to be called the Broadway musical, grew out of and eventually replaced vaudeville. It also was centered in Tin Pan Alley.

In the late 1870s another new form of popular music, called ragtime, was being developed wherever African American musicians performed. Ragtime and its successors, blues and jazz (see Chapter 18), were soon incorporated into the music of Tin Pan Alley.

The advent of recordings in the late nineteenth century provided a powerful means for the distribution of popular music; and the sheet music industry, which had been a flourishing business, began a slow decline. The first recordings of popular music were made early in the twentieth century. By the 1920s all forms of popular music, including songs from musicals, jazz, and blues, were available on recordings.

In the early 1920s a new form of music called hillbilly music began to be recorded. Hillbilly music combined elements of popular song with folk music of English origin, blues, and religious hymns. This music developed into country music, which remains popular today.

From the 1920s through the 1940s a new type of jazz called swing became popular. It was replaced by rhythm and blues in the late 1940s. A major change in popular music took place in the 1950s with the arrival of rock 'n' roll. This music, which developed out of rhythm and blues, rapidly became the dominant popular music in the United States and spread world-wide. It later became known simply as rock, and it continues, of course, to the present time.

Other popular music styles coexisted with rock from the 1960s to the present. There was a folk music revival in the early 1960s, along with a wave of protest songs. A new blend of rhythm and blues called soul music, along with rap and hip-hop, became popular later in the century. With music videos and MTV in the 1980s, popular music was once again a visual as well as an aural medium.

Producing a Commercial Recording

A commercial pop or rock recording is created in several distinct steps. These steps may be accomplished in a single session or in multiple sessions with different musicians. The process can be divided into four general stages: preproduction, recording, mixdown, and postproduction.

Preproduction

A recording begins with selecting works to be included, deciding on their musical treatment, hiring musicians and technical personnel, and scheduling the recording sessions. The **record producer** is the person in charge of these arrangements. In addition, the producer is in charge of arranging licenses for songs and contracts with record companies, and for managing the total budget of the production. The producer remains with the production through all its phases and makes many of the artistic decisions in conjunction with the recording artists.

Recording

The first tracks to be recorded are normally the rhythm instruments: guitars, piano, bass, and drums. A lead vocal track may be recorded at the same time to serve as a reference, but this track will usually be replaced later in the recording process. When the basic tracks are completed, background vocal tracks and instrumental "sweeteners" (strings, horns, additional keyboards, and special instruments) are added. This is accomplished by playing the basic tracks back on headphones for the musicians while they perform their parts. At this point the basic tracks, along with background vocals and instrumental sweeteners, are played for the lead singer or singers, who record their parts.

Mixdown

Once all tracks are recorded, the recording engineers begin the process of creating the **mix.** Various tracks are processed through

The Recording Studio

A recording studio consists of two adjoining rooms: the studio proper and the control booth. The musicians perform in the studio proper, while the recording engineer and producer work in the control booth. A soundproof window and door between the two rooms allow the control room personnel to speak with each other during recording without having their voices recorded along with those of the musicians. A microphone in the control room can be connected with speakers in the studio to allow the control-room personnel to "talk back" to the recording musicians. The studio proper has various portable acoustic baffles to create enough isolation for each instrument to be recorded on a separate track. There may also be an isolation booth within the studio to house very loud instruments, such as the drum set. The control booth houses the mixing console—the "central nervous system" of the studio. The mixing console can be set to connect any microphone in the studio to any track on the multitrack tape recorder and to provide instantaneous control of recording levels. The recording engineer operates the equipment in the booth, and the producer provides general direction and coordination.

Recording studio and control booth
Stephen Frisch/Stock Boston

"effects" units and balanced to create the final two-track stereo version of the recording. It may be necessary during the process of **mixdown** to remove certain sounds and even replace them with others. This process is called **editing.** Digital recording technology has made the process of editing relatively easy, and engineers routinely "improve" original tracks in this way.

Postproduction

Once the final version of the recording is completed, it is delivered to the recording company, which will choose the order of the cuts on the final album and produce the final CD, record, or tape. At this time the marketing strategy is planned, cover art for the jacket is commissioned, and the general appearance of the final product is established.

Listening to a Digital Studio Recording: *Animal Crackers*

A digital recording by Axigally, a local band in Ames, Iowa, is broken down to show various stages in the recording and mixing process. Axigally was formed in 1985 when Eric Warner and Matt Ryan were learning studio work at the Media Arts Workshop in Ames. They began writing music, an activity they took more seriously during college. Eventually the band was made up of the following members: Matt Ryan (lyrics, lead vocals), Jeff Sturges (guitars, backing vocals), John Pursey (keyboards), Eric Warner (keyboards, percussion, backing vocals), and Sophie Ellmaker Sturges (drums and percussion).

Over the years, the band put out eleven albums, the last of which, *Paper Sky* (1995), included the song *Animal Crackers*. The song was recorded and produced in a private studio by two engineers, Rob and Jeff Vallier. *Animal Crackers* received radio airplay all over the United States and even in a radio show in Argentina. Owing to a lack of available practice time, however, the band was unable to capitalize on its brief moment of fame.

The song is about a little girl and her single father growing up together. Matt Ryan is the father of two daughters, so there is some autobiographical sentiment there, but he is not single. The music developed while John Pursey was cycling through new sounds on his keyboard and hit something "just right." Matt explains, "It was one of those songs that just come out of you after that, and you just knew what it should sound like. It took only about four days to write, and remains one of the band's better moments."

The final version of the song is on CD 2, track 7.

LISTENING ACTIVITY

Animal Crackers (Matt Ryan) [CD 2, tracks 3–7]

[CD 2, track 3]   Basic drum track. First you will hear a series of eighteen clicks, setting the tempo. This "click track" is recorded on a separate track and will be used by the musicians to coordinate various layers in the recording. There is a short silence, and then the drum track begins. This click track will not be a part of the final mix.

[CD 2, track 4]   Synthesizer tracks are laid over the basic drum track.

[CD 2, track 5]   Bass and guitars are added.

[CD 2, track 6]   Finally the vocal track is recorded.

[CD 2, track 7]   Finished recording with all tracks mixed and effects added. Can you identify some of these effects?

Text

With her shovel she's digging in the sandbox
With her daddy he watches as she plays
Just the two of them they're happy together
So many different pieces fit the puzzle these days

Like a rock Daddy sinks into the sofa
Baby's been a little monster today
But he knows that these are the days he will remember
Someday he'll look back on these days as the best of his life
His pride in his little girl you could cut with a knife
And safe in her Daddy's arms she sleeps

Baby's animal crackers crumble like daydreams
Home from school now she's watching her TV
She picks up a book by the same Dr. Seuss that he knew
Same Nobody inside the same pants of pale green
And as scared as he is that her childhood isn't just as happy as his
The smile on her face says "Daddy, I love you"

And Daddy's looking back
And Baby grows up so fast
Animal crackers and Dr. Seuss become a thing of the past
(But do they really?)

On her prom night Daddy waves from beneath the porch light
So proud of what his baby's grown up to be
She blows him a kiss and he winks and wonders to himself
Is there any Daddy happy as me?
And as fast as she grew
She smiled and then he knew
The smile on her face still says "Daddy, I love you."

"Ensembles" in Commercial Recorded Music

It is clear from the descriptions above that the concept of an "ensemble" must be considerably expanded when we are dealing with recorded music. In the first place, the members of a recording ensemble may never meet each other and may be unaware of each other's musical role in the final product. Second, the recording engineer has total control over the balance among various instruments, with the result that the balances heard by the listener will have little, if anything, to do with the actual balance of the instruments in the original recording. Instruments may be combined in ways that would be impossible in a concert setting. Third, since the recording engineer controls the addition of "effects" to the various tracks, the performer has less control over the nature of the sounds that appear in the final product than do the performers in a concert setting. The "ensemble" is the creation of the recording engineer and may be more the result of the mixdown than of anything the musicians actually did in the recording itself.

Jonathan Goldman has described the process of creating the "ensemble" that makes up the sonic landscape of *Dolphin Dreams* (CD 1, track 1; see page 6), a "landscape" that was supposed to "sonically re-create what I perceived a dolphin water experience would be like":

> In order to create this sonic environment, it was necessary to find the proper sound elements for the auditory experience I was going to create. I wanted the sound of the ocean, a slow heartbeat, choral voices, and dolphins. I knew I could create most of the sonics in my home recording studio, or use already existing recordings I had in my sound library. The difficulty lay in finding dolphin sounds, which were not available anywhere. I was put in contact with a woman . . . and was offered a recorded tape of . . . two dolphins, as well as other dolphin sounds.
>
> The actual production of *Dolphin Dreams* was made on a number of multitracking reel-to-reel tape recorders and cassette decks. . . . My eight-track reel-to-reel contained the tracks of ocean sounds . . . , a stereo female human heartbeat slowed to 48 beats per minute . . . , the stereo sounds of dolphins Joe and Rosie, and a stereo "Om" sound. . . . A four-track reel-to-reel had the haunting melody of the "angelic choir," with each track featuring a slightly different version of this Ur Song (melodic descending minor) sung by myself and friends. A four-track cassette deck featured other dolphin sounds and whale sounds in stereo. All of these were put through my 24-track mixing board into a Sony Beta Digital stereo mastering machine.
>
> The different elements were introduced sequentially, starting first with ocean sounds, then seagulls, then the heartbeat, followed by the almost subliminal "Om" sound. Next the sounds of Joe and Rosie and

finally the addition of the other cetaceans (whales and dolphin). All these elements appear within the first five minutes and continue for the next 13 minutes or so, before I began to slowly fade them out, until at the end of 23 minutes, the listener is left with only the sound of the ocean.

Modern recording studio technology permits the combining of sounds that could never occur together in nature. But this is not the only difference between image and reality. For example, in 1965 the pop music recording *This Diamond Ring*, by Gary Lewis and the Playboys, skyrocketed to the top of the charts. Gary Lewis (the young, hitherto unknown son of the comedian Jerry Lewis) was soon ranked the eighth most popular singer in the United States, and the song itself ranked as the seventeenth most popular song of the year. But the song, the band, and the lead singer were not what they were advertised to be. None of the members of the Playboys actually played on the recording. Studio musicians recorded the instrumental portion of *This Diamond Ring*. Nor did the group (or any of its members) write the song. Nor did Gary Lewis sing the song by himself. The somewhat strange, otherworldly quality of the lead vocals was not due to Lewis's youth; his inadequate voice was overdubbed by one Ron Hicklin—who was *not* ranked eighth in popularity. The music of other groups such as The Monkees and Milli Vanilli was also created by studio musicians, and the resulting sounds have little, if anything, to do with the persons mentioned on the record jackets.

There is no limit to the number and kinds of sounds that may be combined in a recording. Certain musical genres may have standard instrumentations that may be followed even in recording, but the recorded medium can itself be considered an ensemble. This ensemble has unlimited instrumentation and scope, including all acoustic and electronic sounds, plus the effects that may be added during mixdown and editing.

Music in a Postmodern World

We have become so accustomed to music made in a recording studio that we accept it as the result of a live performance. Concert performances, particularly of popular and rock music, now attempt to duplicate the sounds of the commercial recordings through extensive electronic treatment and the use of prerecorded tracks. This makes it clear that the definitive version of the music is the CD that you buy, not the concert performance.

As a result, live performance is often an inferior means of listening to rock and popular music. Live performance has become a spectacle, with laser light shows and other visual effects taking center stage. The audio portion of some "live" performances (particularly on television) is actually a recording. The musicians on stage only act as if they are singing and playing the music the TV audience hears: their mikes are usually disconnected. Since the development of MTV, the visual portions of live performances attempt to mimic the effects of the videos that accompany the recordings. The purpose of live rock performances has increasingly become promoting the artists and generating record sales. In recent years there has been a backlash against the increasingly "processed" quality of these high-tech performances, and a "new" genre of acoustic (nonelectronic) music has sprung up—a genre that used to be the norm.

Response to the Music

After a look into the world of the recording studio, can you better identify the various elements in the final recording? How much of the emotional impact of the song is due to the recording and mixing process? How do you feel about learning how much "engineering" goes into popular recorded music?

Summary

Recording technology was first developed in the late nineteenth century. During the twentieth century, it became the dominant means of creating and distributing music. As techniques have been developed and improved, the goal of most recording production has changed from attempting to provide an accurate representation of a concert performance to making something that bears little resemblance to any live performance.

You have learned about the process of producing a commercial recording, and you have followed the process through two examples: *Animal Crackers*, a rock song; and *Dolphin Dreams*, a studio-produced "sonic landscape."

Applying What You Have Learned

1. It is worthwhile to consider all the recordings you have listened to up to this point in the book to determine how they have been influenced by the art of the recording engineer. You have heard recordings of three basic types:

   a. **Field recordings.** These recordings are made in uncontrolled situations where background noises as well as the music appear on the recordings. Recording engineers have only limited impact on field recordings. They may do some equalization and cleaning up of background sounds to make the finished product more acceptable to the average listener, but what you hear is very close to what took place at the location where the recording was made.

b. **Performance recordings.** These recordings attempt to accurately reflect what you would hear in a concert hall, but without the audience. In performance recording, the engineer may have played a significant part. Some performance recordings are made with a single set of microphones that reproduce what an audience would hear; others are recorded with multiple microphones directed at each performer or group of performers. In the latter case the final balance of musical elements is controlled by the engineer.

c. **Studio recordings.** These recordings are made in the controlled environment of a recording studio, so what you hear has been selected and mixed by a recording engineer. In true studio recording there is no "performance" to be recorded. The recording is assembled out of multiple tracks that may have been recorded separately. Effects may have been added during the mixdown stage so that the result is different from anything the performers themselves could have produced live.

Consider all the recordings you have on the CDs that accompany this book and place each in one of these three categories.

2. In recent years there has been greater interest in music that self-consciously avoids electronic technology. This music is sometimes called "acoustic" because it makes no use of electronics. Is this merely a reaction against technology, or is there something more fundamental at work? Which kind of music—"acoustic" or studio-produced—do you prefer to listen to? Why?

3. People have always used available technology for musical purposes. Name a new technology that is beginning to be exploited musically. Do you feel that this will result in greater musical enjoyment? Why or why not?

4. Some futurists predict that, with the increased availability of interactive technology, there will come a time when most individuals will create their own music, blurring the distinctions between composer, performer, and listener. Would this be a desirable situation? What would be gained and what would be lost in such a musical culture? Is this more like the way folk music has always been produced?

5. When you listen to popular music, have you been aware of the role played by the recording engineer? Can you name a famous recording engineer?

6. If you have been to a "stadium" rock concert, did the performance live up to or exceed the expectations you formed from hearing the music on CD? If it fell short, why do you think that was so? If it exceeded your expectations, why do you think that was so?

7. What are the advantages and disadvantages of field recordings, performance recordings, and studio recordings? Which do you prefer?

8. Does what you have learned about the production process for *Dolphin Dreams* enhance your appreciation of the work?

Important Terms

phonograph 241
cylinder recording 242
disk recording 242
long-playing record (LP) 242
digital compact disc 242
magnetic tape recording 243
four-track cassette 243

eight-track cartridge 243
recording engineer 244
multitrack tape recorder 245
balancing 245
mixing 245
reverberation (echo) 245
dry 245
delay 245

flanging 245
compressor 245
expander 246
compander 246
limiter 246
record producer 248
mixdown (mix) 248
editing 249

Names preceded by * have short biographies in Appendix B, page 346.

Musicians and Ensembles Mentioned

Enrico Caruso
*Les Paul (Lester William Polfuss)
Mary Ford
*John Lennon
*Axigally
*Eric Warner
*Matt Ryan
Jeff Sturges
John Pursey
Sophie Ellmaker Sturges
*Jonathan Goldman

Gary Lewis and the Playboys
The Monkees
Milli Vanilli

Further Listening Resources

Enrico Caruso, Arias, Club "99" CL99-60 (mono).
History of Jazz, New York Scene, Folkways RF-3 (mono).
The Jazz Arranger, 1928–1940, Columbia Jazz Masterpieces, CJT-45143 (mono).
Chip Davis, *Fresh Aire 7,* American Gramaphone AGCD-777.

Form

in Music

In this part we look at several larger-scale aspects of music, including how the elements come together to create a coherent piece of music. We will also explore the nature of our response to musical stimuli. We will consider two important formal properties—continuity and sectional division—and we will look at music that emphasizes each of these properties. To illustrate the concepts we present, we will examine how they occur in the music we have listened to in previous chapters, as well as exploring new compositions.

Form is one of the more confusing terms in music because it is used in several different ways. Form can refer to the "shape" of a musical composition. Any successful piece of music is "well formed" in the sense of having logic and coherence in the organization of all its materials. Individual compositions may be completely unique in their form or (more often) similar to other compositions.

Form is also used to refer to generalizations about common patterns that recur in many pieces of music. Some of these patterns occur often enough to be given names. When we use the term in this way, we say that a particular piece is "in" a given form (binary, ternary, sonata, blues, etc.), as if the "form" of the work were somehow external to the specific details of the piece. This is inaccurate, of course, because the "form" of a piece is created entirely by all the details and how they relate to each other: there is no "external" shaping element in music.

In the following chapters we use form in both senses defined above—as a general term to indicate the shape of an individual composition and also to refer to common patterns found in many pieces of music. When we use the term in the latter way, we will modify it by naming the specific pattern, for example "sonata form" or "minuet-and-trio form."

Wolfgang Koehler/Corbis

CHAPTER 14   Sectional Forms I **260**
Huachos, Eduardo Villaroel and J. Mercado

CHAPTER 15   Sectional Forms II **277**
Symphony No. 39, Franz Joseph Haydn

CHAPTER 16   Continuous Forms I **297**
Sultan Veled Peshrev, Dogin Ergin

CHAPTER 17   Continuous Forms II **312**
Absalon, fili mi, Josquin Desprez

CHAPTER 18   Improvisation and Form **322**
Suite Thursday, Duke Ellington and Billy Straythorn

Sectional Forms I

🔘 *Huachos,* Eduardo Villaroel and J. Mercado

Will Mosgrove

Without craftsmanship, inspiration is a mere reed shaken
in the wind.

*JOHANNES BRAHMS (1833–1897)
GERMAN COMPOSER

In this chapter we will learn how the musical elements are arranged to create a coherent piece of music. As we discussed in the introduction to Part VI, the organizational plan of a piece of music is often referred to as its **form.** It may seem incongruous to speak of "form" in music, but musicians often apply visual terminology to the more abstract realm of sound.

The form of a piece of music is created using three techniques: repetition, contrast, and variation. In this chapter we will examine repetition and contrast. Variation will be explored in Chapter 15.

Elements of Form: Repetition

We often experience **repetition** in our daily lives. A regular routine that includes a time to get up in the morning, a schedule of activities during the day, and meals at regular times enhances our sense of well-being. We like to know that certain aspects of our lives will be repeated daily, weekly, or on some other regular basis, and we feel disoriented when our routine is broken.

Doge's Palace, Venice, Italy
Adam Woolfit/Corbis

Repetition is also an important aspect of music. When we listen to a piece of music and recognize a melody we have heard earlier in the piece, we feel that there is a plan to the work. When a rhythmic pattern is repeated, we are comfortable, sensing that things are progressing in a predictable way. Composers and visual artists rely heavily on repetition to create unity in their work. Repetition is also an important means for creating a sense of continuity in music. When patterns are repeated, we expect that they will continue to occur, and this gives us a sense of an ongoing process.

We will begin to consider repetition in music by listening again to three pieces we listened to in earlier chapters: *This Land Is Your Land, Redemption Song,* and *Grand Entry Song.*

LISTENING ACTIVITY

This Land Is Your Land (Woody Guthrie) [CD 1, track 17]

Notice the repetition of the melody in the first and second phrases of the first verse of this song. The second phrase has the same melody as the first until near the end of the phrase.

Time	Event
00:00	First phrase: "This land is your land, . . ."
00:12	Second phrase: "From the redwood forest . . ."

Source: *This Land Is Your Land.* Words and music by Woody Guthrie. TRO © Copyright 1956 (renewed) 1958 (renewed) 1970 (renewed) Ludlow Music, Inc., New York, New York. Used by permission.

The rhythmic and harmonic materials in backgrounds and accompaniments are usually quite repetitive. This repetition serves the dual purpose of providing continuity and providing a foil for melodic material. In a musical texture, when some elements are changing and others are repeated with little or no change, the changing elements attract our attention while the repeated elements fall into the background. Thus the repetitious nature of accompaniments allows us to concentrate our attention on the primary melody.

LISTENING ACTIVITY

Redemption Song (Bob Marley) [CD 1, track 5]

Notice the constant repetition of the accompaniment in this song by Bob Marley. The repetitive background provides a foil and a support for the primary melody, which is sung.

Time	Musical Event	Description
0:00	Introduction	Notice the repeated melody in this introduction.
0:18	First verse	The guitar sets up a repeated rhythmic pattern as an accompaniment for the

song. This pattern recurs with minor variation through the remainder of the verse.

Repeated Sections

A common use of repetition in music is repeated complete sections. For example, *This Land Is Your Land* is a song with several verses. The first verse, discussed on page 262, is followed by several other verses that have different lyrics but the same melody. Repetition of sections is a common way of extending musical material while maintaining unity. When sections of a work are repeated, it is convenient to designate them using capital letters—section **A,** section **B,** etc. This method of designating sections will be used from now on in this book.

LISTENING ACTIVITY

Grand Entry Song (Little Otter Singers) [CD 1, track 6]

Superscripts indicate slight variations in the restatement of the melody.

Time	Musical Event
0:11	First statement of the melody (**A**^{1}).
0:59	Second statement (**A**^{2}).
1:48	Third statement (**A**^{3}).
2:37	Fourth statement (**A**^{4}).
3:25	Fifth statement (**A**^{5}).

Elements of Form: Contrast

As much as we need repetition in our lives, we also like a change of pace. Weekends and vacations provide relief from the repetitiveness of daily life. Without the **contrast** of the weekend we would become bored and restless. This is also true in our musical experiences. When music goes on for some time without change, we tend to ignore it and think of other things.

When the character of music changes dramatically, we sense that the music is divided into distinct sections. Thus contrast is an important element in creating a sense of structure in music. Contrasting sections are often followed by repetition of previous sections.

LISTENING ACTIVITY

Oy, Abram! [CD 1, track 8]

In this listening example, two contrasting sections alternate throughout the entire piece of music.

Time	Musical Event
0:00	Introduction. Fast instrumental music (**A**).
0:10	First verse of song. Contrasting tempo, and the singer enters (**B**).
0:49	Introductory material repeated (**A**).
1:00	Second verse of the song (**B**).
1:41	Introductory material repeated (**A**).
1:51	Third verse of the song (**B**).
2:34	Introductory material repeated (**A**).

Sectional Form

A piece of music in **sectional form** is divided into logical units that have definite beginnings and endings. Division into sections interrupts the ongoing flow of the music. Rhythmic, melodic, and harmonic cadences are the primary devices for creating these divisions, but silence before the beginning or after the end of a section is also effective in creating a frame around the unit. Contrasting melodic ideas and changes in key are also used to create formal divisions, as are changes in tempo, changes in timbre, and changes in texture.

Strophic Forms

Among the simpler sectional forms are **strophic forms.** Strophic forms are usually settings of strophic poems—poems that are divided into stanzas of equal length and similar meter. A strophic form has the same or similar music for each of the stanzas of the text. Thus it is divided into sections of equal length with a clear sense of conclusion at the end of each stanza. How many of the pieces that you have listened to in this book are in strophic form?

Verse I	Verse II	Verse III	etc.

Strophic form

Verse and Chorus Form

A variant of strophic form that occurs often is the addition of a chorus section between two verses. The chorus is usually a section in which both words and music are repeated. **Verse and chorus form** sometimes begins with the verse and sometimes begins with the chorus. Can you think of songs you know that are in verse and chorus form?

Verse I	Chorus	Verse II	Chorus	etc.

Verse and chorus form

Bring Me Little Water Silvy (Leadbelly) [CD 1, track 18]

Notice that the performers chose to skip the chorus between the third and fourth verses in this recording. This is a matter of preference and was probably done to provide an additional contrast in the formal pattern.

Time	Description
0:00	First statement of the chorus of the song.
0:15	First verse of the song.
0:30	Chorus restated.
0:45	Second verse of the song.
1:00	Chorus restated.
1:16	Third verse of the song.
1:30	Fourth verse of the song.
1:45	Chorus restated.

A Sectional Work from the Andes

Now that you are familiar with listening for repetition, contrast, and sectional form, we will listen to a piece of music in sectional form that comes from the Andes Mountains in South America. We will first learn something about the history and culture of the region and the musical influences that are present in this piece; then we will actively listen to *Huachos,* performed by the Bolivian group Mallku de los Andes.

South America

The continent of South America is divided into twelve independent countries, with Brazil the largest and Uruguay the smallest. The geography is somewhat similar to that of North America, with a high range of mountains—the Andes—in the west, plains in the center, and lower mountains in the east. The Andes Mountains stretch 5,500 miles from north to south and are the longest mountain range on any of the continents of the world. The Amazon River (the second longest river in the world) runs west to east, from the Peruvian highlands to northeastern Brazil. The huge rain forests between the mountains and the Amazon Basin are in danger of being destroyed by current land-clearing practices.

People have inhabited South America for over 20,000 years. The powerful Andean Inca empire began in the mid-fifteenth century. It became one of the largest and richest empires in the Americas, extending more than 2,500 miles along the western coast of South America and including what are now Peru, Bolivia, Argentina, Chile, and Ecuador.

In the mid-sixteenth century settlers arrived from Europe and conquered the native populations. These settlers, mostly from Spain and Portugal, brought slaves from Africa. There has been extensive intermarriage among these communities, resulting in several distinct ethnic groups. People of mixed indigenous and European blood are called *mestizos;* those of mixed African and European blood are called *mulattos.* Latin American music is a complex mixture of African, indigenous, and European traditions, expressed in differing degrees in different regions of the continent.

People of the Andes Mountains

The Andes Mountains include the second tallest mountains in the world; only the Himalayas are higher. In the Andes Mountains the majority of people are indigenous and a significant minority are *mestizos.* Most of these people are peasants, farming small plots of land. They speak a mixture of Spanish and indigenous languages

South America

(Quechua, the language of the Inca; and Aymara, a pre-Incan language*)* and generally follow indigenous customs. While Roman Catholicism is the dominant religion of most of the areas, many people combine it with elements of their own indigenous religions.

The Music of the Andes

The musical traditions of the indigenous Andeans are the oldest in Latin America. However, the Andean people do not live in cultural isolation, nor have they been isolated for over 400 years. As a result, the music of the Andean region is an intermingling of indigenous and European elements and instruments.

Professionals and nonprofessionals play music in a variety of settings. Large cities and small villages have bars and clubs where bands come to play, and informal musical groups often play in homes. Almost every municipality has its own band. Festivals are another time when a number of informal (and more formal) groups get together to make music. In addition, there are numerous folkloric dance festivals at which musicians play. Public festivities during Semana Santa (Holy Week) are also filled with musical events.

The musicians' repertoire usually includes both traditional Andean music, which is played for celebrations and seasonal ceremonies, and contemporary Andean music, which is music inspired by traditional melodies and rhythms. Some of this contemporary Andean music even includes classical influences and modern jazz (see Sukay and Pachamama in Further Listening Resources).

The music you will be listening to in this chapter is a popular version of traditional Andean festival music that has spread throughout the world. Contemporary Andean music is played everywhere from Carnegie Hall to Native American powwows to European street festivals. It is played by groups ranging from itinerant street musicians to highly trained professionals.

Musical Instruments. Andean musicians play a mixture of indigenous and imported instruments. Some, like the harp, have been used for so many centuries that they are considered "native," although they were brought by the Spanish. Some, like the various panpipes, have both Spanish and indigenous names but were, in fact, native to the Andean region. The lengthy cultural contact among indigenous people, *mestizos*, Europeans, and—especially on the Atlantic coast—Africans has led to the intermingling and adaptation of instruments and musical elements.

A predecessor of the European **guitar,** brought by the Spanish invaders, gave rise to local variants that are distinctive in sound and playing technique. The most common of these local variants is the ***charango,*** which may have an armadillo shell for a body.

Andean ensembles use a variety of drums and shakers. One popular large drum is called a ***bombo,*** a Spanish term for drum; it is thought to be of Spanish origin. A bass drum, called ***wankara,*** made of two hides (often llama skins) stretched across a shell made

Musicians in traditional dress, La Paz, Bolivia
Owen Franken/Stock Boston

Carnival, Turabuco, Bolivia
SuperStock

from a hollow tree trunk, is indigenous. Shakers may be of local origin.

Various flutes of indigenous origin are also prevalent. The most distinctive of these flutes are the panpipes—a raftlike bunching of hollow tubes played by blowing across the top. Unlike the European panpipe, the Andean panpipes are constructed in pairs with the notes of the scale alternating between the two sets of pipes. Panpipes vary greatly in size. The largest tube of the smallest panpipe is 7 inches long; the largest tube of the largest panpipe is 54 inches long.

Bamboo and clay panpipes were used more than 1,500 years ago in Peru and Bolivia. A great variety continues to be played today. One popular bamboo panpipe is called **phukuna** in Quechua, from the Quechua word for "to blow"; in Aymara, it is called *siku.*

Peruvian musicians in a Finnish market square
Lee Snider/The Image Works

Siku is also the Bolivian term for the entire panpipe family. The *zampoñas* (a Spanish term) are usually made of a double row of pipes tied together; the largest tube is approximately 13½ inches long. In Andean communities, groups of four, eight, ten, or even sixty people may gather together to play the panpipes.

Several vertical end-notched wooden flutes, called *quenas* (or *kenas*) or *quenachos,* are also used. These instruments are of indigenous origin.

Musical Elements. Like the instruments, the musical elements of Andean music are a mixture of European

Two *quena (kena)* players with *siku* player
Jean Claude LeJeune/Stock Boston

History of the Inca

15th century	16th century	1825	1950s
Inca empire	Arrival of Spaniards	Bolivia declares independence	Andean music comes to United States and Europe

Indigenous peoples have inhabited the Andes Mountains since before recorded history. In the thirteenth century, the tribe (or tribes) that became known as the Incas started to conquer neighboring groups from their base in the Cuzco region. The powerful Inca empire really took shape in the mid-fifteenth century, when the ninth Inca ruler, Pachacuti, conquered many regions and reorganized political and social life, making the empire much more efficient to rule. The political system struck a balance between central authority and local rulers. Pachacuti and his son ruled one of the largest and richest empires in the Americas.

The Incas spoke Quechua, although different tribes within the empire spoke other native languages as well. They studied the planets and stars, and made complex astronomical observations. They used complex mathematical calculations when they designed buildings, roads, and terraced fields. A number of food products were developed by the Incas, including corn, coca, amaranth, quinoa, *charqui* (beef jerky), and 3,000 varieties of potatoes.

They built a vast network of roads as well as large, skillfully constructed buildings. Although they had no writing, records were kept by officials using the *quipu*, a multicolored knotted cord. Each color and knot represented something; knots of different sizes, spaced at certain intervals, stood for numbers.

In 1532 the Spanish explorer Francisco Pizarro captured and murdered Atahualpa, who was thus the last Inca emperor. No major Inca leader was left alive, so the Spaniards easily conquered the empire and enslaved the people. Although the areas near the coasts became Europeanized, the higher elevations continued to be the domain of a largely indigenous population who kept much of the Inca culture alive. It is in this region that modern Andean music developed.

The Inca heritage remains evident among the indigenous Andean people. Many still speak Quechua and Aymara (there are over 13 million native Quechua speakers today) and use farming methods that go back to the Inca empire. In addition, Inca culture survives in the poncho, in other clothing, and in the elaborately woven textiles produced by highland natives.

Although the Inca had no written language, a good picture of their traditional culture can be deduced from archaeological remains. The music of the Incas probably consisted of singing accompanied by flutes, panpipes, shell "trumpets," and drums. There is no evidence of any stringed instrument among the Incas.

and indigenous elements. The harmonic materials are clearly European, and they are played on the guitar and its local variants. The melodic and rhythmic aspects of the music, however, may be of indigenous origin. It is not possible to trace the history of these materials in detail, but they are quite distinct to Andean music and are not found in European music.

Listening to *Huachos*

This example of sectional form from Bolivia shows the distinctive instruments and musical materials of Andean music. Of particular interest is the section at 2:41 where two panpipe (*siku*) players divide the melody, with each player sounding every other note of the scale. This alternation is most obvious when heard on headphones, since the two players are recorded on different channels. This technique, called ***transando*** in Spanish and **hocket** (or **interlocking parts**) in English, is quite common in music for the *siku*.

It has been pointed out that hocket or *transando* results in the ultimate in social music, since to play a melody, an individual usually needs one or more friends. Another solution is for one player to tie the pipes of a matched set together and then alternate playing the front and the back set. As Quentin Navia explains, "In the Andes, you almost play music to *lose* your identity, to blend with the group."

The group playing *Huachos* is called Mallku de Los Andes. *Mallku* means "chief" in both Quechua, the ancient language of the Incas, and Aymara, the pre-Inca tongue. It also means "condor," so the name of the group can be translated as Condor, or Chief, of the Andes. The group formed in 1980; since that time it has toured extensively throughout Europe and the Americas, performing in colorful ponchos and traditional native costumes.

David Mercado Montano, panpipe player, was born in Cochabamba in 1957. Before forming Mallku de Los Andes in 1980, he founded Ballet Folklórico de Bolivia and played with the group Altiplano. René Carrasco García, playing the *charango*, was born in La Paz in 1953. He is also one of the founders of the group. Previously, he played with his own band, Ukamau; he emigrated to

Hocket

Hocket is not unique to Andean music. There are many examples in music of Western, African, Kuna (Panama Indian), and Indonesian origin. In the thirteenth and fourteenth centuries, hocket occurred in European vocal music. Two voices would sing very short tones in rapid alternation—reminiscent, perhaps, of a hiccup, a word that sounds similar to hocket. Another example of the technique is the performance of contemporary bell choirs. The performers hold one or two bells each and must fit in their tones at precisely the right moment to create the effect of an ongoing melody. The Balinese *gamelan* technique called *kotekan* is also a kind of hocket (see page 236).

Switzerland in 1983 but returned to Bolivia and rejoined Mallku in 1985. Edwin Roberts (b. 1956, La Paz), plays panpipes and *quenas*. He joined the group in 1984 after playing with various South American bands, including his own, and traveling around Europe. Victor Hugo Ferrel Torrico (b. 1959, La Paz), is the guitarist. He joined the group in 1985 after playing with his own band for a number of years. When he was sixteen, he won the title of South America's best young guitarist in a competition in Argentina.

Not only do these musicians make recordings and perform in cities worldwide—they also bring their music to remote places where people haven't heard recorded music. *Huachos* is on their album *On the Wings of the Condor*, one of the more popular Andean recordings ever made.

LISTENING ACTIVITY

Huachos (Tramps) (Eduardo Villaroel and J. Mercado) [CD 2, track 8]

Time	Musical Event
0:00	Introduction on *charango*.
0:13	Section **A**. Melody on guitar; background on *charango* with shakers. The metric structure is two measures of quadruple meter, followed by a measure of triple and a measure of duple meter. This can easily be detected by counting the beats: **1**, 2, 3, 4, **1**, 2, 3, 4, **1**, 2, 3, **1**, 2, beginning with the guitar melody.
0:31	Section **B**. A new melody with the same metric structure as the **A** theme. Flute (*quena*) plays the melody.
0:49	Section **C**. A third melody, with one measure of quadruple, one measure of triple, and one measure of duple. Same instrumentation as 0:31.
1:02	Section **A** repeated, now with both guitar and flute on melody.
1:21	Section **C** by *charango*. Note the "stop time" (moment of silence) in this section.
1:33	Section **A** repeated like opening.
1:52	Section **B**, solo by *charango*.

2:10	Section **C**, flute on melody.
2:23	Section **A**, flute and guitar on melody (like 1:02).
2:41	Section **C**, panpipes (*zampoña*), drums, and shakers. Note hocketing of melody by the *zampoña*.
2:54	Section **A,** panpipes.

The sectional divisions in this music are created by changes in melodic material and also by changes in the instrumentation. The overall formal outline is:

Introduction   **A B C A C A B C A C A**

A rondo is a form of music that features a repeated theme alternating with contrasting sections. See page 281.

This form, which is unique, most resembles a Western form called the rondo. The form of *Huachos* may be based on a common Andean dance style, where people sing part **A** and dance to parts **B** and **C**. (Imagine the indigenous dancers bundled up in heavy clothes, standing close together, stamping their feet and trying to keep warm, breathing hard in the thin high-mountain air.)

Response to the Music

Wherever Andean music is played, it draws a crowd of listeners. What is your response to this music? Think of your physical, emotional, cognitive, and spiritual responses. If you find the music attractive, can you say what the source of that attraction is? Does recognizing the sectional form of *Huachos* increase your enjoyment of the music? If so, how and why?

Summary

In this chapter we have introduced two important principles of musical form—repetition and contrast. We have examined a number of sectional forms including strophic form and verse and chorus form. Finally, we have discussed the music of the people of the Andes and listened to an example of this music that is in sectional form.

Applying What You Have Learned

1. Listen again to *Exodus* [CD 1, track 4] and outline the formal structure of the song. What creates the formal divisions in this music?

2. Listen again to *Gending Petegak* [CD 2, track 2]. What creates the formal divisions in it? How do you see repetition and contrast at work in this music?

3. Name an example of each of the following phenomena in music that you like to listen to:

   a. Repetition of a section of music

   b. Repetition of an accompaniment pattern

   c. Strophic song

   d. Verse and chorus

4. Listen again to *Simple Gifts* (CD 1, track 2) and outline the formal structure, using capital letters to designate the sections. Does the *Simple Gifts* section of *Appalachian Spring* (CD 1, track 3) follow the same formal structure as the hymn? Outline that formal structure and compare the two.

5. How does being aware of the formal structure of a piece of music change your responses (physical, emotional, cognitive, and spiritual) to the music?

Important Terms

form 261
repetition 261
contrast 263
sectional form 264
strophic form 264
verse and chorus
   form 265

guitar 268
charango 268
bombo 268
wankara 268
siku 270
zampoñas 270
phukuna 270

quena (*kena*) 270
quenachos 270
transando 272
hocket (interlocking
   parts) 272

Musicians and Ensembles Mentioned

*Woody Guthrie
*Bob Marley
*Little Otter Singers
*Leadbelly (Huddie Ledbetter)
*Sukay
Pachamama
Eduardo Villaroel
J. Mercado
*Mallku de los Andes
*David Mercado Montano
*René Carrasco García
*Edwin Roberts
*Victor Hugo Ferrel Torrico

Further Listening Resources

If you found the traditional music of Bolivia interesting you might enjoy exploring further the traditional music of Latin America produced by ANS, Sukay World Music, Nonesuch, Folkways, and Smithsonian. Some recordings currently available are:

Grupo Aymara: *Alirina—Live and In Concert* (Flying Fish).
Grupo Aymara: *Soul of Aymara* (World Music Library).
Ukamau, Los Rupay: *Magic Flutes* (Arc).
Savia Andina: *Classics 2 (El Minero)* (Sukay Records).
Eddy Navia: *El Charango* (Sukay Records).
Pachamama (Mother Earth) (Naviandina).

Sectional Forms II

🔘 *Symphony No. 39,* Franz Joseph Haydn

Richard Hamilton Smith/Corbis

A composer is a guy who goes around forcing his will on unsuspecting air molecules, often with the assistance of unsuspecting musicians.

*FRANK ZAPPA (1940–1993)

ROCK MUSICIAN AND COMPOSER

I n Chapter 14 you learned about repetition and contrast as methods of creating form in music, and you learned about some smaller sectional forms. In this chapter you will learn about variation, a third basic technique for creating coherence in music. You will also study the major section types in sectional forms. Finally, you will become familiar with some of the larger sectional forms and listen to one highly developed example: sonata form.

Elements of Form: Variation

Variation combines repetition with contrast. Once a musical idea is stated, it may appear again and again with slight changes. The changes may be in the melody, in the accompaniment, or in the rhythm. If you can recognize the original idea in its new guise, you will have the pleasant experience of both unity and variety at the same time.

We see variation in other areas of our lives. The same clothing design may be available in several colors. The same make of automobile can be purchased in different colors and with different sets of options. Successful films beget sequels (*Die Hard, Die Hard 2, Die Hard: With a Vengeance,* etc.), in which the pattern and characters of the earlier film are reproduced with (often minor) changes in plot details.

When variation techniques are applied to musical materials, the result is often called **development.** The term *development* is also applied to sections of pieces where variation takes place. Variation (or development) provides a pleasing blend of the security and predictability of repetition with the freshness of contrast.

Types of Sections

A sectional work is somewhat like a meal that is served in courses. Each course, from the appetizer to the dessert, has its own characteristic quality. We will first consider four common types of sections: thematic, introductory, connecting, and concluding. Most of the terms we use to describe formal sections have been introduced earlier in the book, but we are bringing them together here to provide a more comprehensive picture of form.

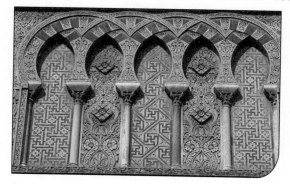

Exterior wall of the mosque, Cordoba, Spain
Peter Wilson/Corbis

Repetition: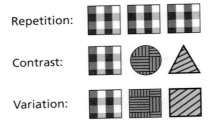

Contrast:

Variation:

Thematic Sections

A **theme** is a section that presents the primary melodic materials of
a composition. There may be several thematic sections in a piece.
The melodic material presented in a thematic section may be new
or may be repeated from earlier in the piece. As we noted in
Chapter 14 (see page 263), thematic sections are labeled with capital letters (**A, B, C,** etc.) in our listening guides and outlines.

Introductions

An **introduction** is a section at the beginning of a composition—
before the first theme—that prepares us to listen to the thematic
material. Sometimes an introduction is as simple as a few measures of the accompaniment pattern, with no melody. In such cases
we learn to know that the theme is coming very soon, and we wait
with anticipation.

In other cases an introduction is an extended section in itself or
even an entire movement separated from the body of a composition
by silence, a change of tempo, or some other major change in texture and dynamics. With an extended introduction, we become
much more involved in the ongoing process of the section itself. In
fact, we may not even realize that we are hearing an introduction.
It may only be in retrospect that we come to understand the introductory function of the music we heard at the beginning of the
composition.

You might think of an introduction as an "appetizer" before the
main course of the composition. The introductory section may be simple or complex, but it will generally be lighter in quality than the
theme.

Connecting Sections: Transitions and Interludes

Between thematic sections there are often sections whose purpose
is connection. Such connecting sections provide a sense of rest
from the thematic presentation and help shape the overall proportions of a composition. Connecting sections have been likened to
open spaces in a sculpture and to the background in a painting.

They set off the thematic material and provide a necessary foil for the themes, much as the "negative space" in visual art provides a setting for the important figures.

One type of connecting section, called a **transition,** has the function of preparing for a theme that will follow. Often, a transition builds a sense of anticipation, which is resolved by the appearance of the following theme.

Another type of connecting section is an **interlude.** An interlude, like a transition, is music that occurs between thematic sections. The purpose of interludes, however, is not so much preparation for the following section as relief from or contrast to the surrounding themes. Relief is often necessary for us to prepare ourselves to listen more intently to the following material. In accompanied vocal music, interludes are usually purely instrumental passages inserted between the major sections of the work.

Concluding Sections: Codas and Codettas

After a thematic section, there is often a concluding section that serves to bring the work or a major part of the work to a close. If the concluding section is at the end of a movement or a composition, it is called a **coda.** If it concludes an internal part of a work, it is called a **codetta.** *Coda* is an Italian word that means "tail," and *codetta* is the diminutive of that term—thus, a "little tail."

It is clear from the descriptions above that introductions and codas have a similar function: creating a "frame" around a composition. Such a frame is desirable because it serves to separate our everyday reality, with its emphasis on chronological time, from the piece of music, which works in psychological time. Introductory and concluding sections are important structural elements in a composition.

Sectional Forms

Most of the standard sectional forms result from some combination of repetition, contrast, and variation. Some of these patterns are so common that they have been given names. **Binary form** is a term describing a work that consists of two sections; **ternary form** refers to a work in three sections. In ternary forms the most common pattern is a return to the first section after a contrasting middle section (**A B A**).

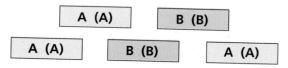

Binary and ternary forms

Compound forms use binary form and ternary form as sections of a larger work. A compound binary form has two major divisions, at least one of which is a simple binary or ternary form. A compound ternary form has three major divisions, at least one of which is a simple binary or ternary form.

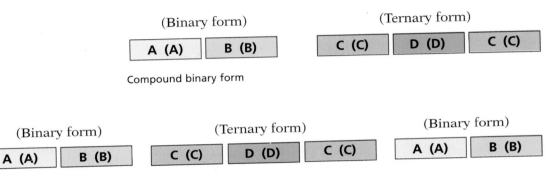

Compound binary form

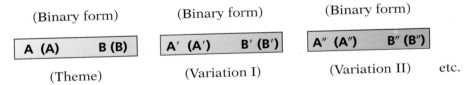

Compound ternary form

Theme and variations is a sectional form in which a theme is stated and then followed by a series of variations, each retaining the general outline of the original theme. The theme is a complete form (binary or ternary) in itself.

Theme and variations form

A rondo is a form based on a single theme, called the rondo theme, that alternates with several contrasting themes, called episodes. The five-part rondo and the seven-part rondo are typical patterns.

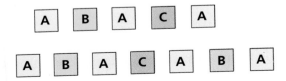

Five-part rondo and seven-part rondo

Sonata Form

When musicians speak of sonata form, they are generally referring to the form of a single movement within a multimovement work. **Sonata form** is a sectional form; in fact, it is the most elaborate of all the sectional forms. It consists of an exposition, a development, and a recapitulation.

Exposition (repeated)	Development	Recapitulation

Sonata form

Exposition

The opening part of a sonata form is called the **exposition.** It presents the thematic material of the piece. The number of themes varies somewhat from piece to piece, but many sonata forms are based on two contrasting themes. The illustration below shows a typical outline of an exposition.

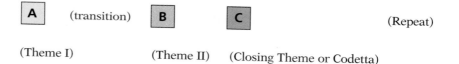

| A | (transition) | B | C | (Repeat) |

(Theme I)   (Theme II)   (Closing Theme or Codetta)

A sonata exposition section

The first theme generally occurs with little or no introduction at the beginning of a sonata form. This first theme may be a single melody or a group of melodies related to each other by being in the same key. If the first theme is a group of melodies, it is often called the first theme group. The first theme is followed by a transition that leads to the second theme or second theme group, which is in a different key from the first theme. This is followed by a closing section that may be simply a codetta or a more extended thematic section. If the closing section is thematic, it is often called the **closing theme.** The exposition section is usually repeated before the development begins.

Development

The **development** is a section in which there is considerable variation of the thematic materials presented in the exposition. Theme follows theme with little transition, and there are contrasts in key and mood. Other developmental techniques available to the composer include new orchestrations, combinations of themes, and even the creation of new material. The development section of the sonata form may be quite long and may rival the exposition in duration. It provides a contrast with the more structured exposition section that precedes it and the recapitulation that follows.

Recapitulation

The **recapitulation** is a repetition of the exposition section with certain modifications. The second theme—which was stated in a contrasting key in the exposition—is now stated in the tonic key. This is necessary so that the movement will end in the key in which it began, a requirement in most tonal music. Other modifications, such as lengthening or shortening of the themes and further development and variation, may also occur, providing additional variety in the recapitulation.

In many sonata forms of the classical period (1750–1825; see page 284), the entire development and the entire recapitulation are repeated. The repeats are marked in the scores, but in practice the performers may or may not choose to play them.

The Complete Classical Sonata

The term sonata has had several meanings throughout the history of Western European art music. In the classical period a standard sonata consisting of three or four movements became the norm for most instrumental music. The work we will examine in this chapter (Haydn's *Symphony No. 39*) is a typical example of the complete classical sonata.

It is important to distinguish between *sonata form,* which is the form of a single movement, and a *sonata,* which is a multimovement work.

A **complete classical sonata** usually has either three or four movements. The opening movement is almost always a sonata form, either with or without an introduction. The second movement is a slower movement, which may be in a variety of forms, including sonata, theme and variation, compound ternary, or rondo. The final movement is a fast movement, often in either sonata form or rondo form. If the sonata has four movements, the additional movement is usually placed between the second movement and the final movement of the work. This additional movement is a dance movement in compound ternary form. In the classical period it was called the **menuet-and-trio** movement.

The complete sonata pattern described on p. 284 was used for most multimovement instrumental works from the late eighteenth century through the end of the nineteenth century. Works with titles such as sonata, symphony, concerto, trio, quartet, and quintet are usually complete sonatas. These titles refer to the instruments the composition is written for, rather than to the form.

Movement	Usual tempo	Typical form
First	Fast	Sonata
Second	Slow	Sonata, theme and variation, compound ternary, or rondo
Third (optional)	Moderate to fast	Compound ternary
Final	Fast	Sonata, theme and variation, or rondo

Plan of a complete classical sonata

The Classical Period

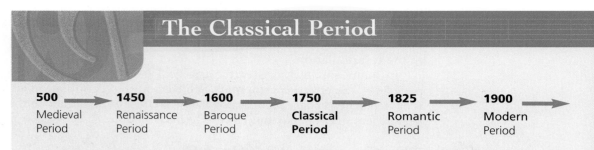

500	1450	1600	1750	1825	1900
Medieval Period	Renaissance Period	Baroque Period	**Classical Period**	Romantic Period	Modern Period

The classical period in Western European art music is frequently called the Viennese classical period because of the dominance of three composers—Franz Joseph Haydn, Wolfgang Amadeus Mozart, and Ludwig van Beethoven—all of whom lived and worked in and around Vienna, Austria. The aesthetic ideals of classicism were objectivity, simplicity, emotional restraint, balance, and clarity of form, along with admiration of Greek and Roman literary and architectural models. These ideals are also present in other periods of music history, but nowhere were they more clearly evident than during this era, especially in instrumental music.

The classical period was marked by contrasts between a privileged aristocracy living in castles and palaces, a rising but still small middle class, and the enraged, desperate masses. Society began undergoing rapid change from monarchy to more democratic forms of government. The American Revolution (1776), the French Revolution (1789), and the Napoleonic wars in Europe were major military expressions of the social and political conflicts of the times.

This was a time that saw an increasing reliance on reason, a belief in natural law and order, and the application of scientific method to political and social issues. The development of the first vaccine, as well as the invention of the steam engine, cotton gin, and electric motors and generators, took place during this time, as did the compilation of the first encyclopedia, Denis Diderot's *Encyclopédie* (1751–1772).

Music in the Classical Period

Instrumental music was more popular than vocal music during this period, and public performances became important. Although operas and sacred and secular vocal music continued to be written and performed, chamber music and orchestral performances gained in popularity. The sonata and the symphony developed, and the string quartet replaced the older trio sonata (see page 176). Improvisation became less important. At the beginning of this period, courts in Germany, France, and Austria-Hungary maintained a staff of resident musicians to provide entertainment in the form of concerts, operas, and dances. Musicians, who were at that time considered servants, often found themselves trading the violin bow for the serving tray in the course of an evening's entertainment. By the end of the era, the musician was an emancipated artist responsible for—and remunerated for—compositions and performances.

The symphony, the solo concerto, the solo piano sonata, the string quartet, and other forms of chamber music dominated instru-mental music. During this time the orchestra expanded in both number and variety of instruments; the piano (invented around 1710) supplanted the harpsichord as the most popu-lar solo keyboard instrument.

Classical antiquity had been an important model for European artists since the Renaissance, but it was particularly admired in the mid-eighteenth century, as a result of fresh archaeological discoveries and wide-spread travel. Thomas Jefferson modeled his design for the state capitol in Richmond on a Roman temple, the Maison Carrée, that he had seen in France.

Virginia state capitol
Michael Freeman/Corbis

The Symphony

A **symphony** is a complete sonata for orchestra. The vast majority of symphonies from the classical period have four movements in

Copper engraving of
Joseph Haydn
Bettman/Corbis

the standard pattern shown on page 284. The three principal composers of classical symphonies were Franz Joseph Haydn, Wolfgang Amadeus Mozart, and Ludwig van Beethoven. Together, these masters of the symphonic form composed about 160 symphonies, which account for most classical-period symphonies still being performed.

The earlier symphonies in the classical period were works of modest dimensions, often twenty minutes or less in duration. (Haydn's *Symphony No. 2* lasts only eight minutes.) Later works of Haydn and Mozart were considerably longer, but Beethoven greatly expanded the duration of the form. By the end of the classical period, single movements were often nearly as long as entire four-movement symphonies had been at the beginning of the period. This trend toward longer and more grandiose works continued into the nineteenth century, and some of the symphonies of Gustav Mahler and Anton Bruckner are over ninety minutes in length.

As you can see, a symphony can vary from a short work for a small orchestra to a work of an hour or more, played by huge orchestral forces. To be able to anticipate what you are likely to hear at a given orchestra concert, you need to know when a work was

Musical Performance in Vienna

There was an abundance of musical performance in Vienna during the time of Haydn, Mozart, and Beethoven, but the settings would seem strange to modern music lovers. Any modern city has various large and small performing spaces, but in Vienna there was no public hall or room dedicated to the performance of music until 1831, well after the end of the classical period. There were theaters devoted to opera and to drama, but no concert halls. Musical performances took place mostly in private settings or in spaces that were rented for specific occasions.

An evening party in the home of a well-to-do family often involved music. The host, the hostess, or a guest would be asked to perform on the piano or a string instrument, or to sing. These performances were amateur, spontaneous, and unrehearsed. At formal parties and at celebrations such as birthdays, professional and amateur musicians often provided music. The music would compete with food, drink, card games, dancing, and conversation for the attention of the guests.

Groups of amateur and professional musicians gathered regularly (usually weekly) to play chamber music. String quartets were their favorite music, but other kinds of chamber compositions, such as trios and quintets, might also be played.

Larger works, such as oratorios, were performed at gala concerts that were sponsored by groups of noblemen who each made a contribution to cover the expenses. Admission to these events was by invitation, and both the nobility and selected members of the middle class received invitations.

A performance of Haydn's oratorio *The Creation* in the audience hall of the old University of Vienna, 1808
Stock Montage

A virtuoso performer with a large following would often arrange a benefit concert. He or she would sponsor it, make all arrangements, hire additional musicians, assume all expenses, and pocket all the profit.

Charity concerts were also arranged, with the proceeds going to a worthy cause. The musicians were often asked to donate their services for such events, and the nobility could be counted on for large donations to cover the expenses.

The Opera

Without doubt, the most important continuing musical events in Vienna were the operas. In Vienna there was a rich diet of *opera seria* (serious operas) and *opera buffa* (comic operas) in Italian, and the *Singspiel*, a German-language light opera with spoken dialogue. The operas ran throughout the winter and spring seasons, except during Advent and Lent, when theater of any sort was prohibited.

Vienna Opera House
Culver Pictures

composed and something about the composer. Knowledge of the history of Western European art music will help you to become a more discriminating listener to this kind of music.

Franz Joseph Haydn

In this chapter we will be listening to a symphony by Franz Joseph Haydn. Haydn was born in 1732 in Rohrau, Austria. He showed unusual musical gifts at an early age and was sent to a nearby city to study before the age of six. He returned home only for short visits. When he was eight years old he became a choirboy in Saint Stephen's Cathedral in Vienna, where he received musical training and education. When his voice broke at age seventeen he was expelled from the cathedral choir and choir school and left penniless and destitute. He lived in Vienna by doing whatever work he could find while teaching himself composition and music theory. Gradually he found work as a musician in the households of noblemen in Vienna. In 1758 Haydn became the musical director of the orchestra of Count Ferdinand Maximilian von Morzin. It was for this orchestra that he wrote his first symphony. When the count's orchestra was disbanded a short time later, Haydn took a similar position with the powerful Esterházy family, a position that he held until his death in 1809, serving three generations of the family. He wrote most of his 108 symphonies for the Esterházy orchestra. Although the Esterházy were his patrons, he also composed for other clients and traveled widely, especially after 1790.

> An *oratorio* is an extended dramatic composition based on a religious subject.

Haydn's musical output is vast. He composed seventeen operas, two oratorios, thirty-seven concertos, sixty-two string quartets, forty-five piano trios, sixty-two piano sonatas, and sixty songs, along with other chamber music and sacred music. He is regarded as the father of the string quartet and the symphony. Many other composers, including both Mozart and Beethoven, studied his works. Haydn achieved international recognition in his lifetime. His crowning achievements were the twelve *London Symphonies*, which he composed between 1791 and 1795 for two extended visits to that city.

Symphony No. 39 was composed between 1765 and 1766. Haydn's symphonies from this period show more emotional depth than his earlier works. A number of these symphonies, including *Symphony No. 39*, are in minor keys.

Three of the four movements of *Symphony No. 39* are in sonata form, although each shows some deviation from the standard outline presented earlier in this chapter. As you will hear, a standard formal outline is not a strict recipe for creating a piece of music, but rather a broad generalization based on the examination of common patterns in hundreds of compositions. Every sonata is shaped by the musical materials themselves, and no two are exactly alike. Studying these three movements will give you an idea of just how varied the sonata form can be.

5-part rondo

LISTENING ACTIVITY

Symphony No. 39 (Haydn) [CD 2, tracks 9–12]

The performance you will hear was recorded by the Academy of Ancient Music in Walthamstow Assembly Hall, London, using modern reproductions of instruments of Haydn's time (see "The 'Early

Music' Movement," page 179). The conductor is Christopher Hogwood.

MOVEMENT I (SONATA FORM) [CD 2, track 9]

Time	Musical Event	Description
Exposition section:		
0:00	Theme **A**	Movement I opens with a rapid melody in a minor key (G minor). Meter is quadruple-simple. There is a short silence after the first phrase, which you will hear repeated in other statements of the theme.
0:25	Transition	This section, which is marked by a sudden increase in dynamic level, prepares for theme **B**.
0:40	Theme **B**	Theme **B** is a variation of theme **A** in a major key. These forms are called **monothematic sonata forms** and are common in Haydn's symphonies.
0:59	Closing theme	This theme, which becomes more important later in the movement, provides punctuation for the exposition section.
1:16	Theme **A**	Entire exposition section is repeated exactly.
1:40	Transition	(see 0:25)
1:55	Theme **B**	(see 0:40)
2:15	Closing theme	(see 0:59)
Development section:		
2:32		Development begins with a variation of theme **A**.
2:42		Theme **A** in a new key. There is an interesting counterpoint between the first and second violins a few seconds into this section. Can you hear that they are playing similar melodic lines separated by one measure?
2:56		Variation of the closing theme.

3:05	Transition	Since this transition leads to the recapitulation (a restatement of theme **A**), it is sometimes called a **retransition.**

Recapitulation section:

A *musical motive* is a short melodic or rhythmic idea that is recognizable when repeated or varied.

3:17	Theme **A**	This restatement is exact for nine measures. Then a loud passage breaks in, cutting the theme short.
3:37	Transition	Here a motive from theme **A** moves through several keys.
3:55	Closing theme	Since theme **B** was only theme **A** in a new key, there is no reason to restate it here. The closing theme serves as the second theme. This is not uncommon in monothematic sonata forms.

Development and recapitulation are repeated exactly:

4:08	Development	(see 2:32)
4:19		(see 2:42)
4:33		(see 2:56)
4:43	Transition	(see 3:05)
4:55	Recapitulation	(see 3:17)
5:15	Transition	(see 3:37)
5:32	Closing theme	(see 3:55)

MOVEMENT II (SONATA FORM) [CD 2, track 10]
Exposition section:

0:00	Theme **A**	Quiet theme in triple-simple time and in a major key. Notice that no wind instruments are playing in this movement. The second movement of a symphony is often lighter in texture than the first movement.
0:15	Codetta	Short closing passage for theme **A.**
0:23	Transition	This passage leads to theme **B.**
0:31	Theme **B**	Introduced by a loud chord, which is repeated several times. Here theme **B** presents a new melodic idea, which is closer to the standard outline for the sonata form.

0:50	Codetta	This passage closes the exposition section.
0:59	Theme **A**	Exposition section is repeated exactly.
1:15	Codetta	(see 0:15)
1:23	Transition	(see 0:23)
1:31	Theme **B**	(see 0:31)
1:50	Codetta	(see 0:50)

Development section:

1:59		Development begins with several variations of theme **A** in a new key. Several keys are visited briefly in this passage.
3:01	Transition	This is a very brief preparation for the recapitulation.

Recapitulation section:

3:05	Theme **A**	Exact restatement of theme **A** for four measures; then some variation begins. (It is not uncommon for the themes in the recapitulation to be treated with further variation.)
3:21	Codetta	Very much like the codetta at 0:15.
3:29	Transition	Very much like the transition at 0:23.
3:36	Theme **B**	This time theme **B** is stated in the key of theme **A**.
3:55	Coda	Like the codetta that closed the exposition section but extended to bring the movement to a close.

Development and recapitulation are repeated exactly:

4:15	Development	(see 1:54)
5:17	Transition	(see 3:01)
5:21	Theme **A**	(see 3:05)
5:36	Codetta	(see 3:21)
5:53	Theme **B**	(see 3:36)
6:12	Coda	(see 3:55)

MOVEMENT III (COMPOUND TERNARY FORM) [CD 2, track 11]

Menuet (rounded binary form):

0:00	Section **A**	This short theme in triple-simple meter and in a minor key is typical of a menuet-and-trio movement.
0:10	Section **A**	(see 0:00)
0:20	Section **B**	Contrasting but somewhat similar idea.
0:40		The entire section **A** is repeated here. A binary form with this internal repetition is called a **rounded binary form.**
0:49	Section **B**	(see 0:20)
1:09		(see 0:40)

Trio (binary form):

1:19	Section **C**	New theme. Again, the theme is short.
1:31	Section **C**	(see 1:19)
1:43	Section **D**	Contrasting but somewhat similar idea.
1:55	Section **D**	(see 1:43)

Menuet repeated:

2:07	Section **A**	(see 0:00)
2:17	Section **A**	(see 0:10)
2:26	Section **B**	(see 0:20)
2:46		(see 0:40)
2:56	Section **B**	(see 0:49)
3:16		(see 1:09)

MOVEMENT IV (SONATA FORM) [CD 2, track 12]

Exposition section:

0:00	Theme **A**	Dramatic theme in quadruple-simple meter and in a minor key. This is the most intense movement in the symphony.
0:19	Theme **B**	Theme **B,** in a major key, is not preceded by a transition. This is another change from the standard formal outline.
0:46	Codetta	Short closing section for the exposition.

Exposition repeated:

0:56	Theme **A**	(see 0:00)
1:16	Theme **B**	(see 0:19)
1:43	Codetta	(see 0:46)

Development section:

1:53	Development	Passage based loosely on theme **A**.
2:09		Variations on theme **A**.
2:29	Transition	Quiet passage that begins the preparation for a return to theme **A**. Later there is a loud passage punctuated by chords.

Recapitulation section:

2:43	Theme **A**	An exact restatement of theme **A**.
3:02	(Theme **B**)	Elements of theme **B**, but not an exact restatement.
3:11	Coda	Closing passage similar to 0:46.

Development and recapitulation repeated exactly:

3:22	Development	(see 1:53)
3:38		(see 2:09)
3:58	Transition	(see 2:29)
4:12	Theme **A**	(see 2:43)
4:32	(Theme **B**)	(see 3:02)
4:41	Coda	(see 3:11)

This symphony has given you three opportunities to hear the sonata form in action. Which movement is closest to the standard outline presented earlier in this chapter?

As you can see, the sonata form is only a set of general principles, not a rigid set of rules. That is true of all the sectional forms. Each individual piece is likely to show some deviation from the standard outline.

The third movement is an excellent example of compound form, in this case compound ternary form. Each section of the work is a complete form in itself. The overall design is ternary.

Response to the Music

How does concentrating on the formal design of these movements affect your physical, emotional, and spiritual response to the music? It is important to listen again to the whole work without following all the details of the listening guides. In that way you will be able to respond more directly to the music itself. Notice, however, that your knowledge of classical formal design helps you to orient yourself within the music. The cognitive response is only one aspect of your enjoyment of music, but it is an important part of the total experience.

Summary

In this chapter you have learned about the technique of variation and about several types of formal sections: themes, introductions, transitions, interludes, codas, and codettas. We have noted that the complete classical sonata form has various manifestations: the symphony, the solo concerto, the solo sonata, and various kinds of chamber music. We have studied in detail a single example of a complete classical symphony: Haydn's *Symphony No. 39*.

Applying What You Have Learned

1. Listen again to *Bay a Glezele Mashke* [CD 1, track 7]. It is a very abbreviated compound ternary form. The first part, in binary form, is (in form) much like the menuet in Haydn's symphony. The second part, however, is much shorter. The return to the opening material is also abbreviated, with only the second part of the binary form present. Make a formal outline of this piece, using capital letters for sections.

2. Listen again to *The Young Person's Guide to the Orchestra* [CD 2, track 1]. The opening part of this work is a theme and variations form. Make a formal outline of the section from the beginning of the work until the second theme enters.

3. Name a work in the CDs accompanying this book that begins with an introduction.

4. Name a work in the CDs accompanying this book that contains an interlude or transition.

5. Does dynamic contrast contribute to the formal structure in Haydn's *Symphony No. 39*? If so, describe the role of dynamics in creating the form.

6. Select another symphony by Haydn or a symphony by Mozart. Listen to the work and try to identify the form of each movement. Select a movement and make a formal outline for it. How do the forms in the work you have chosen compare with those in Haydn's *Symphony No. 39?*

Important Terms

variation 278
development 278
theme 279
introduction 279
transition 280
interlude 280
coda 280
codetta 280
binary form 280
ternary form 280

compound form 281
theme and variations 281
rondo 281
sonata form 282
exposition 282
closing theme 282
development 282
recapitulation 283

complete classical sonata 283
menuet-and-trio movement 283
symphony 285
monothematic sonata forms 290
retransition 291
rounded binary form 293

Names preceded by * have short biographies in Appendix B, page 346.

Musicians and Ensembles Mentioned

*Franz Joseph Haydn
*Wolfgang Amadeus Mozart
*Ludwig van Beethoven
*Gustav Mahler
*Anton Bruckner
Academy of Ancient Music

Further Listening Resources

Mozart: *Sonata No. 13 in B-flat,* K. 333. London 417149-2 LH.
Beethoven: *Concerto in D for Violin and Orchestra,* Op. 61. Angel CDC-47002.
Dvořák: *Quartet in C,* Op. 96. London 430077-2LH.
Brahms: *Symphony No. 4,* Op. 98. DGG 410084-2 GH.
Mahler: *Symphony No. 5 in C-Sharp Minor.* DGG 423608-2 GH.

Continuous Forms I

💿 **Sultan Veled Peshrev,** Dogan Ergin

Hulton-Deutsch Collection/Corbis

Come, come whoever you are,
wanderer, worshiper, lover of leaving
This is no caravan of despair.
It doesn't matter if you've broken your vow a thousand times,
Come, yet again, come.

MEVLANA JALALU'DDIN RUMI
THIRTEENTH-CENTURY PERSIAN SUFI POET AND PHILOSOPHER

In Chapters 14 and 15 you learned about sectional forms. In this chapter and Chapter 17, we will concentrate on forms that do not divide into sections but are based instead on principles of musical continuity.

Continuity

The term **continuity** refers to the way most music seems to flow naturally and logically, keeping us absorbed in the ongoing experience. The musical elements (rhythm, melody, harmony, dynamics, and texture) are arranged in such a way that a continuity is created. The music you are forced to listen to on the telephone when you are "on hold" is often an example of pure continuity. You seem to enter an ongoing stream of sound, and there is no discernible break in the flow until you are connected with another person. In fact, if you are "on hold" long enough, you may discover that this music is simply a passage repeated over and over in a continuous loop.

You are already aware of some of the ways that continuity is created in music: by ongoing beat, by logical harmonic progressions, and by meaningful melodic sequences. In this chapter we will learn how some of these elements function to provide continuity in complete pieces of music.

Continuous forms are musical compositions in which the continuity is seldom broken. These are compositions with few internal divisions or interruptions. Such compositions create an impression of a continuous flow, often with a sense of evolution or development rather than abrupt change. There is often relatively little contrast.

One primary type of continuous form is text-based. Some vocal compositions are based on texts that have no repeated sections and cannot be broken down into verses. **Text-based continuous form** is the subject of Chapter 17, where you will listen to a motet by Josquin Desprez. A second type—**pattern-based continuous form**—is the subject of this chapter.

Pattern-Based Continuous Forms

Some continuous forms are based on musical patterns that are repeated throughout a work. These patterns may be short motives or longer musical ideas, often a phrase or more in length. The patterns may be harmonic progressions, rhythmic phrases, or melodic ideas. Pattern-based continuous forms occur in much of the music of India, the Middle East, and Africa, and in the music of Native Americans. In Western European art music, many compositions such as **preludes, inventions, fugues, passacaglias,** and **cha-connes** are pattern-based, although it is often difficult to anticipate the musical content of a work from its title.

In this chapter you will listen to a pattern-based continuous form, a piece of Sufi music from Turkey called ***Sultan Veled Peshrev.***

Turkey

Turkey is poised between Europe and Asia and is often considered part of the Middle East. Turkey's nearest neighbors are Bulgaria, Greece, Georgia, Armenia, Azerbaijan, Iran, Iraq, and Syria. The Black Sea lies to the north, the Aegean Sea to the west, and the Mediterranean Sea to the south. This land, once called Anatolia, has been settled for at least 8,000 years. Beginning in the eleventh century, the Muslim Seljuk Turks captured much of Anatolia and began building the Ottoman Empire, which reached its high point in the sixteenth century but continued until the twentieth century. In 1923 the empire became a republic, and its first president, Mustafa Kemal Ataturk, brought about massive social and political reforms that separated religion from government and transformed Turkey into one of the most secular of the Middle Eastern nations.

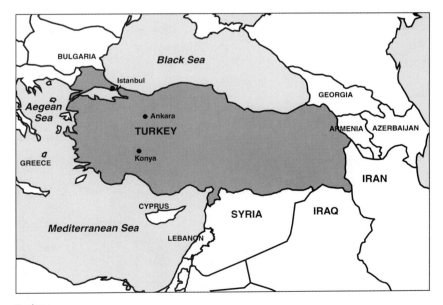

Turkey

Turkish History

The earliest traces of human inhabitants in Turkey—previously called Anatolia—go back to 6000 B.C.E., but the first inhabitants in recorded history were the Hittites, who ruled in Anatolia from 1500 B.C.E. The Roman general Pompey conquered Anatolia in 63 B.C.E., making the region a part of the Roman Empire. In 1071 C.E. the Muslim Seljuk Turks captured most of Anatolia, and the era of the Turkish empire began. In spite of attempts by Christians to drive out the Turks during the first Crusade (1096–1099), and despite an invasion by the Mongols in 1243, the Turkish empire grew. It reached its peak in 1526 when the Ottoman Empire reached the Danube River and threatened all of Europe.

In 1529 European forces successfully turned the Ottoman armies away from Vienna, and in 1571 the Ottoman navy was defeated by the European fleet. This set in motion a gradual weakening of the empire, and one by one its territories were lost. The Ottoman Empire entered the First World War (1914–1918) on

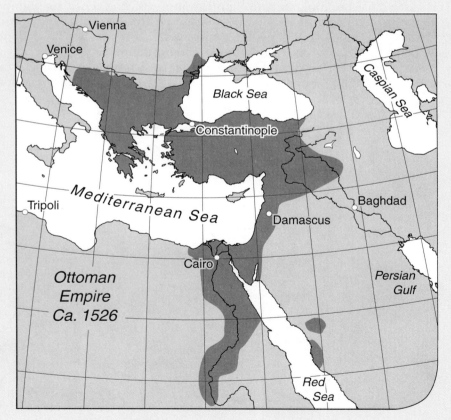

The Ottoman Empire in 1526

the side of Germany and Austria and lost. After the war, the Allied forces broke up the vestiges of the Ottoman Empire.

Mosque of Suleiman I
Adam Turner/The Image Works

In 1923 the Republic of Turkey was formed. It has persisted to the present day, with periodic takeovers by the military. Its first president, Mustafa Kemal Ataturk (1881–1938) (whose name means "Father of the Turks") restored Turkish pride; he also did away with many Islamic traditions, including the Arabic alphabet, Muslim schools, the Islamic legal system, and the wearing of the veil by women and the fez (a brimless, cone-shaped, flat-topped hat) by men. The government also gave women rights, including the right to vote. Turkey is now one of the more Westernized Islamic countries, but tensions between traditional Islamic groups and Westernized Turks continue.

One of Turkey's most important contributions to the arts has been architecture. The sixteenth-century mosque of Suleiman I (the "Blue Mosque") in Istanbul, designed by Koca Sinan, is considered one of the most beautiful examples of Islamic architecture in the world.

Classical Music of Turkey

Turkish classical music has a long history, stretching back at least five hundred years. It is one of the most highly developed musics of the world and includes extensive religious music, which can be divided into music of the mosque and mystical music (such as that performed in the Mevlevi *sema*). Over the centuries, Turkey developed a large repertoire of compositions, notation systems (as early as the thirteenth century), and sophisticated performance practices. There are extensive writings on the theory of Middle Eastern music in Arabic and, later, in Turkish.

Sultan Veled (1226–1312), the elder son of the poet and mystic Rumi (see page 304), is believed to be the composer of the earliest instrumental pieces that still survive. Two other important early composers are Abdülkadir Meragi (also an important theoretician), who died in 1435, and Buhurizade Mustafa Itri (1640–1712), who is regarded as the most important Turkish composer. Turkish heads of state were also composers. Gazi Giray Han (sixteenth century) and

Sultan Selim III (eighteenth and nineteenth centuries) are examples. The repertoire of Turkish classical music includes thousands of compositions. These works are known to modern musicians through notated musical sources. Western music notation was introduced into Turkey in the seventeenth century but came into general use only in the twentieth century.

Turkish music has influenced European music primarily through Turkish military bands, which were popular in Vienna during the classical period (1750–1825; see page 284). See page 209 for a photograph and a description of this ensemble. (Members of Turkish military bands were imposing because of their size and uniforms—an effect that was calculated to strike fear into the hearts of their opponents.) Many European composers in the eighteenth and nineteenth centuries, including Wolfgang Amadeus Mozart and Ludwig van Beethoven, wrote music in the style of the Turkish military bands, which they called "Janissary music" or "*alla turca*" style.

In the nineteenth century, Turkish classical music began to be influenced by European music. Western musical instruments, such as the piano—and the cello you will hear in the recording of *Sultan Veled Peshrev*—were introduced. Western European art music became popular, and a national opera and two symphony orchestras were established. Nonetheless, Turkish composers continued (and continue) to draw upon their own classical and folkloric musical traditions.

Turkish classical music consists of a melody accompanied by drums and other instruments. The melody is played by several instruments, but each plays a slightly different variation, resulting in heterophonic texture.

Makam The basic pitch sets in Turkish music are called **makams.** The *makams* (there are hundreds of them) are somewhat similar to the *ragas* of India (see page 127) in that they include both the idea of a scale and also a set of forms from which melodies are derived. *Makams* also contain a main melodic tone, called **egreti karar,** like the *vadis vara* of *ragas*. The Turkish musician works within these "rules" to create a piece of music. The pitches of the *makams* do not correspond to those of the Western scale—in fact, a number of the pitches lie "between the keys" of the Western piano. If your frame of reference is Western music, this may give you the impression that the musicians are playing "out of tune." But notice that the musicians agree on the pitches they are playing, clearly demonstrating that they are playing "in tune" within their own system.

Unlike Indian classical music, more of Turkish classical music is composed than improvised. There is, however, considerable room

Janissary comes from the name of the elite Turkish troops, the *yeni çeri.*

for improvisation within the composed structure. Another characteristic of Turkish classical music that is different from the classical music of India is the practice of moving from one *makam* to another in the course of a composition. You will hear some of these shifts in *Sultan Veled Peshrev.* In classical Indian music, you will recall, one *raga* is chosen for a piece and is retained for the entire composition.

The Instruments The instruments of Turkish music include strings, winds, and percussion. In *Sultan Veled Peshrev* you will listen to representatives of the three instrumental families. The plucked string instruments you will hear include the **ud** and the **tanbur** (a longer-necked, six-stringed *ud*).

The *ud* is the ancestor of the Western lute. It was brought to Europe when the Moors from North Africa conquered Spain in the Middle Ages. The name *lute* comes from the Arabic *al-'ud*.

The bowed string instruments are the **kemençe**—a fiddle—and the **violonsel,** a cello. The **kanun** is a struck-string instrument like a zither.

The wind family is represented by the **ney**—an end-blown cane flute, originally Egyptian. The percussion family is represented by the **kudüm**—a pair of small kettledrums.

The musical ensemble for Turkish classical music is known as a **mutrip.** It consists of a number of wind, string, and percussion instruments and may have as many as a dozen performers.

An *ud* player
Cameron Powers

Sufism

Sultan Veled Peshrev, which we will listen to in this chapter, is an example of Turkish classical music used by a religious community known as Sufis.

Some say the word *Sufi* comes from an Arabic word, *suf,* which means wool, and refers to the plain wool cloaks worn by these materially poor spiritual seekers. According to some of its adherents, **Sufism** has roots that extend beyond recorded history; others claim that Sufism began at the time of the prophet Muhammad, the founder of Islam, who lived in the seventh century in what is now Saudi Arabia. A Sufi takes literally the Muslim affirmation "La illaha illa'llalh"—"There is no God but God." The central practice of many Sufis is *zhikr* (pronounced "thicker"). *Zhikr* involves repetitive reciting of this affirmation, which is believed to impart an internal

Dervishes (Sufis)
Culver Pictures

realization of the "Unity of Being which annihilates all multiplicity, all separate entities." According to Sufis, it is only an illusion that we see ourselves as separate beings. Sufis perform spiritual practices that are designed to tear open the veil of illusion and bring intense interior awareness of the essential oneness of all creation.

The purpose of Sufism is to convey personal, experiential knowledge of the eternal. This knowledge and the spiritual practices associated with discovering it are passed down within various Sufi orders or "paths." These different orders trace their origins through chains (or lineages) of people that go back to Muhammad. The **Mevlevi** order, the particular branch of Sufism whose music we will be examining in this chapter, was founded by the poet and philosopher Mevlana Jalalu'ddin Rumi (1207–1273). Rumi's poetry has recently become extremely popular in the West, and he is reportedly the best-selling poet in the United States.

The Whirling Dervishes. The Mevlevi have a form of worship called *sema*, a ceremony that centers on a whirling dance. During the *sema* each participant turns slowly in a counterclockwise direction, pivoting on the left leg. Arms are raised out from the sides; the right hand is turned up, receptive; the left hand is turned down, bestowing. In the West these dancers are called **whirling dervish-**

Mevlana is a sobriquet (descriptive name) meaning "our master."

The Turkish word *dervish* comes from the Persian *darwish*, meaning doorsill, suggesting that the Sufi dervish stands at the threshold between spiritual slavery and freedom, seeking the doorway to union with God.

es. Although traditionally only men were trained to perform the whirling dance, the Contemporary Lovers of Mevlana, a Turkish Sufi order, permits women to participate.

Sema. The whirling ceremony is accompanied by vocal and instrumental music. The Mevlevi **semas** are among the most important settings for hearing Turkish classical music.

Specialized garments are worn for the whirling ceremony. The dervish wears a tall, honey-colored cone-shaped, flat-topped felt hat, which symbolizes the tombstone. The dervish also wears a white costume under a long-sleeved black cloak. The cloak symbolizes both the Sufi's worldly attachments and the tomb.

Once the whirling begins, the dervish sheds the black cloak, revealing a white costume with a long, weighted skirt that floats outward in a circle as the whirling continues. This white costume represents the shroud.

The *sema* begins with a eulogy to the prophet Muhammad sung by a soloist. This is followed by a *taksim*, an improvised *ney* solo that establishes the *makam*. Next there is a processional, called *Sultan Veled Peshrev*, in which the dervishes walk three times around the hall, stopping to bow to each other at the sheikh's post. This procession symbolizes the identity and place of humans within a sacred circle. The dervishes look between the eyebrows of the dervish opposite them and "contemplate the divine manifestation within him." At the end of the procession, they drop their cloaks, leaving their tombs and worldly attachments behind, and "prepare to turn for God." This solemn procession is accompanied by instrumental music. The *Sultan Veled Peshrev* you will listen to later in this chapter is one example of this processional music.

Four whirling dances—each called a *selâm*—accompanied by music (see the illustration on page 306) follow the processional. During the whirling, the dancer combines external movement with inner stillness. As Kabir Helminski, a member of the Mevlevis, explains,

> The word *sema* comes from *As-Sami,* one of the ninety-nine sacred names of Allah, meaning "the One who hears all."

> A *shroud* is a burial garment.

> The *sheikh's post* is the place where the leader (the sheikh) is stationed.

Whirling dervishes meditating
Dave Bartruff/Corbis

Whirling dervish at the
Hall of Literature,
Beyoglu, Istanbul, Turkey
*Lee Snider/The Image
Works*

"We are drawn to our inmost center, the point where we are closest to God." The dancers experience themselves as planets in the whirling universe: they are reunited with the cosmic order of things. "They empty their hearts of all but the thought of God and whirl in the ecstatic movement of His breath."

Each *selâm* lasts ten to fifteen minutes. The *sema* ends with a recitation from the Qur'an, the holy book of Islam, by a solo voice.

Listening to *Sultan Veled Peshrev*

"Dervish music cannot be written in notes. Notes do not include the soul of the dervish, they are only to remember the music."

Sultan Veled Peshrev is named after Sultan Veled, the elder son of Rumi, who introduced an opening procession into the *sema*.

Closing the *Tekkes:* Sufi Prayer Lodges

In December 1927, President Ataturk introduced Law 677 into the Turkish Republic, prohibiting among other things the performance of dervish practices, holding meetings in *tekkes*, and Sufi initiations. The tomb of Mevlana Jalalu'ddin Rumi was closed, then reopened as a museum. The *tekkes* were not reopened until the 1960s, following an act of defiance by Sheikh Muzaffer, who reopened the Halveti-Jerrahi *tekke* in Istanbul. In 1953, after lengthy negotiations, a compromise was reached that permitted the dervishes to dance again—not in a religious ceremony but in a public celebration of poetry. After all, the Mevlevi founder, Rumi, was a very popular poet. These ceremonies were performed in public settings.

Over the years, the *sema* has gradually returned to its traditional form. The government permits its performance as long as it is considered a tourist attraction, not a worship ceremony. But to the Mevlevi dervishes whirling in their sacred dance, it is not a show. It is the real *sema*.

Peshrev is the general Turkish name for a musical prelude at the beginning of a classical music performance. *Sultan Veled Peshrev* is a generic name for this type of music; the music you will be hearing was composed by Dogan Ergin, the director of the Mevlevi Ensemble of Turkey.

The music unfolds in long melodic phrases with the drums beating time in the background. Each phrase tends to take up on the pitch that the previous phrase ends with. The phrases are irregular in length and generally conjunct (smooth) in motion. The melodic range is moderate and could be easily sung by a single voice. Although the melodic style is consistent throughout, it is difficult to detect any melody that is repeated. (There is one repeated melody, however, which will be pointed out in the listening guide.)

The rhythmic structure of *Sultan Veled Peshrev* is based on a very long pattern. The rhythmic pattern is fifty-six beats in length, and there are four cycles of this pattern in the composition. This rhythmic structure, called the "grand cycle" (*devr-i kebir*), is the longest rhythmic cycle in Turkish music. The long melodic phrases with little repetition and the long rhythmic pattern contribute to the feeling of continuity of the music. If you begin counting beats with the first drumbeat, you can follow the four cycles of fifty-six beats and hear how the one repeated melodic phrase acts as the conclusion of each cycle. The following TUBS (Time Unit Box System) notation shows the *devr-i kebir* cycle that you will be listening to.

one beat

| L | | L | | H | | H | H | L | | H | | H | H | L | | H | | H | H | H | | H | | H | H | L | |

| H | | H | H | H | | H | | H | H | L | | L | | H | H | H | | H | | H | | H | | H | | H | |

| H | | H | H | H | | H | | H | H | H | | H | | H | H | L | | H | | L | H | L | H | H | | H | |

| H | | H | | L | | H | | L | H | L | H | H | | H | | H | | H | | H | | H | | H | | H | |

L = Low drum

H = High drum

Devr-i kebir cycle

Sultan Veled Peshrev (Dogan Ergin) [CD 2, track 13]

The performance you will hear is by the Mevlevi Ensemble of Turkey under the direction of Dogan Ergin, who also composed the work. Dogan Ergin is a highly respected *ney* player and is considered an authority on *makam.* Performers include: Dogan Ergin, *ney;* Ümit Gürelman, *ney;* Osman Erkahveci, *ney;* Nihat Dogu, *kemençe;* Hasan Esen, *kemençe;* Abdi Coskun, *tanbur;* Necip Gülses, *tanbur;* Ömer Satiroglu, *ud;* Ugur Isik, *violonsel;* and Vahit Anadolou, *kudüm.*

Time	Musical Event	Description
0:00	Phrase I	This is the beginning of the first cycle of fifty-six beats.
0:14	Phrase II	Takes up where the previous phrase ends.
0:39	Phrase III (refrain)	This is the repeated refrain (*teslim*) of each cycle of fifty-six beats.
0:49	Phrase IV	New pitches are added here. The beginning of the second cycle.
1:03	Phrase V	
1:13	Phrase VI	
1:27	Phrase VII (refrain)	Repetition of the refrain concludes the second cycle of fifty-six beats.
1:37	Phrase VIII	Beginning of the third cycle of fifty-six beats. Pitches are more like those at the beginning.
1:51	Phrase IX	
2:07	Phrase X	
2:14	Phrase XI (refrain)	Refrain is repeated, bringing the third cycle to a close.
2:24	Phrase XII	Beginning of the fourth and final cycle of fifty-six beats.
2:38	Phrase XIII	
3:01	Phrase XIV (refrain)	Repetition of the refrain, bringing the final cycle to a close.

Response to the Music

Think about your first impressions of this music. How did you respond to the pitch system and the instruments? Did following the listening guide help to orient you within the music? Could you follow the long, fifty-six-beat pattern? What were your emotional, physical, and spiritual responses to the music?

Imagine a group of dervishes solemnly processing into a large hall, preparing to begin their spiritual practice. Picture them as they circle three times around the room, each pausing to stare into the space between the eyebrows of the dervish opposite him (or her), trying to see God realized in the other dervishes. How does this music contribute to setting the proper mood? What role does the continuous form of the music play in setting this mood?

Summary

In this chapter you learned about two types of continuous forms and the principles of continuity. You listened to an example of pattern-based continuous form—*Sultan Veled Peshrev*—and learned about Turkey and the Mevlevi Sufis, who perform the whirling dervish dance as a spiritual practice. Some details of the structure of Turkish music were presented, including the *makam*, a pitch structure somewhat similar to the *raga* of India.

Applying What You Have Learned

1. Listen again to *Dolphin Dreams* [CD 1, track 1]. Would you describe this work as a sectional or a continuous form? Why?

2. Listen again to *Shango* [CD 1, track 9]. Would you describe this work as a sectional or a continuous form? Why?

3. Name another example of music you have listened to in this book that has heterophonic texture. Compare that work with *Sultan Veled Peshrev*.

4. What would you say is the dominant musical element in *Sultan Veled Peshrev*: rhythm, melody, harmony, dynamics, texture, or timbre? Which of the musical elements are not important in this work?

5. In *The Young Person's Guide to the Orchestra* (CD 2, track 1) the first part of the work is sectional (a theme and variations), and the second part of the work is continuous. Listen again to the second section (CD 2, track 1, 13:44 to the end).

This is a good example of pattern-based continuous music from the West—a **fugue**. The theme of a fugue is called its **subject**. Notice how there are no section breaks from 13:44 until the first theme enters at 15:40. Each instrument enters playing the subject and continues playing counterpoint against the next entry. Make an "ear map"—a listening guide—of the fugue, noting the times when you can hear the subject and when you cannot. Describe how the two sections are different in musical effect. To what extent are the differences due to sectional versus continuous form?

6. Give one example of a continuous form in the music that you know. Describe how listening to continuous forms differs from listening to sectional forms.

7. Both the Shakers and the Mevlevi order of Sufis turn and spin as part of their spiritual practice. Can you name other religious observances that involve movement or dance?

Important Terms

continuity 298
continuous form 298
text-based continuous form 298
pattern-based continuous form 298
preludes 298
inventions 298
fugues 298
passacaglias 298
chaconnes 298

Sultan Veled Peshrev 299
Turkish classical music 301
makam 302
egreti karar 302
tanbur 303
ud 303
kemençe 303
violonsel 303
kanun 303
ney 303

kudüm 303
mutrip 303
Sufism 303
Mevlevi order 304
whirling dervish 304
sema 305
peshrev 307
fugue 310
subject 310

Musicians and Ensembles Mentioned

Sultan Veled
Abdülkadir Meragi
*Buhurizade Mustafa Itri
Gazi Giray Han
Sultan Selim III
*Wolfgang Amadeus Mozart
*Ludwig van Beethoven
*Dogan Ergin
Mevlevi Ensemble of Turkey

Further Listening Resources

Masters of Turkish Music, Rounder Records.
Masters of Turkish Music, vol. 2, Rounder Records.
Ali Ekber Cicek, *Turkish Sufi Music,* Lyrichord.
Kurdistan, *Zikr and Sufi Songs,* Ocora.
Hamza El-Din (a North African master *ud* player), *Escalay (The Water Wheel),* Nonesuch Records.

Indian and Pakistani Sufi music:
Nusrat Fateh Ali Khan, *Traditional Sufi Qawwalis,* Navras.
Sufi Music from Sindhi (Pakistani), Wergo.
Abida Parveen, *Pakistani Sufi Songs,* Inedit.

Continuous Forms II

♪ *Absalon, fili mi,* Josquin Desprez

Scala/Art Resource

J osquin, *don't say the heavens are cruel and merciless*
That gave you genius so sublime.

SERAFINO DALL'AQUILA
POET AND CONTEMPORARY OF JOSQUIN

Text-Based Continuous Forms

Some vocal compositions are based on texts that have no repeated sections, stanzas, or verses. In these cases the music is composed to fit the given text, and the form of the work is created by the form of the text. While there are examples of text-based continuous forms in non-Western cultures, the great majority of the known examples are of Western origin. The primary text-based continuous forms are the **motet** and the **through-composed song.** The motet is sacred music; a through-composed song is usually secular. In this chapter you will listen to a motet by Josquin Desprez called *Absalon, fili mi.*

Motet

Motet comes from the French *mot*, which means "word." Motets are, indeed, word-based compositions. The title *motet* was applied to a wide variety of religious vocal compositions from the thirteenth through the eighteenth centuries, and no single description can encompass all works that carry this title.

History of the Motet

In medieval motets (1220–1450), a short passage taken from Gregorian chant (called the *cantus firmus*) was placed in the tenor voice, and one or two upper parts were composed using a different text, which might be in Latin or in another language. The passage of chant was sometimes stretched out beyond any recognition of the original melody and often had repeated rhythmic patterns applied to it (isorhythm). Each pitch in the chant would be sung or played by an instrument while the upper voices, singing a different text, moved much more rapidly above it. One of the upper voices was called the *motetus*; thus the composition came to be called a motet.

In the Renaissance period (1450–1600; see page 315), motets were generally understood to be polyphonic settings of Latin sacred texts. Thousands of motets were composed during this time, and the vast majority of the works of Renaissance composers such as Giovanni Palestrina, Josquin Desprez, Orlande de Lassus, and Tomás Luis de Victoria were motets. Although most Renaissance motets were intended for church performance, in later centuries they became standard concert pieces. Motets are a part of the repertoire of most college and professional choirs.

By the baroque period (1600–1750; see page 177), the motet had become an "antique" form and the title *motet* could refer to any piece of liturgical vocal music. The influence of the baroque can be seen in many of these motets, which had independent instrumental accompaniments with the characteristic baroque *basso continuo* (figured bass). In later periods, works called motets were composed from time to time, but the popularity of the form had run its course.

Josquin Desprez

Josquin Desprez, recognized by his contemporaries as one of the greatest composers of the Renaissance period (1450–1600), was born around 1440. No information has been discovered about the place or date of his birth. All details of his early life are conjectures based on later documents. The most recent evidence indicates that his birthplace was probably in France, although other places had been proposed in the past. His name appears with a variety of spellings (not uncommon in the fifteenth century), including Juschino, Josse, Jodocus, Pratensis, and Jodocus a Prato. The current preferred spelling is based on an acrostic in the opening lines of one of his motets. No records exist of Josquin's family or of his schooling. In fact, the earliest information we have is from 1459—it indicates that Josquin joined the choir of the Milan cathedral as an adult member. He lived and worked in Italy for many years, in both Milan and Rome.

An *acrostic* is a verse in which the initial or final letters of the lines spell out a word or phrase.

Josquin Desprez
Woodcut from Petrus Opmeer: Opus chronographicum, *1611*

From Italy Josquin moved back to France, serving at several courts. After a short stay at the court in Ferrara, Italy, Josquin moved to Condé, France, where he died in 1521. Composers and literary figures throughout Europe memorialized his death in a number of tributes and laments.

Josquin's compositions became well known throughout Western Europe and were models for many other composers. His works were among the first examples of printed music. (The printing process for music was invented in the 1470s and perfected over the next century.) Another indication of the esteem in which he was held was the practice of attributing the works of other composers to him, perhaps to interest performers. During his life Josquin composed over a hundred motets, eighteen masses, and around seventy secular songs (*chansons*) in Spanish, German, and Italian.

Listening to *Absalon, fili mi*

It is thought that Josquin composed *Absalon, fili mi* in 1497 to commemorate the death of Pope Alexander VI's son, Juan Borgia, who had been murdered. Pope Alexander VI was Rodrigo Borgia, the most

The Renaissance Period

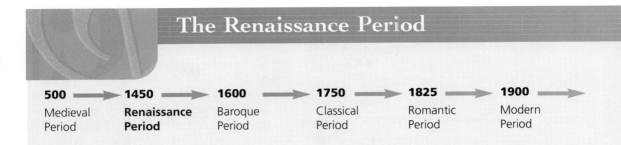

500	1450	1600	1750	1825	1900
Medieval Period	Renaissance Period	Baroque Period	Classical Period	Romantic Period	Modern Period

The term *Renaissance* is derived from the French word for rebirth. It is commonly used to describe European culture from the early fourteenth century to the late sixteenth century and the period of Western music history from roughly 1450 to 1600. The arts of classical antiquity—Greece and Rome—were looked upon as ideals.

The Renaissance was a time of great scientific, literary, and artistic achievement, as well as a time of exploration and discovery, and of emerging nation-states. This period was also known for its humanist emphasis on individual experience and achievement, as well as for the German reformer, Martin Luther (1483–1546), who began what became the Protestant Reformation. Christopher Columbus (1451–1506) lived during this time, as did William Shakespeare (1564–1616). The "universal man" or "Renaissance man"—the many-sided creative genius—is exemplified by Leonardo da Vinci (1452–1519), who was an artist, scientist, engineer, and philosopher.

Music in the Renaissance

In the Renaissance, distinct vocal and instrumental idioms developed as instruments became more popular and numerous. Idiomatic compositions for specific instruments began to supplant the medieval practice of music intended for any voice or instrument capable of the range of a given part.

Vocal music became much more common than in previous periods. Choral music became fully established, although the choruses were usually small, numbering twelve to fifteen singers. The musical forms of the mass and the motet, both liturgical music of the Roman Catholic Church, were developed. Musically trained clergy performed this highly ornate vocal music in Latin, although this was not the native language of the congregations.

One result of the Protestant Reformation (1517–1555) was the formation of a body of religious song in a simpler style. These vocal compositions, called chorales, were intended to be sung by the congregation. Martin Luther—who began the Reformation by posting ninety-five theses on a church door inviting debate over the sale of indulgences—also restructured the relationship between sacred vocal music and congregational singing. Luther composed many chorales, including *A Mighty Fortress Is Our God*, one of the most celebrated works in this form.

Although the Renaissance was dominated by sacred vocal music, many secular vocal works of the period attained an artistic level equal to that of church music. The madrigal, a four- or five-voice musical setting of secular poetry, was popular in Italy and England. Solo songs called ayrs (aires) with lute accompaniment became popular in Spain, France, and England. The works of John Dowland (1563–1626) are perhaps the best known.

Alberti's Renaissance façade, which covers the front of an older church, is governed by a precise system of proportions. The entire

façade can be divided into different whole-number ratios. For example, it is as tall as it is wide (1:1); its upper and lower façade are each one half (1:2) of the whole; and so forth. The result is a symmetry and orderliness reminiscent of classical Greek and Roman architecture, which was also designed with the belief that these whole-number ratios (which also exist in musical harmony) reflect universal principles.

Santa Maria Novella, Florence, Italy, façade by Leon Battista Alberti (1404–1472)
Archivo Iconografico, S.A./Corbis

worldly of the Renaissance popes. He was more of a politician than a religious leader. He fathered many children, including Lucrezia Borgia and Cesare Borgia, and accumulated a huge fortune.

The text for *Absalon, fili mi* is taken from three verses of the Hebrew Bible (Old Testament), each of which deals with the lamentation of a father over the death of his son or sons. The opening lines, "*Absalon, fili mi quis det ut moriar pro te,*" are from II Samuel 18:33, where King David grieves for his son Absalom: "Absalom, my son Absalom, my son, my son Absalom! Would God I had died for thee, Absalom, my son, my son!" The middle line, "*Non vivam ultra,*" comes from the book of Job, where Job laments over the death of his sons: "Let me live no longer." The final line of text, "*sed descendam in infernum plorans,*" comes from Genesis 37:35, where Jacob learns of the death of Joseph and exclaims, "For I will go down into the grave unto my son mourning."

Josquin's treatment of this text is typical of Renaissance motets. Each line of text is given a contrapuntal setting with all four voices usually imitating each other. **Imitative counterpoint** is a polyphonic texture in which all the parts sing the same melody or similar melodies, but each part enters at a different time.

Absalon, fili mi has been the subject of considerable study because of its extremely low pitches and indications in the score that the work fully explored the entire chromatic scale. (Most music in the Renaissance was fairly diatonic.) It is believed that the low pitches and chromaticism were intended to underline the pathos of

Imitative counterpoint

the text. Sung at the pitches indicated in the score, the work would sound very muddy, and some scholars have speculated that the low notated pitches are merely an indication to sing the motet at the lowest pitch possible for a given chorus. The recording you will be listening to is pitched as low as is comfortable for the singers.

Scholars feel that this motet was not intended for religious services but, rather, was performed for the pope in his private chambers. The text, drawn from three different books of the Hebrew Bible, is not a part of the text for the mass. Since the mass has a standard text for each day of the liturgical year, it is unlikely that the text of *Absalon* would have been inserted into religious services.

Absalon, fili mi
quis det ut moriar pro te,
fili mi Absalon.
Non vivam ultra,
sed descendam in infernum
* plorans.*

Absalom my son,
would God I had died for you,
my son Absalom.
Let me live no longer,
but descend into the grave
* weeping.*

LISTENING ACTIVITY

Absalon, fili mi (Josquin Desprez) [CD 2, track 14]

The performance you will hear was recorded in 1983 in Temple Church, London, by the Hilliard Ensemble. This British group was formed in 1974 and explores music of both the prebaroque era and the twentieth century. The members explain that performance of early works "often amounts to re-creations. . . . The constant reinvention of our music is one of the ways we can make very old music live in the present. The music feels different from day to day as we respond to it in new ways, both as a group and as individuals." Since 1974, the membership of the ensemble has occasionally changed. Heard in this recording are David James (countertenor), Paul Elliott and Leigh Nixon (tenors), and Paul Hillier (bass).

Time	Text	Description
0:00	*Absalon, fili mi*	Upper voice (countertenor) enters first, followed by each of the lower voices in order of pitch (tenor, tenor, and bass). All are singing the same melody in imitation. The text is repeated several times and the imitation continues.
1:46	*quis det ut moriar pro te.*	Countertenor leads again, followed by the bass, then the two tenors. Imitation is not strict in this part.
2:25	*Non vivam ultra, sed descendam in infernum plorans.*	Tenor leads in this part, followed by the other tenor. The countertenor and bass enter at the same time. This section is not in imitative counterpoint. On the text *"sed descendam . . ."* a falling melodic motive is introduced in all parts. It is intended to portray the descent into the grave.
3:22	*Non vivam ultra, sed descendam in infernum plorans.*	In this section the previous text is repeated with a new musical setting. The descending motive occurs again on *"sed descendam in infernum plorans."* On the final cadence the bass descends to the lowest pitch of the entire composition.

Notice that in most cases the voice singing a new line of text enters before the other voices have completed their statements. This overlapping of voices keeps the continuity flowing and avoids any sectional break. If you listen carefully you can hear the chromaticism in this setting. Most of the chromatic pitches were not written

Countertenor and tenor parts of *Absalon, fili mi*

Source: From the manuscript copied by Alamire (GB-Lbm Roy. 8. G. VII, f. 56) in *The New Grove Dictionary of Music and Musicians.* London: Macmillan, 1980, vol. 9, p.720.

into the score, and scholars have disagreed as to how they might have been added by singers in the Renaissance. A second difficulty in reconstructing the original performance style has been the way Renaissance music was notated. Instead of full scores showing all the parts, Renaissance musicians wrote their music in **part books,** which show only the music for individual singers.

Another puzzle that must be solved by modern performers is how to place the text on the melodies, since there was little attempt to line the two up in the original scores (see the illustration). What you are listening to is a carefully reconstructed version of *Absalon, fili mi* that attempts to re-create the original composition as nearly as possible (see "The 'Early Music' Movement," page 179).

Response to the Music

Imagine this work being sung in the private chambers of the pope, who is in mourning for his murdered son. What might have been the effect of the music on his mood? What were your emotional, physical, and spiritual responses to the music? Does your knowledge of the historical period and the circumstances of its composition help you to appreciate the work more? What was your reaction to the sound of the countertenor voice? Would you have thought it was a female singer rather than a male? Have you heard this vocal quality before?

Summary

In this chapter you were introduced to text-based continuous forms and to one particular example: the motet. You listened to *Absalon, fili mi,* a motet by the Renaissance composer Josquin Desprez, and learned about imitative counterpoint.

Applying What You Have Learned

1. Listen again to *De sancta Maria* [CD 1, track 10]. Does this music fit the definition of text-based continuous music? Why or why not?

2. Listen again to *Máru-Bihág* [CD 1, track 11]. Does this music fit the definition of pattern-based continuous music? Why or why not?

3. Divide your personal music collection into two categories— continuous forms and sectional forms. You will probably find cases where you are in doubt; indeed, the categories represent a range, with some works having characteristics of both types. On the basis of your survey, does your musical taste incline toward continuous forms or sectional forms?

4. With what texture type does *Absalon, fili mi* begin? What is the texture when the second voice enters? Will this format be the same for all imitative counterpoint? Why or why not?

5. Is dynamic change a factor in *Absalon, fili mi?* If so, where does it occur and what effect does it create?

6. The singers in this performance of *Absalon, fili mi* do not use vibrato. Listen again to a section of *La Bohème* (CD 1, track 12). Contrast the singing in *La Bohème,* where the voices have vibrato, with the singing in *Absalon, fili mi,* where there is no vibrato. What is your impression of the voice qualities without vibrato? Do you find them "dryer," "smoother," "cooler," or "more intense"? In the vocal music you usually listen to, do most singers use vibrato?

7. *Simple Gifts* (CD 1, track 2) is clearly a sectional form. What happens to that form when the tune is quoted in *Appalachian Spring* (CD 1, track 3)? Is it sectional, continuous, or some blend of both? Explain.

Important Terms

motet 313
through-composed song 313
imitative counterpoint 316
part books 319

Musicians and Ensembles Mentioned

Names preceded by * have short biographies in Appendix B, page 346.

*Josquin Desprez   David James   Leigh Nixon
Hilliard Ensemble   Paul Elliott   Paul Hillier

Further Listening Resources

Allegri/Lassus/Palestrina: *Miserere/Missa/Veni Sponsa,* EMI Classics for Pleasure.
Marenzio/Palestrina/Gesualdo: *La Bella Ninfa,* Berlin Classics.
Palestrina, *Missa Aeterna Christ Munera,* Hyperion.
T. L. de Victoria: *Missa and Motet—O Magnum Mysterium,* Hyperion.
Alfred Deller, *English Baroque Songs,* Harmonia Mundi (includes music by John Dowland).

CHAPTER 18

Improvisation and Form

💿 ***Suite Thursday,*** Duke Ellington and Billy Strayhorn

Bettman/Corbis

N*o one had a band like Duke Ellington. No one made music like Duke Ellington. And no one led a life like Duke Ellington. He was truly one of a kind, beyond category.*

JOHN EDWARD HASSE (1993)
BIOGRAPHER OF DUKE ELLINGTON

In Part VI you have been learning about form in composed music. In this chapter we will deal with music that involves extensive improvisation. As you will learn, the basic principles of repetition, variation, and contrast apply to improvised music just as they do to composed music.

Development of Jazz

In the West the primary musical genre that involves extensive improvisation is **jazz.** Jazz developed in the United States from an integration of diverse styles including the blues, hymns, spirituals, ragtime (see page 324), work songs (slave songs), traditional West African music, marches, and waltzes, as well as traditional Spanish and French music. Jazz is a genuinely American phenomenon and an important contribution to world music.

Another influence on the development of jazz was the regimental military bands stationed in and around New Orleans after the American Civil War (1861–1865). Some of the occupying Union regimental bands consisted of African American musicians, who were proficient players of clarinets, saxophones, trumpets, trombones, tubas, and percussion instruments. They owned their own instruments and, as a result, the instruments of the military band became the instruments of early jazz bands, whose members were all African American.

African American Union Military Band, 1860s
Archive Photos

Syncopated rhythm is a rhythm with accents on beats or divisions of beats that are usually unaccented.

A third influence was a popular late-nineteenth-century American music called **ragtime.** The word *rag* refers to a kind of music usually written in compound binary form (see page 281), with syncopated rhythms borrowed from African American banjo music. The **banjo** is a New World descendent of a West African instrument called the **banya.**

New Orleans, Louisiana, the birthplace of jazz, was a major commercial center at the mouth of the Mississippi River. Its population included French, African, and Spanish citizens, and this ethnic diversity provided a rich and varied musical tradition. During the 1890s, almost every town and settlement in southern Louisiana had its own band. Both ragtime and marches were common fare in concerts performed by these local bands.

New Orleans was a major seaport, catering to travelers from all over the world. The numerous taverns, the dance halls, and the infamous prostitution district (known as Storyville) all contributed to the carefree mood of the city. The party atmosphere in New Orleans created a great demand for live music, generating an enormous amount of work for musicians. These musicians were often members of African American parade bands, and they "ragged" march music or combined music from different sources to please their customers. Jazz grew out of this environment. As you can see, it is a truly American art form.

Sears Roebuck catalog, 1914
Culver Pictures

History of Jazz

1865	→	1920s	→	1930s	→	1940s	→	1950s	→	1960s	→	1970s	→
Military Bands		Dixieland		Swing		Bop		Cool Jazz		Free Jazz		Fusion	

Jazz has evolved through several major styles. The essence of early jazz was collective improvisation, a style in which the players of the lead instruments—usually clarinet, cornet (trumpet), and trombone—improvised contrapuntal melodies above a steady rhythm section, usually consisting of banjo, drums, and tuba. These jazz groups of six or seven musicians were called combos, and the style of music they played is known as Dixieland. This term came into use in the 1920s, when musicians in Chicago began to imitate African American music played by musicians from New Orleans—in other words, from "Dixieland."

The New Orleans musicians Joe "King" Oliver, Louis Armstrong, Jelly Roll Morton (Ferdinand La Menthe), and Sidney Bechet are among the first famous jazz innovators. Oliver, Armstrong, and Morton all led bands in Chicago, an active center for jazz during the 1920s. Eventually the Chicago musicians and the transplanted New Orleans musicians mixed with musicians from New York, and by the late 1920s New York also had a very strong jazz scene.

During the 1920s a looser feeling developed in jazz. This change to more of a "swing" effect was gradual and continued into the 1940s (see page 330). Most jazz from the mid-1930s to the end of World War II was called swing. Since most swing was performed by bands of ten or more musicians, this period is often referred to as the "big band" era.

As the bands became larger and the personnel changed more frequently, a need arose for written arrangements. This resulted in a decrease in improvisation, but even in the most carefully scored big band jazz arrangement, there is always space for improvised solos.

Form in Jazz

Most improvisation in jazz is a spontaneous variation on preexisting musical materials. These musical materials create the form of the work, and the performer expands on them without changing the form itself. Three major sources of preexisting materials for jazz improvisation are popular songs, composed themes, and the blues.

Popular Songs. Many popular songs of the 1920s through the 1950s were given jazz treatments. Most of these songs are in ternary form: **A A B A** (see page 280). A typical jazz treatment begins with a rather straightforward statement of the song (sometimes called the **head**), followed by a series of repetitions with improvised solos.

In many such arrangements the head is repeated to bring the work to a close.

Composed Themes. Jazz composers sometimes create **composed themes.** These themes might be in ternary form, like most popular songs, or in another form. In some cases a theme is given lyrics and becomes a popular song in its own right. Once the theme is composed, the general form of the arrangement usually resembles the pattern described above.

The Blues. The **blues** is a secular African American vocal music that developed in the late nineteenth century in the Mississippi delta and east Texas. Originally, the blues was sung without accompaniment, or the singer accompanied himself or herself with a simple instrument such as a washboard, banjo, or guitar. That form became the basis of the instrumental blues form, which is characterized by a twelve-measure harmonic progression repeated throughout the song (see the illustration). The form created is a pattern-based continuous form centering on this harmonic progression. In a jazz arrangement the blues progression is repeated several times, with each performer improvising for one or more repetitions of the pattern. The composer may provide a written head for the arrangement, or there may simply be a series of improvisations. Some melodies based on the **blues progression** have words and, like other popular songs, are given names. Examples are *Beal Street Blues* and *Saint Louis Blues.*

In Duke Ellington and Billy Strayhorn's *Suite Thursday,* which we will be listening to in this chapter, two of the four movements are based on the twelve-measure blues progression.

Duke Ellington

Duke Ellington is one of the most outstanding figures in jazz history. He received numerous awards and citations from around the world, including fifteeen honorary degrees. He and his band were voted the top jazz organization seventy-six times by various periodicals in the United States and abroad. Ellington made significant contributions as a pianist, bandleader, arranger, and composer.

Duke Ellington's Early Years

Edward Kennedy Ellington (1899–1974) was born in Washington, D.C. He would spend much of his life working and living in the nation's capital. His father, James Edward Ellington, had moved there from North Carolina in the late nineteenth century.

Chord I

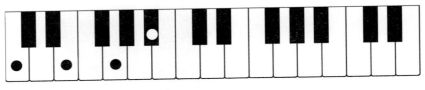

Chord II

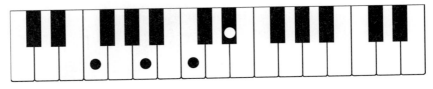

Chord III

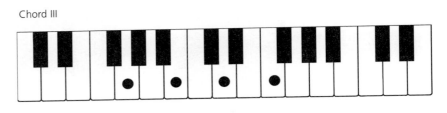

Twelve-measure blues progression:

Phrase 1:	Chord I	|	Chord I	|	Chord I	|	Chord I	|
Phrase 2:	Chord II	|	Chord II	|	Chord I	|	Chord I	|
Phrase 3:	Chord III	|	Chord II	|	Chord I	|	Chord I	|

An example of the blues progression

As a child, Edward Ellington lived a pampered existence. He was, in his own words, "spoiled rotten" by a multitude of relatives, mostly female. A boyhood friend gave him the nickname "Duke" because of his dress and demeanor, and that name stuck with him for the rest of his life.

When Duke was slightly injured playing baseball, his mother arranged for him to have piano lessons. She hoped that studying music would encourage him to participate in less hazardous activities. He skipped as many lessons as he attended, but when he was asked to play at a party and found that pianists attracted girls, he began to pay more attention to music. He soon became an excellent pianist.

Duke Ellington
Bettman/Corbis

Duke's band, Kentucky Club, New York, 1925
Lester Glassner Collection/Neal Peters

Duke Ellington's
orchestra, Chicago, 1932
Culver Pictures

Ellington as a Bandleader

Duke Ellington showed musical and business acumen from an early age. While he was still in high school, he formed a jazz band that played at dances. He was the band's pianist. After having to pay booking fees for his own band, he decided to advertise himself as a music agent. His gracious personality and fair business dealings earned him a great deal of money, and before he was twenty he owned a house and bought his first Cadillac.

In 1922 Ellington and his band attempted to move from Washington, D.C., to New York City, but bookings were tight and they returned to Washington. In 1923 Ellington tried again to get established in New York City. This time the band was well received, and he and the musicians moved to New York, where they were hired on a permanent basis at the Kentucky Club.

In 1926 Ellington began an association with Irving Mills, a small-time impresario who became Ellington's manager. Because Mills was white, he got the band bookings it would otherwise have been denied. He also arranged for its first recording sessions. In 1930 Mills was even able to get the Duke Ellington Orchestra an appearance in an Amos 'n' Andy movie, *Check and Double-check*. In 1927 the band got a permanent engagement in Harlem's top nightclub, the Cotton Club. There, Ellington gradually increased the size of the band from its original nine pieces to the fifteen-piece band of the 1930s.

Duke Ellington's Cotton Club Orchestra attracted the best African American musical talent, and Duke's genius at leadership enabled him to keep all the members working as a team. As a composer he wrote to showcase each musician's unique style and technique. He cared for his musicians financially as well; members of his band were consistently the highest paid in the business. This care was reciprocated by an unprecedented loyalty from the musicians in his band, which

Duke Ellington with Billy Strayhorn
Lester Glassner Collection/Neal Peters

included many of the most famous jazz performers of the first half of the twentieth century.

In 1938 the twenty-three-year-old composer-arranger-pianist Billy Strayhorn (1915–1967) joined the band. In 1939 he submitted one of his tunes, *Lush Life*, for Ellington's consideration. It is now a jazz "standard." Ellington immediately recognized not only Strayhorn's genius but also how attuned to each other they were. Strayhorn soon entered into an association with Duke Ellington that was the closest intellectual and personal partnership in the history of jazz.

The two men absorbed each other's musical and philosophical ideas. Billy Strayhorn composed Ellington's theme song, *Take the "A" Train*, and together they wrote many songs—among the most notable, *Satin Doll*. Strayhorn's classical training combined well with Ellington's "poolroom education," and they produced music that is an engaging blend of academic and self-taught. They also collaborated on many larger works, such as *Suite Thursday* and a jazz adaptation of Pyotor Il'yich Tchaikovsky's *Nutcracker Suite*. Ellington said of Strayhorn, "His patience was incomparable, and unlimited. He had no aspirations to enter into any kind of competition, yet the legacy he leaves, his *oeuvre*, will never be less than the ultimate on the highest plateau of culture."

Ellington the Composer

Duke Ellington wrote more than 900 compositions, including three movie scores, a ballet, three Broadway shows, three sacred concert works for voices and instruments, and twenty-one suites, in addition to songs and individual instrumental works for the band.

Swing is a jazz style in which the division of the beats is uneven and there is considerable stress on the notes that are not on the beat.

His compositions are marked by diversity and a breadth of style not characteristically found in works played by most swing-era big bands. He presents a larger number of themes and more variety than was customary at the time. His work never really fell into any of the usual "fixed" categories of early jazz, swing, or modern jazz. The jazz he created was uniquely his own, and he wrote extensively in this medium for four decades.

Ellington's collaborative methods of composition extended to the members of his band. The trumpeter Rex Stewart recounts the story of a recording session where Ellington appeared with "about one-eighth of a page on which he'd scribbled . . . some notes for the saxophones . . . but there was nothing for Johnny Hodges [the band's lead saxophone player]. Duke had the saxes run the sequence down twice, while Johnny sat nonchalantly smoking. Then Duke called to Hodges, 'Hey Rabbit, give me a long slow glissando against that progression.'" He then asked trumpeter Cootie Williams to try entering with a trumpet growl. To the lead trombone Lawrence Brown he said, "You are cast in the role of the sun beating down on the scene." When he got no

Legato is a musical term for playing a melody in a smooth style.

response he said, "What kind of a sound do you feel that could be? You don't know? Well, try a high B-flat in a felt hat, play it legato, and sustain it for eight bars." This picture of a composition being assembled in the recording studio is far different from the stereotype of a composer writing down every detail of his creation. The compositions of Duke Ellington reflect the imagination and capabilities of his players to an extent few other composers could match.

Duke Ellington and the Suite

Duke Ellington, alone or in collaboration with Billy Strayhorn, experimented with longer instrumental forms such as the concerto (*Concerto for Cootie*, 1940), the tone poem (*Black, Brown and Beige*, 1943), and the suite. The **suite** (see page 25), an extended composition in several movements, had a special attraction for him, and he composed more than twenty suites. Ellington was always fascinated with composing musical descriptions of places and people. The suite provided him with a format for musically depicting characters from literature and experiences from his own life.

In 1944 Ellington and Strayhorn composed *Perfume Suite*, a four-movement musical portrayal of the moods of women under the spell of different fragrances. Ellington's love for the South and his fascination with trains were combined in the *Deep South Suite* (1946), with its six-minute musical train ride called the *Happy-Go-Lucky Local*. Another piece, *Such Sweet Thunder* (1957), was both critically acclaimed and popular. Its twelve movements, lasting nearly forty-seven minutes, are musical miniatures and caricatures of Shakespearean characters, including Lady Macbeth, Hamlet, Romeo, Juliet, Henry V, and Puck.

Ellington and Strayhorn also turned their attention to **dramatic suites** from the Western European orchestral repertoire. In 1960 they devoted an entire album to a big-band jazz version of Tchaikovsky's *Nutcracker Suite*. Edvard Grieg's *Peer Gynt Suites I and II* received similar treatment.

One of Ellington's final major works, *New Orleans Suite* (1970), pays homage to the birthplace of jazz. This nine-section work is a musical tribute to locations and individuals who made major contributions to jazz. Five movements musically depict aspects of life in and around New Orleans, and four movements are individual portraits of the jazz artists Louis Armstrong, Wellman Brand, Sidney Bechet, and Mahalia Jackson.

Listening to *Suite Thursday*

The Duke Ellington Orchestra was scheduled to appear at the third annual Monterey Jazz Festival on 24 September 1960, and

An *independent suite* is a multimovement work that was originally conceived as a suite.

Ellington and Strayhorn were commissioned to produce a work for the occasion. They created a four-movement **independent suite** based loosely on characters in two novels by John Steinbeck, *Cannery Row* and *Sweet Thursday.*

Monterey Bay, California, is an idyllic locale on the Pacific Ocean south of San Francisco. Today Monterey's Cannery Row is a tourist mecca, but in the 1940s—the time of John Steinbeck's novels—it was a smelly, dismal, declining fishery section of the town. Steinbeck found nobility in the down-and-outs who populated Cannery Row. He saw them as individuals who were robustly independent, frequently with hearts of gold, and he made them the protagonists of the two novels.

Major critics for jazz magazines almost unanimously panned *Suite Thursday* when it was first performed at the Monterey Festival. They argued that the four movements, with their light, swinging nature, didn't seem to have any relationship to each other or to Steinbeck. When the recording was released some months later, however, there was nearly unanimous praise from the same publications. This prompted Ellington's biographer Stanley Dance to observe that "jazz critics who clamor for more extended works still appear to lack the qualities needed to judge them at first hearing."

In structure and design, *Suite Thursday* has much in common with a baroque suite. Its four movements follow the slow-fast, slow-fast configuration of the baroque suite, and a single melodic motive is prominent in all movements, tying them together.

Ellington and Strayhorn chose to have the movements—called *Misfit Blues, Schwiphti, Zweet Zurzday,* and *Lay-By*—evoke the moods and personalities of the characters rather than depict Steinbeck's "story." *Misfit Blues* is in twelve-measure blues form and begins with a muted trombone sounding the primary melodic motive. Ellington's piano solo leads to a section in swing style, which he said described John Steinbeck as a "swinger." The fast, flying *Schwiphti* evokes the mood and tempo of Cannery Row. *Zweet Zurzday* is a descriptive piece evoking the Monterey wharf, with its boats and dockside activity. The final movement, *Lay-By,* is also twelve-measure blues. *Lay-by* is a term used in England to describe an emergency parking area.

Suite Thursday is an independent suite, but as in other jazz pieces, there are many opportunities for improvisation within the structure of

Monterey Jazz Festival
Ray Avery

the music. This means that every performance is unique. The performance you will hear was recorded in Hollywood in 1960 by a smaller group from the Ellington band. This recording remained unpublished until 1979, when Columbia Records issued it on an LP record, *Duke Ellington: The Unknown Session.*

LISTENING ACTIVITY

Suite Thursday (Duke Ellington and Billy Strayhorn) [CD 2, tracks 15–18]

Misfit Blues [CD 2, track 15]

Time	Musical Event	Description
0:00	Introduction	Muted trombone begins primary melodic motive. There is little discernable pulse, and the trombone **cadenza**-like line is punctuated by saxophone chords and finger cymbal.
0:24	Introduction continues	Duke Ellington's improvised piano solo breaks in at the end of the trombone solo.
0:35	Introduction continues	Improvised piano solo continues, beginning with the primary melodic motive.
0:59	1st blues chorus	Steady pulse is established with improvised piano solo in twelve-measure blues form, accompanied by bass and cymbals.
1:22	2nd blues chorus	Saxes (saxophones) enter with the blues theme. The theme is shortened to eight bars, however, and repeated (1:37). Accompaniment remains bass and cymbals with piano **fills.**
1:51	3rd blues chorus	Saxes continue, now with the theme in standard twelve-meaure blues form.
2:15	4th blues chorus	Saxes continue; accompaniment becomes heavier with **backbeats** in the drums every other bar.

A *cadenza* is an improvised or written ornamental passage performed by a soloist, usually without accompaniment or accompanied only by a sustained chord.

A *fill* is a short musical idea inserted between phrases of a song.

Backbeats are the second and fourth beats in quadruple meter.

2:38	5th blues chorus	Saxes continue; accompaniment becomes heavier still with drum backbeat every measure. There are added improvised piano fills.
3:00	6th blues chorus	Continuation of previous chorus.
3:22	7th blues chorus	Saxes continue; added trombone fills in call-and-response style.
3:46	Tag ending (coda)	Final four bars repeated; then final two bars repeated (3:53) Bass pizzicato over sax chord (4:01) followed by loud brass chord punctuation (4:04).

Schwiphti [CD 2, track 16]

A *walking bass* is a bass line that moves stepwise in even note values, generally following the beat.

Time	Musical Event	Description
0:00	Introduction	Solo piano (improvised) begins with syncopated figures in a fast, driving swing tempo. The rhythm section enters almost immediately with cymbals and string bass playing a fast-moving stepwise **walking bass** accompaniment.
0:06	Theme	"Tune," a sixteen-measure melody divided into two eight-measure segments, is played by solo piano with rhythm section accompaniment. The first eight measures are played again and interrupted by full band entrance.
0:26		Full band enters—saxes, trombones, and trumpets.
0:37	Interlude	Sax section with clarinet lead (top voice) plays a fast passage. Rhythm section drops out.
0:40	Theme	Rhythm section returns while saxes continue to play the lead line.
0:52		Brass chords punctuate the saxes.
1:17		Piano solo (improvised) with cymbal and walking bass accompaniment; similar to (0:06).

1:30		Full band enters.
1:35	Interlude	Sax section interlude; rhythm section stops; similar to (0:37).
1:38	Theme	Piano solo (improvised) with cymbal and walking bass accompaniment.
1:51		Full band enters; added improvised trumpet solo over full band at 2:04.
2:25		Improvised tenor sax solo over full band.
2:31	Coda	Tenor sax solo continues over heavy, rising brass chords. Trumpets play a **riff** (2:44), then play two, final sustained chords (2:51).
2:59		Baritone saxophone interrupts the final chord, stating the primary melodic motive.

A *riff* is a short melodic idea repeated over and over.

Zweet Zurzday [CD 2, track 17]

Time	Musical Event	Description
0:00	Theme	Solo piano begins with bouncy eight-measure theme based on the primary melody motive, and in a moderate swing. Percussion and bass enter with a Latin beat accompaniment.
0:20	Theme (**A**)	Theme is played by clarinet accompanied by muted trombones and saxes.
0:40	Theme (**A**)	Theme continues with added chordal accompaniment by the sax section.
0:57	Bridge (**B**)	**Bridge** section; clarinet lead accompanied by muted trumpets.
1:16	Theme (**A′**)	Theme is now played in sustained style.
1:33	Theme	Theme continues with improvised trombone solo above.
1:50	Theme	Theme—sax and muted trombone.

A *bridge* is the contrasting section or phrase in a popular song.

Time	Musical Event	Description
2:09	Theme	Improvised tenor sax solo; muted trumpet accompaniment.
2:25	Coda	Clarinet returns with a bouncy riff based on the primary melodic motive (as in 0:20) and continues to play this riff in sequence. Baritone saxophone punctuates (2:43) while the clarinet continues adding short improvised figures, eventually ending on a high note (3:30). Clarinet sustains this high note while muted trumpets (3:31), muted trombones (3:34), and saxes (3:37) build a **pyramid chord**. Sections then drop out in reverse order, leaving the clarinet note at the end.

A *pyramid chord* is a chord built up one tone at a time, usually starting with its lowest tone.

Lay-By [CD 2, track 18]

Time	Musical Event	Description
0:00	Introduction	Piano begins with primary melodic motive in sequence, accompanied by rhythm section.
0:11	1st blues chorus	Primary melodic motive becomes the first part of the twelve-measure blues theme played in moderate tempo by piano and rhythm section.
0:28	2nd blues chorus	Saxes play blues theme with brass punctuations.
0:46	3rd blues chorus	Saxes play new, more lyrical theme over blues progression.
1:03	4th blues chorus	Saxes play first blues theme accompanied only by rhythm section.
1:20	5th blues chorus	Saxes play new lyrical theme accompanied by rhythm section.
1:38	1st solo chorus	Solo violin enters with primary melodic motive, accompanied by rhythm section with piano fills. Some improvisation.
1:57	2nd solo chorus	Solo violin continues with theme played **pizzicato.** Rhythm section emphasizes backbeat.

Pizzicato is a special technique on bowed string instruments: the player plucks the string rather than using the bow.

2:14	3rd solo chorus	Solo violin returns to bowing and continues with improvised solo over rhythm section.
2:32	4th solo chorus	Improvised solo continues with added piano fills.
2:48	5th solo chorus	Improvised solo continues.
3:07	6th solo chorus	Violin returns to pizzicato; improvised solo continues.
3:25	7th solo chorus	Pizzicato violin and pizzicato string bass improvise two-part counterpoint over rhythm section accompaniment.
3:42	8th solo chorus	Violin returns to theme accompanied by two-note riffs in the saxes and brass.
4:01	9th solo chorus	Solo continues as two-note accompaniment riffs become louder and more intense.
4:18	Coda	Violin plays a variation on the theme until the band interrupts with final punctuating chords (4:24).
4:33		Low note on baritone sax and the primary melodic motive in violin pizzicato end the work.

Suite Thursday gives you an opportunity to observe the relationship between composed and improvised music in jazz. Many of the solos were improvised against accompaniments that were either written out or indicated with chord symbols. The music played by the whole band or by sections of the band was all written out. As you can hear, the structure of the work is completely specified by the composed music, and the improvisation occurs within that structure.

Response to the Music

If you have not been aware of which elements in jazz are composed and which are improvised, this listening experience may have been revealing. How has your response to the music been changed by this knowledge? You may not have been aware before of the presence of the blues progression in jazz. Can you now follow the blues choruses as they unfold? Some of the critics seem to have missed the melodic motive that ties all the movements together. Does having this common thematic element brought to your attention alter your perception of the work?

Summary

In this chapter you learned about the history and structure of jazz and the role of improvisation in jazz. Jazz is based on popular songs, composed themes, and the blues progression. These elements create the form of a jazz composition; the improvisation works within that structure. You listened to *Suite Thursday* by the eminent jazz musician and composer Duke Ellington. You learned about his life, his works, and his longtime collaboration with Billy Strayhorn.

Applying What You Have Learned

1. Listen again to *Máru-Bihág* [CD 1, track 11]. This is another example of improvised music. How is improvisation in classical Indian music like the improvisation in jazz? How is it different?

2. Listen again to *This Land Is Your Land* [CD 1, track 17]. Would you say that the performers were improvising in this recording? How is this like and unlike improvisation in jazz?

3. The final movement of *Suite Thursday* (CD 2, track 18) has a solo violin, as does Vivaldi's *Spring* from *The Four Seasons* (CD 1, tracks 14–16). Compare the solo violin parts in these two works. How do they differ in style?

4. Most recorded popular music has little dynamic contrast. Is this true of the recording of *Suite Thursday?* Comment on the use of dynamics in this work.

5. As defined in this chapter, a riff is a short melodic idea that is repeated over and over—usually as a unifying device. Have you heard this device used in other music you have listened to for this course? Did it serve the same function in other pieces?

6. After listening several times to *Suite Thursday,* do you think the four movements belong together? Does the unifying musical element provide a clear connection among them? Or do you agree with the critics' initial reaction that the four pieces are not really related to each other or to Steinbeck's novels?

Important Terms

jazz 323
ragtime 324
banjo 324
banya 324
head 325
composed theme
 326
blues 326

blues progression
 326
suite 331
dramatic suite 331
independent suite
 332
cadenza 333
fill 333

backbeat 333
walking bass 334
bridge 335
pyramid chord 336
pizzicato 336

Names preceded by * have short biographies in Appendix B, page 346.

Musicians and Ensembles Mentioned

*Duke (Edward Kennedy) Ellington
*Billy Strayhorn
*Louis Armstrong
*Sidney Bechet
*Pyotor Il'yich Tchaikovsky
*Edvard Grieg
Wellman Brand
*Mahalia Jackson
Duke Ellington Orchestra

Further Listening Resources

The Music of King Oliver and Kid Ory, Jazz.
Louis Armstrong, *Basin Street Blues,* 1201 Music.
Jelly Roll Morton, Tradition.
Bunk & Bechet in Boston, Jazz Crusade.
Joplin, Piano Music, Biograph BCD-101.
Mahalia Jackson, *Gold Collection,* Fine Tune.

Pronunciation Guide

This list will aid the student in pronouncing names and terms that occur in *Music in Our World*. For the convenience of students, we have used English spellings for these pronunciations rather than the International Phonetic Alphabet. Please be aware that (1) some sounds in other languages do not occur in English and can only be approximated, and (2) even "native" speakers have regional differences in how they pronounce words in English and other languages.

In these pronunciation guides we use the standard sign for long vowels. Thus $\bar{a}$ = **a**ce, $\bar{\imath}$ = **i**ce, $\bar{o}$ = **g**o. We use all capitals to indicate the stressed syllables in words.

a cappella *ah kah-PEH-lah*
Abdelazar *ab-deh-LAH-zuhr*
Absalon, fili mi *AHB-sah-lahn, FEE-lee MEE*
adagio *ah-DAH-jō*
Aida *ah-EE-da*
alap *AH-lahp*
Alceste *ahl-CHEST-teh*
Alcindoro *ahl-cheen-DŌ-rō*
Alfano, Franco *FRAHN-kō ahl-FAHN-ō*
Algonquin *ahl-GAHN-kwin*
alla turca *ah-lah TOOR-kah*
allegro *ah-LEG-rō*
allemande *ah-lā-MAHND*
anacrusis *ah-nah-KREW-sis*
antara *ahn-TAH-rah*
Aquitaine *ah-kwi-TĀN*
Arrien, Angeles *AHN-jeh-lehs AH-ree-uhn*
Aryan *AH-ree-yun*
Ashkenazi *ahsh-kuh-NAH-zee*
avanaddha *ah-vuh-NUHD-uh*
Axigally *AX-eh-gal-ee*
Aymara *ī-MAH-rah*

Ba'al Shem Tov *bahl shehm TŌV*
Bahasan *bah-HAH-sun*
Bali *BAH-lee*
banya *BAHN-yah*
bass *bās*

bass clarinet *BĀS kler-eh-NET*
basso cantante *BAH-sō kahn-TAHN-teh*
basso continuo *BAH-sō con-TIN-oo-ō*
basso profundo *BAH-sō prō-FOON-dō*
bassoon *bah-SOON*
Bay a Glezele Mashke *BĪ ah GLĀZ-uh-luh MAHSH-keh*
Bayreuth *BĪ-royt*
Bechet, Sidney *SID-nee beh-SHĀ*
Beethoven, Ludwig van *LOOD-vik fahn BĀ-toh-vuhn*
Berg, Alban *AHL-bun BEHRG*
Bernstein, Leonard *LEHN-uhrd BURN-stīn*
Bocelli, Andrea *ahn-DREH-ah bō-CHEH-lee*
Bohème, La *lah bō-EHM*
Boito, Arrigo *ah-REE-gō bō-EE-tō*
Borgia, Juan *WAHN BŌR-zhuh*
Borgia, Lucrezia *loo-KRET-seeah BŌR-zhuh*
Brahms, Johannes *yō-HAHN-ehs BRAHMS*
Brhaddeshi *bruh-huh-DEH-sheh*
Bruckner, Anton *AHN-tahn BROOK-nuhr*

caelestium *cheh-LESS-tee-oom*
Café Momus *ka-FĀ MŌ-moo*
cantor *KAN-tuhr*
cantus firmus *KAN-toos FEAR-moos*
Caritas, Lady *LAY-dee KAH-ree-tahs*
Carreras, José *hō-ZĀ kah-REH-rahs*
Caruso, Enrico *ehn-REE-kō kah-ROO-sō*
Causae et Curae *COW-seh eht COO-reh*
cellos *CHEH-lōs*
chaconne *shah-KŌN*
chansonnier *shahn-sōn-YĀ*
charango *chuh-RAHN-gō*
claque *klak*
Colline *kō-LEEN-eh*
coloratura *kō-lō-rah-TOOR-ah*
concerto grosso *kahn-CHAIR-tō GRŌ-sō*
Copland, Aaron *EH-ruhn KŌP-lund*
courante *koo-RAHNT*
Cro-Magnon *crō MAN-yon*
cymbals *SIM-buhls*

Dafne, La *lah DAF-neh*
dalang *DAH-lahg*
De Operatione Dei *deh ō-peh-RAHT-see-Ō-neh DEH-ee*
Debussy, Claude *CLAWD deh-boo-SEE*
Desprez, Josquin *jahs-KAN deh-PREH*
devr-i-kebir *DEHV-ree-kah-BEER*
doina *dō-EE-nah*
Domingo, Plácido *PLAH-see-dō dō-MEEN-gō*
Don Giovanni *dōn jō-VAHN-ee*
Dylan, Bob *BAHB DIL-uhn*

egreti karar *EH-reh-tee kuh-RAHR*
Equiano, Olaudah *ō-LAU-dah eh-kwee-AH-nō*
Ergin, Dogan *dō-AHN EHR-gehn*
Eroica *ehr-RŌ-ee-kuh*
Esterházy *EHS-tuhr-hot-zee*
Evita *eh-VEET-ah*

Festival Te Deum *FEST-eh-vahl teh DĀ-oom*
Florentine Camerata *FLŌR-ehn-teen KAM-uhr-RAH-tah*
Freischütz, Der *dehr FRĪ-shoots*
fugue *fyoog*

Gahbow, Pete *PEET GAH-bō*
gamel *KAM-uhl or GAM-uhl*
gamelan *kam-uh-LAHN or gam-uh-LAHN*
García, René Carrasco *ruh-NĀ cuh-RAHS-kō gahr-CEE-ah*
gat *gut*
gender barangan *kuhn-DEHR bah-RAHN-guhn or guhn-DEHR . . .*
gender gede *kuhn-DEHR GEH-deh or guhn-DEHR . . .*
gender wayang *kuhn-DEHR WĪ-yoon or guhn-DEHR . . .*
Gending Petegak *ken-DING PEH-tee-gak or gen-DING . . .*
Gesamtkunstwerk *geh-SAHMT-koonst-vehrk*
ghana *GUH-nuh*
ghatam *GUH-tuhm*
Gianni Schicchi *JAHN-ee SKEE-kee*
gigue *zheeg*
Gitche-Manidoo *GIT-chee MAHN-eh-doo*
Gluck, Christoph Willibald *KRIS-tōf VIL-i-bahld GLOOK*
Grieg, Edvard *ED-vahrd GREEG*
Guarneri, Andrea *ahn-DREH-ah gwahr-NEH-ree*

guru *GOO-roo*
Han, Gazi Giray *GAH-zee gehr-ī HAHN*
harmonie *ahr-MŌ-nee-eh*
Hasidic *hah-SEE-dik*
Hasidim *hah-SEE-deem*
Haskalah *hahs-KAH-luh*
Haydn, Franz Joseph *FRAHNS YŌ-sehf HĪ-duhn*
Heldentenor *HELD-dehn-ten-ōr*
heterophony *het-ur-RAH-fōn-ee*
Hildegard of Bingen *HIL-deh-gahrd of BING-uhn*
Hindustani *hin-doo-STAN-ee*
Homme armé, L' *LUM ahr-MĀ*
homophonic *hō-mō-FAH-nik*
Hornbostel *HORN-boss-tuhl*
Huachos *WAH-chōs*
Huguenots, Les *lā HYU-guh-no*

iconography *Ī-kuhn-AH-gruhf-ee*
idiophones *ID-ee-ō-fonz*
Indes Galantes, Les *lehs EHN-dees gah-LAHNT*
Iphigénie en Aulide *ehf-eh-JEHN-ee ehn ō-LEED*

Janissary *JAN-iss-ehr-ee*
Jesus-Christus-Kirche *YĀ-soos KREES-toos KIR-kuh*
Jhaptal *JAHP-tahl*
jor *jōr*
Josquin Desprez *jahs-KAN deh-PREH*
Jung, Carl *KARL YOONG*

Kabuki *kuh-BOO-kee*
kanjira *kuhn-JEH-ruh*
kanun *KAH-noon*
Karajan, Herbert von *HEHR-buhrt fōn KEH-reh-yahn*
Karnataka *kuhr-NAHR-tee-kuh*
kemence *kuh-MEHN-chuh*
kenas *KĀ-nahs*
Khan, Hazrat Inayat *HAS-raht eh-NĪ-uht KHAN*
Khan, Ustad Allaudin *oo-STAHD uh-LAUD-din KHAN*
Kiowa *KĪ-ō-wah*
klezmer *KLEHS-muhr*
klezmorim *klehs-mō-REEM*
Koca Sinan *KAH-juh SEE-nahn*

kotekan   *kō-TEH-kuhn*
Kremer, Isa   *EE-sah KRĀ-muhr*
kudüm   *koo-DOOM*

la illaha illa'llah   *LAH ee-LAH-hah IL-ah-lah*
Lac Court Oreilles   *LAK coort ō-RĀ-yehz*
Lassus, Orlande de   *ōr-LAHN-deh deh LAH-soos*
Liber Vitae Meritorium   *LEE-behr vee-TAH-eh meh-ree-TŌ-ree-oom*
libretto   *lee-BREH-tō*
Lully, Jean-Baptist   *ZHAHN bab-TEEST LOO-lee*

maestro di violin   *MĪ-strō dee vee-ō-LEEN*
Mahabharata   *MAH-hah-bah-RAHT-tah*
Mahler, Gustav   *GOOS-taff MAH-luhr*
makam   *mah-KAHM*
Mallku de los Andes   *MĪY-koo deh lōs AHN-dehs*
Manon Lescaut   *MAN-ōn lehs-CŌ*
Marcello   *mahr-CHEHL-ō*
marimba   *mah-RIM-bah*
marsang   *MUHR-sang*
Máru-Bihág   *MAH-roo bee-HAHG*
Matanga   *muh-TUNG-uh*
mazurka   *maht-ZOOR-kuh*
melismatic   *mel-iss-MAT-ik*
membranophones   *mem-BRAH-nuh-fōnz*
Menominee   *muh-NAH-muh-nee*
Menotti, Gian Carlo   *JAHN KAR-lō meh-NAH-tee*
Menuhin, Yehudi   *yuh-HOO-dee MEN-oo-ehn*
Meragi, Abdülkadir   *ab-DOOL-kah-DEHR meh-RAH-jee*
Messa di Gloria   *MEH-sah dee GLŌ-ree-ah*
mestizos   *mess-TEE-zōs*
Mevlana Jalalu'ddin Rumi   *mehv-LAH-nah jah-LAH-luh-den ROO-mee*
Mevlevi   *mehv-LEH-vee*
Meyerbeer, Giacomo   *JAH-kō-mō MAH-yuhr-behr*
mezzo-soprano   *MET-zō sō-PRAN-ō*
Milan   *mee-LAHN*
Mille Lacs   *MEEL LAHK*
Minnesinger   *MEHN-eh-zing-uhr*
minuet   *min-yoou-ET*
Misérables, Les   *LEH mi-zay-RAHB*
Mithila   *MEH-teh-luh*
monophonic   *mah-nō-FAH-nik*

monophony   *mah-NAH-fō-nee*
Montano, David Mercado   *dah-VEED mehr-CAH-dō mōn-TAH-nō*
Monteverdi, Claudio   *KLAH-dee-ō mōn-teh-VEHR-dee*
mot   *mō*
Mozart, Wolfgang Amadeus   *VUHF-gahng ah-mah-DĀ-oos MŌT-zahrt*
mridangam   *mreh-DUNG-uhm*
Msnagdim   *mehs-NAHG-deem*
mulattos   *moo-LAH-tōs*
mutrip   *moo-TRIP*

Nachtanz   *NAHK-tahnz*
nagaswaram   *NAH-guh-swar-uhm*
Natya Shastra   *NAHT-yuh SHAHS-truh*
Nayadeva   *NĪ-yah-DEH-vuh*
Neanderthal   *nee-AN-duhr-tahl*
neumes   *newmz*
ney   *nā*
Noh   *nō*

Ojibway (or Ojibwe)   *ō-JIB-weh*
Olatunji, Babatunde   *bah-bah-TOON-dā ō-lah-TOON-jee*
om   *ōm*
opera buffa   *Ō-puhr-ah BOOF-ah*
opera seria   *Ō-puhr-ah SEH-ree-ah*
oratorio   *ōr-ah-TŌ-ree-ō*
Orfeo   *ōr-FĀ-ō*
Ospedale della Pietà   *ohs-peh-DAH-lah DEH-lah pee-eh-TAH*

Palestrina, Giovanni   *jō-VAH-nee pah-leh-STREE-nah*
Parpignol   *pahr-peen-YŌL*
passacaglia   *pah-suh-KAHL-ee-ah*
Pavarotti, Luciano   *lewch-AH-nō pah-vah-RŌ-tee*
Peer Gynt   *peer GEHNT*
Peri, Jacopo   *YAH-kō-pō PEH-ree*
phukuna   *foo-KOO-nah*
Physica   *FIZZ-ee-kuh*
piccolo   *PIK-ō-lō*
pizzicato   *pit-see-KAH-tō*
polyphonic   *pah-leh-FAH-nik*
potlatch   *POT-latch*
Prélude a 'L'aprés midi d'un faune'   *PREH-lood ah lah-preh meh-DEE doon FAHN*
Prete Rosso, il   *eel PREH-teh RŌ-sō*

Previn, André   *AHN-drā PREH-vuhn*
Puccini, Giacomo   *JAH-cō-mō poo-CHEE-nee*
Purcell, Henry   *HEN-ree PUHR-suhl*

Quechua   *KEHT-chwah*
quenachos   *kā-NAH-chōs*
quenas   *KĀ-nahs*
quipu   *KEE-poo*

raga   *RAH-guh*
Rameau, Jean-Philippe   *ZHAHN feh-LEEP rah-MŌ*
Rampal, Jean Pierre   *ZHAHN pee-AIR rahm-PAHL*
Rastafari   *rahs-tah-FAH-ree*
rebec   *REH-behk*
reggae   *REH-gā*
renaissance   *reh-neh-ZAHNS*
revelationum   *reh-veh-LAHT-see-Ō-noom*
Rig Veda   *rig VEH-duh*
Rodzinski, Artur   *AHR-toor rod-ZIN-skee*
Rondine, La   *lah RAHN-dee-neh*
Rosenkavalier, Der   *dehr RŌ-sehn-kav-uh-leer*
Rüdesheim-Eibingen   *ROOD-ess-heim Ī-bing-ehn*

Sachs   *zahks*
sadhana   *SAH-duh-nuh*
Salassie, Haile   *HĪ-lee suh-LAH-see*
sam   *sum*
saraband   *SAH-rah-bahnd*
Sarasvati   *sah-ruh-SWAH-tee*
sarod   *suh-RŌD*
Scala, La   *lah SKAH-lah*
Schaunard   *shō-NAHRD*
Scivias   *SKEE-vahs*
selam   *suh-LAHM*
Seljuk   *SEL-chook*
sema   *SEH-mah*
Sephardic   *suh-FAHR-dik*
shahnai   *shuh-NĪ*
shaman   *SHAH-mahn*
Shango   *SHAHN-gō*
Shankar, Ravi   *RUH-vee SHUHN-kur*
Shiva   *SHEE-vuh*
shishya   *SHEH-swuh*
siku   *SEE-koo*
Sinfonia da requiem   *sin-FŌN-ee-ah dah REH-kwee-ehm*

Singspiel   *ZING-shpeel*
sitar   *sit-AHR*
slendro   *suh-LEHN-drō*
stile rappresentativo   *STEE-leh rah-preh-zehn-tah-TEE-vō*
Stradivari, Antonio   *ahn-TŌ-nee-ō strah-deh-VAH-ree*
Strauss, Richard   *REE-kahrt SHTRAUS* (rhymes with "house")
strophic   *STRŌ-feek*
Sufi   *SOO-fee*
Sultan Veled Peshrev   *SOOL-tahn VEH-led pehsh-REHV*
Suor Angelica   *SWAHR ahn-JEL-lee-cah*
sushira   *suh-SHEH-ruh*
Sybil   *SIB-uhl*
syllabic   *sil-AB-ik*
symphonia   *sim-FŌN-ee-ah*

Tabarro, Il   *EEL tah-BAH-rō*
tabla   *TAHB-luh*
Tafelmusik   *TAH-fuhl-moo-ZEEK*
tala   *TAH-luh*
talam   *TAH-luhm*
tambourine   *tam-boor-EEN*
tambur   *TAM-buhr*
tambura   *tam-BOO-ruh*
Tanz   *tahns*
Tchaikovsky, Pyotor Il'yich   *PEH-tuhr IL-yich chī-KOF-skee*
tekke   *TEHK-keh*
timbre   *TAM-bur*
timpani   *TIM-pan-ee*
Torrico, Victor Hugo Ferrel   *BEEK-tōr OO-gō feh-REHL tō-REE-kō*
Tosca   *TŌS-kah*
Toscanini, Arturo   *ahr-TOO-rō tōs-kah-NEE-nee*
Trittico, Il   *eel TREET-tee-kō*
troubadours   *TROO-bah-dōr*
trouvères   *troo-VEHR*
Turandot   *TOO-ran-dōt*

ud   *ood or oot*
vadi svara   *VAH-dee SWUH-ruh*
Verdi, Giuseppe   *joo-SEHP-eh VEHR-dee*
Vesti la giubba   *VEHS-tee lah JOO-bah*
Vicenza   *vee-CHEN-zah*
Victoria, Tomás Luis de   *tō-MAHS loo-EES deh beek-TŌ-ree-ah*

vina *VEE-nuh*
vinaya *VIN-ī-yuh*
Vinci, Leonardo da *lee-ō-NAHR-dō dah*
  VEEN-chee
viola *vee-Ō-lah*
violonsel *vee-ō-lawn-CHEHL*
Vivaldi, Antonio *ahn-TŌN-ee-ō vee-VAHL-dee*

Wabanoon *WAH-buh-noon*
Wagner, Richard *REE-kahrd VAHG-nuhr*
wankara *wahn-KAH-rah*
Wayang Kulit *WĪ-yoon koo-LEET*

Weber, Carl Maria von *KARL mah-REE-ah*
  fōn VĀ-buhr
Weill, Kurt *KOORT VĪL*
Winnebago *win-nuh-BĀ-gō*
Wozzeck *VUHT-sehk*

xylophone *zī-lō-fōn*

Yiddish *YID-ish*

zampoña *zam-PŌN-yah*
zhikr *THICK-er*

Musician Biographies

[Note: A name preceded by an asterisk has a short biography in this appendix.

Although the term "American" can include South American and Canadian, we are limiting its meaning here to the United States.]

Alfano, Franco
(1875–1954) Italian composer

He studied in Naples, then moved to Berlin and Paris. His early work was in the *Puccini tradition. Alfano composed operas, songs, string quartets, symphonies, and violin and cello sonatas. He was chosen to complete Puccini's *Turandot,* but his ending was cut by *Toscanini and not heard in full until 1982.

Almanac Singers, The
(formed in 1941, disbanded after World War II)

American folksinging group originally formed by Pete Seeger, Lee Hays, and Millard Lampell. Later members included Pete Hawes, Sis Cunningham, Arthur Stern, Gordon Friesen, and Bess Lomax Hawes. The group often performed and recorded *Woody Guthrie's songs; sometimes Guthrie played with them. They often played at union halls, farm meetings, etc.

Armstrong, Louis ("Pops"; "Satchelmouth"; "Satchmo")
(1900–1971) African American bandleader, trumpeter, singer

After an arrest on a minor charge as a boy, Armstrong was sent to a home for boys, where he was taught to read music and play several instruments, most notably the trumpet. Following his release, he found work in Storyville, the notorious brothel district in New Orleans, where, in 1921, he became part of "King" Oliver's Jazz Band. In 1925, Armstrong formed his own band, the Hot Five, which would later become the Hot Seven. His skill at playing the trumpet, as well as his unusual voice, combined with a phenomenal stage presence and a charming personality, won him admirers all over the world and earned him national recognition as a cultural ambassador.

Axigally
(founded in 1985)

*Eric Warner and *Matt Ryan founded the band Axigally in Ames, Iowa, when they were in high school and learning studio work at the Media Arts Workshop. They began writing music although they had had less than two years of instrument lessons and knew no theory. Later band members include Jeff Sturges, John Pursey, and Sophie Ellmaker Sturges. They have recorded at least eleven albums, including *Paper Sky*, which includes the song *Animal Crackers*.

Bach, Johann Sebastian
(1685–1750) German composer

J. S. Bach was born into a family of musicians and had a largely uneventful childhood. He showed skill in both Latin and music. At the age of eighteen he took a position as organist in the Neukirche in Amstadt, the first of several positions he would hold as organist. It is, however, as a composer that Bach is remembered. He wrote roughly 200 church cantatas; more than 22 secular cantatas; and a vast number of chorales, toccatas, preludes, fugues, suites, concertos, and other works. In all, his compositions number well over 1,000 and include such masterpieces as the *Well-Tempered Clavier, B-minor Mass, Saint Matthew Passion,* and *Brandenburg Concertos.*

Beatles, The
(1961–1970) Pop music's most celebrated group

They began as rock 'n' rollers in Liverpool, England, and went on to enjoy worldwide adulation in the 1960s. Their music was originally inspired by the American rock musicians Chuck Berry, Bill Haley, and Buddy Holly. The original group was made up of *John Lennon, Paul McCartney, *George Harrison, and Stu Sutcliffe. Sutcliffe died of a brain hemorrhage and was replaced by Pete Best, who was locally popular but sought different musical directions from the rest of the group. Best was replaced by Richard Starkey, who took the stage name Ringo Starr. Their manager, Brian Epstein, transformed them into the legendary group that turned "Beatlemania" into a household word. Their songs included *Love Me Do, Please Please Me, She Loves You,* and *I Want to Hold Your Hand.*

Lennon and McCartney—the Beatles' writing team—were responsible for most of their hits. They produced two well received films, *A Hard Day's Night* (1964) and *Help!* (1965). As they gained financial security, they experimented with electronic music effects. The band broke up in 1970 and its surviving members (Lennon died in 1980) have made their own solo careers with more or less success.

Bechet, Sidney
(1897–1959) American-born jazz musician, master of the soprano saxophone

Bechet began playing at age six; by age seventeen he had played with a number of notable New Orleans bands. He moved to New York City in 1919, then toured Europe. He worked briefly with *Duke Ellington in 1925, then toured Europe again. From the late 1940s he was based in Paris, where he attained a great deal of fame. He was a master of musical drama and "note blending" (critically timed deviations in pitch).

Beethoven, Ludwig van
(1770–1827) German-Austrian pianist and composer

Beethoven belonged to the Viennese classical period and also the early romantic period. Born in the Rhineland town of Bonn, he showed exceptional musical talent quite early. He settled in Vienna in 1792, and he lived there the rest of his life. His rough manner contrasted with his brilliance as a pianist, and he fascinated the Viennese aristocrats, who provided him with a steady income. Worsening deafness (first acknowledged in 1802), along with the distressing Napoleonic Wars, made Beethoven increasingly moody and difficult. His musical greatness was recognized before he died, however, and 10,000 people attended his funeral.

Berlin, Irving
(1888–1989) American songwriter

A Russian-Jewish immigrant to the United States, he began his career in Tin Pan Alley (New York's music district), working as a street singer, singing waiter, and song plugger. He played from memory, since he couldn't read music. He went on to write over 1,500 popular songs, including *God Bless America*, *There's No Business Like Show Business*, and *White Christmas*. He often wrote both lyrics and music. He wrote for many New York revues and operettas, and for film musicals, including *Annie Get Your Gun*. He is considered one of the most versatile and successful twentieth-century writers of popular songs.

Bernstein, Leonard
(1918–1990) American conductor and composer

As the United States' first classical music superstar, this multitalented musician was a successful composer, conductor, pianist, and lecturer. He was educated at Harvard University and the Curtis Institute of Music. His career encompassed the worlds of both concert music and show business. He served as assistant conductor of the New York Philharmonic and became a star at age twenty-five when he conducted at the last minute for an ailing Bruno Walter. His opera *Candide* (1956) won the New York Critics Award; his musical *West Side Story* (1957) was a smash hit, and its film version (1961) won the Oscar for best picture. He was music director of the New York Philharmonic from 1958 to 1969. Bernstein made numerous recordings as conductor and piano soloist with most of the world's major symphony orchestras. He was also an excellent speaker and writer about music, and his series of television programs, called *Young People's Concerts,* is still in use today.

Bocelli, Andrea
(b. 1961) Italian tenor

Bocelli, disciple of *Pavarotti, has been called the "fourth tenor" (Pavarotti, *Carreras, and *Domingo being the other three) and is considered one of the most exciting new operatic voices. Unlike most opera singers, he has been equally successful as a pop ballad singer, recording popular duets with Celine Dion and *Sarah Brightman, among others. Bocelli grew up on a farm in Tuscany. He began piano lessons at age six and later studied flute and saxophone. His eyesight was poor, and he became totally blind at age twelve because of a soccer accident. Although obviously musically gifted, he earned a doctor of law degree at the University of Pisa before pursuing a career in music. While studying voice, he supported himself by performing in piano bars.

Bocelli's first big break came in 1992 when he recorded *Miserere* with Pavarotti. In 1995, he toured Europe. His first two albums showcased his operatic singing; his third featured famous arias and traditional songs from Naples; his fourth, *Romanza* (1997), featured pop music, including a hit duet with *Sarah Brightman, *Time to Say Good-Bye.*

Boito, Arrigo
(1842–1918) Italian composer and librettist

Boito is little remembered as a composer, although he wrote an opera based on *Doctor Faustus.* He was, however, influential in establishing the career of *Giacomo Puccini and, most importantly, he was the librettist for Ponchielli's *La Gioconda* and *Giuseppe Verdi's *Otello* and *Falstaff.*

Boulanger, Nadia
(1887–1979) French composition teacher

Nadia Boulanger was the sister of the composer Lili Boulanger. Both her father and grandfather were teachers at the Paris conservatory. She studied composition with Gabriel Fauré and graduated with awards in both organ and theory. She spent some time composing but could not compete with her sister, so she turned to teaching, where she firmly established her place in music history. Among her students were such notables as *Aaron Copland, Roy Harris, Walter Piston, Ellie Siegmeister, Cole Porter, and *Leonard Bernstein. During World War II she came to the United States and taught at Wellesley and Juilliard. In 1946 she returned to her beloved Paris, where she taught as long as her health permitted.

Brackett, Elder Joseph
(1797–1882) A member of the Shakers who "received" the song *'Tis a gift to be simple* as a spiritual gift.

Brahms, Johannes
(1833–1887) German composer

Brahms's father, a musician, gave him his first instruction, after which he received private instruction in piano. He first appeared publicly as a pianist at the age of ten. During his teens he earned a living by playing piano in public houses and taverns. In 1853 he went on a concert tour, during which he made the acquaintance of both Franz Liszt and Robert Schumann; the latter called him a genius. Brahms's notable works include four symphonies; four concertos; and several large choral works, including *A German Requiem.*

Bridge, Frank
(1879–1941) English composer, violist, and conductor

Bridge taught *Benjamin Britten. His own more adventurous music, composed in the 1920s and 1930s, was not much regarded until the 1970s.

Brightman, Sarah
(b. 1960) English singer

Brightman studied ballet and music as a child and made her first theatrical appearance at age thirteen. She sang with a punk-rock band before she auditioned for the original staging of *Andrew Lloyd Webber's *Cats* in London; she got the part, and she married Lloyd Webber. Under his direction she embarked on a classical career, singing with *Placido Domingo in Lloyd Webber's *Requiem* and starring in his *Phantom of the Opera*. After divorcing Lloyd Webber, Brightman moved to the United States and began a solo singing career. Her duet with *Andrea Bocelli, *Time to Say Good-Bye*, became a worldwide hit. Brightman enjoys singing both operatic arias and popular music.

Britten, Benjamin
(1913–1976) British composer

(See page 212.)

Brown, James
(b. 1933) African American rhythm-and-blues vocalist and composer

Brown achieved great popularity in the late 1950s through the 1970s with his combination of blues and gospel traditions, his rhythmic delivery, and his strong showmanship. He released a hit single, *Please, Please, Please,* in 1956; this was followed by other million-selling hits, including *I Can't Stand Myself, Papa's Got a Brand New Bag,* and *It's a Man's, Man's World.* Brown had a major role in getting white people to listen to African American popular music.

Bruckner, Anton
(1824–1896) Austrian composer

Bruckner, the son of a village schoolmaster and organist, studied organ, violin, and theory at Saint Florian monastery when he was thirteen. He later taught there and he became its organist in 1851. He wrote masses and other sacred works during those years. In 1855 he became organist at Linz Cathedral and began studying counterpoint. In 1863 he came into contact with *Richard Wagner's music, which moved him in new directions. He became a theory teacher at the Vienna Conservatory in 1869 and began writing complex symphonies, with mixed success. Only in the 1880s did he enjoy real success, receiving honors and patronage.

Buffalohead, (Alvin) Harry
(1926–1992) Native American singer and composer

Buffalohead was born near Ponca City, Oklahoma. His Indian name was Uh'ge ti, meaning "the beginning and the end" referring to the first tipi in the traditional circle. He was a Ponca singer and composer of songs. He was well known throughout the powwow world and served as head singer of the Ponca Powwow fifty-seven times. He credited his great-grandfather with teaching him the ways of the drum and the many songs he knew. Buffalohead began learning at age five and became the youngest head singer among the Ponca at age seven. During his career he learned many of the old songs that had been handed down from generation to generation. He was a member of the Baptist, Native American, and Bahai faiths.

Carreras, José
(b. 1946) Spanish tenor

Carreras studied at the Barcelona Conservatory. In 1971 he performed in a concert in London; his American debut was in 1972. Since then he has sung at the New York Metropolitan Opera House, London's Covent Garden, and other important opera houses. He is one of the most popular lyric tenors of his generation, famous for his sweet timbre and pure phrasing. (He, *Pavarotti, and *Domingo are known as the "Three Tenors.")

Carrasco García, René
(b. 1953) Bolivian musician

Carrasco is one of the founding members of *Mallku de Los Andes. He plays *charango*. (See page 272.)

Caruso, Enrico
(1873–1921) Legendary opera tenor of the early twentieth century

Caruso was born in Naples, Italy, and made his early reputation singing Italian opera roles, mostly in Europe. During his later career he sang more than 600 performances at the New York Metropolitan Opera House. His pioneer recordings for early gramophones made him one of the first music superstars and enormously wealthy.

Coltrane, John
(1926–1967) African American jazz saxophonist, bandleader, and composer

Coltrane was one of the most innovative and widely imitated jazz saxophonists. He was a soloist with Miles Davis before leading his own bands.

Copland, Aaron
(1900–1990) American composer

As a young man, Copland took piano lessons from Victor Wittgenstein and lessons in counterpoint from Rubin Goldmark. In 1921 he went to Paris, where he studied composition with *Nadia Boulanger until 1924. He was notable for his use of folk and folk-like motifs in grand, sweeping works, such as *Rodeo, Billy the Kid,* and *Appalachian Spring.* Also exceptional among his works are the perennial favorites *A Lincoln Portrait* and *Fanfare for the Common Man.*

Debussy, Claude
(1862–1918) French Impressionist composer

Debussy, who graduated from the Paris Conservatory, made pilgrimages to *Richard Wagner's opera house in Beyreuth but abandoned Wagner's technical excess, weight, and emotional richness for the tenets of the Impressionist artists and symbolist poets. Debussy's works usually have a pictorial or evocative effect. *La Mer, The Sunken Cathedral,* and *The Girl with the Flaxen Hair* are among his better-known works.

Desprez, Josquin
(See Josquin Desprez.)

Domingo, Plácido
(b. 1937) Spanish tenor

Domingo is regarded as one of the leading lyric-dramatic tenors of his time. Born in Madrid, Spain, he began his career in Mexico in 1950. He sang with the Israel National Opera for four years, then performed at the New York City Opera in 1965. He has sung at the New York Metropolitan Opera and many European houses, performing diverse roles. He has great vocal gifts and a warm, outgoing stage personality. (He, *Carreras, and *Pavarotti are known as the "Three Tenors.")

Dowland, John
(1563–1626) Prolific London-born composer, virtuoso lutenist, and singer

He traveled widely, serving the English ambassador in Paris, then returned to England and earned a bachelor of music degree at Oxford in 1588 before traveling again in Europe. Dowland became a lutenist at the English court in 1612. He earned a doctorate in 1621. He was a gifted, highly original composer whose eighty-four *ayrs* for voice and lute raised the level of English song.

Dylan, Bob
(b. 1941) American singer and composer

Born Robert Allen Zimmerman in Duluth, Minnesota, Dylan led the urban folk music revival of the 1960s and 1970s. He was heavily influenced by the folksinger *Woody Guthrie and early in his career imitated Guthrie's vocal style and lyrics. Dylan became a leading composer and singer of songs of protest, many with powerful, poetic, metaphorical lyrics.

Some of his songs—*Blowin' in the Wind* (1962), *The Times They Are a-Changin'* (1964)—were anthems of the civil rights movement. Originally a solo performer, in 1965 he began playing electronically amplified instruments and using the rhythms of rock 'n' roll. His albums *Highway 61 Revisited* (1965) and *Blonde on Blonde* (1966) established him as a leading figure in rock. Later albums were more country-and-western in style. He continued to perform in the 1970s, and in the 1980s he experimented with reggae rhythms.

Ellington, Edward Kennedy "Duke"

(1899–1974) African American jazz composer, pianist, and band-leader

(See page 326.)

Ergin, Dogan

(twentieth century) Turkish *ney* (flute) player, composer, and conductor

(See page 308.)

Ferrel Torrico, Victor Hugo

(b. 1959) Bolivian guitarist

Ferrel Torrico is a member of *Mallku de Los Andes. (See page 272.)

Foster, Stephen

(1826–1864) American song composer

Foster, who was self-taught, wrote some 200 songs, beginning in 1844. These include *My Old Kentucky Home, Jeanie with the Light Brown Hair, Beautiful Dreamer, Oh! Susanna, Camptown Races,* and *Old Folks at Home.* He composed simple, sentimental songs, strongly rhythmic minstrel songs in black dialect, hymns, and Sunday school songs.

Gahbow, Pete

(b. 1965) Ojibwe drummer and singer

Gahbow was born on the Mille Lacs Reservation in Minnesota. He is a founding member and lead singer of the Little Otter Singers. (See page 67.)

Garcia, Jerry

(1942–1995) American rock musician and counterculture icon

Garcia personified the hippie counterculture for three decades as the leader of the rock band *The Grateful Dead, based in San Francisco. Garcia was the singer, songwriter, and lead guitarist of the group, which became one of the most successful touring bands in the nation. Garcia was the gentle, laid-back patriarch of the Deadheads—the group's fans. He struggled with heroin addiction and died of a heart attack at a drug rehabilitation center.

Gershwin, George
(1898–1937) American composer

Gershwin began as a song plugger and accompanist in Tin Pan Alley (New York's music district). His first hit song was *Swanee,* sung by the vaudeville singer Al Jolson. Gershwin also composed stage musicals; his brother Ira was usually the lyricist. *Rhapsody in Blue,* a concerto for piano he wrote in 1924, made him famous, and he began writing more "serious" compositions. He also wrote the American folk opera *Porgy and Bess.* Gershwin synthesized jazz and classical traditions, as well as black folk music and opera.

Goldman, Jonathan
(b. 1949) American writer, musician, and teacher

Goldman has been a rock 'n' roll musician, songwriter, and recording artist, as well as a professional disc jockey, freelance writer, and newspaper editor. He is an authority on sound healing, a pioneer in the field of harmonics, and a lecturing member of the International Society for Music and Medicine. Goldman has studied with masters of sound from scientific and spiritual traditions. Over twenty years ago, he founded the nonprofit Sound Healers Association, which is dedicated to education about and awareness of the uses of sound and music for healing. Goldman has published several books about sound, including *Healing Sounds* and *Shifting Frequencies.* He has released a number of CDs, including *Dolphin Dreams, Trance Tara, Gateways,* and *Chakra Chants.* Goldman teaches Healing Sounds Seminars and workshops at universities, hospitals, holistic health centers, and expos throughout the United States and Europe. (See page 8.)

Grateful Dead, The
(founded mid-1960s) San Francisco-based psychedelic rock band

*Jerry Garcia was lead singer and guitarist; *Mickey Hart was percussionist. Fans, known as "Deadheads," often followed the band from concert to concert, forming spirited temporary communities. The band regained fame in the late 1980s, when a new generation of young fans, along with nostalgic baby boomers, combined to make it more popular than ever.

Gregory I, Pope
(540–604) Pope, 590–604

Gregory I restructured the liturgical music of the Catholic church. Popular medieval mythology suggested that the Holy Spirit had, in the guise of a dove, whispered Gregorian chant into Gregory's ear, but in fact, he probably completed work which had been begun by his predecessors, codifying the whole of the chant and composing some of it.

Grieg, Edvard
(1843–1907) Norwegian composer

Grieg's early works were influenced by early Romantic music. In 1864–1865 he had a stylistic breakthrough and began composing folk-inspired music. He promoted Norwegian music through concerts, teaching, conducting, and helping to found the Christiania Musikforening. Although chronically ill, he toured as a conductor and pianist. He was a lyrical composer and a pioneer in impressionistic uses of harmony.

Guthrie, Woodrow Wilson "Woody"
(1912–1967) Oklahoma-born folksinger and composer

He left home at age fifteen and traveled the country by freight train, playing his guitar and harmonica in hobo and migrant camps. The son of a professional fighter and musician, Guthrie became involved in the labor movement during the Great Depression, and at this time his leftist politics became ingrained. He became a spokesman for the common people and their struggles. He composed over 1,000 songs.

Guthrie became the colleague of *Pete Seeger and other folksingers, with whom he worked from time to time. About 1957, Guthrie developed Huntington's disease, a degenerative disease of the nervous system. In an unusual move—given Guthrie's politics—the United States government gave him an award of merit in 1966, calling him "a part of the American landscape." And he was indeed a legendary folk figure. He was the father of Arlo Guthrie, who carries on the folk tradition of his father. (See page 191.)

Harrison, George
(b. 1943) English singer, songwriter, and guitarist, member of the legendary *Beatles

Harrison joined *John Lennon and Paul McCartney in the Quarrymen band in 1958; this group became the Beatles, and Harrison became lead guitarist. Among other songs, he wrote *I Need You, Taxman,* and *Something.* In 1965 he became a pupil of the noted Indian sitarist *Ravi Shankar and pursued Indian-based spiritual values. Eastern influences soon permeated the Beatles' music. After the Beatles' breakup in 1970, Harrison began releasing well-regarded solo albums and became involved in the production of several films. He organized the 1971 Concert for Bangla Desh, in part as a result of his relationship with Ravi Shankar.

Hart, Mickey
(b. 1943) Percussionist and musicologist

Mickey Hart was the percussionist of the rock group *The Grateful Dead for more than twenty-five years. After becoming interested in percussion and its relationship to ritual and anthropology, he met with the comparative mythologist Joseph Campbell and began researching percussion instruments and their playing techniques throughout history. The result was two books, *Drumming at the Edge of Magic* (1990) and *Planet Drum* (1991). In addition, Hart serves on the board of the Smithsonian Institution's Folkways Records, and he produces *The World,* a series of recordings from around the world for Rykodisk.

Haydn, Franz Joseph
(1732–1809) Austrian composer

Haydn was the son of a wheelwright and grew up in a musical home. His father was a self-taught harpist and accompanied the family in song. At the age of eight, Haydn was engaged as a boy soprano in the Cathedral of Saint Stephen in Vienna. Eventually, he came under the patronage of the Esterházy court, where he would spend some of his most fruitful years. His legacy is vast. It is generally accepted that he wrote 108 symphonies in addition to oratorios, masses, numerous dramatic works, and a great number of string quartets, as well as various other works. (See page 288.)

Hildegard of Bingen
(1098–1179) German abbess, composer, and mystic of the Middle Ages

(See page 104.)

Hill, Lauryn
(b. 1975) Award-winning recording artist, actress, and activist

Hill started her career as lead singer of the Fugees. In 1996 they released their million-seller album, *The Score,* and they began their first world tour. In 1998 Hill released her first solo album, *The Miseducation of Lauryn Hill.* She won five Grammy Awards in 1999, including album of the year, best new artist, best female rhythm-and-blues (R&B) vocal, best R&B album, and best R&B song. She is founder of a nonprofit organization, the Refugee Camp Youth Project.

Inayat Khan, Hazrat
(1882–1927) Indian composer, musician, and spiritual leader

Pir-o-Murshid (a term that means Honored Teacher) was born in Baroda, India, into a family of well-known musicians. At an early age he showed outstanding musical talent as a singer and as a *vina* player. He began performing and won many awards, but at the same time he was searching for a spiritual guide. He found that guide, the Sufi mystic Mohammed Abu Hasan Madani. Madani eventually gave Inayat Khan the task of bringing Sufism to the West in a way that would be both accessible and acceptable to non-Muslims.

In 1910 Inayat Khan left India for Europe and the United States, giving concerts and, later, lectures on the inner life. He founded the Sufi Movement International, which has its headquarters outside of Paris, France. His many lectures have been published in the volumes of *The Sufi Message* and other books.

Itri, Buhurizade Mustafa
(1640–1712) Considered the most important Turkish classical composer

He is said to have composed more than 1,000 works, although only 42 have survived. His *na't* is the best known and later came to be sung as the opening to the Mevlevi ceremony.

Jackson, Mahalia
(1911–1972) African American singer known as the "queen of gospel song"

Jackson sang in the church choir of the New Orleans church where her father was preacher. She learned sacred songs as well as blues. She moved to Chicago at age sixteen and worked at various jobs while touring with a gospel quintet. In the 1930s her extraordinary voice first received widespread attention when she took part in a cross-country gospel tour. She made her first recording in 1934. Her records went on to sell millions. She appeared at New York's Carnegie Hall in 1950, as well as on radio and television; she toured in the United States and abroad, joining *Duke Ellington at the 1950 Newport Jazz Festival. Jackson was active in the civil rights movement and sang at the rally in Washington, D.C., in 1963—the rally where Martin Luther King gave his famous oration, "I have a dream."

Jefferson, "Blind Lemon" (Lemon)
(1897–1929) African American country blues singer, guitarist, and songwriter

Born in Texas, Jefferson was blind from birth. In his teens, he became a traveling entertainer, singing prison songs, spirituals, blues, and dance songs throughout the South. He moved to Chicago in the 1920s. He became one of the first successful black folk-blues singers, and he recorded for the Paramount label from 1926 to 1929. *Leadbelly (Huddie Ledbetter) was his disciple. Jefferson's vocal style, guitar technique, themes, and lyrics became staples of the blues. He reportedly suffered a heart attack and died of exposure.

Josquin Desprez
(b. about 1440; d. 1521) Northern French composer

Josquin is considered the greatest composer of the high Renaissance. What we know about him is a bit uncertain, but he was a singer at Milan Cathedral in 1459 and in the papal church choir (in Rome) in 1486. He left the choir by 1501 and went to France, where he became a very highly paid singer in the Ferrara court chapel. He also wrote masses and motets. Because of the plague, he left Ferrara and went north in 1503, to Notre Dame at Condé. He may have been connected with Margaret of Austria's court from 1508 to 1511. A portrait of him by Leonardo da Vinci survives. Josquin's works became known through Western Europe; many composers and theorists used them as models. Along with motets and eighteen complete masses, he composed secular *chansons*. (See page 314.)

Karajan, Herbert von
(1908–1989) Austrian conductor

Herbert von Karajan's international career was launched in Berlin in 1937 with a performance of *Tristan und Isolde*. The war impeded his career, but from 1947 on it grew rapidly. He recorded with a number of prestigious orchestras, including the Berlin Philharmonic. He was based in Berlin and Vienna. From 1956 to 1960 he was artistic director of the Salzburg Festival; from 1967 he was in charge of the Salzburg Easter Festival, at which he conducted a number of operas.

Khan, Hazrat Inayat
(See Inayat Khan, Hazrat.)

Larson, Jonathan
(1960–1996) American composer and lyricist

Larson created the book, music, and lyrics for *Rent,* based on Puccini's tragic opera *La Bohème.* He was posthumously awarded the Pulitzer Prize for Drama for *Rent.*

Lassus, Orlande de
(b. about 1530–d. 1594) Franco-Flemish composer

He served Gonzaga of Mantua from 1554 or so, traveling with him to Sicily and Milan. Lassus later moved back to Rome and became *maestro di cappella* (chapel master) of Saint John Lateran in 1553. Again he traveled, this time to Mons and Antwerp, where his early works were published. In Munich, he joined the court chapel of Duke Albrecht V of Bavaria as a singer. He took over the court chapel in 1563 and served the duke and his heir for over thirty years. Lassus traveled frequently and had many works published. He was one of the most prolific (over 2,000 works) and versatile of sixteenth-century composers, publishing in almost every genre. His works include masses, motets, psalms, and private devotional pieces, as well as secular works, including madrigals and *chansons.* He is considered one of the most significant musical figures of the Renaissance.

"Leadbelly" (Huddie Ledbetter)
(1888–1949) African American blues singer and guitarist

Leadbelly was born in Louisiana, raised in Texas, and led a hard life. His music was an important bridge between nineteenth-century African American field hollers and twentieth-century blues. (See page 196.)

Lennon, John
(1940–1980) English rock 'n' roll musician and composer

Lennon was born during an air raid on Liverpool. He showed an early tendency toward music, learned the guitar as a teenager, and formed, with Paul McCartney, *George Harrison, and Stu Sutcliffe, the original *Beatles. After the breakup of the group in 1970, Lennon went on to enjoy a successful solo career, writing both by himself and with his second wife, Yoko Ono.

In 1980, Mark David Chapman, a crazed fan, gunned Lennon down in front of his apartment house in New York. Lennon is survived by Yoko Ono and by two children—Julian Lennon, his son by his first wife, Cynthia; and Sean Ono Lennon, his son with Yoko Ono. Lennon's death, more than any other single incident, defined the loss of innocence of the Woodstock generation.

Lind, Jenny
(1820–1887) Swedish opera singer

Lind, who was nicknamed "the Swedish nightingale," began her operatic career in Stockholm in 1838; soon she made triumphant appearances in Germany, Austria, and Britain. She was known for her acting ability and for the extraordinary power and purity of her soprano voice. In 1850 she began an extended tour of the United States; in 1858 she settled in England. In 1883 she gave her last public performance.

Little Otter Singers
(founded in 1979) Prize-winning Ojibwe drum group from Minnesota

(See page 67.)

Lloyd Webber, Andrew
(b. 1948) English composer

Lloyd Webber was born into a musical family. He went to Oxford University but dropped out after his first year: he wanted to compose. He joined with Tim Rice, lyricist, to create the hit musical *Joseph and the Amazing Technicolor Dreamcoat* in 1969. This was followed by other hits: *Jesus Christ Superstar* (1970), *Evita* (1978), and *Cats* (1981). *Cats* became the longest-running musical in history. After *Cats*, Rice and Lloyd Webber separated as a team. Lloyd Webber went on to create *Starlight Express* (1984), *The Phantom of the Opera* (1986), *Sunset Boulevard* (1992), *Whistle Down the Wind*, and a requiem. *Sarah Brightman starred in several of his musicals while they were married; he wrote the part of Christina in *Phantom* for her.

Luther, Martin
(1483–1546) German religious reformer and musician

Although best known as the man who started the Reformation, Luther was also a musician. He was an ordained Catholic priest who protested against what he saw as the corruption of the church. Beginning in 1512, he lectured and preached about the Reformation throughout Germany. He was a fine singer, and he played the flute and lute. He had contact with *Josquin Desprez during a visit to Rome (c. 1510). Central to his reformation of the church was a change in the role of music. He created plainchant in which there was a close association between words and music—reflecting his belief that music was "the excellent gift of God." He composed or arranged numerous hymn melodies as well as two four-part polyphonic sacred pieces.

Mallku de los Andes
(founded in 1980) Bolivian musicians

The band Mallku de los Andes is internationally known and respected for Andean-style music. Its members include *Victor Hugo Ferrel Torrico, *David Mercado Montano, *René Carrasco Garcia, and *Edwin Roberts. (See page 272.)

Mahler, Gustav
(1860–1911) Austrian composer

At fifteen, Mahler entered the Vienna Conservatory. He also studied at the University of Vienna. In 1880, he took his first post as a conductor at the opera in the Austrian town of Halle. In 1891 he was named conductor of the Hamburg opera, and in 1897 he was offered a position with the Viennese court. In order to accept this offer, he was forced to convert from Judaism to Catholicism, the prevalent religion in Vienna. He held his position with the Viennese court for ten years; during much of this time he also conducted the Vienna Philharmonic orchestra. His compositions represent what was essentially the finale of the Romantic movement, at the same time foreshadowing the nontraditional harmonies of later musical styles.

Marley, Robert Nesta
(1945–1981) Jamaican rock musician

Bob Marley became the first third world superstar and spread reggae around the world. (See page 42.)

Menotti, Gian Carlo
(b. 1911) American composer

Menotti is of Italian origin. He first won success with a comic one-act opera, *Amelia Goes to the Ball* (1937), performed by the New York Metropolitan Opera. He proceeded to write a number of other operas, ranging from chamber opera to comedic to political melodrama. *The Saint of Bleeker Street* (1954) and the Christmas piece *Amahl and the Night Visitors* (1951)—the first opera composed for television—have become very popular. His later works include more operas and orchestral pieces, including works for children. He founded the Spoleto Festival of Two Worlds in 1958.

Menuhin, Yehudi
(1916–1999) American violinist

Menuhin, an internationally famous violin virtuoso, made a historic recording of Elgar's Violin Concerto at age sixteen with its composer conducting. Menuhin's career had amazing breadth, ranging from jazz to concerts with the Indian sitarist *Ravi Shankar. Bela Bartók wrote a sonata just for him. He settled in England, where he directed the Bath Festival and founded a music school.

Montano, David Mercado
(b. 1957) Bolivian musician

Montano was founder of *Mallku de Los Andes (1980) and Ballet Folklórico de Bolivia (1975–1980). He is a panpipe player. (See page 272.)

Morton, Ferdinand Joseph LaMenthe "Jelly Roll"
(1885–1941) African American jazz and blues musician

Born of French-American and African parents, Morton grew up in a relatively well-to-do home, surrounded by musical instruments. He was exposed to opera at an early age. He took up the piano and, against his parents' wishes, became a professional musician at age fifteen in Storyville, New Orleans's brothel district. He left New Orleans in 1907, touring the country playing ragtime and jazz. Morton was a habitual gambler, though much less successful at that than at music, losing several fortunes over time. His notable compositions include *King Porter Stomp* and *Jelly Roll Blues*.

Mozart, Wolfgang Amadeus
(1756–1791) Austrian composer

Mozart was the son of Leopold Mozart, himself a noted violinist and composer. Wolfgang was composing by the age of five, and Leopold commercially exploited his son's talent, displaying him at most of the influential courts of Europe. Wolfgang went to Paris with his mother in 1777 but was less than successful there. In Paris, his mother died, and Mozart returned to Salzburg. There he entered the entourage of the archbishop, a position which he neither wanted nor adapted well to, and one which he left under less than ideal circumstances. In 1782 he married Constanze Weber, against his father's wishes. The growing rift between Mozart and his father had a profound influence on his music. Mozart died at thirty-five of acute nephritis.

Netsky, Hankus
(b. in twentieth century) American multiinstrumentalist, composer, and teacher

Netsky was founder of the Klezmer Conservatory Band. (See page 80.)

Olatunji, Babatunde
(b. in twentieth century) West African drummer and teacher

He has toured the world playing and teaching West African drumming techniques and has also collaborated with *The Grateful Dead's percussionist *Mickey Hart on several ethnic percussion recordings. Olatunji's album *Drums of Passion* (1959) was perhaps the first stereo recording of traditional West African drumming in the United States. He has also produced an instructional video on West African drumming that details his GUN, GO DO, PA TA vocalization method. (See page 93.)

Orff, Carl
(1895–1982) German composer

Orff wrote in a generally expressionistic style until he became aware, in 1937, of the existence of a collection of secular Latin poetry known as *Carmina Burana*. He set this to an angular, percussive score; this was the work by which he would essentially be defined, although he composed many other works. His most notable accomplishment aside from *Carmina Burana* was the creation, in collaboration with Dorothee Gunther and Jacques Dalcroze, of a school for introducing music to schoolchildren, the *Orff-Schulwerk*, based on rhythm-focused instruction.

Pace, Mike
(b. 1946) Singer, drummer, dancer, and lecturer on Delaware traditions

Pace is past assistant chief and current treasurer of the Oklahoma Delaware Tribe. Born in Los Angeles, California, he now lives in Oklahoma.

Palestrina, Giovanni Pierluigi da
(b. about 1525; d. 1594) Italian composer

He began his musical career as a choirboy in Rome and later became organist of Saint Agapito. In 1551 he began publishing his first works. He also served as *maestro di cappella* (chapel master) at several important Roman churches, and he taught music at the Seminario Romano. His fame and influence spread rapidly during the 1560s and 1570s, owing to the wide dissemination of his compositions. He was so famous that he was commissioned to rewrite the church's plainchant books according to the Council of Trent's guidelines. He was one of the greatest Renaissance masters; his works became the classic model of Renaissance polyphony.

Paul, Les (Lester William Polfuss)
(b. 1915) American musician and guitar designer

Les Paul was the partner of the singer Mary Ford. He is best known as an innovator in electronics and recording technology. He contributed significantly to the development of the electric guitar, altering and helping to perfect the magnetic pickups that allowed it to be overdriven. Paul may have been the first person to utilize intentional distortion of the electric guitar as a musical technique. He was also responsible for the creation of a new guitar body type with particular resonant properties. As a recording innovator, Paul pioneered the technique known as layering or "overdubbing."

Pavarotti, Luciano
(b. 1935) Italian tenor

Pavarotti is considered one of the finest and most appealing Italian tenors of the twentieth century because of his rich, vibrant voice, splendid high notes, and fine musicianship. He made his debut in Italy in 1961, then began singing outside Italy in 1963, including at London's Covent Garden and in Australia. He made his debut at La Scala opera house in Milan, Italy, in 1965 and his American debut at the New York Metropolitan Opera House in 1968. (He, *Carreras, and *Domingo are known as the "Three Tenors.")

Pears, Peter
(1910–1986) English tenor

Pears had a wide repertory ranging from the sixteenth to the twentieth century. Benjamin Britten wrote all his major tenor roles for Pears, who was his lifetime companion.

Previn, André
(b. 1929) German-born American composer, conductor, and pianist

Previn studied in Berlin and Paris but moved to Los Angeles in 1939. His early career included working as a jazz pianist. In 1963 he made his conducting debut; he has conducted with a number of orchestras, including the Houston Symphony Orchestra and the Pittsburgh Symphony Orchestra. In 1986 he became music director of the Los Angeles Philharmonic Orchestra. In addition, he has composed musicals, orchestral pieces, and chamber works.

Puccini, Giacomo
(1858–1924) Italian opera composer of the late romantic period

(See page 147.)

Purcell, Henry
(1659–1695) English composer of the baroque period

Henry Purcell is considered one of the greatest composers of the baroque period and among the finest of all English composers. His illustrious musical career included posts as keeper of the king's keyboard and wind instruments, organist at Westminster Abbey, and organist of the Chapel Royal. He composed one of the most famous English operas, *Dido and Aeneas;* instrumental works; and incidental music for more than forty Restoration plays.

Rampal, Jean-Pierre Louis
(1922–2000) French flutist

Born in Marseilles, he studied at the Paris Conservatory. He began touring internationally in 1947. After playing at the Vichy Opera and the Paris Opera, in 1968 he joined the faculty of the Paris Conservatory. He was devoted to chamber music and founded several chamber music groups. He also recorded extensively. His clear, mellow tone is best heard in his authentic interpretations of eighteenth-century music, especially *Bach and *Mozart. Rampal brought new prominence to the flute as a concert instrument.

Reagon, Bernice Johnson
(b. 1942) African American singer, educator, and museum curator

Bernice Johnson Reagon founded the African American a cappella gospel quintet *Sweet Honey in the Rock in 1973 as part of the Black Repertory Theater Company. Daughter of a Baptist minister in rural Georgia, she had already served in a historic African American vocal group, the SNCC (Student Nonviolent Coordinating Committee) Freedom Singers, formed during the civil rights struggles of the 1960s. As a member of that group, she had toured the country, singing civil rights anthems and freedom songs handed down from black churches.

She is currently Distinguished Professor of History at American University in Washington, D.C., and Curator Emeritus at the Smithsonian Institution. She has produced fourteen recordings with Sweet Honey in the Rock, eight recordings of African American songs, and six documentary films and videos about the history and literature of African American folk music.

Rich, Buddy
(1917–1987) American jazz drum virtuoso

Rich's parents had a vaudeville act, and he began dancing in it at eighteen months. By age eleven he was leading a band. He began playing jazz in 1938. Rich accompanied major big bands, including Tommy Dorsey's and Harry James's, and then formed his own popular big band in the 1960s. From 1967 to 1974, he led a band of sixteen young musicians, playing jazz arrangements of rock and popular music. He was a brilliant swing drummer.

Roberts, Edwin
(b. 1956) Bolivian musician

Roberts is a member of *Mallku de Los Andes. He plays panpipes and *quenas*. (See page 272.)

Ryan, Matt
(b. 1971) Founder, with *Eric Warner, of the band *Axigally

Along with playing music, Ryan is the proprietor of an independent Internet board game site, Envelope Games (www.netins.net/showcase/envgames/), and a retail manager at a software store in Ames, Iowa. (See page 250.)

Schafer, R. Murray
(b. 1933) Canadian composer

Schafer was a student at the Royal Conservatory in Toronto. He later became associated with the Canadian Broadcasting Corporation. He is an innovator in electronic music and music for orchestra and tape and has written several innovative textbooks for teaching music theory.

Schwartz, Abe
(nineteenth–twentieth century)

A Jewish immigrant from Eastern Europe, the violinist and bandleader Abe Schwartz was signed by Columbia Records in the early part of the century to record klezmer music.

Seeger, Pete (Peter)
(b. 1919) American folksinger, composer, and virtuoso five-string banjo player

Seeger's father was the important musicologist Charles Seeger. Pete left Harvard University after two years, in 1938, and began hitchhiking around the country, collecting songs, ballads, and hymns. In

1940 he organized the *Almanac Singers, who played at union halls, farm meetings, etc.; sometimes the group included *Woody Guthrie. In 1948 Seeger formed the Weavers, who played on college campuses and made several records. However, the group was black-listed as a result of Seeger's left-wing politics and labor activities. The Weavers disbanded in 1952 but reunited in 1955 for a Christmas concert at Carnegie Hall. Seeger was convicted of con-tempt of Congress in 1961 for his refusal to answer questions asked by the House Committee on Un-American Activities in 1955. His conviction was overturned in 1962, but major networks blocked his appearance on TV for several years.

His informal, personal style encouraged the development of the "hootenanny," a gathering of performers playing and singing together. He sustained the folk music tradition and was the princi-pal inspiration for younger performers in the folk revival of the 1960s. Songs that he wrote alone or in collaboration include *Where Have All the Flowers Gone, If I Had a Hammer, Kisses Sweeter Than Wine,* and *Turn, Turn, Turn.* In the 1970s and 1980s he became active in environmental and antinuclear causes.

Shankar, Ravi
(b. 1920) Northern Indian sitar virtuoso and composer

Ravi Shankar was director of All India Radio at the time of India's independence (1948) and until 1956; he worked then to restore national pride in Indian classical music. His performances with the violinist *Yehudi Menuhin and with *George Harrison of the Beatles were important in popularizing Indian music in the West. (See page 132.)

Strayhorn, Billy
(1915–1967) African American jazz composer, pianist, and arranger

Strayhorn was a musical collaborator with *Duke Ellington. Strayhorn's classic compositions (composed alone or with Ellington) include *Lush Life, Take the "A" Train, Chelsea Bridge, Passion Flower,* and *Johnny Come Lately.* Strayhorn had both jazz and classical training, and Ellington described him as his most dependable critic. (See page 330.)

Sukay
(founded in the mid-1970s) Andean musical group, educators, and record producers

Founded by Quentin Howard (Navia), the group now includes Eddie Navia, a renowned Bolivian *charango* player and composer. The group is considered expert in Andean music. It has played at

Carnegie Hall and Lincoln Center and has released a number of recordings, including one with its crossover band, Pachamama, that includes modern jazz. Sukay has given educational programs and produced a video and workbook on making and playing Andean flutes.

Sweet Honey in the Rock
(founded in 1973) African American women's gospel quintet

This group was founded by *Bernice Johnson Reagon. It has made at least fourteen recordings and is committed to black music as a force against oppression. As well as vocalists, the group includes a sign language interpreter. (See page 197.)

Tarras, Dave
(1897–1989) Clarinetist

Originally from Eastern Europe, Tarras arrived at Ellis Island in 1921, fleeing economic hardship and persecution. This legendary clarinetist was a highly trained musician, famous for his smooth, elegant style. He became one of the most celebrated klezmer musicians of his generation.

Tchaikovsky, Pyotor Il'yich
(1840–1893) Russian composer

The son of a mining inspector, Tchaikovsky studied music as a child but showed no particular tendency toward greatness. In 1861, he entered a newly founded musical institute, from which he graduated in 1865. Shortly thereafter, he began composing prodigiously, leaving the world twelve operas, three ballets, six symphonies, numerous overtures—including the famous *1812 Overture*—and a plethora of smaller works and choral pieces. He died in 1893 after drinking unboiled water during a cholera outbreak, despite warnings to the public not to do so.

Tosh, Peter
(d. 1987) Jamaican reggae musician

Tosh was a member of the original *Wailin Wailers. He left the band in 1974 to pursue a successful solo career. (See page 42.)

Toscanini, Arturo
(1867–1957) Italian conductor

Toscanini began as a cellist. At nineteen he made his conducting debut in Rio de Janeiro, where he conducted *Aida*. He returned to Italy and became music director of the famous La Scala opera house in 1896; from 1908 to 1915 he was music director of the Metropolitan Opera in New York. In the 1920s his career was centered in Italy, and he toured Europe and North America with the La Scala orchestra. In 1937 he conducted the newly formed NBC orchestra, where he remained until 1954 and where he made most of his recordings.

Veled, Sultan
(1226–1312) Turkish composer

Veled, the elder son of the poet and mystic teacher Rumi, introduced the use of the opening procession, called *peshrev*, into the Mevlevi ceremony. Turkish art music is considered to date back to the founding by the mystic Rumi of the Mevlevi Order in Konya, in central Anatolia, in the thirteenth century. Two very old instrumental pieces that have survived until the present are believed to have been composed by Sultan Veled. (See page 301.)

Verdi, Giuseppe
(1813–1901) Italian opera composer

Born near Parma, the son of an innkeeper, Verdi began helping a local organist at age seven. His initial struggles as an organist and opera composer were discouraging. His first opera, *Obeto*, was accepted at La Scala, but his next failed totally. With *Nabucco* (1842), he finally met with success and fame. He was identified with the movement for Italian unity and independence and was elected to the first Italian parliament. Among his most popular operas are *Rigoletto, Il Trovatore, Aida, Otello,* and *Falstaff.* When he died, 28,000 people lined the streets as the funeral procession passed by.

Victoria, Tomás Luis de
(1548–1611) Spanish composer

He began as a choirboy at Avila cathedral, then was sent to the Jesuit Collegio Germanico in Rome, where he may have studied under *Palestrina. He was singer and organist at Santa Maria di Monserrato (1569–1574). He also taught at the Collegio Germanico (1571 to 1576–1577), during which time he became a priest. In the 1580s he returned to Spain as chaplain to the dowager empress Maria, whom he served at the Descalzas Reales convent in Madrid from 1587 to 1603. He remained there as organist until he died. He is considered the greatest Spanish Renaissance composer and is among the greatest composers in Europe of that period. He composed only Latin sacred music, including a number of masses, *magnificats,* psalms, and *motets.* He is best remembered for his masses and motets, composed in a serious, devotional style.

Vivaldi, Antonio
(1678–1741) Italian composer of the baroque era

Vivaldi, a remarkably prolific composer, was known as the "Red Priest."

(See page 174.)

Wagner, Richard
(1813–1883) German composer

Wagner, who was born in Leipzig, had some early training in music, but it was sporadic. When he was seventeen, his *Overture in B-flat* was premiered at the Leipzig theater. The next year, he entered the University of Leipzig. In 1835, he married Minna Planer, an actress, who eventually left him (in 1859). Shortly thereafter Wagner married Cosima von Bülow, the daughter of Franz Liszt. Until Wagner became romantically involved with Cosima, she was the wife of Hans von Bülow, the conductor who championed Wagner's operas.

Wagner's work represents the pinnacle of German Romanticism, and the bulk of it consists of operas that reflect his philosophical ideal of *Gesamtkunstwerk*, or total art. Wagner would attempt the ultimate expression of this ideal with the creation of his great theater at Bayreuth and with his crowning achievement: the opera cycle *Der Ring des Nibelungen*. Wagner died of a heart attack in 1883.

Wailer, Bunny
(b. ?) Jamaican reggae musician

An original member of the Wailin Wailers, he left the band in 1974 to pursue a successful solo career.

Wailin Wailers
(founded in the mid-1960s) Reggae group

*Bob Marley, *Peter Tosh, and *Bunny Wailer formed the Wailin Wailers. The producer Lee Perry joined them with the drum and bass duo Carlton and Aston Barrett; together they recorded two great early reggae albums, *Soul Rebels* and *African Herbsman*. In 1972 the group signed with Island Records; it was relaunched in 1974 as Bob Marley and the Wailers. Peter Tosh and Bunny Wailer soon left for successful solo careers. Marley died in 1981. (See page 42.)

Waller, Fats
(1904–1943) African American composer, pianist, organist, singer, and bandleader

He had a brief but extremely active career, during which he made nearly 500 discs and many piano rolls and composed some 400 pieces. His songs included *Honeysuckle Rose* and *Ain't Misbehaving*.

Warner, Eric
(b. 1971) Recording artist

Born in San Diego, California, Warner grew up in Ames, Iowa. In 1985 he founded the band *Axigally with Matt Ryan. Warner wrote, sang, and played keyboard and bass. He graduated from the University of California, San Diego, with a degree in applied mathematics and is now a programmer analyst at a computer visualization software company. (See page 250.)

Webber, Andrew Lloyd
(See Lloyd Webber, Andrew.)

Zappa, Frank
(1940–1993) American rock musician

Zappa released over fifty albums in styles ranging from rock to jazz to avant-garde. He began studying music in the 1950s and was a drummer in high school. Then he switched to the guitar. Along with performing, he wrote movie scores. His group became known as the Mothers and then as the Mothers of Invention. It disbanded in 1969, reformed in 1971, and was renamed Zappa in 1979. Zappa also produced satiric works, with some scatalogical lyrics. His album *Jazz from Hell* won a Grammy award in 1988; his sound track for *200 Motels* was performed by the Los Angeles Philharmonic under the direction of Zubin Mehta in 1970. *Valley Girl*, a parody of California slang, became his greatest commercial success.

ENDNOTES

Prelude

Page 8   "This sonic environment . . ." Jonathan Goldman. E-mail communication, subject, *Dolphin Dreams,* 4 December 1999.

Chapter 1

Page 14   "There have been more . . ." Leonard Bernstein, *The Joy of Music.* New York: Simon and Schuster, 1959.

     22   ". . . from full participation . . ."; "the World's" music; "divine inspiration." Daniel W. Patterson. Liner notes for *Early Shaker Spirituals,* Rounder CD 0078.

Chapter 2

Page 35   "For traditional Puerto–Rican–American Catholics . . ." Phone conversation with Justo Gonzales II, Puerto–Rican–American ordained minister, May 1999.

     36   "This arrangement [the Tree of Life] . . ." Z'ev ben Shimon Halevi, *Introduction to the Cabala Tree of Life.* York Beach, Maine: Samuel Weiser, Inc., 1991, p. 184.

     36   "One of the aspects . . ." *The Sufi Message of Hazrat Inayat Khan,* Volume XI. London: published for the International Headquarters of the Sufi Movement, Geneva, by Barrie and Jenkins, 1964, pp. 101–102.

     36   "My research has demonstrated . . ." Angeles Arrien, Ph.D., *The Four-Fold Way, Walking the Paths of the Warrior, Teacher, Healer, and Visionary.* San Francisco: Harper San Francisco, a division of HarperCollins Publishers, 1993, p. 7.

     36   "If we envisage the cosmos . . ." Alain Daniélou, *The Myths and Gods of India.* Rochester, Vermont: Inner Traditions International, 1985, pp. 15–17.

Chapter 3

Page 55   The authors are indebted to Mike Pace and Pete Gahbow for their input and suggestions.

     56   ". . . any large gathering . . ."; "cultural rejuvenation." Chris Roberts, *Powwow Country.* Helena, Montana: American and World Geographic Publishing, 1992, p. 14.

     56   ". . . a time to get together . . ." "Denver Gathering Starts a Round of Dance," *Denver Post,* March 19, 1999, pp. 1E.

     57   "One legend about the jingle dress . . ." Ibid., p. 35E.

58 "... an acknowledgment to the Creator ..." Written communication from Mike Pace, November 1999.

58 "... help them keep count ..." Telephone conversation with Pete Gahbow, 30 November 1999.

58 "Being a member ..." Richard Cornelius and Terence J. O'Grady. "Reclaiming a Tradition: The Soaring Eagles of Oneida," *Ethnomusicology,* Spring/Summer 1987, pp. 261–272.

58 "... powwow dancers choose their own dances ..." Linda Raczek, *Rainy's Powwow,* Rising Moon Publications, 1999.

61 "There are no really old ..." Personal communication from Mike Pace, June 1999.

61 "When I'm singing ..." From video, *Into the Circle: An Introduction to Native American Powwows.* Tulsa, Oklahoma: Full Circle Communications, 1992.

66 "It is a warm night ..." Excerpted from the program notes by Thomas Vennum, Jr., to the album for *Honor the Earth Powwow,* Ryko RCD 10199.

67 "We thought it was ..." Pete Gahbow, telephone conversation, 30 November 1999.

69 "Since the song was ..." Pete Gahbow, telephone conversation, 30 November 1999.

Chapter 4

Page 77 "... the most important music of the Askenazi Jews ..." See Henry Sapoznik, "Klezmer Music: The First One Thousand Years," in *Musics of Multicultural America,* ed. Kip Lornell and Anne K. Rasmussen. New York: Schirmer Books, 1997, pp. 49–72. See also Henry Sapoznik, *Klezmer! A Very Social History of 100 Years of Yiddish Music in America.* New York: Schirmer Books, 1998.

78 "... further enliven their gatherings." Hankus Netsky, "An Overview of Klezmer Music and Its Development in the U.S.," unpublished, p. 2.

78 "wailing sound reminiscent of ..." Ibid., p. 1.

80 "inspired not only Jewish ..." Ibid., p. 4.

Chapter 5

Page 87 In this chapter, rhythm is shown in Time Unit Box System (TUBS) notation, developed by Alan P. Merriam for African rhythms.

87 The authors wish to thank Dr. John Galm, ethnomusicologist at the University of Colorado, Boulder, for his advice on this chapter. However, any errors or misconceptions are the responsibility of the authors.

88 "From the African perspective ..." Personal communication from John Galm, 10 December 1999.

89   "Sub-Saharan Africa . . ." Thomas Turino, "The Music of Sub-Saharan Africa," in *Excursions in World Music*, Bruno Nettl et al. New Jersey: Prentice Hall, 1992, pp. 165–195.

90   "We are almost a nation . . ." Quoted in Eileen Southern, *The Music of Black Americans*. New York: W. W. Norton, 1971, pp. 6–7.

91   "In such a pair . . ." Personal communication from John Galm, 10 December 1999.

92   "many words may share . . ." Thomas Turino, "The Music of Sub-Saharan Africa," in *Excursions in World Music*, Bruno Nettl et al. New Jersey: Prentice Hall, 1992, p. 187.

92   "Drums may also be used . . ." J. H. Kwabena Nketia, *The Music of Africa*. New York: W. W. Norton, 1974, p. 198.

94   "The Yoruba tribesman . . ." Betty Warner Dietz and Michael Babatunde Olatunji, *Musical Instruments of Africa*. New York: John Day, 1965, p. 2.

94   "With thunder and lightning . . ." From the liner notes of *Olatunji! Drums of Passion*. (Columbia CK 8210), written by Akin Akiwowo and Babatunde Olatunji.

Chapter 6

Page 105   "When I was forty-two . . ." Quoted in Matthew Fox, *Illuminations of Hildegard of Bingen*. Santa Fe, New Mexico: Bear and Company, 1985, p. 9.

106   "the present in such depth . . ." Ibid., p. 9.

108   "He had silenced . . ." and "Those who choose . . ." Ibid., p. 9.

109   "The goal of creation for Hildegard . . ." Brendan Doyle. Quoted in *Hildegard of Bingen's Book of Divine Works*, Matthew Fox, ed. Santa Fe, New Mexico: Bear and Company, 1987, p. 664.

113   "It is said that . . ." Sequentia recording group, *Voice of the Blood* liner notes (Deutsche harmonia mundi 05472 773462), 1995, p. 6.

113   "Through the power of hearing . . ." Quoted in Matthew Fox, *Illuminations*, p. 115.

114   "all sacred music . . ." quoted in Layne Redmond, *When the Drummers Were Women*. New York: Random House, 1997, p. 162.

115   "rebounding to the celestial . . ." Quoted in Matthew Fox, *Illuminations*, p. 9.

115   "Her poetic effects are . . ." Peter Dronke. Sequentia recording group, *Symphoniae* liner notes (Bayer Records 100 116 CD), 1985, p. 9.

Chapter 7

Page 124   "The Music of India." The authors are indebted to Chaitanya Kabir for his input and advice on Indian classical music.

127   "Guru, as many people know . . ." Ravi Shankar, *My Music, My Life.* New York: Simon and Schuster, 1968, pp. 11–12.

Chapter 8

Page 141   "high art . . ." *The Rough Guide to World Music.* London: APA Publ., 1994, p. 466.

141   "The aristocratic *Noh* . . ." For a more detailed description of *Noh* and *Kabuki*, see Isabel K. F. Wong, "Japan," in Bruno Nettl et al., *Excursions in World Music.* Englewood Cliffs, New Jersey: Prentice Hall, 1992, pp. 105–133.

151   Plot synopsis of *La Bohème:* Summary by William Weaver, used by permission.

154   Text of *La Bohème:* Adapted from the translation © 1966 by William Weaver, used by permission.

Chapter 9

Page 174   "The family must continue . . ." John Julius Norwich, *A History of Venice.* New York: Knopf: distributed by Random House, 1982, pp. 594–595.

175   "Every Sunday and holiday . . ." Edward Wright, *Some Observations Made in Traveling Through France, Italy, etc. in the Years 1720, 1721, and 1722.* London, 1730 (2 volumes), vol. 1, p. 79.

179   "The 'early music' movement . . ." Eric Hobsbawm and Terence Ranger, eds. *The Invention of Tradition.* London: Cambridge University Press, 1983.

182   Sonnet for *Spring,* translation by H. C. Robbins Landon.

Chapter 10

Page 194   "These songs here aint . . ." Woody Guthrie, *Pastures of Plenty.* New York: HarperCollins, 1990, p. 45.

196   "the rich tradition of nineteenth-century . . ." Charles Wolfe and Kip Lornell, *The Life and Legend of Leadbelly.* New York: HarperCollins, 1992, p. 4.

196   "In fact, Ledbetter was . . ." Ibid., p. 265.

197   "For a singer in Sweet Honey . . ." Bernice Johnson Reagon, *We Who Believe in Freedom.* New York: Anchor Books, 1993, p. 35.

198   "July and August is hot . . ." In Moses Asch and Alan Lomax, eds. *The Leadbelly Songbook.* New York: Oak Publications, 1971, p. 60.

Chapter 12

Page 230   "*Gamelan.*" Our thanks to Dr. John Galm, ethnomusicologist at the University of Colorado, Boulder, for his assistance. Any errors remain the authors'. Additional resources include Sumarsam, *Gamelan: Cultural Interaction and Musical Development in Central Java.* Chicago:

University of Chicago Press, 1992, 1995. See also Michael Tenzer, *Balinese Music*. Berkeley-Singapore: Periplus Editions, 1991.

230 "It has been said ..." Personal communication from John Galm, 6 December 1999.

230 "After casting the largest gong ..." Personal communication from John Galm, 10 December 1999.

232 "The gamelan was ..." Personal communication from John Galm, 6 December 1999.

234 "The 'male' instruments ..." William P. Malm, *Music Cultures of the Pacific, the Near East, and Asia*. New Jersey: Prentice Hall, 1996, p. 56.

Chapter 13

Page 244 "I moved to Los Angeles ..." Les Paul, quoted in Tom Wheeler, *American Guitars: An Illustrated History*. New York: Harper and Row, 1982, p. v.

245 "The device was called an ADT ..." Peter Dogget, *Let It Be/Abbey Road: The Beatles*. New York: Schirmer Books, 1998, p. 69.

250 "It was one ..." E-mail communication from Matt Ryan, 29 November 1999.

252 "In order to create ..." E-mail communication from Jonathan Goldman, 3 December 1999.

253 "For example, in 1965 ..." For a more complete description, see David Brackett, *Interpreting Popular Music*. Cambridge: Cambridge University Press, 1995, pp. 1–9.

Chapter 14

Page 268 "Music of the Andes." The authors wish to thank Dr. John Galm, ethnomusicologist at the University of Colorado, Boulder; Quentin Navia of Sukay World Music; and Dr. Loren Stafford for their assistance with this chapter. We take responsibility for any inaccuracies that may remain.

268 "A bass drum ..." Phone conversation with Quentin Navia, musician and Andean music specialist, Sukay World Music, 10 December 1999. Sukay World Music has been bringing Andean music to the United States and Europe for over twenty-four years and is considered an expert in the field. Website: http://www.sirius.com/~sukay

270 "A great variety ..." For more detail, see John M. Schechter's chapter, "America/Ecuador," in *Worlds of Music*, pp. 376–427. See also *Music in Latin American Culture*, ed. John Schechter. New York: Schirmer Books, 1999. *Garland Encyclopedia of World Music*, vol. 2: *South America, Mexico, Central America, and the Caribbean*, eds. Dale Olsen and Daniel Sheehy. New York: Garland, 1998.

270 "One popular ..." John M. Schechter, "America/Ecuador," in *Worlds of Music*, 2nd ed., ed. Jeff Todd Titon. New York: Schirmer Books, 1992, p. 383.

270 "in Aymara, it ..." Ibid., p. 386.

270 "*Siku* is also ..." Phone conversation, Quentin Navia, 10 December 1999.

270   "These instruments are . . ." Ibid.

272   "In the Andes . . ." Ibid.

274   "Imagine the native dancers . . ." Written communication from John Galm, 6 December 1999.

Chapter 16

Page 297   "Come, come whoever you are . . ." Mevlana Jalalu'ddin Rumi, thirteenth century Persian Sufi poet and philosopher. Translation in *Singing the Living Tradition,* the Unitarian Universalist Hymnal (Boston: Beacon Press, 1993).

301   "Classical Music of Turkey." The authors are indebted to Chaitanya Kabir and John Galm for their input and advice on the classical music of Turkey.

301   "Sultan Veled . . ." *New Grove Dictionary of Music,* vol. 19. London: Macmillan, 1980, p. 268.

304   "Unity of Being . . ." Laleh Bakhtiar, *Sufi: Expressions of the Mystic Quest.* New York: Thames and Hudson, c. 1976, reprinted 1991, p. 9.

305   "contemplate the divine . . ." Ira Friedlander, *The Whirling Dervishes.* New York: Collier Books, 1975, p. 91.

305   ". . . prepare to turn to God . . ." Ibid.

306   "We are drawn . . ." Kabir Helminski, *The Knowing Heart.* Boston: Shambhala, 1999, p. 188.

306   "They empty their hearts . . ." Friedlander, p. 26.

306   "Dervish music cannot be written . . ." Ibid., p. 134.

307   "The following TUBS . . ." from John Galm.

Chapter 17

Page 315   "Alberti's Renaissance facade . . ." Thomas Buser, *Experiencing Art Around Us.* Cincinnati, Ohio: Thomson Learning, 1995, p. 175.

317   "often amounts to re-creations . . ." The Hilliard Ensemble Biography on the Website http://www.ecmrecords.com/ecmlbio/43.html, copyright 1995–1998, Mediapolis, Inc.

Chapter 18

Page 330   "His patience was . . ." Duke Ellington, *Music Is My Mistress.* Garden City, New York: Doubleday, 1973, p. 161.

330   "about one-eighth of a page . . ." quoted in Richard Crawford, *The American Musical Landscape.* Berkeley: University of California Press, 1993, pp. 186–187.

332   ". . . jazz critics who clamor . . ." Stanley Dance, quoted in Derek Jewell, *Duke: A Portrait of Duke Ellington.* New York: W. W. Norton, 1977, p. 100.

INDEX

A cappella, 198
Abelard, Peter, 105
Absalon, fili mi (Josquin Desprez), 316–321
Academy of Ancient Music, 289
Accented beat, 55
Acrostic, 314
Active listening, 6
Adagio, 180
Adami, Giuseppi, 150
African American music, 42, 195–198, 323–338;
    see also Blues; Jazz
African music, 87–96
Agogo, 91, 95
Aida (Verdi), 143
Akiwowo, Akin, 95
Alap, 135
Alberti, Leon Battista, 315, 316
Alceste (Lully), 143
Alexander VI, Pope, 314
Alfano, Franco, 150, 346
Allegro, 180
Almanac Singers, 193, 346
Altiplano, 272
Amahl and the Night Visitors (Menotti), 143
American popular music, 247
American vernacular music, 191–194
Anacrusis, 84
Anchoress, 105
Andean music; *see* Native American music;
    South America
Angeloni, Carlo, 147
Animal Crackers (Ryan), 250, 251, 254
Appalachian Spring (Copland), 21, 24–28, 50,
    275, 321, 353
Aria, 154
Armstrong, Louis, 325, 331
Arrien, Angeles, 39
Art music, 19
Ashkenazi Jews, 77–79
Atahualpa, 271
Ataturk, Mustafa Kemal, 299, 301, 306
Axigally, 250, 251, 254, 347, 367, 372

Bach, Johann Sebastian, 178, 347
Backbeat, 333
Background music, 18, 19
Balancing, 245
Bali; *see* Indonesian music
Band, 207, 323, 325
Banjo, 324, 326
Banya, 324
Bar, 74
Bar line, 74
Barbarossa, Frederick, 105, 106
Barbershop quartet, 190
Baritone, 146
Barker, Mildred, 25
Baroque period, 27, 177, 178, 313
Barrett, Aston, 371
Barrett, Carlton, 371
Bartók, Béla, 363
Bass baritone, 146
Bass clarinet, 211
Bass drum, 212
Bass voice, 146
Basso cantante, 146
Basso continuo, 180, 313
Basso profundo, 146
Bassoon, 211, 218, 222
Battle Hymn of the Republic, The, 247
Bay a Glezele Mashke, 80, 81, 83, 138, 187, 200,
    224, 295
Beal Street Blues, 326
Beat, 55
Beatles, 34, 122, 347, 356, 360, 368; *see also*
    Harrison, George; Lennon, John;
    McCartney, Paul
Bechet, Sidney, 325, 331, 348
Becket, Thomas à, 105
Beethoven, Ludwig van, 14, 15, 34, 284, 286,
    289, 302, 348
Belasco, David, 149
Believers; *see* Shakers
Bell choir, 272
Bells, 67
Berg, Alban, 143
Berlin, Irving, 98, 193, 348
Bernard of Clairvaux, 105

Bernstein, Leonard, 14, 348, 350
Berry, Chuck, 347
Best, Pete, 347
Bible, 316, 317
Binary form, 280, 293
Blackwell, Chris, 43
Blessing prayer, 64
Blues, 42, 196, 326; *see also* African American
    music; Jazz
Blues progression, 326
Bocelli, Andrea, 142, 166, 349, 351
Bohème, La (Puccini), 143, 147, 148, 151–165,
    187, 225, 321, 360
Boito, Arrigo, 148, 349
Bollywood, 134
Bombo, 268
Bop, 325
Borgia, Cesare, 316
Borgia, Juan, 314
Borgia, Lucrezia, 316
Borgia, Rodrigo; *see* Alexander VI, Pope
Boulanger, Nadia, 4, 350, 352
Bound for Glory (Guthrie), 193
Bow, 210
Bowdich, Thomas, 90
Brackett, Elder Joseph, 25, 350
Brahms, Johannes, 20, 260, 350
Brand, Wellman, 331
Brass instruments, 209, 211, 212
Bressler, Judy, 82, 83, 186
Bridge, 335
Bridge, Frank, 213, 350
Brightman, Sarah, 166, 349, 350, 361
Bring Me Little Water Silvy (Leadbelly), 191,
    197–199, 225, 265
Britten, Benjamin, 143, 206, 212–225, 350, 351
Brown, James, 97, 351
Brown, Lawrence, 330
Brubeck, Dave, 208
Bruckner, Anton, 286, 351
Buddhism, 229
Buffalohead, (Alvin) Harry, 61, 351
Bulgarian Women's Chorus, 200
Bülow, Cosima von; *see* Wagner, Cosima Liszt
    von Bülow
Bülow, Hans von, 371
Burgess, Marie, 25
Bustle, 59

Cabala, 36, 37
Cadenza, 333
Call and response, 17, 18
Calypso, 42
Campbell, Joseph, 357
Camptown Races (Foster), 247
Canby, Edward Tatnall, 243
Candide (Bernstein), 349
Cantor, 77
Carnatic; *see* Karnataka style
Carr, Frances, 25
Carrasco García, René, 272, 352, 362
Carreras, José, 142, 349, 352, 353, 365
Caruso, Enrico, 149, 153, 242, 352
Cats (Lloyd Webber), 145, 350, 361
Cauley, Karlyn, 22
Cephas, John, 194
Ceremonial setting, 14
Chaconne, 299
Chamber music, 285–287
Chamber orchestra, 224
Charango, 268, 272, 273
Charles II, King of England, 216
Charles VI, Holy Roman Emperor, 176, 178
Chartres Cathedral, 112
Childbirth, 8
Children's dances, 65
Chimes, 212
Chinese music, 165, 209
Chord, 171, 336
Chorus, 207
Christian, Tom, 64
Christianity, 64, 76, 105–116
Christianity (Protestantism), 21–24, 315
Christianity (Roman Catholicism), 267, 268,
    313, 315
Chromatic harmony, 173
Chromatic scale, 173
Civil War, American, 323
Claque, 149
Clarinet, 211, 218, 222
Classical period, 27, 284, 285
Classical sonata, 283
Closing theme, 282
Clowns, 63, 64
Coda, 280
Codetta, 280
Cognitive response, 33
Coloratura soprano, 146

Colores, De, 35, 36
Coltrane, John, 132, 352
Columbus, Christopher, 315
Compander, 246
Competition dances, 65
Composed theme, jazz, 326
Compound beat division, 75
Compound form, 281
Compressor, 245, 246
Concerto, 174, 178, 180
Concerto grosso, 179
Conjunct melody, 103
Continuity, 298
Continuous form, 298
Contrabassoon, 211
Contralto, 146
Contrast, 263, 264
Cool jazz, 325
Copland, Aaron, 21, 24, 26–28, 350, 352
Cotton Club Orchestra, 329
Counterpoint, 219
Countertenor, 146
Country music, 208
Creation, The (Haydn), 287
Crosby, Bing, 244
Cunningham, Sis, 346
Cylinder recording, 242
Cymbals, 212

Dafne, La (Peri), 143
Dalang, 233
Dalcroze, Jacques, 364
Dall'aquila, Serafino, 312
Dance, Indian, 126, 127
Dance, Jewish, 78–80
Dance, Native American, 58–67
Dance, Stanley, 332
Dante Alighieri, 150
Dave Brubeck Quartet, 208
Davis, Miles, 352
Debussy, Claude, 227, 232, 353
Definite-pitch percussion, 212
Delaware people, 58
Delay, 245
Dervish, whirling, 304–306
Development, 278, 282
Diatonic harmony, 173
Diatonic scale, 173

Diderot, Denis, 284
Digital compact disc, 242
Dion, Celine, 349
Disjunct melody, 103
Disk recording, 242
Dixie, 247
Dixieland, 325
Doina, 78
Dolmetsch, Arnold, 179
Dolphin Dreams (Goldman), 6–9, 27, 70, 187, 252, 254, 309, 355
Dominant triad, 173
Domingo, Plácido, 142, 349, 351–353, 365
Don Giovanni (Mozart), 143
Dorsey, Tommy, 367
Double bass, 209, 218
Dowland, John, 315, 353
Dramatic mezzo-soprano, 146
Dramatic soprano, 146
Dramatic suite, 25, 331
Dramatic tenor, 146
Drone, 125
Drum, 57–61, 64, 66–70, 91–95, 130
Drums of Passion (Olatunji), 93, 364
Dry, 245
Dunn, Elizabeth, 25
Duo, 207
Duple meter, 74
Dust Bowl Ballads (Guthrie), 194
Dylan, Bob, 20, 353, 354
Dynamics, 221–224

Early Music Movement, 179, 289, 320
Echo, 245
Edgar (Puccini), 148
Edison, Thomas A., 140, 240–242
Editing, 249
Egreti karar, 302
Eight-track cartridge, 243
Elizabeth II, Queen of England, 215
Elk Boy, Clevland Holy, 54
Ellington, Edward Kennedy "Duke," 80, 322, 326–338, 348, 354, 359, 368
Elliott, Paul, 318
Ellis, Don, 132
Emotional response, 32–34
Encyclopédie (Diderot), 284
English horn, 211

Ensembles, 207–209, 252, 253
Epstein, Brian, 347
Equal temperament, 101
Equiano, Olaudah, 90
Ergin, Dogan, 307, 308, 354
Eroica Symphony (Beethoven), 14, 15
Esterházy family, 289, 357
Ethnomusicologist, 66
Eugenius III, Pope, 106
Evita (Lloyd Webber), 143, 145
Exodus (Marley), 44–47, 70, 274
Expander, 246
Exposition, 282

Fanciulla del West, La (Puccini), 149
Fanfare (Robbins), 215
Fauré, Gabriel, 350
Ferrel Torrico, Victor Hugo, 273, 354, 362
Field recordings, 54
Figured bass; *see* Basso continuo
Fills, 190, 333
Film, 145
Film, India, 134, 135
Filmi, 134
Fishman, David E., 82, 83
Flag song, 64
Flanging, 245
Florentine Camerata, 142
Flute, 211, 218, 222
Fontana, Ferdinando, 148
Ford, Mary, 244, 365
Form, 258–265, 278–284, 290–294, 298
Foster, Stephen, 247, 354
Four Seasons, The (Vivaldi, 179–185, 338
Four-track cassette, 243
Free jazz, 325
Freischütz, Der (Weber), 143
French horn, 212
Freni, Mirella, 154
Frequency, 101
Friesen, Gordon, 346
Fugue, 299, 310
Function of music, 19–21
Fundamental frequency, 101
Fusion, 325

Gahbow, Pete, 58, 67–69, 138, 200, 354
Galilei, Galileo, 177

Galm, John, 232
Gamel, 230
Gamelan, 227, 229–238
Garcia, Jerry, 204, 354, 355; *see also* Grateful Dead
Gary Lewis and the Playboys, 253
Gat, 135
Gender, 234
Gender barangan, 234
Gender gede, 234
Gender roles, 58, 59
Gender wayang, 233, 234
Gending Petegak, 236–238, 274
German Requiem, A (Brahms), 350
Gershwin, George, 143, 355
Gershwin, Ira, 355
Gesamtkunstwerk, 142
Ghatam, 131
Ghiaurov, Nicolai, 154
Gianni Schicchi (Puccini), 150
Gillette, Grace, 56
Giraud, Anna, 176
Giraud, Paolina, 176
Giveaway, 66
Gluck, Christoph Willibald, 143
God Bless America (Berlin), 193, 348
Gold, Didier, 150
Goldman, Jonathan, 6, 8, 9, 252, 254, 355
Goldmark, Rubin, 352
Gong, 94, 230, 232
Gong-gong, 91
Goodnight Irene (Leadbelly), 197
Gourd dance, 62
Gozzi, Carlo, 150
Graham, Martha, 24
Grand entry song, 62–64
Grand Entry Song, 68–70, 96, 120, 187, 200, 262, 263
Grateful Dead, 34, 93, 208, 355–357, 364; *see also* Garcia, Jerry; Hart, Mickey
Great Tradition (Indian music), 125, 127
Green, Minnie, 25
Greenblatt, Marjorie, 193
Gregorian chant, 109, 111–113
Gregory I, Pope "the Great," 109, 111, 356
Grieg, Edvard, 331, 356
Guarneri, Andrea, 211
Guitar, 262, 268, 274, 326
Gunther, Dorothee, 364
Guru, 127

Guthrie, Arlo, 193, 356
Guthrie, Charley, 191, 192
Guthrie, Mary Jennings, 192
Guthrie, Nora, 191, 192
Guthrie, Woodrow Wilson "Woody," 189, 191–196, 200, 262, 346, 353, 356, 368

Haile Selassie I, 41, 44
Haley, Bill, 347
Han, Gazi Giray, 301
Harmonic progression, 172
Harmonic rhythm, 172
Harmonizing, 190, 191
Harmony, 171–174, 185, 190, 191, 326
Harp, 218
Harris, Roy, 350
Harrison, George, 122, 132, 347, 356, 360, 368; see also Beatles
Hart, Mickey, 52, 69, 93, 355, 357, 364; see also Grateful Dead
Harwood, Elizabeth, 154
Hasidic Jews, 79, 80
Hasse, John Edward, 322
Hawes, Bess Lomax, 346
Hawes, Pete, 346
Haydn, Franz Joseph, 284, 286–295, 357
Hays, Lee, 346
Head, 325
Hearing, 6
Helminski, Kabir, 305
Henry II, King of England, 105
Hercalitus, 5
Heterophony, 235
Hicklin, Ron, 253
Hildegard of Bingen, 100, 104–110, 113–119, 357
Hill, Lauryn, 33, 42, 357
Hilliard Ensemble, 317
Hillier, Paul, 318
Hinduism, 229
Hindustani style, 127
Historical periods, 27
Hocket, 272
Hodges, Johnny, 330
Hogwood, Christopher, 290
Holly, Buddy, 347
Homme armé, L', 20
Homophonic texture, 220
Homorhythmic texture, 221

Honor beats, 58
Horn, 212
Houppelande, La (Gold), 150
Howard, Quentin, 272, 368
Huachos, 266, 272–274
Huguenots, Les (Meyerbeer), 143
Human attributes, 36–39
Hymn, 14, 21

Iconography, 106
Idiophone, 90
Imitative counterpoint, 316, 317
Improvisation, 128, 181, 303, 325, 338
Inayat Khan, Hazrat, 39, 358
Inca Empire, 271
Incidental music, 216
Indefinite pitch percussion, 212
Independent suite, 332
Indes Galantes, Les (Rameau), 143
Indian music, 123–136
Indigenous religions, 38, 39, 64, 267
Indonesian music, 227–237, 272
Inferno (Dante), 150
Instrument classification, 130
Instruments, Andes region, 268–270
Instruments, Indian, 130–132
Instruments, Indonesian, 230–235
Instruments, Turkish, 303, 308
Instruments, Western, 209–212, 217–219
Interlude, 81, 279, 280
Intertribal music and dance, 56, 57, 60, 62, 64
Introduction, 81, 279
Invention, 299
Iphigénie en Aulide (Gluck), 143
Irregular phrase, 115
Islam, 88, 229, 301, 303; see also Mevlevi order; Sufism
Itri, Buhurizade Mustafa, 301, 358

Jackson, Mahalia, 331, 358
Jamaica, 39–44
James, David, 318
James, Harry, 367
Janissary music, 302
Japanese music, 141, 208
Jazz, 42, 129, 181, 323–338; see also African American music; Blues
Java; see Indonesian music

Jefferson, "Blind Lemon," 196, 359
Jefferson, Thomas, 285
Jewish music, 76–83
Jhaptal, 136
Jobson, Richard, 90
Jolson, Al, 355
Jor, 135
Josquin Desprez, 312–320, 359, 361
Judaism, 76–80
Jung, Carl, 39
Jutta, 105

Kabbala; *see* Cabala
Kabuki, 141, 142, 165
Kandel, Harry, 80
Kanjira, 131
Kanun, 303
Karajan, Herbert von, 154, 359
Karnataka style, 127
Kemençe, 303
Kena; *see* Quena
Kentucky Club, 328
Key, 173
Khan, Ustad Allaudin, 132
King, Martin Luther, 359
Kiowa people, 62
Klezmer Conservatory Band, 79–83, 186, 364
Klezmer music, 76–83
Klezmorim, 76
Kotekan, 236, 272
Koto, 208
Kremer, Isa, 82
Kudüm, 303

Ladysmith Black Mambazo, 200
Lamb, Charles, 170
LaMenthe, Ferdinand; *see* Morton, Jelly Roll
Lamon, Jeanne, 183
Lampell, Millard, 346
Language, 13
Larson, Jonathan, 152, 360
Lassus, Orlande de, 313, 360
Lay-By (Ellington/Strayhorn), 336, 337
Lead, 60
Lead singer, 58
Leadbelly, 191, 195–200, 225, 265, 359, 360
Leap, 103

Ledbetter, Huddie; *see* Leadbelly
Lee, Ann, 21
Legato, 331
Lennon, John, 245, 347, 357, 360, 361; *see also* Beatles
Lennon, Julian, 361
Lennon, Sean Ono, 361
Lewis, Gary, 253
Liber Vitae Meritorium (Hildegard of Bingen), 107
Librettist, 142
Libretto, 142
Limiter, 246
Lind, Jenny, 361
Listening, 6
Liszt, Franz, 350, 371
Little Otter Singers, 67–69, 263, 354, 361
Little Red School House Chorus, 194
Little Tradition (Indian music), 125
Liturgical year, 114
Lloyd Webber, Andrew, 143, 350, 361, 372
Lockspeiser, Edward, 227
Lomax, John A., 196
London Symphonies (Haydn), 289
Long-playing record, 242
Louis, Armstrong, 331, 346
Love Drum Talk (Olatunji), 93
Lullaby, 7
Lully, Jean-Baptiste, 143
Lush Life (Strayhorn), 330, 368
Luther, Martin, 315, 361, 362
Lyric baritone, 146
Lyric mezzo-soprano, 146
Lyric soprano, 146
Lyric tenor, 146

Madama Butterfly (Puccini), 148, 149
Madani, Mohammed Abu Hasan, 358
Madonna, 146
Maffeo, Gianni, 154
Magnetic tape recording, 243
Mahabharata, 233
Mahler, Gustav, 286, 362
Major key, 173
Major scale, 102, 173
Makam, 302
Malcolm X, 93
Mallku de Los Andes, 266, 272, 274, 352, 354, 362, 363, 367

Manley, Michael, 43
Manon Lescaut (Puccini), 148, 149
Marimba, 212
Marley, Rita, 43
Marley, Robert Nesta (Bob), 36, 39, 41–49, 224, 262, 362, 371; *see also* Wailin' Wailers
Marsang, 131
Martin Luther King, Jr., 93
Máru-Bihág, 134–137, 187, 320, 338
Mary, mother of Jesus, 109, 114, 115
Mazurka, 78
McCartney, Paul, 347, 357, 360; *see also* Beatles
McCool, Elsie, 25
Measure, 74
Medieval period, 27, 104–116
Mehta, Zubin, 372
Melba, Nellie, 153
Melismatic style, 113
Melody, 101, 103, 112, 113, 147
Membranophone, 91
Memorial prayer song, 64
Menga, Pan, 236
Menominee people, 66
Menotti, Gian Carlo, 143, 362
Menuet and trio movement, 283
Menuhin, Yehudi, 132, 363, 368
Meragi, Abdülkadir, 301
Mercado, J., 273
Messa di Gloria (Puccini), 147
Mestizo, 266
Metal bar percussion, 230
Meter, 74, 75, 80
Mevlana, 304
Mevlevi Ensemble of Turkey, 307, 308
Mevlevi order, 304, 305; *see also* Islam; Sufism
Meyerbeer, Giacomo, 143
Mezzo-soprano, 146
Middle Ages; *see* Medieval period
Mighty Fortress Is Our God, A (Luther), 315
Military band, 323, 325
Milli Vanilli, 253
Mills, Irving, 329
Minor key, 173
Minor scale, 103, 173
Minuet; *see* Menuet
Miseducation of Lauryn Hill (Hill), 42
Misérables, Les, 145
Misfit Blues (Ellington/Strayhorn), 332–337
Mix, 248

Mixdown, 249
Mixing, 245
Modern period, 27, 214, 215
Mohejo-daro, 125
Monkees, 253
Monophonic texture, 109, 219
Monothematic sonata form, 290
Montano, David Mercado, 272, 362, 363
Monteverdi, Claudio, 143
Morton, Ferdinand Joseph LaMenthe "Jelly Roll," 325, 363
Morzin, Count Ferdinand Maximilian von, 289
Motet, 313
Motivational music, 18
Moustache, James "Pipe," 67
Mozart, Leopold, 363
Mozart, Wolfgang Amadeus, 143, 168, 284, 286, 289, 302, 363
Mridangam, 130
Mulatto, 266
Multitrack tape recorder, 245
Mürger, Henri, 148
Music definition, 8, 9
Musical instruments; *see instruments headings*
Musicals, 145, 146, 152
Mutrip, 303
Muzaffer, Sheikh, 306

Nagaswaram, 131
Native American music, North America, 55–66
Native American music, South America, 266–274
Navia, Quentin; *see* Howard, Quentin
Nayadeva of Mithila, 129
Netsky, Hankus, 80–83, 186, 364
Neumatic style, 115
New Age, 17, 104
New Orleans, 324
New Orleans Suite (Ellington), 331
New York Pro Musica, 179
Newton, Isaac, 177
Ney, 304
Nixon, Leigh, 318
Noh, 141, 165
Nonet, 207
Northern style (Indian music); *see* Hindustani style

Northern style (Native American music), 61, 69, 127
Northwest Coast peoples, 66
Norwich, John Julius, 174
Nutcracker Suite (Tchaikovsky), 25, 330, 331

Oboe, 211, 218, 220, 222
Octet, 207
Odo, Master, 113
Ojibwe people, 66–69
Olatunji, Babatunde, 86, 93–96, 364
Old Folks at Home (Foster), 247, 354
Oliver, Joe "King," 325, 346
Omaha people, 56, 57
Ono, Yoko, 360, 361
Opera, 142–147, 165, 287, 288
Operatione Dei, De (Hildegard of Bingen), 107
Oratorio, 289
Orchestra, 207, 224
Orchestration, 215
Orfeo (Monteverdi), 143
Orff, Carl, 364
Ospedale della Pietà, 175, 176
Oy, Abram!, 81, 83, 137, 186, 264

Pace, Mike, 58, 61, 364
Pachamama, 369
Palestrina, Giovanni Pierluigi da, 313, 364
Panerai, Rolando, 154
Part book, 319
Passacaglia, 299
Pattern-based continuous form, 298
Paul, Les, 244, 365
Pavarotti, Luciano, 142, 154, 349, 352, 353, 365
Pawnee people, 56, 57
Pears, Peter, 213, 365
Peer Gynt Suites (Grieg), 331
Percussion instruments, 90, 131, 209, 212, 230, 231
Performance recordings, 255
Peri, Jacopo, 143
Perry, Lee, 371
Peshrev, 307
Peter Grimes (Britten), 143
Phantom of the Opera, The (Lloyd Webber), 145, 351, 361

Phonograph, 241, 242
Phrase, 104, 115
Phukuna, 270
Physica (Hildegard of Bingen), 107
Physical response, 31, 32
Piano, 285
Piccolo, 211, 218, 222
Piston, Walter, 350
Pitch, 101
Pitches sound, 101
Pizarro, Francisco, 271
Pizzicato, 336
Plainchant; *see* Gregorian chant
Plainsong; *see* Gregorian chant
Planer, Minna; *see* Wagner, Minna Planer
Planet Drum (Olatunji), 93
Playback singers, 134
Polfuss, Lester William; *see* Paul, Les
Politics, 40, 43, 44, 68, 78, 144, 192
Polyphonic texture, 219
Polyrhythm, 87, 88
Ponchielli, Amilcare, 349
Popular music, US, 247, 248
Porgy and Bess (Gershwin), 143
Porter, Cole, 350
Potlatch, 66
Powwow, 55–66
Prayer, blessing, 64
Prayer song, memorial, 64
Prehistory, 12–13
Prelude, 299
Prélude à l'après-midi d'un faune (Debussy), 227, 232
Previn, André, 132, 365
Prévost, Abbé, 148
Program music, 182
Protestantism, 21–24, 315; *see also* Christianity
Puccini, Giacomo, 143, 147–165, 225, 346, 349, 360, 366
Puppet theater, 233–235
Purcell, Henry, 215, 216, 366
Purpose of music, 16
Pursey, John, 250, 347
Pyramid chord, 336
Quadruple meter, 75
Quartet, 207
Quartet, barbershop, 190
Quartet, string, 284–286, 289
Quena, 270, 273

Quenacho; *see* Quena
Quintet, 207
Qur'an, 306

Raczek, Linda, 58
Raga, 127–129, 134–136, 302
Ragtime, 324
Rama, 131
Rameau, Jean-Philippe, 143
Rampal, Jean-Pierre Louis, 132, 366
Range, 103, 146
Ras Tafari; *see* Haile Selassi I
Rastafari, 40, 41, 45–47
Rattle, 91, 92, 94
Reagon, Bernice Johnson, 198, 200, 366, 369;
    see also Sweet Honey in the Rock
Recapitulation, 283
Record producer, 248
Recording engineer, 244
Recording studio, 249
Recording technology, 241–249, 252–255
Redemption Song (Marley), 47–50, 119, 120,
    185, 186, 224, 262
Reformation, 315
Regalia, 56
Reggae, 41, 42
Regular phrase, 115
Religion; *see* Christianity; Indigenous religions;
    Protestantism; Roman Catholicism
Renaissance period, 27, 314–317
Rent (Larson), 152, 360
Repetition, 261, 262
Retransition, 291
Reverberation, 245
Rhythm, 55, 74–76, 87, 88
Rhythm and blues, 42
Rice, Tim, 361
Rich, Buddy, 132, 367
Ricordi, Giulio, 148
Riff, 335
Ring des Nibelungen, Der (Wagner), 143, 145,
    371
Robbins, Jerome, 215
Roberts, Edwin, 273, 362, 367
Roman Catholicism, 267, 268, 313, 315; *see also*
    Christianity
Roman Empire, 76
Romantic period, 27, 144, 145

Rondine, La (Puccini), 150
Rondo, 274, 281
Rosenkavalier, Der (Strauss), 143
Round, 219
Round dance, 64
Rounded binary form, 293
Rubinstein, Arthur, 20
Rumi, Mevlana Jalalu'ddin, 297, 304, 306, 370
Ryan, Matt, 250, 251, 347, 367, 372

Sadhana, 127
Saint Louis Blues, 326
Sancta Maria, De (Hildegard of Bingen), 104,
    115–120, 187, 320
Sapoznik, Henry, 77
Sarod, 130
Saxophone, 211
Scale, 102, 103, 173
Schafer, R. Murray, 30, 367
Schumann, Robert, 350
Schwartz, Abe, 367
Schwiphti (Ellington/Strayhorn), 334, 335
Scivias (Hildegard of Bingen), 106, 107, 110
Sea chantey, 17
Seaga, Edward, 43
Second, 60
Second chorus, 60
Second Coming, 21
Sectional form, 264
Seeger, Charles, 367
Seeger, Pete, 192–195, 197, 199, 346, 356, 367
Sekehe Gender Bharata Muni, Sading, 236, 237
Selim III, Sultan, 302
Sema, 305, 306
Sénéchal, Michel, 154
Senter, I Nengah, 236
Sephardic Jews, 77
Septet, 207
Sequence, 104, 115
Setting, 14
Sextet, 207
Shanai, 131
Shakere, 91, 92, 95
Shakers, 21–24
Shakespeare, William, 177, 315, 331
Shamanism, 16, 92
Shango (Olatunji), 93–96, 138, 187, 309
Shank, Bud, 132

Shankar, Ravi, 122, 127, 132–136, 357, 363, 368
Siegmeister, Ellie, 350
Siku, 270, 272
Simmer Down, 42
Simple Gifts, 21, 24, 50, 96, 120, 172, 275, 321
Sinan, Koca, 301
Sioux people, 64
Sipon, Pan, 236
Sitar, 130, 132, 135, 137
Ska, 42
Slendro tuning, 234
Snare drum, 212, 218
Sonata, 176, 283
Sonata form, 282, 283, 290–294
Song picturization, 134
Sonnet, 182
Soprano, 146
South American music, 266–274
Southern style (Indian music); *see* Karnataka style
Southern style (Native American music), 60, 61, 69, 127
Spiritual response, 34–36
Spring (Vivaldi), 180–185, 338
Starkey, Richard; *see* Starr, Ringo
Starr, Ringo, 347
Steinbeck, John, 332, 338
Stern, Arthur, 346
Stewart, Rex, 330
Stradivari, Antonio, 211
Strauss, Richard, 143
Strayhorn, Billy, 326, 329–338, 368
Streisand, Barbra, 99
String bass, 26
String instruments, 26, 130, 209–211
String quartet, 284–286, 289
Strophic form, 264
Studio recordings, 255
Sturges, Jeff, 250, 347
Sturges, Sophie Ellmaker, 250, 347
Subject, fugue, 310
Sub-Saharan African music, 88–96
Sufism, 303–306; *see also* Islam; Mevlevi order
Suite, 24, 25, 331, 332
Suite Thursday (Ellington/Strayhorn), 326, 330–338
Sukay, 368, 369
Suleiman I, 301
Sultan Veled Peshrev, 299, 302–309

Sumeria, 14, 16
Suor Angelica (Puccini), 150
Sutcliffe, Stu, 347, 360
Sweet Honey in the Rock, 191, 194, 195, 197–200, 366, 369
Swing, 325, 330
Syllabic style, 113
Symphonia Harmonie Caelestium Revelationum (Hildegard of Bingen), 113–118
Symphony, 285, 286
Symphony No. 39 (Haydn), 289–295
Symphony orchestra, 207, 224
Syncopation, 324

Tabarro, Il (Puccini), 150
Tabla, 130, 135–137
Tafelmusik Baroque Orchestra, 183
Take the "A" Train (Strayhorn), 330, 368
Tala, 128–130
Talam, 131
Talking drum, 91
Tam-tam, 212
Tambourine, 212, 218
Tambura, 125, 130, 136
Tanbur, 303
Tape recorder, 244
Tarras, Dave, 73, 369
Tchaikovsky, Pyotor Il'yich, 25, 330, 331, 369
Technological revolution, 215
Technology, 241–246, 248–250
Temple blocks, 212
Tempo, 55
Tenor, 146
Tenor drum, 212
Teri, Pak, 236
Ternary form, 280
Terraced dynamics, 224
Text-based continuous form, 298
Texture, 109, 204, 219–221, 235
Theme, 279
Theme and variations, 281
This Diamond Ring (Lewis), 253
This Land Is Your Land (Guthrie), 191, 193–195, 262, 263, 338
Threepenny Opera, The (Weill), 143
Through-composed song, 313
Timbre, 204

Time to Say Goodbye, 166, 349
Timpani, 212, 223
Tonal harmony, 171
Tones, 92
Tonic, 103
Tonic triad, 173
Tosca (Puccini), 148
Toscanini, Arturo, 75, 149, 369
Tosh, Peter, 42, 43, 369, 371; *see also* Wailin' Wailers
Townsend, Ken, 245
Transando, 272
Transition, 279, 280
Tremolo, 184
Triad, 171
Triangle, 212
Trio, 207
Trio (menuet), 283
Triple meter, 74
Trombone, 212, 218
Tuba, 212, 218
Turandot (Puccini), 150, 151, 346
Turkish music, 209, 299–307

Ud, 303
Uh'ge ti; *see* Buffalohead, (Alvin) Harry
Ukamau, 272
United States; *see* African American music; American popular music; American vernacular music; Blues; Jazz
Unpitched sound, 101
Ursula, Saint, 114
Utility of music, 17

Vadi svara, 128
Vallier, Jeff, 250
Vallier, Rob, 250
Variation, 278
Veled, Sultan, 301, 306, 370
Vennum, Thomas Jr., 66, 69
Verdi, Giuseppe, 143, 147, 349, 370
Vernacular music, US, 191
Verse and chorus form, 265
Vibration, 101
Vibrato, 235
Victoria, Tomás Luis de, 313, 370
Vienna, 286

Villaroel, Eduardo, 273
Villi, Le (Puccini), 148
Vina, 130
Vinaya, 127
Vinci, Leonardo da, 315
Viola, 26, 209, 218, 222
Violin, 26, 131, 182, 209, 218, 222
Violoncello, 26, 209, 218
Violonsel, 303
Vivaldi, Antonio, 173–176, 178–185, 224, 338, 371
Vocables, 58
Voice ranges, 146
Volmar, 106

Wagner, Cosima Liszt von Bülow, 371
Wagner, Minna Planer, 371
Wagner, Richard, 142, 143, 145, 165, 351, 353, 371
Wailer, Bunny, 42, 43, 371; *see also* Wailin' Wailers
Wailin' Wailers, 43, 369, 371; *see also* Marley, Robert Nesta (Bob); Tosh, Peter; Wailer, Bunny
Walking bass, 334
Waller, Fats, 80, 371
Wankara, 268
War dances, 64
Warner, Eric, 250, 347, 367, 372
Watson, Doc, 194
Wayang kulit, 233, 234
Weavers, 368
Weber, Carl Maria von, 143
Weill, Kurt, 143
West African music, 90–96
West Side Story (Bernstein), 349
Whirling dervish, 304–306
Williams, Cootie, 330
Winnebago people, 66
Wittgenstein, Victor, 352
Woodblock, 212
Woodwind instruments, 209, 211
Work song, 17
World War I, 150, 214, 300
World War II, 79, 193, 214
Wozzeck (Berg), 143
Wright, Edward, 175
Wright, Frank Lloyd, 215

Xylophone, 91, 212

Yiddish, 76
Young Person's Guide to the Orchestra (Britten),
    212–225, 295, 309

Zampoñ, 270, 274
Zappa, Frank, 277, 372
Zimbabwe, 43, 89
Zimmerman, Robert Allen; *see* Dylan, Bob
Zweet Zurzday (Ellington/Strayhorn), 335, 336